James Hingston

The Australian Abroad

Branches from the Main Routes Round the World

James Hingston

The Australian Abroad
Branches from the Main Routes Round the World

ISBN/EAN: 9783744720175

Printed in Europe, USA, Canada, Australia, Japan

Cover: Foto ©ninafisch / pixelio.de

More available books at **www.hansebooks.com**

THE BOER BUDDHA TEMPLE.

THE AUSTRALIAN ABROAD.

BRANCHES FROM THE MAIN ROUTES ROUND THE WORLD.

By JAMES HINGSTON,
("*J. H.*" of the "*Melbourne Argus.*")

DOMESTIC LIFE IN CHINA.

London:
SAMPSON LOW, MARSTON, SEARLE, AND RIVINGTON,
CROWN BUILDINGS, 188, FLEET STREET.
1879.

> "The cloud-capp'd towers, the gorgeous palaces,
> The solemn temples, the great globe itself;
> Yea, all which it inherit."
>
> SHAKESPERE.

PREFACE.

THE following notes of travel are the outcome of a long holiday taken by an Anglo-Australian, who, after twenty-five years of active occupation in Melbourne, was enabled to indulge his long-cherished desire of making a tour of the globe. Without companions, save those whom he found by the way, and unassisted by guide-books, he travelled through most of the principal countries in each of the world's five divisions, and recorded the impressions made upon his mind by all that he saw and heard while they were still fresh. The chapters in their present shape were actually written in the localities which they describe, and thence posted to a newspaper in Melbourne. In the columns of the *Argus* they have appeared at regular intervals during the last three years. Thus written, the Author ventures to think that they convey a more faithful description of the scenes and people visited than if they had been subsequently elaborated from the rough material of a diary, assisted by reference to the works of other travellers.

The kindly welcome eagerly accorded to them in their serial form by his fellow-colonists has induced him to offer them collectively to the acceptance of a larger public at home. The present volume relates to those stages of his journey which began after leaving the American Continent, embracing the route through Japan, China, Malasia, Sunda, Java, and Australia, to New Zealand. The illustrations have been engraved from photographs obtained at the several places selected.

The remaining notes of his travels through Asia (including Ceylon, India, Syria, and Palestine), Europe (including Great Britain, Italy, &c.), America and Africa, will furnish materials for one or two succeeding volumes.

Sept., 1879.

CONTENTS.

CHAPTER I.
INTRODUCTORY 1

CHAPTER II.
THE TYCOON'S TOWN 10

CHAPTER III.
THE JAPANESE SPHINX 23

CHAPTER IV.
THE MIKADO'S CITY 35

CHAPTER V.
AN EASTERN VENICE 45

CHAPTER VI.
LIFE WITH THE JAPS 56

CHAPTER VII.
THE INLAND SEA OF JAPAN 70

CHAPTER VIII.
A LAST LOOK AT JAPAN 81

CHAPTER IX.
THREE DAYS AT SHANGHAI 92

CHAPTER X.
THE CHINESE PORTS 103

Contents.

	PAGE
CHAPTER XI. A LOOK AT CANTON (No. 1) .	114
CHAPTER XII. A LOOK AT CANTON (No. 2)	124
CHAPTER XIII. IN CHINA .	134
CHAPTER XIV. IN COCHIN CHINA .	145
CHAPTER XV. SINGAPORE AND THE STRAITS	155
CHAPTER XVI. IN NETHERLANDS INDIA.	166
CHAPTER XVII. THE SUNDANESE CAPITAL	176
CHAPTER XVIII. BUITENZORG AND THE HILLS.	188
CHAPTER XIX. SANDANGLAYA TO SAMARANG (SUNDA-JAVA)	198
CHAPTER XX. SOLO AND JOCKIO (JAVA).	208
CHAPTER XXI. THE JAVANESE UPAS	219
CHAPTER XXII. THE BOER BUDDHA TEMPLE.	230
CHAPTER XXIII. SAMARANG TO SOERABAYA	240
CHAPTER XXIV. SOERABAYA TO SOMERSET (TORRES STRAITS)	251

CHAPTER XXV.
New South Wales: Sydney 266

CHAPTER XXVI.
New South Wales: The Blue Mountains 275

CHAPTER XXVII.
South Australia: Adelaide 283

CHAPTER XXVIII.
New Zealand: West Coasting and Landing . . 290

CHAPTER XXIX.
Eastward Ho! on Wheels 300

CHAPTER XXX.
Close Quarters with Royalty 306

CHAPTER XXXI.
The "Square" City—and People 315

CHAPTER XXXII.
The Maori-land Bird—The Moa 325

CHAPTER XXXIII.
The Maories "at Home"—to Dinner . . . 332

CHAPTER XXXIV.
East Coasting, and Coaching 346

CHAPTER XXXV.
North and South Contrasts (Auckland—Dunedin) . . 354

CHAPTER XXXVI.
Cook's Straits—"The Middle Passage" . . 361

CHAPTER XXXVII.
Picton and the "French Pass" 368

CHAPTER XXXVIII.
The Maori Family—"in Town" . . . 376

CHAPTER XXXIX.

IN THE RICHEST OF ALL GOLD-MINES—THE CALEDONIAN . 388

CHAPTER XL.

THE "SILVER THAMES"—WITH GOLDEN BANK . . . 396

CHAPTER XLI.

THE WATER-KING'S HEAD-QUARTERS 402

CHAPTER XLII.

THE PAKEHA'S PROGRESS 409

CHAPTER XLIII.

THE MAORI'S DECLINE 417

LIST OF ILLUSTRATIONS.

	PAGE
The Boer Buddha Temple	*Frontispiece*
Japanese Waggoners	4
The Jinrickishaw	5
Ascent to Heights (eighty-six steps) of Tokio	12
A Japanese Temple	17
Fusiyama	23
Dai Butsa	26
Ehmidji Castle	29
Japanese Street	33
Temple at Kioto	43
Japanese Wrestlers	51
Female Musicians (Japan)	56
Japanese Lady	61
Ladies' Outdoor Dress	62
Dress of Japanese Lady	63
Japanese Almanac	82
Two Sides of a Merchant's Card	90
Tea House, Shanghai	99
Amoy Harbour	103
Chinese Palanquin	115
A Chinese House	117
Domestic Life (China)	128
Macao from the Bay	134
Javanese Carriage-chair	178
Javanese Musical Instruments	180
Weaving the "Batuck"	182
At Prambanan	213

List of Illustrations.

	PAGE
Emperor's Residence (Soerakajarta)	217
Native Musicians (Java)	220
The "Gamelong"	221
The Hotel Verandah (Soerabaya)	244
Port Darwin	251
An Aboriginal	253
A Native King	254
A Native Queen	255
Native Mia-mia	257
Waterfall, Otira Gorge (New Zealand)	303
A Maori Lady	306
Amelia Tanui Arahura	308
The Maori Type (Male)	338
The Maori Type (Female)	339
The Maori Type (Female)	340
Maori Dress (Male)	376
Maori Dress (Female)	377
Artistic Tattooing (1)	379
Artistic Tattooing (2)	380
Maori Woman	383
The Maori and his Pipe	425

BRANCHES FROM THE MAIN ROUTES ROUND THE WORLD.

CHAPTER I.

INTRODUCTORY.

THE wharf at San Francisco has, I find, steamers of largest size leaving monthly for Japan. They lie alongside those leaving the same wharf monthly for Australia. An Australian has thus the choice of returning to his adopted country by way of Honolulu and Fiji, or by way of Japan and Singapore, at which last-named port he can monthly meet with the Torres Straits mail. There can be little question which route offers the greater attraction to the traveller. Japan is a country but sixteen years opened to the world. There are now three European settlements upon its shores. From all parts of Europe settlers have gone thither. Scarcely an Australian but can remember some one from some part of Australasia who has made Japan a home. To see how they are all doing there, and the wonders of the newly-opened country, are attractions that outweigh many other considerations. Life should not be all business, any more than all beer and skittles. Pope tells us that it "can little more supply, but just to look about us and to die." The world has accredited him with wisdom, knowledge of life and of human nature beyond that of most men. His opinions, therefore, carry weight. I went accordingly to "look about" in Japan, and have to tell something of what can be seen there.

The "City of Tokio," a steamship of the large size of 5500 tons register, made a pleasant passage of twenty-one days. On the voyage, the 15th of December was dropped out of the calendar, so that I never saw that birthday of mine. The coloured steward of our vessel was a sort of Uncle Tom in his opinions. He did not see, he said, how man could interfere with Providence, and take a day out of the week of seven days that the Creator had given us. It reminded me that, when the calendar was reformed in our grandfathers' days, a party in Great Britain clamoured against it on religious grounds, resolving to adhere to the "old style," and wanting back "the days taken from them" by Act of Parliament.

Yokohama is our landing-place—a pleasant-looking stone-built seaport, with very clean and macadamized streets. The three of them that lie parallel with the sea beach make up the white settlement. Behind those is a busy settlement of Japanese, a native town of 40,000 or so, that have come down from Yeddo, twenty miles distant, to live upon the white settlers, who had come thither to live upon them. These whites are not now more than 2000 in number at Yokohama. Looking at the fact that the town is only sixteen years old— that not a building stood upon the low, flat-lying spot in 1860—it is really a surprising place to the stranger, and looks at least three times its age. On the "Bluff," to the left of the settlement, are the villa residences of the Europeans—comfortable places, surrounded with gardens, and, but that they are all bamboo-fenced, very like the villas of South Yarra.

Commodore Perry came here in 1860, with the compliments of President Fillmore, and a gunboat. He presented a respectful letter to the Tycoon, and, for himself, added that he would take back only a courteous answer. The port must be opened to American traders, or the refusal taken as a declaration of war. The officials told him to go away down to Nagasaki, where the Dutch had a settlement, on the island of Decima; but the commodore pointed to his guns, and dropped his anchor. That resolute behaviour had its effect. The Tycoon granted him permission to land at Yokohama, and make a settlement there, but to come no nearer to Yeddo—the London of Japan. Other countries followed suit, and got similar permission, and thus was the shut-up Japan, the Great Britain of the East, opened to the world. The miserable Dutch had, for two hundred years, had a trading settlement at Decima, and submitted there to every possible indignity for the sake of the dollars made by the small trade that the Japanese permitted them to do. Left to Dutch enterprise, Japan would have continued as closed to the world as the neighbouring Corea still is.

Fortunes are no longer made quickly in the white settlements of Japan. A steady jog-trot trade is now done, similar to what might be done at any of the New Zealand ports. The Japanese manufactures have been hitherto works of art in metal, porcelain, cottons, and silk. These have been exported largely, and the demand has now decreased. The bronzes, vases, and curious porcelain wares have become not the curious and expensive things that they once were, and no longer pay the profits they did. The mines of Japan have not been found profitable up to the present. Japan is five-sixths hills and mountains. Sheep and cows are almost unknown in it. The hill-sides are cultivated but little. Round the base of a few are to be seen the graded rice-fields, with which the land abounds. Rice and fish are the staple of Japanese food. In fish everything is eaten—the shark and octopus included. The latter, which is the great curiosity of British aquariums, is a common article in Japanese fish-markets. The drink of the country is a weak tea, taken without milk or sugar, and drunk throughout the twenty-four hours. Fires are of charcoal only, and made in square boxes lined with metal. Chopsticks are used instead of knives and forks. After the first day I bought a spoon, and used that, failing to make any progress in taking up rice curries with two penholders.

The Japanese are a small race. The men are rarely over 5ft. 4in., and the women usually under 5ft. They are the most polite, cheerful, and pleasant of people. It is easily accounted for. They eat the most easily digested of all food, and drink nought but that which cheers but not inebriates. They are strong people in the way of endurance, of which I saw notable instances. If a Victorian were to tell me that he could run forty miles—say, from Melbourne to Kyneton—at six miles an hour, stopping but three times, for a short half-hour each time, on the way, I should think that he

JAPANESE WAGGONERS.

romanced, and that he altogether over-estimated human powers if he told me that he could also drag me after him in a light hansom. Yet the Japanese do that all through Japan. They have no horses. The palanquin was the mode of conveyance until the Japanese saw an American buggy, and the way of making light wheels and springs. Seven years ago this ingenious people made the jinrickishaw (man-power carriage), which is a cross between a perambulator and a small hansom. One man could, between the shafts of this conveyance, do the work that two had done hitherto with the palanquin. This new pull-man car is now the national vehicle of Japan. I went forty miles with ease in one day in one of these, and the same conveyancers brought me back forty miles the next day. In these long journeys two men will go, one as an emergency man, to occasionally take a turn in the shafts, and uphill pull at a rope in tandem fashion. At first it looks objectionable to be dragged about by one's fellow-beings in place of horses. The traveller, however, gets used to everything in time, and comes to look upon whatever is as being right. Our prejudices and predilections are all

THE JINRICKISHAW.

accidents of birth. Our thoughts, beliefs, and tastes are of education.

Travelling in Japan would be all the pleasanter if one knew the language. The little Japanese guide would be a philosopher and friend as well, if he could. His knowledge of English is very limited, but he speaks it better than the Chinese, and does not invent new words that belong to neither language, as the Chinaman does in his "pigeon English." Living in Japan is very cheap indeed, and so is locomotion. For the forty miles' journey I was only charged 10s. a day, and the bills of the tea-houses on the road came to a mere nothing. The tobacco-smoking of Japan is as mild a thing as the eating and drinking. It is the weakest of all tobacco to begin with. The pipe-bowl is less than a child's thimble in size. Three whiffs exhaust its contents, and that is enough smoking for three hours for a Japanese. His liver being always in good order, his ideas are so likewise. His religion is, like his eating and drinking and smoking, a mild and cheerful thing. He stops at a temple and washes his hands at a small tank in front. He then ascends the steps, prostrates himself for four minutes, mutters a formula of prayer, and advances to a wooden trough in front of the image of his deity. Into this trough he drops two or three coins of a value that go 200 to an English shilling. That done, he pulls a rope that rings a bell, and calls the attention of the gods to his donation. The service is now ended. The lavation, the prostration, and the donation have taken six minutes only. He goes away light-hearted and happy. No Scotchman who has stood or sat through a sermon of an hour long could be happier. He that "keeps the keys of all the creeds" can alone say what form of worship, of all the thousand forms extant, is the right one. I will not judge that I may not be judged.

Yeddo, now called Tokio, is a fine, busy, bustling city, with goodly-sized streets, and not the narrow chinks that disfigure the cities of the Chinese. The number of the inhabitants has been much over-estimated—especially by Lord Elgin. It is nothing like three millions. I doubt if it approaches more than half that number, and the secretary to the resident British Minister, who had best means of knowing, shared my doubts. The city, being mostly of wooden houses, of one or two storeys, is very liable to fires. One that occurred there on New Year's Day of the present year destroyed some thousands of buildings. It was, however, thought nothing of. Other parts of the city showed signs of similar disasters. New wood-built houses are rapidly raised to replace the burnt ones. Here and there, on the scenes of these fires, stand up two-storey buildings that appear as if built of polished black slate. In these buildings, which are fire-proof, the neighbours store their valuables. They are, I was told, built of clay, coated with a cement that takes a polish. After a fire these buildings stand about—dozens in number—among the surrounding blackened stumps of the burnt houses, and have a curious appearance, like to a concourse of funereal mutes scattered over a large graveyard.

The Japanee is the cleanest of mankind. Cleanliness is, so to speak, more than godliness with him. Though he has no soap, he washes all over at least once a day. He worships but once a week. His candles are made of vegetable wax. He uses a cotton coverlid, well stuffed and padded, for bed covering and mattress. A sort of stereoscope case—made of wood—makes his pillow. He resorts to that, and so do his wife and daughters, that their carefully arranged hair may not be disarranged during sleep. No head-covering is worn by the Japanese. No nation dresses the hair so tastefully. Usually it is with the men shaved in sections. They are coming now to wear it in European fashion. They are adopting all European customs. On *levée* day I saw the reception at the Mikado's palace in Yeddo. Every one presented had to come in European full dress. That dress does not become the Japanese figure. He looks awkward in it. His legs are too short. The tails of his claw-hammer coat drag on the ground, and the black dress trousers wrinkle up and get baggy around his feet. His European-fashioned clothes have been sent out ready made from America or England, and in no case did I notice anything approaching to a good fit. Yet he smiled and looked happy, though he could not get his heels halfway down his wellington boots, and his hat was either too large or too small for his head. He always smiles and looks pleasant. Nothing can make him grumble, and he has not learnt to swear. He is satisfied to be paid his due, and never asks for more. As a London cabman he would be the very man that London wants.

Railways, gas, schools, telegraphs, barracks, and military

drilling, directed by Europeans, are spreading throughout Japan. A Melbourne man, who had been a "super" at the Theatre Royal, was, I found, tutor at an up-country school at 200*l.* a year. He intended to stay in the country. Educated Englishmen are thus utilized by the Japs. Japan is opening all its cities and ports to the world generally. It was for some time doubtful about opening Yeddo, but that being done, everything followed. The Mikado was brought down from his sacred city of Kioto and set up in Yeddo, in place of the Tycoon, who was then and for ever abolished. Kioto is now open to the visitor. The way thither is by steamer to Kobé, a thirty hours' journey. Here a second Yokohama is seen, with a native settlement called Hiogo in its rear. A good line of rail takes one in an hour to Osaca—a Japanese Venice of many hundred bridges, and the most commercial city in Japan. Some of these bridges—I was told that they numbered 848—are of stone and iron, and well built, but the majority are of wood, and some of very curious build. Osaca is more surprising to the visitor than is Yeddo. Another hour's railway ride, and I am in Kioto. To get thither a passport from the British Consul was necessary. For what reason is not so very apparent, except that one is getting into the heart of the country, and is supposed to want more looking after than when on the seaboard. No traveller now requires any guard beyond his guide. He is welcomed everywhere with smiles and politeness. There is nothing to spend much money upon. The theatres and shows are like to what one supposes them to have been in Britain 500 years ago, in the time of the tournaments and the hawkings, and the jesters and the Joyous Life, before avarice had eaten into the heart of the world, and made money-making the end, aim, and object of existence. Avarice has not got hold of the Japanese as yet. He is careless about money, so long as his daily wants are supplied. Frugal, temperate, and happy, he takes little thought for tomorrow, and none for the day after. Any overplus he may have he spends in some exhilarating amusement. Of that

Japan shows plenty. Jugglers are at the street-corners, open-air dramas are performing in the market-places, and the Eastern story-teller sits under his umbrella and tells his tales, wherever an open space will afford him room to gather his laughing audience. I wished I could understand the farces I saw thus acted, and the stories I heard told. They must have been good. That was evident from the interest they created. I subscribed when the dish came round in place of the hat, for the novelty of the sight was worth paying the two-hundredth part of a shilling for. A shilling goes a long way in Japan, but one has to get one's guide to carry the coin. Five shillings' worth of copper "cash" would seriously impede one's progress.

From Kobé I take steamer and pass down the inland sea for another thirty hours' journey to Nagasaki—the third of the white seaboard settlements in Japan. It has more seaport characteristics than either Kobé or Yokohama, and is more of a resort for shipping in want of ship stores and repairs. For the latter purpose it has a graving-dock and other ship-repairing conveniences. Here is the little Decima, the wretched island on which the Dutch settlement stood, as dirty a hole as one can see anywhere. The beauty of the inland sea is something surprising. It is like to Sydney harbour, stretched out for a thirty hours' steamboat journey. I don't think that any description could convey a better impression of its beauty than those few words. The white settlers at Nagasaki are less in number than those at Kobé or Yokohama, and more in a ship-chandlery and boat-building way. It has not that appearance of cleanliness and respectability which characterizes the two other white settlements. Its surrounding scenery is, however, far superior. In a land-locked basin, surrounded by tree-covered hills, and goodly Japanese temples and well-built houses, it forms a striking picture to the traveller's eyes, and well repays a visit—as indeed does every place in Japan.

CHAPTER II.

THE TYCOON'S TOWN.

OF the characteristics of the pleasant Japanese land, the first is the Tycoon's town—the London of Japan. This Jeddo, or Yeddo, is now called Tokio, "the Eastern capital." It is a town of many hundred thousand inhabitants. There is no certainty as to how many, but the number is very large. Its streets have the great blessing of good width, fine length, and well-kept roadways. There is not much to speak of in the way of side-walks, but all is smooth and clean.

The working King of the Japanese, called the Tycoon, made this city his residence until late years, when the idle and mysterious other sovereign left his seclusion at Kioto, and came down to Yeddo to change its name, to govern in person, and henceforth do the Tycoon's work. The Tycoon thereupon quietly retired into private life, which he still adorns. The feudal lords of Japan, called Daimios, were then deprived of their territories, and made pensioners on the state. Their pensions are generally reduced every year. They bear the reduction as quietly as if they were Victorian civil servants. There are exceptions to all rules, and a recalcitrant Daimio stood out and fought for his own hand, causing some little trouble for the time. Generally, however, all the many wondrous revolutions made and making in Japan are quietly effected. Folks are all pleasant and complaisant there—born philosophers, who seem to think that all institutions must change, or end, some time or other, and that there is nothing in this world much worth fretting or fighting about. They have a

way of keeping their heads cool—by wearing no covering—
that perhaps goes a long way in helping to an easy mind.
The head is also well washed daily, and its top tastefully laid
out by a barber, who has the skill of a flower-bed gardener.
The bodies of the general run of Japanese are covered with a
blue blouse, tied with a sash around the waist. Of all things
in the world they wear mostly blue serge tights for the rest of
their dress, and blue cloth shoes with thick paper soles to
them. Arrayed in this attire the happy Japanee looks like to
a Christmas pantomime sprite, with a mixture of blue and
white hieroglyphics and heraldry stamped upon his back.

Wandering about Tokio, looking at its scenes, I came upon
the tombs of the Tycoons. They are situated at Shiba, the
enclosed grounds of several small temples. Here was something different in the way of tombs to what I had seen in
other Eastern lands. Large bronze vases here stood upon
blocks of granite under wooden canopies. From the little
English I could get out of the Japanese boy who was with
me, I could not ascertain whether it was the vase or the stone
beneath it that enclosed the remains of the deceased. The
effect was very good. Nothing gaudy, but something solid
and appropriate seemed these tombs of the Tycoons. In
their graves, as in their dwellings, the Japanese do not make
any useless display. The palaces and castles of Japan are
substantial but very unpretentious places. Very different are
they in that respect to those of other Eastern nations. In
Hindoostan the splendour of the palace is mostly equalled by
that of the tomb. Near to these tombs of the Tycoons was a
small temple, in which I found three of the sweetest sounding
bells that were ever made. The bells of Shandon, in the
church of St. Mary, at Cork, were still in my remembrance for
their pleasant sound when I heard these at Shiba, which were
certainly the sweeter.

Atago Yama is a sort of hill in Tokio from which a splendid
view of the whole city can be obtained. To get to it I had to
mount one hundred very steep steps of a foot and a half high
each. They were of roughly-hewn granite, and from their

width and steepness reminded one unpleasantly of getting up the Pyramid of Cheops. From the tea-house on the top of this mount all Tokio can be seen. It is not a fine sight. The city stands on a dead flat. The houses are all roofed with dark-coloured tiles, and are of similar design, and destitute of chimneys. It all looks too flat and plain, and wanting in variety. A church steeple, or a few hundred of them, or bulbous domes of mosques, or graceful minarets or turrets, would have been a real relief to one's eyes. The temples have all plain-ridged roofs, are low in height, and squat-looking

ASCENT TO HEIGHTS (EIGHTY-SIX STEPS).

things seen from any eminence. The vastness of Tokio could be well seen from this position, but the eye failed in singling out objects that would arrest attention. For a variation from the tasteless tea, I took at the tea-house on this mount some "sakura-ya." It is a drink made of salted cherry-blossoms steeped in hot water—a mild Japanese drink, no doubt, and quite an acquired taste; one, too, that seemed likely to take some time to acquire.

The River Simoda is the Thames of Tokio, and I was told runs up, in navigable size, twenty miles from the sea. From that bridge all distances are measured in and about the city, as they used to be in London "from where Hicks's Hall formerly stood." A good idea of the size of the teeming city could thus be obtained. To the north a line could be drawn three miles through streets and houses, and to the south for five miles. To the east a line could be extended six miles, and for four miles to the west. A goodly city, measuring nine miles by eight, but a bad one for a stranger to be lost in. My Japanese boy (Kampadgi) was so like every other Japanese boy, that on stopping to look at the wares on the different shop-boards I could not always again recognize him amongst the crowd that soon surrounded me. I had a mob around me whenever I stopped. They never tired of looking at the hairy face, the stove-pipe hat, and the European clothes. I feared several times that I had lost Kampadgi, and if I had I might have probably wandered in Tokio to this day. To avoid that trouble we handcuffed ourselves together by the wrist, and I adopted that plan henceforth. Any one who has ever been lost in a strange city, where no one could be made to understand a word one says, will appreciate my foresight. I got lost in Jerusalem once, and wandered, with another Englishman, for two hours and more, vainly asking the way to Joppa Gate. When I looked at the size of Jerusalem and its form on the map, it seemed quite impossible that any one could be lost for so long in it, but the fact nevertheless remained. The name, in Syrian, that I should have said for "Joppa Gate" was something that took nearly half a day to learn. When seen on paper, no clue was afforded to the sound when spoken. The Frenchman reads "Ironmonger-lane," only as "Ereen-mongjeelarney." He fails to make Londoners understand that when asking for the place.

In looking into a larger-sized building than usual, in a street leading out of the great road called "Ginza," I observed this pleasant inscription :—

NOTIS.
NO CHITS.
ONE
DRINK
15
CENTS.

Here was English at last. I found that something similar was spoken by several of the inmates, and concluded to stay there while I was in Tokio. The "no chits" I found meant "No I O U's taken"—a sort of Eastern polite way of saying "No trust."

My first evening at this new lodging was disturbed by a large fire that broke out in a distant part of the city. It disturbed dinner very much to see the flames reddening the sky more and more, every five minutes. My host had a vein of humour in him, and was quite inanimate about fires. He had seen too many of them. I need be in no hurry to go, he said; if I waited long enough the fire would possibly come to me; very probably too, if the wind changed towards our quarter. Five or six thousand houses were nothing in one Tokio fire's consumption.

After "chow," as Japanee calls his meals, I took a jinrickishaw, or pull-man-car, and went to the great fire. To avoid the trouble of taking Kampadgi, and looking after him in his separate vehicle—a pull-man only comfortably holds one—I entrusted myself to the guidance of the centaur, only getting Kampadgi to inform him that I was bound for the fire and back again. It was about three miles or so distant, and the crowd gathered thicker as I neared the place. It got soon unpleasantly thick. Half the jinrickishaws in Tokio appeared to be going to Asakusa, where the fire was. It was soon dangerous travelling in so thick a crowd. It was also unpleasant to meet every now and then a dead man carried on the shoulders of men coming from the fire. On all sides, and back and front, I was shut in by thousands upon thousands of men, women, and vehicles. The vehicles often collided. Mine was wheel-locked twice, which perhaps saved it from being thrown on one side altogether. At last the shafts and front bar of a vehicle running behind mine came through the back of it, and pitched me violently forward on to the back of my man in the shafts.

We both rolled on the ground. The lantern that he carried —as all these men do at night—in his hand at once caught fire on its paper sides, and we had hastily to rise to avoid catching fire also from the flaming oiled paper. Merry Japanee only laughed at the disaster. He took another lantern from beneath the seat I had sat upon, lighted the candle, and resumed his trot. I wished very shortly that I had not gone to this fire: but, having got into it, I was, like to Macbeth, "stepped in so far that . . . returning were as tedious as go o'er."

The crowd of vehicles increased, and some ran with reckless haste—drawn by two men in tandem fashion. In that case, the foremost man ran six feet or more in advance of his fellow in the shafts, and pulled by a rope or a strap over one shoulder and across the back under the other. Such a waste of power in drawing so far off from the load showed great ignorance on Japanee's part. He ran well for all that, and shouted as he ran. This shouting added new terrors to one's troubles. It was a strange shout in an unknown tongue, and therefore bewildering. More dead men now went by on stretchers. Strangely-attired men, whom I afterwards learnt were firemen, came rushing by, having on their heads that unheard-of thing in Japan, a head-dress. They dragged a small machine, about the size and appearance of a washing-tub, on wheels, with a churn in it. That was the Japanese fire-engine. It was only calculated to extinguish the fire in a dog-kennel or some dwelling of similar size. Bamboo-made ladders followed in plenty. The flames now became apparent, and soon our progress on wheels came to a deadlock. My centaur took his car into a tea-house, and I handcuffed him carefully to my wrist, to his great amusement, and went forth to thread street after street filled with crowds all looking aflame with the glare from the great fire, which reddened also the water running in the gutters.

This fire at Tokio, on New Year's night, consumed 6000 wooden houses. I found that it extended over streets and cross streets for more than a mile onwards in a straight line. The earth was strewn everywhere with smoking and smouldering wood ashes, reddened now and again into a glow as the wind came their way. The fireproof stores or go-downs stood out in bold black relief over the frightful scene, and looked like to giant monsters standing sentry in the fiery, infernal regions. The smoke was unbearable to the eyes, making them smart and water in a way that stopped all progress through the streets of this fire quarter. Away on every hand it looked a wilderness of flame and smoke and burning logs —a painful sight to look at, and equally so to think of. Now to get away from it.

The tea-house had to be found at which our carriage had been put up, and then tea was of course served to both self and centaur, and paid for with a few cents. The stuff was warm and wet, and that was all that could be said of it. It was the only thing that was to be had thereabout. My centaur again put himself in the shafts, and started homewards. Our road was lighted by the glimmer of thousands of hand lanterns that showed like to large glow-worms. It was worse returning than in going. In that going journey my vehicle was on the same way as all the others—going with the tide. Now it was going half with and half against it, and centaur had often to pull up very short and make sharp turns that nearly upset him, to avoid collisions. At last, in some soft spot, he slipped up and fell flat on his back, and as the shafts dropped I pitched forward full length on to him and his prostrate lantern.

We were again all on fire, or nearly so, and had to burn our hands, and my handkerchief, to extinguish the blazing paper of the lantern. This lantern was of value now, as being our last one. The other had been burnt on the downward journey. My stove-pipe hat was crushed in on the side, and presented a stranger sight than it did before to the mob of laughing Japanese around, but the centaur only laughed at our troubles, as he did before. The Japanese laugh at everything. He again got between the shafts, and by midnight, or after, I got back to No Chits' house, and to shelter. I don't think that I shall go to another fire in Japan.

The timber trade ought to flourish in this land. The

frequent fires must promote that industry. Where wood is not used, the walls are built of stones that are cut so as to lean inwardly and gravitate towards each other. No mortar seems to be used in the walls of Japanese buildings.

The kites that nearly every fifth old man or boy seems to be flying are of square shape, and have two tails. Another and live kite that is seen in plenty is a dark-brown bird that hovers over all the cities of Japan, and has eaten up all the sparrows, if there were ever any about.

The Tori-i, a stone gateway-like erection in front of every

A JAPANESE TEMPLE.

temple, is a feature of the streets of Japanese towns that one soon comes to take notice of. The word translated means "bird rest," and is a distinctive feature of Japanese temples —no resemblance to which had I seen in any other Eastern land. The Great Temple of Asakusa, that was formerly one of the sights of Yeddo, is no longer to be seen there. It was a Buddhist temple, and the Sintoo religion having become the one encouraged by the Government, it was sought to turn many of the temples of Buddhism, and that of Asakusa amongst them, into the worship of Sintoo,

C

"the religion of the gods." Let it be recorded to the honour of the priests of Asakusa, that they would not submit to such a desecration. They burnt down their temple—the finest in the city—and, as martyrs, they afterwards forfeited their lives for the act.

"Saiyoken" is, I find, the proper name of the house I am staying at. It is a very comfortable place—for Tokio. In addition to the notice in English to which I have referred, the Japanese proprietor makes other attempts at propitiating the foreigner. Stoves are placed in the bed-rooms instead of the pans of charcoal. As, however, the stoves have no chimneys to them, they are as bad as the open charcoal boxes, or worse. Although it is very cold, I bundle my stove outside the door of a night before going to bed. The door is of course represented by a sliding sash panel in the window-frame. I might awake alive in the morning without taking this trouble overnight, but it looked too much like an attempt at a French suicide to sleep with a stove of lighted charcoal in a closed-up room twelve feet square. I was told that it never caused any inconvenience to the Japanese, and that they often took a pot of charcoal to bed with them and placed it between their feet, in warming-pan fashion, and so slept. The top rim of the pot would keep the coverlid from touching the burning charcoal at the bottom, but such a sleeper must needs never turn or kick about.

There is, perhaps, plenty of coal in Japan, if proper means were taken to find it. The everlasting hills that one sees all around wherever one goes have surely something in them! The sterility of their exterior warrants that supposition. The Japanese, however, fall back entirely on charcoal for their fuel. Pots of it stand about everywhere. In my bed-room is the novelty of a polished steel mirror in a blackwood case, raised at the sides to save the surface from scratches. It has a handle bound round with strips of bamboo. A wooden stand is made to hold it, in which is a niched half-circle. This mirror is quite as good a reflector as the best of silvered glass. I could fancy myself an ancient Roman as I handle it, but for the queer Japanese letters at the back of it. As these articles are very cheap, I invest in half a dozen small ones for presents in distant lands.

The trees that meet one's eyes everywhere that I have gone are pines and firs, that seem to be taken great care of. There are a few cocoa-nut palms also to be seen, and bamboos abound everywhere, as do cherry-trees in the orchards.

It is the day after New Year's Day, and a general holiday in Tokio. The lattice-work is put up on the shop-fronts. Such answers the purpose of shutters here. New clothing appears on the backs of everybody. The Japanese flag, a white ground with a red ball in the centre, is flying everywhere. Boys and old men are sending up kites in hundreds. Girls are outside every second house playing at shuttlecock. Every one seems happy and contented. There are no signs of poverty or misery about, and no beggary. The sun is shining, and the sky is blue, and the air clear. As I get warm with walking, I begin to feel that it is a good thing to be alive and well. Were I able to express to Kampadgi what I want, I think I would buy a kite, and try the sensation of flying it, as I did ever so many years back, when happy as a Japanee.

Crowds in market-places and at street-corners soon attract one's attention. Here, under a canopy, rapping a baton now and then, and gesticulating like a Frenchman, sits a cross-legged real Oriental story-teller on a raised bench, telling some thrilling tale, and enchaining the attention of between 100 and 200 folks who understood his language. In another place I find a similar crowd witnessing open-air theatricals by a company of strolling players. It is some farce that is performing, and three of the *dramatis personæ* are all that are upon the ground at the time. It must be very amusing, from the merriment it excites; as far as the pantomime is concerned, I can see that it is well done, and wish that I could understand more of it. The only thing that mars the appearance of the merry faces all around are the blackened teeth and shaved eyebrows of the married women. When they smile they are quite repulsive. In Victor Hugo's *Les Misérables*, the reader's horror is excited by Cosette's mother selling her two front teeth to a dentist for bread, and leaving an ugly dark hole in the front of her mouth. A double row of blackest teeth is, however, a more disgusting sight. The love of the Japanese wife for her husband must be something great to make her so sacrifice her comeliness, for the disfigurement is done to please him. How many of the women of the western world could be induced to commit such a sacrifice? to so put an end to all hope of flirting henceforward?

Further on I came upon a juggler, who has been, all unassisted by tables, assistants, or apparatus, amusing an immense crowd. To make himself look very distinguished, he had got on some cast-off European clothes that by no means fit him. The trousers are a foot or more too long for his short legs, and much too tight around the waist. He has burst them in several places, but seems quite unconcerned about that. The coat, also, is too long in the sleeves, which are turned up nearly to the elbows. He has a bell-topper hat on, and appears to hail my appearance in a similar one as that of a brother, as he makes some allusion to me that causes a roar of laughter. Before I recover from the attention so suddenly brought upon me, he comes up and musters all his English to say, "Give me money." He would, I know, being a Japanee, be more polite if he knew other form of words. That the performances may proceed I comply with his request, and see him go on with his wonders. He appears to be able to do anything and everything in the way of sleight of hand, and has a world of ready pattering talk, like to a British cheap Jack, by which he keeps his large audience in good humour, and gets showers of coppers thrown to him. By an allusion that he makes when he comes to me again for a contribution, I perceive that he takes me for an American. I lose some faith in his powers being supernatural after that mistake, and go away to something else.

This time it is to some acrobats who have erected an open-air gymnasium, and have covered up the back with rush matting. Here are long bamboos at work balanced on the chests of those who carry them, with boys thirty feet up in the air performing all kinds of break-neck things at the other end of the stick. Occasionally the boy would leave the bamboo and take a rest on a trapeze which was made to oscillate with him, while he clung to it with his feet—with one foot—with the back of his heels on his chin. He could no doubt have hung on by his eyebrows, but I did not witness that.

Down below, top-spinning was going on, and the drawing out of a bale of cloth from the interior of a small box. Then followed the ground tumbling, and the elevation of a boy on the top of some twenty half-barrels, supported on the soles of the feet of a performer who lay upon his back. When the half-barrels, piled up one after another, reached a great height, they were kicked away from beneath the boy, who stood on the topmost one, and he then alighted, quite naturally and easily, on the soles of the feet of his fellow-performer. All these performances were to be seen for nothing. Contributions were quite voluntary, and were plentifully made.

To see something that one had to pay for, I went into a sort of hall, at which twopence, or its equivalent, was charged for admission. A gong was beating at the door. The check handed to me in return for the money was made of wood, and was about the size of a bootjack. Some hieroglyphics were inscribed on it. Had there been a chance of carrying such a thing in one's bag, I would have kept the check as a curio, and cleared out the front way, and missed the performance. But the curio was too big. Such a check as that was worth twopence to handle. I gave mine to Kampadgi to carry along with his own. Such checks for a whole family would have needed a hand-barrow. The hall had no seats. I forgot that Japanese houses have no chairs or stools. I stood with the rest. The curtain had gone up, and a Japanese gentleman, in squatting attitude, was making an oration from the stage. It was impressive but not intelligible. A lady performer then came on who made a top walk across an open fan, and did other wonders, followed up by elongating her neck some ten feet, and looking down upon us in a swan-like manner from that elevation. Her hands remained in her lap as before, and she now looked down upon them as they proceeded to keep half a dozen little balls in motion at once. It was a very short but a novel and entertaining performance for 2d. With another speech from the orator we were bowed out, and the gong sounded for the entrance of a fresh batch of visitors.

CHAPTER III.

THE JAPANESE SPHINX.

FUSIYAMA, or Fusinayama, the volcanic mountain of Japan, is to be seen from everywhere about Yokohama and Tokio. It is in winter (as I see it) covered with snow, rearing its graceful conical shape in midday sunshine and in the glow of

FUSIYAMA.

evening sunset, with frosted silver casing and crown. With the exception of Mount Egmont, on the Northern Island of New Zealand, a more perfectly-shaped mountain it would be difficult to meet with. Its foot can be reached from Yokohama or Yeddo in an easy day's journey. The ascent and escent is usually divided by a night's rest on the mountain. The height of it I could not find any two folks to agree about. It was variously stated as being from 8000 feet to 12,000 feet. To ascend it in the winter time was an impossibility. To avoid seeing it was also impossible. It came next to the sun and moon in that respect.

The traveller soon understands why this majestic mountain has so entered into the Japanese mind. In this part of the land the volcano is always in full view. At sunset it receives the last gilding rays of the setting luminary. Twice I saw it resplendent with this gilded glory. Rays of light seemed, aurora-like, to shoot out from its crown. No wonder, then, that the Japanese make it their characteristic emblem on their lacquerware, in their drawings, paintings, and printings, their inlaid work, their vases of bronze and porcelain, and in their figured silks. The mountain of Fusiyama is to the traveller in this part of Japan similarly impressive. He calls attention to its varied aspects from his fellow-traveller. It is the first thing that is looked at in the early morning, and it claims the last look from one in the starlit brightness of the night.

Next to Fusiyama, the great sight of Japan is one of the works of man—of many hundreds of men. It is a great work of metallic art, perhaps the greatest of such works. Very appropriate is it, therefore, in a land that is famous for such labours. It is a gigantic bronze-built Japanese sphinx-like figure, much larger than what is now to be seen of the Egyptian one. This sitting figure of Buddha has its place away in loneliness among the hills, twenty-three miles from Tokio. Its name is "Dai Butsa," which in common talk is pronounced as "Dieboots." It is one of those sights that the traveller is forbidden to leave unseen. It is the greatest of the metallic curios that Japan has to offer for one's admiration, and it was for actual sacrilegious sale but a few years back. All through the East I had seen figures of the calm, contemplative Buddha in all the temples, but here was one of fifty feet high to be seen—an antique too, and seated in a wilderness away from temples, and as if dropped there from the clouds in the ancient days when Vulcan and the Cyclops might have worked at the making of it. It is possible, on looking at it, to believe that they did so.

The snow covered the ground, and the day looked very unpromising, but those who regard the clouds will miss seeing much on their travels. I found a companion who would join me in the cold journey, though he at first spurned the idea. A good example was, however, too much for him, so he kicked off his slippers and went for his overcoats. It was certainly nippingly cold in the open jinrickishaws. The snow soon again began to fall, and a biting wind blew it in our faces and into our perambulators. I quite envied the man in the shafts, who by running could keep himself warm, as could also the one who ran in tandem fashion in front of him. The snow had to be cleared out of the vehicles every hour of the six long ones that the journey down occupied. At those times I took exercise by running behind the vehicle for a spell when it again started. The snow, however, froze as it fell, and made walking and running very slippery work to one who had not walked on snow but once lately, at Kansas city, for a quarter of a century. The chance of getting snowed up altogether seemed imminent. The beauty of the country round about would have been most attractive in fine weather. As it was, one's face had to be covered up from snow and cold wind, and I wished Dieboots at the deuce before our journey was over, so wretchedly cold and desolated did I feel, and perhaps deserved it, running after strange gods as I was doing. The tedious journey came to an end at last. Surrounded by hills that greatly dwarf its tall appearance, we found the solitary Buddha sitting—sphinx-like—in the wild scene. A temple appears to have covered this majestic statue at one time, but only bits of the foundations are now left. The grand figure is of fine bronze, and is about fifty-six feet high. Its appearance altogether fascinates the spectator. The sweet, placid expression, the downcast eyes, the look of deep thought, or rather serene contemplation, that appears on the face of this figure, are things that bid you regard it, make you continue to gaze at it, and come back again and again to look at it, until you finally unwillingly leave it. The sight was voted between us as being a full recompense for the journey we had taken, unpleasant though that had been. The face of this figure measures ten feet from chin to forehead. It is thirty feet in width across the shoulders. The head is covered with knots or knobs of metal of the size of

DAI BUTSA.

large apples to represent curls. The fine materials of which the metal is made seem to ensure it from decay. It looks quite untouched by time, and as durable as the hills that surround it. All the statues of Buddha that I had hitherto seen in those strongholds of Buddhism, Ceylon and India, were as nothing compared to this one. This really looked like something to be worshipped. It commanded admiration from the alien. There was something awe-inspiring in its gigantic size. In its look were peace, contemplation, and eternal rest—the great majesty of repose. As our centaurs knelt before it and bowed their heads to the earth, we thought that they had quite sufficient cause for doing so. Had the figure stood in a building, every one would naturally uncover before it. It enforces respect, and has altogether a veritable " presence "—distinctly to be felt.

A mile or more from this statue of Buddha stands a temple, wood-built, dedicated to Kuanon, the Goddess of Mercy. It enshrines a gigantic full-length figure of the goddess, forty feet in height, and richly gilt. The miserably small temple is not one-fifth large enough to show this fine statue to advantage. Standing against its walls, one has even to bend the head far back to get a full view of it. The walls are not anywhere ten feet from the statue. Insufficient light is admitted also. The figure appears to be holding something like to a crown and sceptre in its hands. From what little could be seen of it in its dimly-lighted prison, I thought that it deserved a far finer dwelling. It would be the greatest sight in Tokio were it to be removed thither. Speaking of removals, I heard on every hand that it had been proposed by the Japanese Government, instigated by the Sintoo priests, to sell the great statue of Dai Butsa for its weight as old metal. It seemed incredible that such vandalism could have been thought of, but it is understandable when one learns that the Sintoo religion is the present ruling one in Japan. Its priests, therefore, desire to insult Buddhism to the utmost, and counselled the sale of its grandest idol. Threepence per pound was the price asked. No buyer was found to offer more than $1\frac{1}{2}d$.—an enterprising American offered that—so that no sale was effected. The figure has been made in many castings, and could be taken down and reunited. The interior can be explored by a staircase, from which I learnt its construction. As fine bronze alone, no doubt largely mixed with silver, it was well worth the price asked. I wonder if the Khedive will ever offer the sphinx for sale at so much per pound?

He wants money, and is parting with an obelisk to America just now.

The physical endurance of the Japanese was well shown in this journey and another long one that I had, though the latter was not in the snow. The journey had been a good one on such a day, even for a strong horse and buggy. The two little Japanese fellows had got through with it apparently easy, and came in quite light-hearted. All the refreshment they had taken on the journey was a cup of tea at two wayside houses, and "chow," consisting of fish and rice, at Kamakurd. No two Europeans could have run for forty-six miles, dragging a light hansom with 11 st. of weight in it. Man is truly an adaptable animal. I had never seen him more like an animal than when engaged in this novel conveyancing business. The Japanese is, however, a born conveyancer. For untold years his forefathers ran with the heavy palanquin, here called a "Noriwon," until some happy genius, seven years back only, invented the jinrickishaw, in which the wheels take all the burden off his shoulders, and leave only half of it on his hands.

Returning from Tokio to Yokohama, I take ship southwards for Hiogo, and land at Kobé thirty hours afterwards.

These ports of Japan are all similar—a foreign settlement with a native town at its back. Hiogo is the native town here, and Kobé the foreign one. It is, if possible, a cleaner, brighter-looking settlement than Yokohama. Its river-side, or "bund," as it is called here, is planted with trees and flanked with grey stone buildings of two storeys. The streets are wide and well paved. Altogether, Kobé looks as bright as Bath when one sees Lansdowne-crescent on a sunshiny day. But then Bath wants the fine bay of Kobé to complete the comparison.

The voyages to all places on the Japanese coast are made pretty well in sight of land. The hilly coast, dotted with small fishing-stations, is always visible, and so are the boats. These "sampans" are engaged trading or fishing, but mostly in fishing, at the little villages. The boats, with their yellow sides and large sails, produce a pretty effect as seen from the deck of the coasting vessels. In these little villages, half the people cultivate their rice and grain at the foot of the hills, and the other half go fishing, and all are happy, or seem so. The fish and rice together make the "chow," which is the staff of life to the Japanese. In some such way our ancestors lived before we got vitiated and smoke-dried, mistook our ways in the world, and the objects of life.

A good hotel at Kobé is kept by an English widow, who conducts it with admirable attention to business and the com-

EHMIDJI CASTLE.

fort of her guests. With a guide supplied by her hotel, I started on a visit to the great castle of the Prince of Akashi, forty miles distant, at Ehmidji.

The Castle of Ehmidji is reached at the end of a long day's ride, much of which is along the sea-shore. Its white sides can be seen upon the plain against a dark background of hills many miles before it is reached. It was night when I got there. The novelty occurred on this journey, and near to the city of Ehmidji, of crossing a river otherwise than by a bridge.

Bridges are the specialities of Japan. They seem to grow over the rivers naturally, so numerous are they. The river in this case had resisted embankment, and spread about all over the place, like to the rivers of New Zealand. After crossing the well-washed stones, that indicated a river's bed, for some distance, I came upon the water, now making another course for itself, and had there to be ferried across. It was the only instance of a ferry I met with in Japan.

In the morning I left the tea-house, in which I had formed the usual bed by spreading a padded quilt on the floor and heaping two others above it, and took my way through the town. It was a large place this town, and had grown up around three sides of the walls of the great castle. One street of it ran directly down to the sea in a straight line, a distance of fully eight miles. The streets were all wide and clean, and the place looked prosperous and comfortable—quite Japan-like.

I came now in view of the castle walls, surrounded by a wide moat, in which grew the lotus, covering the water with its now dead leaves. At the castle gate I was stopped by the outcoming of fifteen separate bands of soldiers for morning exercise in the neighbouring parade-ground. It was so cold standing about, and they filed out so slowly, that I wished I had stayed for breakfast before coming. When I essayed to go in, I was stopped by the sentry. My native boy was here useful, and so was my passport. It had to be taken in first and overhauled, and then I was fetched in and introduced to the potentate of the place, who appointed a body-guard for me, and passed me on. If any one will take the buildings seen on the willow-pattern plate, and multiply them to the height of 200ft. by putting walls beneath them for the first 40ft., and then putting the buildings one on top of another, decreasing in size as they go upwards, a good idea of the Castle of Ehmidji will be obtained. The timbers of the castle are stout and strong, but very roughly finished. The doors are covered with sheet iron. Rude staircases mount from floor to floor. I counted about a dozen flights of stairs, and then lost count. No attempt at finish or fine work was anywhere to be seen. The place was as plain as a barrack, and nearly as rough as a barn. Its lord and master, who had given up the revenues of Ehmidji, and now lived in Tokio on a pension, did not evidently care for luxuries, at least not in the way of a residence.

The view from the summit of the Castle of Ehmidji was a sight worth seeing. On that fine, clear morning, everything was visible for miles around. The view over Ehmidji from that castle, like to the view over Tokio, was not befogged in any way by coal smoke. Let that much be said in favour of the use of the wretched pots of charcoal. From that castle-top I might, ten years or less ago, have, with permission of the Prince of Akashi, looked upon a feudal scene such as I might have looked upon in England hundreds of years ago. Round this large castle had grown up the great town. Within the castle walls I was shown the foundations of the houses in which had dwelt the hundreds of armed men, "Saumarai," who were the body-guard of their lord and daimio. They had gone now, their houses had followed them, and the great castle was a Government barrack. The prince was a pensioner, but what had become of his vast body of two-sworded fighting-men I could not learn. Providing for this large number of disbanded semi-soldiers has been one of the troubles of the Government. They are of too advanced an age to learn to run about with the perambulators, and they know nothing of agriculture or fishing. Some were perhaps among the soldiery that I had seen defile out at the gate. It was really a novel and goodly sight all around on that morning, and kept me on the castle-top much longer than I thought to be there. Shut in by hills on nearly its three sides, the whole town beneath, and the country right away to the sea in front, seemed to lie at one's feet, as it had for centuries done at the feet of the owner of this lordly place.

On the way back to Kobé, I passed through the village of Akashi—a small place, in which is situated another castle of the same great prince, now deserted and going to ruin. The part of it that had been used for residence is now occupied as a local school-house. The schoolmaster's English tutor had no doubt written the following notice. It appears on a board just within the castle gate:—" Notice.—All hountings are prohibits in the limite. hyoyoken." It is meant to warn off sportsmen.

Inside this castle gate of Akashi, and at the back of it, I found steps leading to a room over the gate. Here were two big drums and an immense bronze bell of excellent sound. The sticks lay near that had, in times gone by, beaten a call to arms on these drums and this bell. My native boy ran to prevent my striking either, in fear, I suppose, that I might alarm the little township. Inside the inner moat I found most of the buildings pulled down, and the rest going to ruin —a melancholy sight altogether this deserted Castle of Akashi. One of the Saumarai was here pointed out to me. On the back of his blue blouse was a white stamp about the size of a five-shilling piece. On the back of the lower orders are hieroglyphics the size of a frying-pan. Were the blouses of a whitish colour, the wearers would look, on the rear-view, like to prisoners from some gaol bearing the Government brands on their backs. The Japanese had run with the vehicle these two days eighty miles—two men to each—and they did not seem fatigued in any way. I had heard before of men outrunning horses, and now saw proof of it.

Temples are the sights to which foreigners usually pay most attention in Japan. They are, however, but second-rate compared to those of India, and about on a par with the Buddhist temples of Ceylon. The bell is, however, a speciality in these Japanese temples, as is also the money-box. The first is shaped like to a pope's hat, and the latter is an oblong trough, railed over, and with slanting shelving within, that the amount of the "collection" may not be seen from the outside. A worshipper washes his hands in water from a neighbouring stone tank, and wipes them upon a blue cotton cloth suspended near to the tank. He then drinks water from the same tank in a wooden scoop, and, having thus washed his mouth and

hands, he mounts the steps of the temple, pulls the rope of
the bell to call the attention of his deity, and then throws his
money-offering into the trough. After that he kneels, clasps
his hands, and mutters a formula of prayer, for about a minute
only. His worship then seems to be over for the week. The
Eastern world is generally fanatically religious, but the
Japanee is French in his politeness and in his religious feelings. The female Japanee does not seem either to be more
devout than the male. The European custom of observing
the seventh day is gradually being introduced in Japan,
together with the European system of almanacs and time-

JAPANESE STREET.

keeping. Hitherto the Japanee has stolen a march on the
Western world by observing as a holiday one day out of six,
instead of one out of seven only. Perhaps to that is to be
credited his greater jollity as a nation, and his happiness as
an individual.

The smooth roadways and the light-running jinrickishaws
with their unshod drawers, avoid much of the clatter, rumble,
and roar that offends the ear in London, New York, and other
cities. In the latter city it is difficult to hear conversation in
the streets. Tokio is a busy city indeed, with many thou-

sands—it is said fifty—of these little hansoms running about, but it is not a noisy one. The Japanee is a quiet and low-voiced man. His laugh is full of fun, but not boisterous. There is no smacking of whips heard, nor any calls to horses. Nobody is run over and killed. No "bolts" occur in which a frightened horse is seen dashing through a crowded street with a rocking vehicle and its screaming occupant behind. No collisions occur, and no breakdowns. A mild cry from one centaur warns another on which side he is about to pass, and there are no blocks in the crowded streets, no stoppages, and no swearing of car-drivers, omnibus, and cabmen. That vehicles should be drawn by men between the shafts is not a pleasing sight to a European, but it obviates many troubles that occur in the use of horses, and one never has to fear that one's steed may be vicious or badly broken to harness.

CHAPTER IV.

THE MIKADO'S CITY.

I WANTED a guide at Hiogo who would accompany me for a week or more on an up-country journey to Kioto, the formerly reserved city of the mysterious Mikado. This place is some seventy miles from the coast. A passport is imperatively necessary to those who visit it. I was advised to apply at the post-office for a guide, which I did, and saw one there who was introduced as an English scholar. Next day I was waited upon by a young Japanee, who handed me the following note:—"Sir, I have the honor to send you the barer as gide. Cannot say mugh for his Englis, but he as knowledg of the plas you go too, and is best I find at present thoug not number one.—Yours, &c., J. N. January, 1877." In the Japanese ideas of English, everything good is called "number one." It was the opinion of my friend, it will be seen, that the gentleman sent to me did not classify as such. My hostess of the Hiogo Hotel, a blooming widow, took all the interviewing business out of one's hands, and interrogated Minerva—for such was the nearest approach I could make to my guide's name—in this style :—

"You been long in Kobé and Hiogo, and where?"

"Been six years; most with Nicolas and Jawbreaker."

"You been to Kioto with pigeons?"

"Many time; last time two year."

"How long you take to show this pigeon Kioto?"

"Three days. I go everywhere that time."

"Where will you sleep him?"

"At naughty Maria's!"—so it sounded.

"No, you take him to Marianna's. Mind that!"

I thought of Tennyson's Moated Grange at this last name, and did not like the associations that such recollection and these feminine-sounding names called up. My lady resumed :—

"You take him to buy things and you not squeeze him— no commission now! This pigeon is cousin of mine," which I was certainly not, nor anything like a pigeon either.

"All right. I do as you say."

"How many days you take to show pigeon Osaca? You know Osaca, boy?"

"No; I know all about it. I take three days go everywhere."

"Where you sleep him at Osaca?"

"I go to Judie's, up town." More feminine-sounding names.

"No! You go to Judie's on Concession—mind that! And now, I see everything this pigeon buy; and mind, if you let him be squeezed, I take care that you never take another one away from here. If you do well, I get you plenty others. Boys are always wanted from this hotel."

"No; I do well." Minerva frequently said "no" when he should have said "yes," but many of us also do that.

"Now, boy, what he pay you?"

"One dollar a day and chow."

"Yes—likely! Now you shan't go. A dollar a day and chow indeed! Nicholas and Jawbreaker never gave you that for a week."

"I was told to ask a dollar a day and chow!"

"Well, I tell you to ask half a dollar a day and your chow. If you don't take that, I send one of my boys, and you can come here and work in his place at that rate!"

"No! I go!" And so the bargain was concluded.

I could understand now how Lady Hester Stanhope had, all alone in the East, established her great authority over the native Syrians. There is something sublime in female nature when it developes itself in the form of bounce! My hostess had dwelt for fifteen years among the Eastern people, and had learnt to subdue them with that powerful mind and tongue of hers in a way that I could only wonder at. All the Japanese that I saw her deal with quailed before her. On my return from a visit to Ehmidji and its castle, I had asked of my centaurs who had dragged me there and back what was to pay to the four of them, and was told fifteen dollars, which seemed reasonable enough for eighty miles' work for two days and two vehicles. My hostess, however, stepped in between us.

"You shall pay nothing of the sort. Did you pay for their chow?" she said.

"Yes, I paid for their meals all the way along, and for their lodging, if it was charged for. I paid four dollars."

"They squeezed you, then!—it did not come to that. They must be paid a dollar a day only. That's what I pay a day when I travel."

Now, my fair hostess of forty was buxom to boot, and very much heavier than myself. It looked a species of cruelty to animals, not to say men, to ask them to take 4*s.* a day for running forty miles between the shafts with such a load as herself behind them.

I said then that I would take a middle course, and give half what was asked, and double what my hostess spoke of.

"You shall do nothing of the kind. You will spoil the market for others. I will settle with them, and charge to you."

"No, no; I shall pay them what I say. They have been good fellows, and have earned their money well. It is about half what a horse and trap would have cost elsewhere."

That would not, however, satisfy this weighty and careful woman. As she looked on at the folly I committed in paying a fair price, as things went, for the hardest day's work men ever did, she said, "All right! If I don't take two days' ride out of those fellows for nothing, and so square it, I'm not a woman."

She said that, too, in the presence of the men, who knew enough of her, and of English, to understand what was in store for them. They were Japanese, and therefore merely smiled. I wonder what an English—or, better still, an Irish—cabman would have said on such a matter. Madame would then have met her match.

All throughout the East—in Ceylon, India, Egypt, Syria, Japan, and China—the natives are accustomed to such rough language and overbearing treatment from the English as I have narrated in this little matter. Bounce, bluster, and abuse all through.

I went with Minerva to Kioto, and entered that city, which up to two years before had been as shut up and as sacred as Mecca or Medina. It was plain to see that a European, or one in European costume, as I was, was still a novelty in the place. I had a little following everywhere of those who were attracted by my outlandish appearance. It was all innocent curiosity, however. Their native politeness shamed them for it. When the crowd darkened the shop-boards, and I was forced to look up for light, not an eye would then be looking at me. Oh dear, no! The articles round about, or the appearance of the sky or the sun, were all that these people were then looking at!

Kioto was not in the best condition for a visitor at that season. Its river—the Kanagawa—was quite run dry. Its wide, stony bed was being used for bleaching purposes. To look at it from any of the bridges was very unsatisfactory—too much like to a general washing-day appearance. The Mikado was there upon a visit, however, and holding a *levée* or reception, to which, as at Tokio on New Year's Day, every official was going in the regulation European dress suit and stove-pipe hat. It might have been the 5th of November, looking at the Guyish appearance presented by the majority of these folks. Scarcely the hat, coat, or boots of one of them fitted, or came near to a fit. These clothes could scarcely have been made by any Western tailors, so grotesquely were they fashioned. The hats were either too small or too large, and were only balanced on the head in the first case, or padded up with paper in the second. Nearly all of them had been crushed in some way, and their rims were stuck up or bent down, or levelled all round in a stiff outstanding circle—a fearful and wonderful sight in the way of hats. The coats were mostly too long, and the tails trailed at the wearers' heels. In the cases in which the coat was short, it mostly came up too high in the neck. The waist was, in that case, somewhere between the shoulders, and bursting at the seams. The trousers were never turned up at the feet when too long, but worn in folds and ridges about the leg, from the knee downwards. When too short, it was equally ridiculous to see the wearer's comical appearance, especially when he could not get his heels down in his boots. That was very often the case, and a trouble that the trouser legs, when too long, helped often to conceal. Scarcely a pair of these leg coverings but what had burst somewhere before or behind Nothing, however—not even misfitting boots—troubles the serenity of a Japanese! He smiled at me as I smiled at him; and when he bowed, I could not but do the same in return, and wish that the Mikado had ordered the clothes for these folks when he issued the order for the wearing of them. It was really a shame to put people so ready to please and be pleased into such uncomfortable misfits as they had been, by necessity, forced thus to wear. The Japanese figures, male and female, are not adapted for showing European costumes to advantage, but that does not trouble them.

Plenty of time was given to study the appearance of the folks of Kioto on that day. The police, which the Japanese have adopted in imitation of European fashions, kept nearly all the crossings barred on the line of road along which their Majesties were to pass. The Empress was to be there also, but I could not hear the proper title of this feminine Mikado. I noticed that those going about in *levée* dress were allowed by the police to pass through the barriers, so that I pinned up, with Minerva's help, the half part of the tails of a frock coat, and then looked in regulation dress costume, and passed muster, and so onwards.

Like to most Japanese cities, this up-country capital stands on a small plain shut in by adjacent hills. It looks almost imprisoned by the surrounding heights. They give it a walled-in and oppressed appearance. Lying there among the hills, all shut in, as it appears to be, it was the very city for the dwelling of the mysterious Mikado—the hereditary King of Japan, who reigned but did not govern—whose kingly functions were exercised solely by the working king, the Tycoon down at Yeddo. The Mikado's palace here, now untenanted, called Goshio, is an unpretending place compared with some of the daimios' castles. His semi-sacred character was, I suppose, sufficient protection to him. Goshio would otherwise have stood but a very sorry chance if built to resist an attack.

Minerva, away from my hostess's feminine influence, which had oppressed him down at Kobé, reasserted his right of judgment, and took me to Nackamarya's house. It was, I found, a tea-house at the foot of the hill, and had the blessing about it of a boy who spoke a little English. The landlord with the long name could only bow me a welcome. The boy brought me, whilst waiting for a mid-day meal, the quaintest of guide-books among the hundred or so that I had happened upon in my travels. This guide-book to Kioto was by a Japanese who had got hold of a little English, and had also got a little of wood engraving done to help it out. The price of the book was a dollar, but had it been more, the price had not parted me from such a gem as this queerest of guide-books! Each page is headed with a rough woodcut, which occupies half of it. The balance of the page is funny letter-press, in language the like of which is worth sampling. Take the page headed "Biwa," the cut at the top of which is meant to represent a lake-side. This pretty chapter is as follows (the only punctuation is in the long dashes between some of the words, as copied) :—

"BIWA.

" Biwa the lake in the east of Kioto is a very nice lake with many fine views all round——The beauties of the lake are eight in number——First the strange fir tree in Karasaki——Second the view of the flying down of wild geese——Third Awatsu——Fourth the moon lighting night in autumn in Ishiyama and Fifth the evening in Sheta——Sixth the boats sailing to Yabashe. Seventh the snow mountain, Hira, evening sight. Eight If you go to the Mediera you will see nearly all of them."

The book and the city it illustrates are well matched. It would be a shame to publish any other guide-book to Kioto in place of it. I copy further from it another chapter—the heading to which is a woodcut of an enormous tree:—

"KARASAKI.

"The firtree in Karasaki, as I said before, is one of the eight remarkable things round the lake——The tree is grown near the shore of the lake, and its branches are spreading far over the water——It is said that the tree is at least two or three hundred years old. The rain dropping from branch to branch, and at last in the water, makes a peticular sound."

The chapter on Sheta and Ishiyama is also as good as any. The woodcut heading it represents a long wooden bridge:—

"SHETA AND ISHIYAMA.

" The bridge Sheta which crosses the outlet of the lake is a most famous and large one——The sight of the evening is very pretty and many visit it when the sun is set——The finest scene is when the wind blows and the sun shines——The waves of this lake then look very pretty like silver——The temple Ishiyama stands on the hill near the outlet of the lake and the lower part of it can be best looked over from here ——The place is visited in the autumn by many people who pass a moonlight night."

In Kioto I found a bird of the duck species, the drake of which is more prettily feathered than any bird I have seen. It is difficult to believe that it has feathers, so closely do they lie, and so fantastically are they cut and shaped by nature. I thought at first that the bird had surely been covered with fancifully cut paper, and then painted and lacquered up. This bird is called the Oshee Tori as nearly as I could get to the sound. My inquiries for a stuffed one were numerous, but I failed to obtain it. It was swimming about with its mean-looking and plain-feathered ducks in a pond at a small menagerie. In the background of that place I came also upon a sad sight. It was a young Australian kangaroo that had gone stone blind. The poor thing was in bad condition, its bones being all too prominent. I fed it with some cut turnips, and fondled it with that feeling which one Australian exile must naturally feel for another. What misfortune had drifted the poor wretch from the green plains of pleasant Australia to this out-of-the-way corner of the world? Why had its eyesight gone? In the cold air of the winter weather here among the bleak hills it was visibly shivering, equally with myself. It stood up to take the cut turnips I offered, and held my hand with its little hand-like fore-paws as if it would detain me. It was the only Australian that I met with in that city of Kioto, and it is characteristic of travelling Australians to greet each other gleesomely.

The Mikado and his wife came at last—in a closed English brougham drawn by two horses, and driven by a coachman dressed as he would be in an English city. The Japanese might have thought it grand, but it looked to me very shabby—this plain turn-out, with its coachman and two out-riders in European costume, where nearly everybody else was orientally dressed. A British consul might have made such a modest appearance on a special day, but for the Mikado to visit his old stronghold in such style was very disappointing —to me. The English do not travel to see English fashions reproduced in second-hand sort.

The temples of this Kioto divide honours with those at

Nikko, in the north of Japan. There is much of sameness about them, and great want of height and impressiveness. In the eyes of the Japanese they are of course sublime. Near to one of them I came upon something more interesting—a large cemetery, fenced in as an English one would be.

The cemeteries of Japan are very like those of Europe. Each grave has its grave-stone. The stones have their inscriptions also cut into them. It would look almost as if space was economized in a country where all available land is cultivated, by reducing the length of these graves to about

TEMPLE AT KIOTO.

4 ft. only. Of that length only a flat stone is laid upon each grave. On the centre is then placed upright a stone of 4 ft. high by 1 ft. side measurement. The thin head-stones seen in English graveyards are not used here. Some of these graves are fenced in with wooden palings, and by each of them stands a stone vase of narrow form, in the mouth of which a sprig of some evergreen was always apparent. The appearance of these graves and their short coverings lead one to the idea that the dead are interred in a sitting posture. To protect the inscriptions from the weather, many of

these little monuments had domed caps to the top of the upright stone, from which the rain would drain off clear of the writing beneath. This cemetery stood near to the *Kiomesya* Temple.

The Japanese doorways are made to suit folks of not more than 5 ft. 8 in., and these not with stove-pipe hats on. I was continually getting mine knocked off whilst in Japan. The Japanee is short. He wears no hat, and shaves the crown of his head, or parts of it. I would have abandoned my British hat in favour of the fashion of the country, had a head-dress existed. The blue rag, with hieroglyphics on it, which the lower orders wear on holidays, does not look well with European costume. It wants the blue blouse to match with it, and the brown Japanese face.

Some fine lacquer-work and some lovely thin egg-shell china were for sale at Kioto. Had my luggage afforded room for it, I felt that I had purchasing inclination to any extent in the rich and rare things to be seen around one. It was quite the city for a man to come to with a wife of good taste—he having a good purse to back it. About a dozen well-filled packing-cases would be the result; one of them of large size, to hold the famous fire-screens that these Japanese make, and which at Kioto are to be seen in best form.

In the neighbourhood of Kioto I was shown the measured ground—about a mile in extent—in which unfaithful wives are doomed to walk between a guard of soldiers until they can walk no more—until the pricking of spears will no longer goad them onwards or move them upwards when they fall, there to lie and die of hunger, thirst, and over-exertion—a sad sight to any single man.

CHAPTER V.

AN EASTERN VENICE.

OSACA—lying midway between Kioto and the port of Hiogo—is a city of bridges. They number, it is said, 840. It is the Venice of Japan, and yet Venice only in the way of water—not of gondolas. The pull-man car maintains its supremacy. The traffic on the endless waters is restricted to merchandise.

Minerva—my boy guide—has a patriotic feeling, and takes me to that native hotel (Judie's) which is situated in the city, and it is, I find, a large two-story tea-house with a splendid water frontage. If I don't like it, I am to go to that other Judie's, which is in the foreign settlement of Osaca, called the Concession. It is a dark night, and I have to walk through unlighted streets for two miles or more before I reach this tea-house. It is a cold and freezing night too; my upstairs room overlooks a river on one side, and a square courtyard, with leafless trees in it, on the other. I cannot get warmth from the square box with the charcoal in it. The bedroom, with this box and nothing else for its furniture, looks cold, and indeed feels so. I go to bed to forget all about it, and am soon in the solace of sleep, for which the long walk and the cold night well provided.

All is different when daylight comes, and the morning sun glamours and gilds everything. The balcony overhanging the river affords fine views of wide water. On an island to the right are some hospital buildings of neat appearance. River craft and coasting boats are passing on their way, propelled by hand labour, or trusting to their queer-looking sails. I can see three bridges from this position—two of wood and one of stone. The piers are substantial, but the arches too narrow and numerous to suit English taste. Japanese boats, however, make their way through all difficulties. They could otherwise never get into or out of the crowded state in which they lie on some parts of these Osaca rivers. To enable large vessels to get to their destinations, some of these bridges have a swing or a turnstile on one of the central supports that is easily opened and closed.

I hang about on some of these Osaca bridges with ceaseless gaze on the scenes before, behind, and around me. The rivers of Osaca, called the Cowa and the Ajacowa, divide into many branches, forming forks and islands which builders have been busy upon. No land is wasted in Japan. The seas, the mountains, and the rivers take up so much space that the Japanese have to be economical with that little of level earth that is left to them. Economical they are, and nurse and nourish and improve their patches of land as they do their families.

From the bridge that crosses to the foreign quarter, "The Concession," some good water views are to be had. The grand water view is, however, from the great bridge called the "Tinsinbash," or some similarly sounding name. It is the greatest bridge of the 840. From its sides, dividing streams are to be seen either way. The great river here parts itself into two streams, each seemingly little less large than itself. Each of these is spanned by many bridges. The setting sun was on the waters when I looked upon the scene from this bridge. I went again next day to see the same sight at high noon, but found that the view of the previous evening, seen by the setting sun, had been by far the finest one. Wide, clean waters, filled with craft of novel form, are here to be seen flanked by the queer-looking water-side houses of the Japanese merchants. The view that the traveller obtains at sunset at this bridge of Tinsinbash is one that will be retained without effort, and recalled always with pleasure. I stayed over next day to see its grandeur again.

I wander from this bridge towards the next one, that has midway for support an island or an artificially-made and stone-faced central earthwork. That is planted with trees and shrubs, and has a picturesque appearance. A fine view of the greater and undivided bridge of Tinsinbash is obtained from this one, which appears to be the most expensively-built of all the bridges of Osaca. The ironworker has had his share in this bridge work. Several of those I saw were of his construction.

From the bridges I pass on, with Minerva's help, to the Sinsidori—the leading street of Osaca. To get thither I go through a highly respectable-looking street, in which are some broad-faced buildings, with large open doors, and nothing exhibited in front. I cannot understand from Minerva what these places are. He endeavours to prevent my entering them. I must not go in, he says. He has, however, said that so often at other interesting places, that I immediately resolve on going in, and do so. The buildings prove to be Japanese banks. The clerks are squatting on the floors, but a large outer counter acts as a barrier between them and the customer. They bow a welcome to me as I look about the place. Minerva must have been brought up to look upon it as wrong to go into any place whereinto business had not called him. He stayed my progress also into a large building, which turned out to be a gigantic general store—a sort of Japanese "Stewart's" of New York—where everybody, one hundred at least, seemed very glad to see me, as a probably large customer.

The Sinsidori of Osaca is quite a Cheapside in respect of width and length and traffic. The absence of glass to the shop windows, and of a side-walk, is, of course, a difference, and so is the absence of tall houses, omnibuses, and horses. All, however, is bustle and business with the bare-headed and blue-bloused crowd. Everything that a body can want is for sale here, save milk, butter, soap, beef, mutton, and beer, and a few such like superfluities of life. Any Englishman walking this street may say, as he may say indeed in any of the leading streets of the world, "How much there is there that I don't want!" It all looks so useful, and much of it so pretty, that it is almost a pity that one can do without any of it.

Brown, a mercantile man from New Zealand, who is passing through Osaca with me, observes, "If I were not gone out of business, and retired from its bother, I could purchase in this city, and ship to Australia and New Zealand for 500*l.* what would sell there for 1500*l.*" My unmercantile ideas had some hazy notion of this kind in all the cities I had passed through in Japan. The same sort of things are seemingly imported by everybody into those two countries Brown had named. The markets must be glutted and clogged with such wares. Here in Japan are all new articles to tempt the best class of buyers, and those are they who buy only to spend their money, and not to satisfy the mere daily wants of life.

"How many other ways have you seen, Brown, by which a fortune could be made during your Japanese travel?"

"Fully half a dozen. I wish I had come here fifteen years ago, instead of going to New Zealand."

We had by this time got to the street devoted to theatres and shows, a quarter of the town where theatres large as the minor ones of London are at one end of the street, and a sort of English country fair going on in full swing at the other. The theatres were entered, notwithstanding Minerva's strong objection to such intrusions, through the unfastened doors. We found them to be large, clean, theatrically-shaped places. Benches, raised one foot only from the floor, covered the lower part. A gallery (one only) ran round the three sides of the building half-way between the floor and the roof, after the fashion of an English chapel. On a seat, a foot high only, Japanee sits easier than he would on a common chair. We rest the foot only upon the floor. He prefers to rest the leg from the knee downwards, in the older fashion of the earlier nations of the earth. One empty theatre after another was explored in this manner, no one interfering with me. The good manners of Minerva would not allow of his venturing further than the doorstep, where I always found him tremblingly waiting my return.

Outside the theatres were gorgeously-painted boards, largely lettered with announcements of the performances for the next evening. None were to take place that evening. The boards took the place of printed playbills. Japan has not got to bill-printing and sticking as yet. The walls of Osaca are not defaced by paste and placards. No men are seen sandwiched between advertising boards. The public vehicles here are undefaced by the huge advertisements that make those of England and America hateful to one's eyes. These theatrical performances are not satisfactory to the traveller. There is little to speak of in the way of scenery. The theatre and stage is lighted with candles. Exits and entrances are made from doors at the back of the stage. The music is very queer, and not pleasing to English ears, and goes on, too, strange to say, while the speakers are declaiming. After twenty minutes of such a theatrical evening one feels that one is quite satisfied, and wishes to retire. The thirst for knowledge in that direction is slaked. You feel as if you had seen it before, and did not want to see it again—a feeling of full satisfaction.

If the theatrical part was all dumb show and noise to us foreigners, we had no such cause of complaint among the shows and showmen at the other end of Theatre Street. We were quite at home there. A wax-work exhibition first claimed attention. Coins equivalent to 2d. each were paid, and Minerva loaded up with the planks of wood, given as checks, in return. Outside the show the attraction was wax figures in motion. Inside we found that the motion was given by wooden wheels turned by hand-power. Quite a mound of machinery was made in the middle of the show by this rough mechanism. The various tableaux were arranged around this motive power, and numbered about twenty groups, equal in execution to anything to be seen at Madame

Tussaud's, or any other waxworks show. Not all of them were pleasing sights to European eyes. A revengeful man had destroyed another's house, and had his foot upon his prostrate victim's neck, whom he was about to brain with an uplifted door-post. He had previously plucked out the eyes of the fallen man, which lay now upon his cheeks—a horrible sight! Minerva explained, from the handbill, price one cent, that this group meant "Vengeance." Mechanism was here used to make the eyes of the destroyer roll in his head, and this was most effectively done. The next group represented two soldiers in pursuit of the man who had, in the preceding group, been seen taking revenge into his own hands. In the third group Nemesis had overtaken him. He was here seen suffering the dread penalty of the law. Enclosed between two upright boards, the executioners were seen sawing him in half from the neck downwards. The waxwork was good. The exhibition had certainly a moral to it, and a good one, too. The machinery, in the case of the last group, moved the saw. The whole was a great sermon against murder.

The finest group in this waxwork show was that of the wrestlers. It was really worth buying and exporting. The figures were full life-size—the size of Japanese wrestlers, who are the biggest men of Japan. These men are fed and trained as athletes, and reserved for wrestling, as the Roman gladiators were for fighting. The Japanese training has on them a very different effect to what is outwardly produced by European training. In the Western world, the man trained is reduced in weight, and looks, when stripped, of a spare and sinewy shape. These Japanese athletes are very bulky men, with heavy limbs and stomachs. If the object has been to develope weight and bulk, it has been most successfully done. The man who is heaviest is considered, I suppose, as the most difficult one to throw.

In the group now on show, two heavy men, of fully 16 st. each, are represented as publicly wrestling for a prize. A small, tightly-strapped bandage round the hips is their only covering. Close to them followed, with bent form and eager eyes, the umpire whose duty it is to see that the rules of the ring are complied with, and that the fall that we see impending shall be a fair one. The perspiration that is starting from every pore is well shown in the waxwork of this group, and waxwork perspiration was new to me. Good also are all the anatomical details. One man has been got upon the hip of the other, but holds fast with one foot around the other's leg, and one arm around his neck. The struggle seems to be for life itself. The features of each show strength tested to the utmost—every muscle and nerve strained to bursting. It is

JAPANESE WRESTLERS.

all so very real, the skin so well coloured, the hair, eyes, and teeth so perfectly natural, that one waits to see the fall which is so imminent. In this case, the machinery is used to make the group revolve only. It is impossible to get away from these wrestlers under half-an-hour. If the model could be got into a portmanteau instead of requiring a ship's cabin for its conveyance, not many visitors would leave it unpurchased. Wrestling is one of the great sports of Japan. It is perhaps, therefore, less wonderful that the modeller has so well succeeded in his life-like rendering of this group.

E 2

It is very cold weather, and I get gladly to the charcoal fires at one end of this waxwork show, and sit down on the raised bench to take hot tea, warm my hands, and see a theatrical performance by wax figures that will take place on the raising of the curtain opposite to me. It differed from other marionette shows in the figures being life-size, and the performance consisting of three tableaux only. The groups were raised through a trap in the stage, and disappeared through another in the roof, after the fashion in which Marguerite is seen leaving the stage, and the world, at the end of "Faust." What the tableaux meant I could not guess; the playbill was silent about them, and Minerva was ignorant, and objected to ask questions to enlighten others or himself. He had nothing of the inquiring mind in him—a pattern of placidity and self-satisfaction—a happy Japanee.

A monkey show came next, in which monkeys were to be seen doing everything that would help to illustrate the Darwinian theory, but not more than one sees done in such sights elsewhere. Japan has not developed monkey power any further than the general European showman. It has got on about as well only with birds. The bird saloon was very crowded, as the payment was left to the option of the visitor—a plan that it would be best to adopt at all places of amusement. People then pay in proportion as they are pleased. The bird proprietor found the system to answer well. He got the people in crowds, and then trusted to his cleverness and that of his birds to charm the payment from his visitors' pockets. Not one left, I think, but paid something.

Acrobatic shows on raised platforms and scaffolds brought up the finish of this street of amusements. As a fit conclusion to it, some enterprising Japanee had erected a tall platform, like to a fire look-out, from which, for a cent, the traveller could see Osaca as a bird does. The timbering of this structure, so to speak, was of bamboo only. It was strong enough, no doubt, but looked, at its 60 ft. level, a very light and skeleton affair to trust one's self upon. The Venice of Japan lay now all before one, clear in its smokeless air, and flat-looking in its uniformity of houses, destitute of chimneys, towers, spires, turrets, or minarets, but grand, indeed, in its waters and bridges.

On one part of the river, near to this perch, shipbuilding was going on to an extent that reminded one of the Clyde-side at Glasgow. The six or eight iron hulls that are there to be seen building in one builder's yard were represented here by the same number of wooden vessels, called sampans, of large size and clumsy build. They are built, however, for dwelling-houses, as well as for ordinary ship purposes. Convenience and utility are therefore studied before clipper qualities. In a distant part of this large city we saw the smoke of a fire that might grow to the size of that terribly-devastating one which I had seen at Tokio on New Year's Eve. A fire is, I should think, one of the usual features of a bird's-eye view of a Japanese city.

Minerva stopped our course near to this point that he might go and pay his weekly ten minutes of worship at a neighbouring temple. Having washed his hands from a stone tank that was in front of it, and drunk a little of its water afterwards, he proceeded to pull a rope that hung in front of a sitting image. The rope pulled a bell to call the attention of the idol to what was coming. That was the deposit of some copper coin in a trough in front of the figure, and afterwards the kneeling, bowing, and muttering a prayer by Minerva, who now wiped his hands on the interior of his frock. He said that he felt better for it, and looked so.

If the gift of Tokio or of Osaca were offered to one, the choice would probably be with most travellers in favour of Osaca. Its revenues may not be so large; the Mikado does not live there, but it is a large, bustling city, and its fine rivers and multitude of bridges give it a more interesting and more picturesque appearance than any other of the cities of Japan. Its chief defect lay in its unlighted state at night. The population do not seem, as they do in Tokio, to move much about the streets after dark, carrying each his pretty lantern, nor do the shopkeepers, as in the former city, do evening business, and court it by hanging large lanterns, bearing their names and signs, over their doors.

Minerva took me now to Judie's other house in the Concession, the foreign settlement of Osaca. This settlement is a very clean and well-built place, and on a large and growing scale. The hotel here was different to the tea-house that I had stayed at on the preceding night. The rooms were better warmed, and for that reason perhaps were more favoured by mosquitoes. These little torments I hailed as Australian friends, and slapped them about on their backs as often as they gave me the opportunity. Their existence in such cold weather was probably no pleasure to them. It was certainly none to me, as the bed was curtainless.

The oysters brought to me for supper at Osaca seemed to bleed, a peculiarity about oysters that I had not noticed elsewhere.

That night Brown and myself bought lanterns that folded up, with bamboo ribs, and could be easily shut and carried in the crown of one's hat. These lanterns had handsome hieroglyphics on them in red letters, and were altogether dandy affairs. The candles put into them were of vegetable wax, and the wick made seemingly of a rush, round which cotton had been twisted. The candles burnt well, and shed a good light through the oiled paper on the pathway, and about four feet along it, that we were treading. The lanterns were of no weight, and no inconvenience whatever. Armed with them and a walkingstick, we, much to the disgust of Minerva, who wanted to smoke and sleep, or to go and see his sweetheart, explored something of Osaca by night. How its governing powers can permit it to lie in the state of darkness it does after sundown passed our understanding.

"Brown, what do you say to a gas company here? Easy to lay the pipes, plenty of craft to bring coals up to the river side, good levels, no opposition, and no need to create the want!"

The want was but too conspicuous, as Brown, in listening to my argument, had run his lantern against a post and extinguished the candle. As he had with him a box of matches, that evil was soon remedied, and suggested a new thought.

"All these matches are imported, Brown! Labour and material are plentiful here, and yet most Japanese have to use the old flint and steel. Join a match factory to the gas one!"

"That makes about ten industries that you have mentioned to-day. Make it a dozen before we get back!"

It was really difficult to go about this Japanese Great Britain and not see what great wants existed that European enterprise might supply—seeing also how readily all European ideas had been adopted by the people as soon as started. It was impossible to walk about thus with a Japanese lantern to lighten the darkness, and not to think of Londoners' lanterns and their whale-oil lamps in the streets fifty years ago, and then of the gas that had changed all that state of things there as it might do here.

CHAPTER VI.

LIFE WITH THE JAPS.

THE singing and music-playing girls of Japan are quite an institution there. They are in request at all little convivial

FEMALE MUSICIANS.

meetings, such as I saw at the tea-houses. At these meetings in the evenings three girls generally gave their services, and added a game of forfeits to their singing and playing that caused much merry laughing. It consisted in two girls

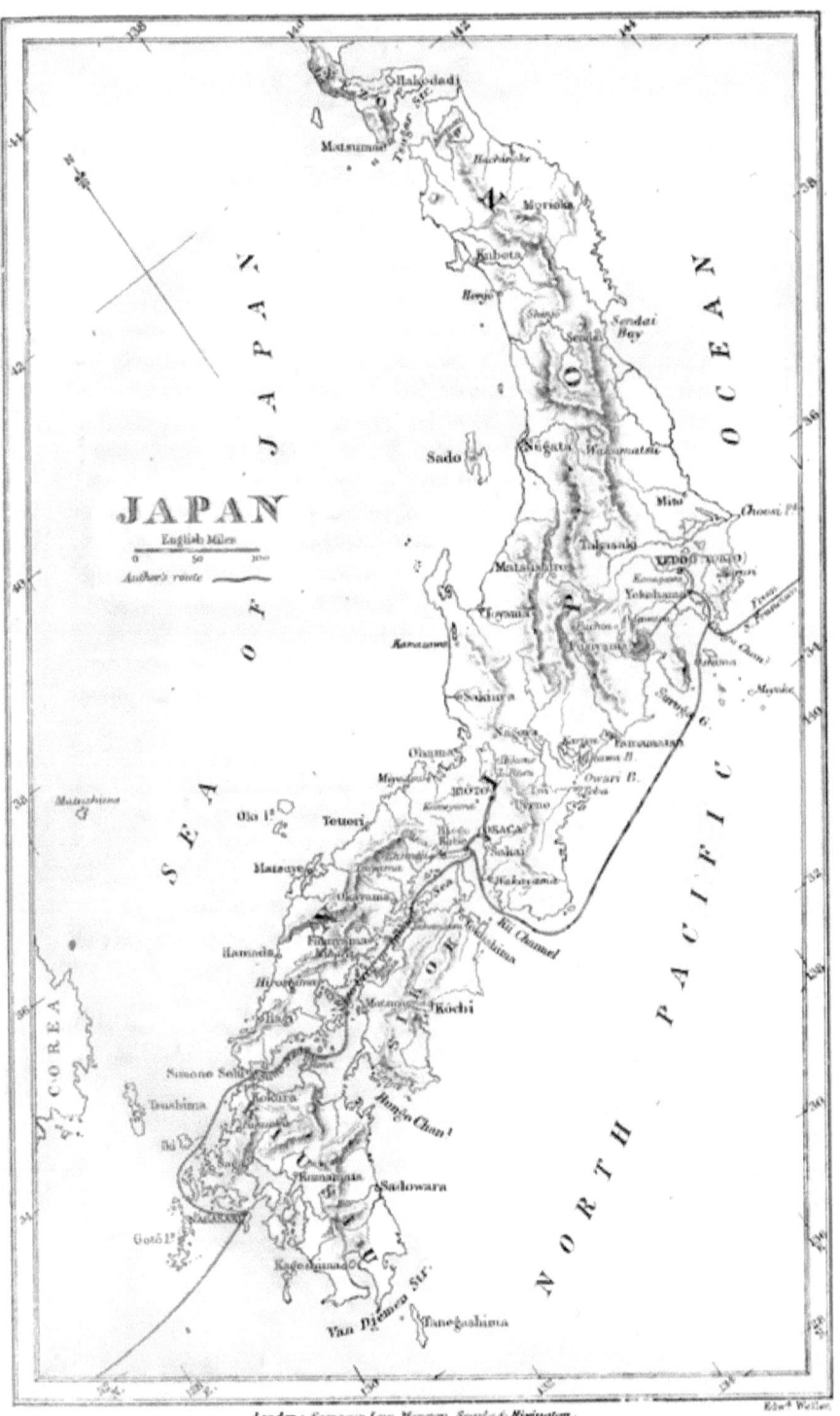

repeating some little rhyme, and keeping time by alternately clapping their own hands and then those of each other. A failure to keep time was followed by merriment and the payment of some counter or other substituted trifle as a forfeit. Occasionally an excited Japanee would drop his pipe and cup of saki, and rise and "declaim a piece," as the Americans phrase it. These tea-house convivialities are mild substitutes for English tavern evenings, with the addition of three dolls of girls sitting on the table. For "dolls" these little Japanese musicians appear to be, as they sit there in their gay-coloured dresses, with painted lower lips, powdered faces, and decorated hair—that hair which the Japanese woman is so careful of, and ornaments so very tastefully. That it may not be disarranged, she sleeps, I was told, with her neck on a stereoscope-case-shaped "pillow," at the risk of making it stiff. Similarly, in the old time of the Georges in England, it was customary for ladies whose heads had been elaborately puffed, pasted, bolstered, and powdered up in the fashion of the period for some ball or party, to sleep the night before in an easy chair, that the head-dress might not be disarranged. The musical girls are to be easily recognized as they pass along by their superior dress and the accompanying coolie girl who carries the music and the zither. The lower class of men and women —the working class—are in Japan, as elsewhere in the East, called "coolies."

Among the customs of the Japanese that are curious in strangers' eyes is that of planting trees on New Year's Day in front of their dwellings. The plantation is not intended to be permanent. At the end of a few days the little bush or sapling has died, and is removed. My host at the Seiyoken Hotel at Tokio celebrated New Year's Day by an extra good dinner to his lodgers and some outside friends. He is evidently bidding for British patronage, introducing chairs and tables, bedsteads, pillows, soap, and suchlike matters into his house. Wood ashes have been used, instead of soap, hitherto in Japan. The Japs are a cleanly folk, and bathing-houses are features of every town. In the bathing-houses the simplicity of sinless times still prevails. One bath suffices for all, and males and females bathe at the same time. By-and-by they will perhaps divide or institute bathing costumes, when they learn that such is European fashion. Very strange dishes came upon the board at our New Year's dinner. A preliminary pipe of mild tobacco was handed around. The tobacco was too mild an affair altogether to take the edge off one's appetite—if intended for that purpose. The first course consisted of sweetmeats, served upon lacquered plates. The whole meal was of a Frenchified character. Balls of golden, scarlet, and green jellies were among the things in this dish; rice, flour, and sugar made up the constituents of the other parts of it. Saki (rice spirit) and the ever-present tea were then served round. The second course consisted of soup, into which were shredded hard-boiled eggs. This was served in bowls, but without spoons. I had, however, my purchased spoon, fork, and knife, always upon me, and so escaped trouble. Then came a very strange dish. It was a collop cut from a living fish wriggling on the sideboard. The Japs are a great fish-eating folk, and this raw fish-eating is quite common. The steak cut for Bruce from the living ox, told of in his Abyssinian travels, occurred to one's memory. The live tit-bit is supposed to be eaten with the Japanese "Soy," a sauce that makes everything palatable, but I let my portion of it pass. It is not possible to comply with all Japanese fashions at once. Time is necessary to the acquirement of taste. Cooked fish was next served, and that in great variety, including shell-fish. A sort of lime or small lemon was used as the flavouring to this dish. Then came boiled beans, with ginger roots, and some fried fish and horseradish. To follow that came boiled fish and clams, the latter cut up and served with pears. Rice, in tea-cups, followed, and then a salad, and the dishes were ended. The hot saki and tea-cups were sent round after each course. The health of our landlord was proposed in Japanese, and drunk in saki. He then rose to reply. I thought that he would never have done bowing before he began to speak. He appeared to speak very well, and elicited the approbation of those who understood Japanese. I could differ from him in nothing that he said.

The climate of Japan is in heat and cold something like to that of Great Britain, but knows less of fogs and nothing of the east wind. The ground was covered with snow for several days at a time during my stay. The islands that make up Japan are nearly of the size and shape of those of Great Britain, and the population very little larger. Religious differences do not seem to have caused so much bitter misery and hatred and trouble, as is the case elsewhere. The Japanee is not a religious fanatic. There is nothing of the Hindoo or Mahometan in his nature. He will, unlike the Hindoo, eat and drink with any one, and not smash his plate after meals, nor drink out of his hands to save defiling his lips with any vessel that may have been touched by infidel fingers. He does not scowl at one of another faith with looks of hate, as does the Mahometan, nor believe that sending you quickly to your heaven will help him in getting to his own. Japanee is again like to the Frenchmen in religious matters—they do not much trouble him. Neither do they trouble his wife.

"A light heart and a thin pair of—pants" have been mentioned as ingredients of an Irishman's jollity. They are exactly those of the Japanee. When he wears anything on his legs beyond the blue cotton napkin that he mostly prefers to wrap them in, it is, as before observed, a closely-fitting pair of pantaloons or stage "tights" of the thinnest blue cotton. His legs are not particularly adapted to this fashion, as they are but seldom seen straight and well cut. In the case of the draymen, however, it is different, and one sees then the outline of legs that nothing could upset the owner of. It is so with the trained wrestlers here, who are wonders of muscular development. Japanee is, however, not particular about much clothing, and makes a little of it go a long way, and answer many purposes. Blue is the favourite colour with him. His blouse or sack is of blue cotton, enlivened on the back and sides with curious white circles and stripes, that give him a piebald appearance. His head-gear, when it is raining, is anything that comes handy. He prefers, however, to wear none, that he may show the elegant appearance of his half-shaved and sectioned scalp. A rudimentary tail is made out of the back hair and brought to the crown, and there tied and waxed and fastened down, pointing at you across the bald head like to a small revolver. All this is not done to be covered up and hidden. The European fashion of wearing the hair has, however, been lately decreed, and in time will prevail with all, as it does now with many, and then hats and head-coverings will follow. In the way of hats, the Mikado has decreed in favour of the English chimney-pot, which, with English evening dress, is the costume only permitted at his *levées* and receptions. That will be the fashion that Japanee will run after, and, like to the stage Irishman, he will be seen in the next generation in a claw-hammer coat and a tall hat. He has already got the tight continuations.

About his foot-coverings Japanee is very undecided and easily satisfied. It does not distress him to go barefoot, though he usually has something of a sock or sandal. A dark-blue cotton sock is the most usual wear. The sole is made of thick blue canvas or thick paper, and looks made to last about a week or two, but really lasts a month. These things fasten with hooks and eyes at the back, and are divided at the toes into two parts. One is for the great toe, and the other for what remains. So covered, the foot of Japanee appears like to a cloven hoof. His sock is one that would become well a stage Mephistophiles, and should be imported for those who at fancy dress balls are so fond of assuming that character. Was there ever a F.D.B. that had not two or three Mephistos? This sock is varied in colour to red for children, and white for those who can afford extra outlay. The sock alone with its canvas sole is considered quite enough foot-covering by many, and even the hard-running centaurs often wear nothing else. Sandals are, however, very common. The first to be noticed as most common is of plaited straw, a mere solepiece, with a triangular-shaped loop that goes over the foot below the instep, and between the opening in the toe-part. In nine cases out of ten this sandal is too short for the foot, and the wearer's heel hangs over it. Another sandal is of thick wood, like to the sole of English clogs, secured over the toes in a similar way to the other. The third style is for snowy or sloppy weather, and is a patten sole mounted upon two pieces of thin wood of four inches high and standing six inches apart. This very queer-looking patten is secured in the same way as the others. Some clog soles are to be had with leather toe-pieces, but I never noticed them in use. The

JAPANESE LADY.

sock seemed to be considered sufficient covering for the upper part of the foot. I speak, of course, of the population as I had opportunity of noticing it out of doors. The four-inch patten support is of great advantage to the Japanee and his wife and daughters, as to European eyes the Japanee is altogether too short, and his wife and daughters particularly so.

The female Japanee behaves in no way like to the females of other Eastern countries. No "yashmak" hides her face, nor does she hide within doors from her bridal to her burial. She does not beautify herself with henna on the finger-nails and lampblack to the eyebrows. She looks like the chubby daughter of an English country farmer, and is a buxom little round lump of a thing that one mistakes for twelve years old until told that she is eighteen or twenty. The round full faces of these girls would become women of 5 ft. 8 in., and they look out of place on little beings of 4 ft. 6 in. Figure, to speak of, the female Japanee does not possess. She could not easily wear a corset, and her dress seems to be altogether planned to make her look as broad as

LADIES' OUT-DOOR DRESS.

she is long. A thing like to a little knapsack is worn on the small of the back outside of the sack jacket. It gives the appearance of almost a deformity, and is a strange idea of producing a hump for and in place of a Grecian bend—if such be the intention of the wearer. This excrescence is made of folded cotton, or cotton-padded silk. The "kodomo," as the baby Japanee is called, is carried in a sort of hood, on the back of its mother or sister—sister I generally thought, from the small size of the being carrying the baby—but I am not sure that in many of these cases I did not make mistakes.

Very neatly indeed does the female Japanee dress her hair. It always goes uncovered, and therefore the skill bestowed upon it is not hidden. There are no Japanee blondes. Jet black hair is the rule, and I saw no exception. Rosy cheeks, laughing eyes of dark-brown colour, pearly teeth, and dumpling forms make up the unmarried female Japanee. When engaged to be married, she proceeds to make herself hideous—that no

DRESS OF JAPANESE LADY.

other man may fancy her. She succeeds beyond belief. Her white teeth are dyed a hideous black, and her pretty arched eyebrows are all plucked out with tweezers. The effect is horrible. If her intended husband was now to alter his mind, as he might reasonably do, what would become of the bride expectant? No other suitor would be found to fancy the now ugly little Topsy. Such trouble must happen sometimes, and yet the disfigurement is not postponed until after marriage, as one would think would be best and prudent.

In shopkeeping, the female Japanee, when a wife, takes a Frenchwoman's part in the business, and does all the work. With her hideously black mouth and fringeless brows she is on the shopboard all day, and her husband, when about, generally appeals to her as to the prices of everything, and the policy of accepting half the price that has been asked. The half price is generally taken, but not until the "soroban" has been consulted—that is the calculating board, without which no Japanee seems to be able to tell the price of anything that he has to sell, or to say what six pictures of three cents each amount to in the gross. He learns no multiplication table. This board, with its twenty-one bars, on each of which slide six perforated marbles, does all his cyphering. The topmost row of the marbles is cut off from the other five rows by a bar running the whole length of the soroban. Each of the marbles in that row counts as five of the others. Calculations up to millions can be made on this wooden ready reckoner. It is made of all sizes, from that of a sideboard to that of 3 in. by 1 in., and is alike used by both the Chinee and the Japanee. A long schooling is necessary, however, to the working of this oracle by a foreigner. An adult white has never been known to adopt it.

The Japanee is careful never to soil with his feet the fine rush-made matting that he spreads for a carpet to his house and a shop-board for his goods. He requests me to take my boots off before entering his shop. At his tea restaurants he proffers the same absurd request; but that is not to be complied with. I am there to purchase as a customer, and if he will not take me as I am, I threaten to go elsewhere. It is winter weather, and I cannot stand about with cold, unbooted feet. He gives way, and I enter his tea-house. My first visit to such is memorable. There is nothing but the floor, rush-matted, for me to sit upon. I must squat like to a tailor, or a Turk, if I sit, and sit I must to have tea, and to take the other strange things that are given to one in these restaurants. So I sit on the matting, cross-legged at first, and then with legs to the left and then to the right, and then with straightened knees, on which I rest the cup. It is all very uncomfortable. One of the fire-boxes is brought to me by one of the stumpy girls, who then proceeds, under my nose, to put a small frying-pan on it, into which she tumbles a mass of meat cut up to the size of dice. Some similarly cut-up vegetables are then added, and the affair is set to stew on the sticks of charcoal. While that is going on I am handed a teacupful of saki, that tastes much like to warm and weak sherry, with a pinch of salt in it. The meat is soon after turned out into a small basin, which is handed to me, together with a pair of skewers. These things are "chopsticks," and I am to feed myself with them alone. No knife, fork, or spoon is provided. I had noticed that the meat was already cut up into mouthfuls. Two other chubby-faced, stumpy girls had now come into the room, which was destitute, like to all Japanese rooms, of any article of furniture. I had to make a maiden effort to eat with chopsticks in presence of these three girls. It was dreadfully uncomfortable. The French philosopher said that "Men have mercy, but women have none," the remembrance of which gave me very little courage in my efforts to eat with those six eyes upon me. The sticks would divide widely instead of coming together. Nohow could I grab a mouthful with them out of the basin until five or six failures had been made. The maidens were waiting to change dishes and bring in a second course. Of these courses there were half a dozen to come. Had there been a napkin handy, I might have remembered that fingers were made before forks or chopsticks, but napkin there was none; so I had to take a stick in each hand, and then had a little better success. It was of course a dreadful breach of etiquette, but necessity knows no manners. What did I care for the moon-faced maidens that looked on me as a clumsy clown? They would never, probably, see me more, and I this way got my "tiffin." This Indian word has been brought into use in Japan. Rice followed the meat, but that I passed. Catch me trying to pick up grains of rice with two rounded skewers before three laughing girls! A lot of other messes followed, that I more or less failed with, and then came sweet preserves and the everlasting Japanee warm-water tea. My legs fairly began to ache by this time, and I stumbled about somewhat with stiffness on getting up. For all this entertainment only 1s. 2d., or its equivalent, had to be paid. On the first opportunity I had, as I said before, I bought a knife, fork, and spoon, and henceforth carried them, wrapped in paper, in a side-pocket, and was done with chop-sticks. Had my stay in Japan been long, I should have had a folding-chair made, with a "practicable" table-top to it. To do at Rome as Rome does is very well to talk about, but does not apply to Japan. The Romans did not require me to eat with skewers.

There are no doors to Japanese houses. Sliding sashes, glazed, so to speak, with paper, serve for doors and windows. When I had to sleep in one of these houses up the country, I found that my bed was the rush matting of the floor, my bed-clothes a quilt only, and my pillow a piece of wood—the aforesaid stereoscope case. That extraordinary "pillow" quite bewildered me. I took it at first for a joke, to ask me to rest my neck on a wooden block eight inches high, and about two inches broad. To accommodate me, the top was covered with a padded roll of paper that was tied upon the block. It looked then like to a tailor's large iron goose held by a big iron holder. A stiff neck could be produced by this instru-ment after one application, supposing it possible in sleep to keep it balanced. I at last rolled an overcoat round it, and that somewhat accommodated matters.

Japanee is not luxurious about his bed or his bedchamber. He withstands the cold of winter much better than the European. His house is full of draughts and emptiness, and is wholly destitute of fireside comforts. Yet he is happy. It is the privilege of the Japanee *not* to grumble—a privilege that he rather abuses than otherwise.

How careful, too, is the Japanee in sanitary matters! His

rivers and canals are all unpolluted by sewage. His land—best manured of all lands—is rich in verdure. The drainage matter is carefully collected, and daily removed for manuring purposes. Not a stench from sewage matter can be found in Japan save at the sewage depôts. The smell of some of the cookery is not nice to European noses, but there is nothing worse than sourkrout amongst it all. What clothes Japanee does wear he is careful to keep washed and clean, and now that he is going to wear all his hair, he ties a handkerchief round it on windy days to keep it in order. He is as careful as a Hindoo to wear a sash twisted round his loins, but it is always a plain and useful one, and not a gay shawl-like thing such as the Hindoostanee folks adopt.

Yokohama, having been slow in building, is numbered by its houses only, in the European quarter. Its streets are not named in any address given. "No. 88, Yokohama" is a proper address, though it reads as strangely as "No. 1, London." The new settlement can count three foreign and one native newspapers. A fortnightly mail from England, viâ China, and another from France, and a monthly one from America, keep its folks well acquainted with news. One street in the town is nicknamed as "Curio Street." In that the Japanese do a thriving business with the foreigner. In looking at the contents of the shop, he is, however, liable to run against the wooden-walled wells which are here sunk in the centre of the footpath, with long bamboo-handled dippers floating twenty feet below. In Curio Street the traveller will find the wonders of native art in which the Japanese have hitherto delighted. To produce the fanciful, and not the useful, appears to have been the aim of the artist. He has succeeded to a marvel. Here are wonders in metal-work that fifty and eighty guineas are necessary to purchase—for chimney-piece and sideboard ornaments. Vases of porcelain, exquisitely painted; vases of porcelain and metal intermixed; vases of copper, inlaid with groundworks of flowers, and filled up with hardened coloured cements; vases of all shapes, sizes, and designs, and of all metals and materials, here delight the eye and confuse the mind of the visitor. He is shown teacups thin as egg-shell, and nearly transparent—teacups with bas-reliefs upon them—teacups with figures enclosed with doors—teacups with a tortoise at the bottom, that floats at the top when the tea is poured in, and yet cannot be fillipped out with a spoon. China and pottery in all shapes and forms, in bewildering variety, are here on hand, and lacquered ware that one can hang over and admire for a day or a week. This is the place to buy wedding presents for one's friends—the sort of things that are shown in the ante-room after the bride and bridegroom have gone forth on their tour—the sort of things to send to a maiden aunt from whom one has great expectations. Here are boxes of flowers, too, that look like to pipelights, but expand into leaves and blossoms when thrown into basins of water. Here, also, are carved ivory and metallic monsters for all the mantelpieces of the lovers of the grotesque, and all old maids that love pugs and monkeys. Curio Street, Yokohama, is one of the streets of the world, and a day may be as well spent in it as in Regent Street or Broadway, if one does but take care not to take much money along.

Japan is getting lines of railway now, and steam-vessels, and has been buying cannon and rifles and revolvers. Japanee will turn his artistic labours in a practical direction for the future, and, sad to think, will produce the useful and neglect the fanciful. England is starting schools of design for the teaching of all that Japanee has known and delighted in for all the ages, and which, in the "regeneration" Japan is now so strangely undergoing, he will for the future neglect for those arts which have advanced Europe and America, if advanced they are, while he has been dozing and dreaming—learning only how to be contented and happy.

There is but little doubt, comparing the millions of Great Britain and those of the Japanese isles, that the greatest happiness of the greatest number—which has been defined to be the end and aim of civilization and legislation—is by no means certain to be found in Queen Victoria's kingdom as against that of the Mikado. There are those who will make it a question, but there are those again in plenty who, having seen both territories, will make no question about it.

"The sin of great cities," as some one has phrased it, is to be found in Japanese towns, but not in the streets. The Government, finding it irrepressible, have regulated it, and reduced it—as they have done everything else—to system and order. No one is tempted to vice by the sight of it in the busy thoroughfares. No pestilence walks at noonday in Japan. It must be sought in the quarter reserved for it in every city of the empire, and it is not allowed to go forth in brazen bravery to offend the modest and allure the unwary. In the quarter to which it is relegated it is caged within doors, and visitors there walk the streets as they would the grounds of a zoological garden, and are fully made to feel that they tread upon dangerous ground when in the "Yoshawarroh" quarters.

I have written thus of what I observed of the fashions of Japan. The subject might be extended to any length, and made quite tiresome. I may notice, as a fit conclusion to the matter, that the favourite mode of suicide—the "hari kari," or disembowelling—is performed mostly by those who conceive that they have suffered an injury, and think by their death in this form to cause remorse to the one who has injured them. Goldsmith, in one of his poems, expresses a similar notion of revenge when he tells the deserted maid that—

> "The only art her guilt to cover,
> To hide her shame from every eye,
> To give repentance to her lover,
> And wring his bosom—is to die."

CHAPTER VII.

THE INLAND SEA OF JAPAN.

THE Inland Sea of Japan! Who has not heard of its beauty? Nothing in the way of sea-coast scenery that I ever expatiated upon with enthusiasm but was wet-blanketed by "Oh! you should see the Inland Sea of Japan." Sydney harbour and its beauties had brought forth my loud admiration, as they bring forth that of every one who first sees them; but the ship's captain, anxious to show his superiority to such weakness, said, "Nothing to the Inland Sea of Japan!" In the pretty harbour of Madeira I heard the same exclamation from a *nil admirari* fellow-passenger, whose life seemed to lie all in the past or the future. With such it is always yesterday or to-morrow, and never to-day. For the study of those is the wisdom of the proverb, "Take the good the gods provide you."

It was upon this inland sea that I now embarked, upon leaving Hiogo and its seaport Kobé, to go to Nagasaki, a southern port of Japan. It was there that the first settlement of foreigners had taken place, the Dutch getting a footing there two centuries ago. It was scarcely a footing, however, for they were restricted to a small island joined to the mainland by a well-guarded bridge. Too much of interest attached to such a place to leave it unvisited, especially as the attraction of a voyage for two days down the inland sea was added to it.

The "Tokio Maru" was the steamer on which I embarked, with about 200 others, mostly Japanese. It was a side-wheeled vessel of 3000 tons, belonging to the Mitsu Bishi (three diamonds) Company, subsidized by the Government of Japan. It was Japanese midwinter, windy and freezing, with occasional gusts of sleet and snow. The captain's seat at the table was always vacant. The intricacies of the passage demanded all his care, and the taking of his meals in his deck-house. The land was visible, and sometimes almost touchable, as islands studded the way down this sea for the whole length of it. There were too many of these altogether, and they were sometimes destitute of trees and bushes. The shore-line showed hills and valleys, and then valleys and hills again. The valleys were very small, but always fully populated by those who grew rice round the foot of the hills and caught fish in the waters of this sea. The fishing-boats about everywhere along shore made a prominent feature in the beauty of the scene. A great sameness about it was soon, however, observable, producing even the usual effect of monotony—wearisomeness. There was too much of it altogether. Sydney harbour is quite large enough. Just sufficient is seen there to please to the limit of pleasure, and leave no sense of satiation. It is so also with the harbours of Rio and Cork. Every one is delighted with the drives around Galle and the delightful Ceylon scenery there to be met with—cocoa-nut and banana-trees alternating with pineapple and palm. If led on to take the journey from Galle to Colombo, for seventy miles, through a road full of such delightful scenery, the delight is found to get less with every mile after the first ten. At the twentieth mile the traveller yawns, and at the thirtieth he sleeps. "This is the end of every man's desire."

It was something, of course, against the enjoyment of the scene that the wind was bitterly cold, though the air was clear and the sun generally to be seen. The wind disturbed the waters too much for one's enjoyment of sea life. That state of things got worse, and on the evening of the second day the plate and dish washers had a holiday of it. No one came to dinner save the ship's officers. Others had no appetite, and at 7 p.m. the cold saloon was deserted, and miserable landsmen went to their beds as early as do naughty children. A horizontal position is best for qualmish stomachs, and warmth can be got from blankets and rugs.

Those destined to misery dream of delights. It is said that the condemned criminal, whose dance upon nothing is to take place at eight o'clock the next morning, sleeps peacefully through his last night, and dreams of happy picnics and dances upon sunny slopes. I know that I dreamt of the inland sea, and of beauties thereon and thereabout that I had missed seeing by daylight. Just awakened from the long sleep that attends a cold night and an empty stomach, I was collecting the facts of my position from the fictions of dreams, when there came, in the horror of utter darkness, a grating and scrunching sound beneath one's bunk that suspended all thought, movement, and even breathing for the instant. Another scrunch, and then another, and the sound of the ever-going paddles ceased altogether. There was no need to inquire what had happened. That inner consciousness, from which it has been said that the German can develope the appearance of the camel that he has never seen, told me what the strange sounds meant. The "Tokio" had run upon rocks! I have omitted the "Maru" in thus naming her, as that word is placed after each ship's name by the Japanese, and merely means "ship." The feeling that I experienced was as appalling as that of an earthquake which had once shaken me out of a sleep when up country in Java.

It was not yet five o'clock, and nearly two hours to daylight. The lamps had been taken from the cabins at eleven at night, but I struck a match and looked at my watch, sitting up in the bunk to do so. As the match expired I felt my head bumped against the bottom of the bunk above me, and lay down again instead of turning out. No one else occupied the cabin. The one next to me was also empty, the season of the year being that in which much travelling is avoided by those not on business. I lay endeavouring to think what to do, but the remembrances of similar cases of running upon rocks and the dread results came uppermost, and crowded out all thoughts of action. The vessel now bumped with each wave. The waves seemed to try and lift her over the rock, and, failing in the attempt, to let the burden fall again. This bumping and thumping became soon a sickening sensation, and also rendered movement awkward, troublesome, and dangerous. I found that much as I now tried to turn out and dress.

Ten months before this, when at Ceylon, I had met the survivors of the wrecked ship "Strathmore," who had been landed there after seven months of suffering upon the Crozet Islands, and were returning to their friends as from the grave. Their description of the shipwreck and their survival I had taken down and transmitted to the journals. Our disaster had occurred at a similar hour in the morning, and had been accompanied with similar sounds and movements of the ship. Thinking of that, and feeling in the darkness for articles of dress with one hand, holding on to the bunk-side with the other to steady myself, I heard footsteps coming down towards the cabin-door, and the voice of Allen—a fellow-passenger, a shipwright going to the Chinese port of Foochow—"Get up at once, and save what light things you can, and dress and come on deck. We have run on the rocks at the mouth of the inland sea, thirty miles from Nagasaki." The voice from out the darkness then ceased, and the footsteps hurried away. Curses were that morning heaped upon those who take lamps and candles out of cabins and leave folks to darkness and death in such cases as ours. The cabin steward had taken away my boots, and as I trod about on the icy cold oilcloth, my feet were freezing. I found somehow waistcoat and trousers, and got on deck, where I at once fell at full length. The sleet had frozen during the night, and rendered the boards too slippery to walk upon had the ship been even level and quiet.

As she lay there on the rocks, she was all on a slope of many feet from stem to stern. The stern was rising upon every wave, and thumping down again into the water. In the darkness I could at first discern nothing, but gradually came to perceive two sugarloaf-shaped rocks between which the

"Tokio" had run, instead of going into the clear sea-room on either side. A ledge that connected the two rocks ran beneath the water, and it was upon this that the forepart of the vessel had gone, and where she stuck fast, canting over to one side in an unpleasantly perceptible manner.

Scrambling down below again, I got from one of the stewards a small lantern that showed more of darkness than light, and managed to find coat and boots and head-covering. The only things that I thought of securing from the travelling-bag were thick socks and buckskin gloves that seemed now likely to be of great value. If we had to get upon the precipitous rocks on either side of the ship, it seemed to be almost a necessity to hold on to their craggy sides to keep a footing. As I looked at the other things in the bag, and saw the collection of curios from Japan, and thought of the trunkful there behind from other countries, the present state of things seemed a sorry ending indeed. Even the Mexican dollars, that in this part of the world were the only coins valued, were of no use now. They must be left behind as too weighty for the pockets of one who expected to have to jump on to rocks or into water before trouble was all over. Standing, or rather staggering, over that bag on that dark morning, with the dim lantern in one's hand, was the most miserable five minutes of life that I can now recall. If the passengers should save themselves only, their bag and baggage would then be either lost altogether or rifled by those who might succeed in getting them. A ship upon the rocks is fair game for wreckers. Had we been upon the coast of China, or of Cornwall for the matter of that, the Philistines of the sea would have been upon us shortly. Meantime through all the trouble, thump, bump, bump, thump, went the "Tokio" upon the rock's edge. How long she would thump about like that and not go to pieces was the question. The "Strathmore" had broken up in half an hour's time.

The "Tokio" was a wooden vessel, well-coppered, and stood the trouble she was now in better than an iron ship would have done. The grim figure of the carpenter came lantern in hand, every three minutes to the saloon, where, through a hole in the floor, he measured with foot-rule-shaped measure the depth of the water in the hold. It was good to hear of only a few inches increase at each measurement.

The saloon passengers did not number more than twenty. The Japanese and Chinese, forward, made up the bulk of our number. These were, with difficulty, kept out of the saloon, into which they wished to crowd, as if more safety lay there than forward. Knots of passengers collected round any one who had a lantern, and discussed what in French phrase is called "the situation." One of them showed me a small bottle labelled "poison" that he had taken from his trunk. He had kept it, he said, for years to avoid a lingering death when hope might have gone. There seemed now a probability of his wanting it. He quietly said that there was enough for two! I don't recall whether I had the good manners to thank him for such courtesy. A bluff, burly-looking Irishman from the States had another drink that he dragged me to his cabin to partake of. He seemed already to have largely taken of it himself. "Sure, man," he said, "take a glass or two of it, 'twill put spirits into you." There was no denying that two glasses of Irish whisky would put spirits into any one who drank them, but I had a stomach empty for twenty hours, and sense enough left to know that the warmth that spirits give is followed by the greater cold and prostration. I pleaded that I had had a drink already offered me, and would go back to it, and come to my hospitable present friend for the next one.

The captain had ordered the forward cargo overboard to lighten that part of the ship. That work was going on promptly, and the paddles resumed their work in reversed order to drag the ship backwards. Crates, barrels, and boxes were flying over on both sides, and being gulped down by the tossing waters. The coals were going out also in bags, buckets, and shovelfuls. The cannon—a 24-pounder—went overboard with a huge splash and a thundering noise that seemed to protest against such a sacrifice. Ten boxes of treasure were got out, and placed on the middle deck, to be the first thing cared for after the lives of the passengers. The grim phantom with the lantern and the measuring-rod came upon us oftener now, but the ship's officers and stewards surrounded him, and he departed in silence to report to the captain the progress of the rising water below. We were not to hear the bad news he had to tell.

Daylight dawned at last. It had never seemed so long in coming, and, perhaps, never will again, to those who were on board the "Tokio" that morning. A boat was put off from the side of the ship and despatched with six rowers and a steersman to Nagasaki for help. It was a five hours' journey for them. As the provisions and bottles of water were given out, we looked on with a sort of personal interest. The same thing might be doing with ourselves in a short time if the vessel showed signs of not holding together. The state of things around could be now discerned. No landing-place was apparent upon the two rocks near to us, about 200 ft. only from the sides of the ship. If any existed, it must be upon the outer sides of these most inhospitable-looking crags. How the ship could have got into such a narrow place, with rocks ahead to warn the ship's look-out man, it seemed difficult to guess at. The watch had been that of the second mate, and the blame lay between him and the Japanese pilot, who pleaded that he had set all things right and gone below to get a drink of tea. Japanese, men and women, drink tea at all hours; they have the strange ability, too, of taking it scalding hot.

The lightening of the ship still went on. Not a sail came in sight anywhere, though for the two preceding days we had seen the native sampans about in scores. The captain, who was now approachable, seemed quite calm about the state of things. "If I cannot get her off in an hour or so, you can be landed on that rock. There is standing-room on the other side." That to us—who were freezing, and wanting warmth and a breakfast! The prospect of a bleak rock with a bitingly cold wind and sea spray for long hours, until a tug could come from Nagasaki—some time in the next night! The Irishman, on hearing that news, went back to his whisky bottle, button-holing me on the way. "Look here, man, we must be friends now. Here's my card, and these boxes and bags have my name on them. If I don't get out of this and you do, I have written a name on the back of that card that you will write to, and tell all about it. Take a drink now. Sure I'll do the same for you if you like. Drink, me boy."

It was a strange time to be taking duties upon one when the grasshopper would be a burden added to one's load of present trouble, but there was no resisting my friend and his required promise. His bottle I could stave off. I took my share of it in a couple of phials that some preceding passenger had left in the rack of the cabin. A sort of idea crept upon me, that had I finished my friend's bottle, it had been better for him, however it might have been for me. He began to get demonstrative, and to look very moist about the eyes. He said, "I niver thought, me boy, to get a watery death: shure I always hated it!" This anti-teetotal remark was quite needless, and, in other circumstances, might have been humorous. Things were too unsettled now for smiling at anything.

After four hours of work at lightening the "Tokio," the captain resolved upon a movement that had its intended effect. The forward passengers and the crew were all to be rushed aft in a body, and extra power applied to the paddles. The move was successful. We now, with gladness for which joy is no name, heard a scrunch, and then another, and then a third! And the "Tokio" floated backwards, and was free of the rocks! I might put a hundred or two of notes of exclamation to signify what our feelings and exclamations were upon that event. It was necessary only to keep the pumps going to get safely along. The Irishman now brought out another bottle, and insisted upon drinks round. He had never, "Niver, me boys," had a doubt about all being right. The peaceful way in which he soon afterwards slept was, perhaps, due—not wholly due—to reaction of the nervous system.

A new lease of life seemed to be given to each of us. Those used to sea troubles, perhaps, think but little of such escapes. To the landsman, however, the past four hours—two of them in the darkness—had been an interview with Death after the manner in which Farmer Dobson, in the old story, had seen him on his wedding-day, and got a similar reprieve.

The inland sea of Japan, and especially the entrance to it, is likely to be well remembered by the passengers of the "Tokio" on that trip. Towards the afternoon we got into the harbour of Nagasaki, and found ourselves safe upon shore. The foot-plate of the vessel had been torn off, and it was necessary to keep the pumps going to keep the water down before the vessel went on the slip for repairs, and that convenience existed fortunately at this port.

Nagasaki had an especial interest for us of the "Tokio." Had it been a cinder-heap, it would have been pleasant to those who little expected a few hours before to have seen it so soon—perhaps ever to have seen it. It was the land of Beulah to which we had got after passing the Valley of the Shadow of Death. Of all the settlements—native and foreign—that I had seen in Japan, this one was in reality the least pleasing. It is not large and clean, like to Yokohama; nor small and well built, like to Kobé. It has a sort of common shipping-port look about it, and is troubled with many of the drawbacks of shipping ports—pot-houses and mean streets. In position it is grandly situated in a bay surrounded on three points of the compass with fine hills, on the sides of which trees and rice-fields are seen, with other signs of cultivation and industry.

That part of Nagasaki most attractive to the foreigner is the old Dutch settlement of Decima that is here to be seen. It is now an overcrowded and very dirty quarter, separated from the mainland by a long bridge that formerly was well guarded. The native element appears to have taken possession of this place now, and made a sort of Wapping of it. This was, then, the small beginning of the wonders that foreigners had wrought in Japan! The Dutchman had not to be thanked for anything, however. He would have muddled on here for another 200 years very likely, content to do as his fathers had done—make a little money by merchandise and take all the snubbing that the brief authorities for the time being liked to give to him. It was to Englishmen, as represented by their eldest son in America, that the opening of Japan trade and travel was due. Had Commodore Perry not gone to Yeddo in 1860, with his letter of introduction from President Fillmore, and his man-of-war to back up the letter, it is quite certain that the Dutch would not have gone in his place. The evil would have resulted that mere travellers for health or pleasure would have seen nothing of all the beauties of Japan and all the surprises that it has in store for the traveller from the Western world. That Western world, and the world generally, would have been deprived, also, of all benefit and delight that the curious merchandise and manufactures of Japan have given to them; also the amusement that its native actors, conjurors, and acrobats have created wherever they have been seen. One walks about at Nagasaki with disgust, to think how long the Dutchman had the partial entry of this place, and never got himself better established in the land.

The specialty of Nagasaki, apart from its shipwrights and wharfside business, seemed, with the Japanese, to be the manufacture of tortoiseshell into articles of utility and ornament. Every visitor takes such things away from the place as some souvenir of a visit to this first or last port of Japan.

Another port between Nagasaki and Kobé is to be shortly opened to foreign trade. It is known as Simoneseki. From the open roadstead, whence we saw it the day before entering Nagasaki, it looked a populous seaside place, with a large crowding about it of native boats. None, however, came near to the ship. The "Tokio" had merchandise to land there, and anchored for that purpose. The weather proved to be too rough for doing so. One of the anchors was lost and the other taken up, and the merchandise taken on to be lost about the rocks off the island of Otata—for that was the locality of our shipwreck troubles—in the manner I have told.

There will be fine fishing for native boats about those rocks for many a day to come. Barrels, boxes, and chests will be fished up yet. Some fine day the cannon may be got up also. It is pleasant to think that of the "Tokio's" cargo that is all that the fishers may get. The sea thereabout has not in our case to give up its dead.

CHAPTER VIII.

A LAST LOOK AT JAPAN.

"THE land of the rising sun" fades from view as I leave Nagasaki, but its memory is indelible; its almost perfection of a climate and varied scenery of hill and dale, mountain and lake, woodland and plain; its rich foliage and fair flowers, its hill-sides clothed with firs and pines; all its novelties of nature and art, and its peculiarities, political and personal; its cheerful, pleasant, and frugal people; their cleverness of hand and simplicity of mind; that patience and politeness which makes them more than the Frenchmen of the Eastern world in all that is pleasant in French character!

Imperilled as Japan now is by the financial troubles consequent on her many reforms, nothing but what is pleasing in prospect seems to lie before her. It seems impossible that a people who have given themselves so seriously to education and improvement can now sink among the nations of the world. They have proved themselves so easy to lead and to govern in their ignorant state, that in their new state of knowledge they must needs be difficult to drive, and impossible to enslave. Not much troubled as yet by religious dissensions, and not trammelled, as is India, by the inexorable laws of caste, it is not to be imagined that any other nation can subdue them, and retain over them a supremacy such as the Hindoos endure.

The language of Japan, hitherto expressed in character similar to the Chinese, is quite a distinct tongue. Efforts are now in progress to express the sounds of its forty-seven syllables in Roman characters, avoiding the many hundreds of semi-Chinese characters that have hitherto been required to express them.

The laws of the Japanese are now in process of codification, by French assistance. The common practice of torture to enforce confession is to be forthwith abolished. The practice

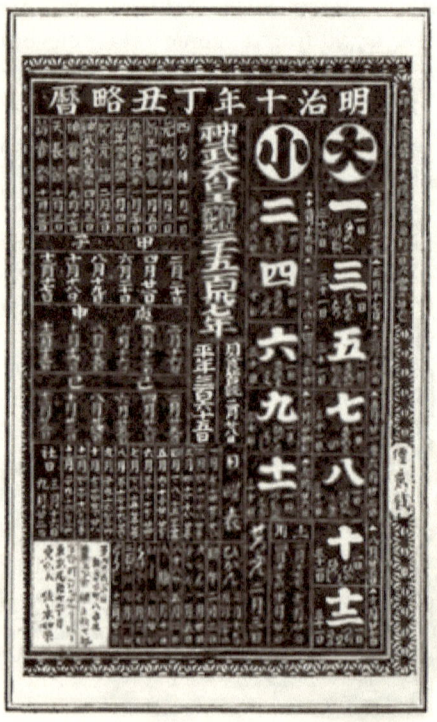

JAPANESE ALMANAC.

of the "hari kari" mode of suicide is also passing out of fashion. Disappointed politicians will no longer disembowel themselves. Everywhere progress is making towards European customs. If such progress should prove to be slow, it is still in the right direction.

Though my visit to Japan had been made in its winter, I

had seen little but blue skies and bright sunny weather. The snowstorm that I had experienced on the journey to Kama Kura, and the rough weather on the second day of the inland sea journey, had been the only exceptions to the bright and beautiful days. In such a climate, walking became a pleasure, and exercise of any kind delightful. Pleasant weather had been supplemented by cheerful companions. I had gone on all my journeys with Japanese company, of whose language I was ignorant, but whose courtesy and sympathy made me feel quite easy and confident. Their cheerfulness was contagious, I believe. Long journeys seemed to lose all tedium in such companionship.

In native tea-houses, far away from English settlements, I had eaten, and drunk, and slept in novel ways that gave a zest to the appetite and soundness to repose. Cleanliness of the greatest and attention the most assiduous were to be found everywhere. The bowing politeness was not marred by extortionate after-charges. I never found it charged for in any of the ridiculously small accounts that I was called upon to discharge. If I had not found it easy at first to eat with chopsticks the French-like tit-bits that made up the meal, I had afterwards carried a pocket knife and fork that, bought long years before in a far-off land, now became of the greatest utility.

Wrapped in overcoat and rug, I had found journeying in the cold but sunny days to be not unpleasant. At first it did not seem a manly thing to go into a perambulator, of larger size, and be run about with, dragged by a man as children are; but the fashion of the country in that way soon subdues all feeling against it, and one realizes without difficulty Cowper's description of his youthful journeys in a similar manner:—

> " And where the gardener Robin, day by day,
> Drew me to school along the public way;
> Delighted with my bauble coach, and wrapp'd
> In scarlet mantle warm and velvet capp'd."

There is no choice but so to travel, or to take to the lumbering palanquin and its two bearers. In such travel in Japan, variety is fully enjoyed and all sense of danger is lost. A word ("Matti") stays the progress of the vehicle, and one gets out to notice any matter of interest, to make any purchase, or to stretch oneself by half an hour's walking. As the floor of the jinrickishaw is only a foot and a half from the ground, the danger of an upset is out of the question. One's sense of humanity is soon satisfied by finding that one wearies sooner than do those who run with us, and we call upon them to stay that *we* may rest. *They* never seem to tire.

Travel is made pleasant in Japan also by its good roads and its numerous towns and villages. At all of these the traveller finds tea-houses, in which rush-matted rooms await his coming. These matting floors are so clean that he is expected not to tread them with boots on. Mats are brought for his seat, his feet are placed in a square hole in the floor made to accommodate them, jointly with a pot of charcoal; a large rug is placed over both, and warmth is at once obtained by the traveller, who waits for his meal while cooking is going on. Two rugs padded with cotton make the softest of beds, and two more the warmest of covering; another one, folded up, serves for pillow. A Sybarite might sleep in such a bed. A bath-house is ready in the morning, with the option of warm or cold water. There is no boot-cleaning certainly, and no soap, but then there is no soap to be found in French or Italian bedrooms. The traveller learns to carry that little necessary in the France of the East as he does in that of the West.

In Japan, one's native company never get drunk. The peril of having a drunken driver is out of the reckoning. The tea-houses, at which a stoppage is made for drinking every two hours or so, are things for which the traveller is thankful. He joins in the drink also. It is warm and wet, and costs next to nothing. After a day or two he begins to like Japanese tea, which is as mild as French soup or English small beer—mere yellowish water. Destitute of milk or sugar, it is rather insipid at first, but the taste for it is soon acquired. It is evidently invigorating by the work that one sees done upon it. It is cheering also by the mirthfulness it evolves from one's friends in the shafts. It leaves no sense of thirst or prostration afterwards, and is evidently, and very soon evidently too, a better drink to travel upon than beer, or wine, or spirits. For the first week or so of travel the foreigner will take a flask with him. He gradually gives that up, and finds that the natives will not share its contents with him. At last he astonishes himself by drinking tea when they do, and takes his flask home as full as he brought it out. Henceforth he leaves it behind him, but can never understand how Japanese can drink the tea in such a scalding state.

There is no real trouble of any sort for the traveller in Japan. A little money goes a long way in living expenses, and in travelling and in purchasing power. The currency is so small that one soon forgets such monstrous sums as sovereigns and half-sovereigns. A dollar is 4s., and in Japan is looked upon much as a pound is in the Western world. It is of no use to go out with dollars in one's pocket. Change would not always be obtained. Half-dollars, quarters, and eighths are the coins to be carried in silver, and then the smaller subdivisions, the cents, in copper. Stoppage is not made at the halfpenny, however. There is another coinage smaller than the cent or the farthing, the half-cent. That coinage is a metallic disc with a rim bit, and a square hole in the centre. It is between a halfpenny and a farthing in size. Ten pieces of this "cash," as it is called, make one cent. Cash is the old original currency of this cheap and pleasant land.

When cleaned up, this cash of Japan has a neat appearance. Pretty Japanese letters and figures appear between the rim and the centre hole. This coinage is carried in strings of a hundred or two hundred and odd. The larger quantity would be a shilling's worth. One sees then the use of the central hole. The string that keeps this bank of money together goes through that. One's native guide takes care of this native money, and tells you when it is all expended. It is wonderful what a way it goes, this Japanese cash. There are no beggars in Japan—at least I saw none. Had there been such, charity might have revelled in distributing happiness by the handful—of cash. To those of a benevolent disposition, who feel the blessing that is promised to the liberal, Japan would be a most satisfactory country. Plenty, in the shape of cash, might be scattered over the smiling land with a prodigal hand, and no fear of a prodigal's fate await the happy doer.

The pretty paper coinage lately introduced in Japan, and called "yen," is eclipsing the attraction of the hitherto potent Mexican dollar. The mint established at Osaca has been bought from the authorities at Hong Kong, who appear to have found the making of money for the Chinese and the foreign visitors to Hong Kong not a profitable thing. It may be found yet that the mints established in other English colonies besides that of Hong Kong will not yield a profit—may, perhaps, cause a great loss. At all events, the Hong Kong people tired of money-making in that shape, and Japan has taken over the business as a national undertaking, and the Mexican dollar is now doomed in that country. The great, clumsy thing is cursed by the traveller, who has to exchange the light moneys of other countries for this cart-wheel currency, cumbersome to the pocket and to the baggage, and only to be bought by a sacrifice of better money.

The Japanese "yen" is an improvement on the United States' greenbacks. The paper is thicker, and the notes well printed in good colours, and of the size of small playing-cards, such as the Spaniards use. The notes go down as low as five cents. A pocketful of this currency is of no weight. The same amount in silver and copper would require a hand-basket or the services of a coolie.

Japan has not yet got the blessing or the burden of a national debt. It is a million, perhaps two millions, in debt, to some of the foreign banks there, and will have to become further indebted before its financial affairs are put straight. Its last budget shows a big balance of expenditure as against income. The country has, however, immense borrowing power, and is worth a hundred Turkeys or Egypts to those who expect principal and interest from national loans. No money is wilfully fooled away in Japan, as in Egypt, on the building of splendid palaces for ladies of the seraglio. The Mikado dwells in the plainest of dwellings. That which is expended in Japan will be, as it has been, on the most useful and reproductive of works. The Japanee is honest and staunch and true in his nature, and not a mixture of a gipsy and a Maori, as is the lazy, designing, and brutal Turk. In dealing with a Japanee you are dealing with one of nature's gentlemen.

For nature's gentlemen are the Japanese, made in the older fashion of the world before money-grubbing had soiled the souls of men, cankered their hearts, and driven chivalry and enjoyment of life out of their nature! If one would know how the people of Britain lived in the days of old, when there were maypoles and morris-dancers, and caps with bells to them; when the theatres were open to the sky, and when there were tiltings and jousts and tournaments; when folks were educated to excel in sports and manliness, to play at quarterstaff, to wrestle, play at singlestick and fence, to tilt at the quintain, and go hawking and hunting and fishing, as the chief occupation of a "joyous life," we may go to Japan, look at the Japanese, and learn all.

Frugal in his habits, the Japanee has but few wants and makes no waste. He toils a little, and his wife spins for a time—sufficient work to make pleasure piquant. He never saves money, takes but little thought for the morrow, and none for the day after. He seems to know nothing of care. A few yards of blue cloth make his covering, a little rice and fish are his "chow chow," taken but twice a day. The drink that "cheers but not inebriates"—the everlasting tea—is always at hand. Sorrow and sin seem never to trouble him. Since he kicked out the Jesuits, 200 years ago, the religion of fear has not yet got at him, and made him a fanatic or a misanthrope. His religious duties are duly and lightly observed, and he is content to let others observe theirs also.

His religious offerings are made in coin. He thinks that such contribution to the gods is the true basis of all other religions as it is of his. He is travelling now, and will write and tell us his knowledge of the world, when he gets it, and whether his ideas on religion have altered. All remorse is foreign to his nature, so that regret for the ejection of the Jesuits is not likely to be acknowledged by him—should he ever feel it. .

The Japanese may not have been willing that their happy life—shut in from the world and its worldly trouble—should have been disturbed; that they should have been compelled to open their sea-doors, receive and make visits, and do business with the rest of the nations. As war, and threats of further war, made such necessary, they are trying to make improvement result from innovation. They resisted improvement because it was innovation; but, having been forced to that, they wisely endeavoured to get the best return for it. As a change had to be made, this hitherto steady-going, never-changing nation has resolved to have radical changes, "to reform it altogether." In feminine language, the house of the Japanee has been turned out of windows rather than set in order. The governmental system of many hundreds or thousands of years was upset at once to begin with. The Mikado was, as the real king, brought down from his contemplative position at Kioto and set up in Yeddo, which was then rechristened Tokio, an act equivalent to calling London or New York by a new name. The Tycoon that had reigned there as working king was set adrift altogether, and sent to pursue country amusements for the future. A representative House of Parliament was started, and the feudal system abolished. From Oriental Government to this sort of thing in a year or so was like the transformation scene in a pantomime. Change, having begun thus precipitately, goes on with a like rapidity in this new constitutional empire. Every visitor will pat the lively Japanee on the back, and wish him and his pleasant country good speed.

It is certain that the visitor to Japan, especially if the visit has been made in winter-time, will desire to renew the call upon this new member of the family of nations, and see it in its pleasant spring, summer, or autumn appearance—also to send his friends on the visit. The visit to Japan has been made an easy one to the dweller in Great Britain since the opening of the Pacific Railway across the continent of America. A ten-day sea passage from Plymouth, or Liverpool, or Cork, lands the traveller at New York. Seven days of further travel, in sleeping cars, across the continent takes him to San Francisco. Fifteen days of steaming across the smoothest of oceans brings him to Japan. The journey across America may, and no doubt will, be protracted by visits to its cities and places of interest. No journey could well be less monotonous than such a one to Japan. Its summer and winter months are those of Great Britain. Leaving London in July or August, a month's pleasant excursion will land the traveller in Japan in the beginning of its autumn. Leaving London in the beginning of English winter would not be so pleasant for travelling. It would necessitate crossing America in the time that snow is apt to encumber the railway, and cold weather to make the journey an irksome one.

Mercantile travellers will find a good account in a visit to Japan. No one who goes thither will quit it empty-handed. The purchases are likely to cause more anxiety for space in one's luggage than about the call made on the purse by them. The handsome Japanese screens and tasty cabinet work will tempt all visitors. So will the lacquer ware of Kioto and Osaca and the copper and bronze work to be found in other places. The vases alone, by their beauty and cheapness, will necessitate the purchase of an extra packing-case or two. Much may, however, in the way of Satsuma china and other porcelain rarities, be stored within these vases. The Japanese are excellent packers. Their maps and picture-books will not escape notice. The thinness of the paper and binding renders their carriage easy and inexpensive.

But not only to the mercantile traveller will Japan be a land of profit. All who travel will similarly benefit by it. The artist will find in it scenes of rare natural beauty. In its scenery of mountain, lake, and glen, the pencil will find its finest field. It is the land of the picturesque. Those who seek health will find it their best resource. Japan is the land

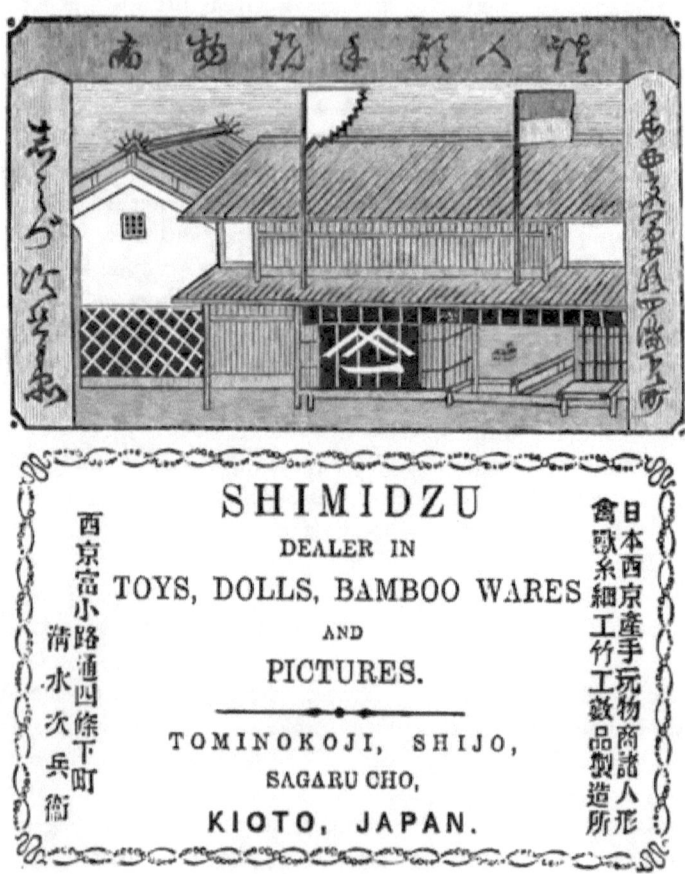

TWO SIDES OF A MERCHANT'S CARD.

of health—of all climates, the nearest to perfection. Those who travel for the pleasure of seeing the world will here find a new one recently opened out. The seeker after new ideas, manners, and customs will find them all here. The lover of sport and the seeker for pleasure will find Japan the country for both. Those who wish to save money or to spend it can satisfy, in Japan, either wish. Its roads afford equally good travelling to all. On foot, with knapsack and native companion, no land could afford more delight. To those who wish to travel otherwise, the means are varied, and all equally inexpensive and satisfactory. Any one who wishes to get away from himself for a time—to seek "fresh woods and pastures new"—will find the newest and freshest in the land of the Rising Sun.

CHAPTER IX.

THREE DAYS AT SHANGHAI.

ON his return journey to Australia, *viâ* America and Japan, the next port that the traveller touches at after leaving Nagasaki is Shanghai. "Far Cathay," China itself, bursts suddenly upon the stranger's eyes at this port. As regards general characteristics, Shanghai is but a smaller Calcutta. It is similar to the Indian city in the situations of its foreign and native settlements, save that in Calcutta the native town is not a walled and gated affair, as at Shanghai.

A fine bay into which my Japanese steamer ran, two and a half days after leaving Nagasaki, introduces a full view of the large semi-circular Bund, or water-side street of Shanghai, and affords also a fine show of the many varieties and strange looks of the numerous Chinese sailing-craft—the sort most usually seen having one tall mat-made sail of towering height and most awkward appearance to European eyes. The first sight of these queerly-rigged boats is as impressive as is the first view of the many-decked, piled-up steamers that greet one's wondering eyes in the harbour of New York.

Shanghai, as far as its foreign settlement is concerned, is but the growth of about seventeen years. It numbers only 2000 or so of Europeans. Looking at the large number of substantially-built stone houses filling many streets and long suburban roads, the visitor will be apt to estimate the white folks there at a large number. Every such inhabitant would certainly seem to have one to himself. I say himself, because the white female population did not count up to more than 300 in February, 1877. I fear that I thus point out a marriage market that may yet rob Melbourne. I can remember, too, what a matrimonial mart Calcutta once was. The native ladies will excite no jealousy. Competition by them is out of the question. I see no pretty Chinese women here.

Here, in Shanghai, I first saw the famous Chinese compressed female foot. Those so disfigured are recognized by their wretched hobbling attempts at walking. The impression on the stranger is exactly that made by one trying to walk on one's heels only. It is most unpleasant. The foot appears to have been squeezed up, heels and all, into the ankle, and the toes only left on which to tread. These small feet, or hooves, as they really are, are luckily not common sights. The fashion never became general, like to the growing of pigtails by the men. Every Chinaman shaves nearly all his head to give strength to the back hair, which is twisted about to form the tail. To make this excrescence longer and thicker, silk is intertwisted with it. The longer the tail the more admirable. When not hanging behind, a proper pigtail should twist three times round the neck. It is finished off with a silken tassel. A Chinaman would as soon lose his life as part with this useless but, to him, highly ornamental article. You touch his honour and dignity if you touch his pigtail.

A new national conveyance is soon perceptible hereabout. To every one palanquin that one sees about Shanghai there are a dozen wheelbarrows used as conveyances. To make one of these, the wheel of a common barrow should be made three times the usual size, and the seats placed on each side of it in Irish jaunting-car fashion. The vehicle has the appearance of a veritable wheelbarrow, and is wheeled in the same way. It is, of course, springless. When one passenger only is carried, it tilts to one side to preserve the equilibrium. So mean a conveyance does it look, that some courage is required with Europeans to make use of it. The palanquins are more in favour with the foreign population, who leave the barrows to the natives. Of all the vehicles that I had seen in the world, these appeared to be the meanest. To think of being carried on a wheelbarrow!

The settlers in this seventeen-years' old Shanghai have their history. They tell of the past, even at so short a date, and speak of it as better than the present. The halcyon days, when wealth was widely distributed, and easy to be had! "When a hundred dollars were as easily to be got as one is now!" "When Cokem came from Australia here with a circus company, and set up a tent there, opposite where Jannsen's Hotel stands, and made a fortune of 20,000*l*. in a few weeks!" "When Lorara was a great man here, and made nothing of thousands! Poor fellow, he went to poverty and Lisbon at last, and died in an asylum there!" Such are the little recollections that crop up and come out when Shanghai folks talk. With every community it seems to be thus—always yesterday or to-morrow, and never to-day, as the day of prosperity.

To get to Shanghai I had passed some little distance up the Yangtze-Kiang river, and became acquainted with one cause of the greatness of China and the prosperity of its hundreds of millions. It is another America for majestic rivers. With such natural facilities for water traffic, supplemented by numberless canals, the favoured land of China grew naturally to greatness, and prospered until outside interference by England shook its stability, and has now left it, like to a great whale, floundering in shallow water, nearly helpless. This river with the long name is navigable for a thousand miles from the Yellow Sea, from which I entered it, up to Nanking.

From the great river a divergence is made into the lesser Wangpo, on the passage to Shanghai, and the walled town of Woosung has to be passed on the way. From Woosung to Shanghai a railway has recently been opened—the first that was made in China. The Chinese do not favour these innovations. They are not like to the Japanese in that respect. A Chinaman's conceit is something enormous; all that does not originate with his nation is to him worthless. Since I was at Shanghai last year, this railway has been bought by the Chinese and destroyed.

There are many pleasant characteristics about Shanghai in addition to its noble bay, filled with shipping and picturesque craft of all kinds. On the crescent-shaped sand around this bay are to be seen the different divisions of the town—the English quarter, the French, and the native. The range of buildings so distributed around this bay frontage must be some three miles in extent. The population of the foreign kind is mixed up of all nations, similarly to that of the Japanese ports. The winter weather, at the time of the year I was there—the beginning of February—was cold, but no snow was visible, as at Japan. An overcoat was, however, a desirable addition to one's clothing. The walks and drives around Shanghai are numerous and pleasant, the Bubbling Well road particularly so. The race-course is passed on this road. It is on well-selected ground, and has a tolerable grand-stand, that is not likely, however, from the good views to be had of the racing all round, to be much patronized.

The Bubbling Well is a curious wayside well of 5 ft: diameter. The water upon which one looks therein is ever bubbling—in a single bubble at a time. The cause of this phenomenon is not agreed upon. Here a fine opportunity is afforded for the exercise of fancy, and the display of learning, in defining this inexhaustible and most definite of the bubbles of the day. It is of Nature's concoction. There is no humbug about it. As enduring and reliable as Niagara, this little one of Nature's water-wonders bubbles ever on and on, welling its single bubble as regularly as the beatings of the human heart or the ebb and flow of the tide. In any other country but that of Confucius, a temple would have been erected over this well, a sacred legend have been attached to it, and a large income derived from devotees! Here, at Shanghai, the Bubble Well is a miracle wasted—blushing, not unseen, but wasting its sweetness in producing no profit. At Benares it would bring in a large revenue. With a good legend attached to it, fame may yet draw the world to see it. It goes to look at far more trumpery things than the curious Bubbling Well of Shanghai.

The native town is walled to the height of about 20 ft. The wall is surrounded by a moat. If the walls were 10 ft. higher, the town would have much of the exterior appearance of Jerusalem. The gate by which I entered is very like to the Joppa gate of Solomon's city. Inside, also, the resemblance to Jerusalem is kept up by the narrowness and filthiness of the streets. How different to the wide streets and clean ones of tidy Japan! The gaudily-painted signs that are protruding everywhere, showing Chinese characters and hieroglyphics, soon tell me, however, that I am not in Palestine. The city is busier than is Jerusalem, and is far more densely populated. Busy bees are all around me, and I take leave to watch their movements. Time is too precious for them to suspend their work because a stranger is looking at them.

Here are all the characteristics of a Chinese town, in this old city of Shanghai, to be seen in every particular. Some of these particulars are not very pleasant. There is, to begin with, a very oppressive sense of overcrowding. One feels that at once in endeavouring to walk about the 10 ft. wide streets. The stones that pave them have been worn to a slippery condition by the bare feet of the million that jostle each other in their ceaseless traffic. "Million" is, by the way, a fitting term indeed when speaking of a Chinese population, they are so plentiful and so prolific. Scarcely one of the little squeezed-up shops in these crowded alleys but appears to have as much of family as of goods in it. All work seems to be done in full view of the public; the wood-carver in his huge spectacles is busy at his minute labour at his open stall, with the noise of the multitude that pass his door, or jostle each other in front of it, ever in his ears. Privacy does not appear to be valued. The dyer, the silk-worker, the weaver, and the miller, are all to be seen at their avocations, carried on in places in which there scarcely appears space enough to swing around their arms. The habit that we see the Chinese have in American and Australian settlements of overcrowding themselves has been learnt in their crowded and overcrowded native towns, and habit, we know, is stronger than nature—bad habits especially so.

That no time may be wasted, or money either, in going to temple-worship, a little shrine, holding the figure of Buddha or some other deity, is placed in a corner of most of these little hives of industry. The sticks of incense, at a penny a dozen, are lighted up before the image when evening comes on, so that worship goes on with business—as it ought to do, all good Christians will say. Cleanliness and godliness do not go hand-in-hand in this case, however. There is reason for their not doing so. The struggle for bare existence is so hard with these people that time cannot be wasted in fetching water and much washing. What few hours can be spared from labour is too often wanted for sleep.

Do I not see the sleep of the tired ones all around me? The Chinese are not particular where they rest when nature can no longer hold out. Like dogs, they lie about on doorsteps and under any shady place—any out-of-the-way corner that gives them six feet by two of space. As no vehicles run about in these narrow alleys and crowded lanes, there is no danger from passing wheels. All travelling not done on foot is performed by two bare-backed men carrying a sedan chair, slung upon two bamboos, in which chair sits the traveller, carried along at a "Chinaman's trot" of between four and five miles an hour. Though these carriers have but little breath to spare from this intolerably hard labour, they have to spare some of it in shouting loudly to warn the crowd of their coming, that space may be made to let them pass with their burden. Only long practice can have given their bare feet the foothold which they unfailingly seem to have. Booted, as I was, I slipped about everywhere on the greasy and polished stones, but never was a slip made by these chair-bearers, all naked as their feet were.

The native city of Shanghai must be an ancient place. It bears every mark of time about it. Its temples are black with age and decay. The smoke of the incense sticks has had something to do with the blackening perhaps, but, allowing for that, it is still an antiquated town. It is probable that nearly all of it has been rebuilt many times. Fire is so active in these crowded Chinese cities that building is always going on to replace that which the fire has destroyed. For that purpose only is the builder seemingly required. In these crowded walled towns there has been no spare ground left for building upon. It would be difficult to find space enough to put up a pump. Most of the buildings are of brick.

Wandering about with that prime necessity, a guide, in this crowded, mazy place, I pass into its temples and through its markets, and along its streets, and into this shop and that, until I come to near about the centre of the city. In Jerusalem I should have now arrived at Solomon's Temple, or the Mosque of Omar, that at present stands on its site; but here, at Shanghai, was "something more exquisite still," something worth Solomon's Temple twice over. It was a tea-house, in the centre of a large pool, with zigzag wooden roadways leading from the land across the water under the overhanging trees. "Only that and nothing more."

What is it, then, that makes one stop and rub one's eyes and open one's mouth? Why am I silent and standing stock-still looking at that tea-house? The guide says nothing, and moves not. He has seen the same state of things with other travellers, and has come to understand it—so far as a Chinaman can understand emotion and sentiment. Will one's eyes never cease staring? It is to be feared not, for they are looking at the original of the earliest thing that British human eyes can remember seeing, at what they looked at three times a day or so, and at the time when the brain best receives lasting impressions. They have seen the scene now before them until it has been foremost of all things in the memory of the eye. It can be recalled at any time to the mind's eye by closing the outer vision, and will remain a vivid picture when memory of all other pictures and paintings, seen but now and then, have faded—for I am gazing now at the original of that well-known view in the willow-pattern plate. All the rest of native Shanghai is as nothing to this. Towers and palaces and gorgeous temples it has none. Its temples are rough and ugly, and dirt-begrimed; but here, in this water and willow tea-house, Shanghai holds a shrine that makes a pilgrimage to it as excusable as any pilgrimage ever made. No traveller has ever told of it. None have brought home the slightest news about it. The source of the Nile and the locality of the North Pole have had too much of attention altogether. In point of advantage and value to the world they will confer no greater benefit when, if ever, found, than will the know-

TEA-HOUSE, SHANGHAI.

ledge of the whereabouts of the famous Tea Temple among the water and willows of Shanghai, with its winding, wooden approaches.

To me no more a fiction, but a pleasant reality, foremost among the sights of the world, is that tea-house temple. I had thought it, as others have no doubt done, but the mere fancy of the artist, and yet the enduring nature of that million-multiplied picture might have told me that its stronghold was in the foundation of fact. The countless millions of copies of it that have circulated through the world have made it the best-known of pictures. How many of them have we not broken and been beaten for breaking? Nothing approaching to it in the way of pictures has been so multiplied and distributed. At Damascus, early in 1876, I was served at dinner in Dhemetri's Hotel off a willow-pattern plate. There, in the oldest city of this world, as in the mushroom town of yesterday's growth, has this nursery story of a picture found its place. It will have another place now. I do not remember that I ever saw this picture framed and glazed. That shall now be done. In circular rosewood frame it will look well. The word "Shanghai" beneath it will be all that will be necessary to recall the scene as one of the greatest surprises that awaits the traveller who seeks astonishments.

I enter upon the crooked water-walk, and cross to the tea-house. Before I enter it I look around. I am in the centre of an oblong reserve of which the tea island forms the middle part. There is a piece of fenced-in grass at one end, in which a deer is browsing. The place has evidently seen better days. The water was not always of the clayey colour it is now, and the tea-house and its approaches had a gayer appearance in the days that were, and when its picture was painted for our dinner-plates.

Entering this house of houses, I take a seat with the Chinamen who are drinking tea there, and eating curry with chopsticks. I get some tea, and wait until its scalding-hot state has abated. It is sugarless, of course, and without milk, but what of that? Its surroundings will make it taste like unto nectar, served as it is in that wondrous tea-house—a place that my young eyes had looked upon as a paradise, and my infant fancy pictured as the great pleasure-spot of the world. I had now come to it, and, like to all the other fine things of this world that the traveller seeks, it did not improve on acquaintance. Venice looks much better in pictures than it does to the traveller's eyes. Calcutta is not a city of palaces, and very far from being so. You do not want to die after seeing Naples. The Blarney-stone is a swindle, and so is the Logan Rock. No disappointment can be greater than that one experiences in looking at the Sphinx and the Church of the Holy Sepulchre. The "splendid city of Benares" that the traveller expects to see, from what he has read, does not exist. A decaying and dilapidated town is what he does see, walking and stumbling about as he does over that part of it here and there which has fallen, and lies as it fell. Nothing —not even Niagara—equals expectation. Why, therefore, should the willow-pattern plate tea-house be an exception?

Shanghai city closes its ancient gates sternly at 8 p.m. After that none can enter it. The native element has outgrown its protection, however, and is largely distributed around it and through the settlement generally. The Tazmaylew, or big road, is a highly picturesque street in the English part of Shanghai. It has the advantage of good width, so that the Chinese signs with which it is hung from end to end on each side show to advantage. This street leads out to the pleasant Bubbling Well road, all along which fine views are obtained of the surrounding country. Shanghai is built on the edge of the great plain of Kaing See—the largest of the plains of China. It is said to be in extent 3000 miles by 12,000, and to be the very garden of the land of China.

This garden of China is much bedotted with mounds of earth that are untouched and uncultivated. In many cases these mounds make up as much as a fourth of the field in which they stand. They are the graves of former proprietors, and are held as sacred and untouchable by the present owners.

"These graves take up much of the land," I said to the kindly friend who was driving me around the country.

"Oh, yes, they do indeed. Cremation would be the salvation of China—would place so much more land in cultivation. These large graves about the fields are great drawbacks to the profits of the cultivator of the land."

"Yet I suppose he would rather perish than level the ground and cultivate the spot."

"He holds the grave of his ancestors as sacred as his own pigtail, and so helps to starve himself by his superstition."

The settlement of Shanghai appears to have a pleasant future before it. It is an increasing and prosperous place. The Chinese are not to be feared. As a nation they are the weakest of warriors, and incapable alike of aggression and defence. They need the protection of a strong power like England. It is well that a company like to the aggressive East India Company have not found a footing among them. The fate of India would have been that of China ere now. Its wonderful system of civilization and government held it together, as a nation, until its constitution was broken by the rude shocks of war made by the British in 1842, 1869, and 1872. The power of China was, by the first of these shocks, so injured that the Taeping rebellion gradually gained strength thereafter, and grew to formidable results that have desolated many populous parts of the empire, and threatened it with dissolution. China, as a nation, is as weak and defenceless now as a milch cow. To keep the nation together should be the aim of the rest of the world ; for, if it falls to pieces, its millions will take to emigration, and flood the labour-markets of the world. There is no such cheap labourer as a Chinaman, and none so dangerous as a competitor with Western workfolk.

CHAPTER X.

THE CHINESE PORTS.

PASSING down to Foo-chow, a great tea-shipping place, and Amoy, a similar one, in one of the boats of Holt's line, I am taken thence to Hong Kong and landed at the smallest colony

AMOY HARBOUR.

that Great Britain possesses. It is, I was told, but thirty-six miles round. The extravagant salary of 5000*l.* a year is paid to its lucky governor. Time was when Melbourne was the golden thing in governorships. Looking at the thing all round, the "plum" would appear now to be Hong Kong— one-twentieth the size of little Tasmania, and no bother of responsible government and playing at Parliament.

Hong Kong is like to Madeira in the first look which the traveller gets of it—a white town at the foot of a mountain. Seen at night, lighted up, it has a pretty appearance indeed to those who then approach it by its land-locked and winding harbour. To go into Hong Kong in foggy weather must be impossible. Winding about among the rocks and their narrow passages, this Gibraltar-like place is reached at last, long after the traveller has seen the flag that waves at the look-out station on the top of the o'erhanging mountain.

There is no separate native town at Hong Kong, as at Shanghai. There is advantage in this to those who like to see the Chinese brought to comply with European customs and to live in wide and clean streets. Except around the water's edge, wheeled vehicles are not much used in Hong Kong. The sedan chair carried on the bamboo is the favourite form of moving about. The cold winter weather of Shanghai had been now quite left behind. At the end of January, Hong Kong was too warm for one's liking. The mosquitoes were troublesome, and all walking about out of the question.

Having taken a drive out to Happy Valley to see the race-course, and declined the fatiguing journey to the flagstaff-house, the sights of Hong Kong proved to be exhausted. I walked through its native market in the early morning, and left its fine white stone houses and the green waters of its pretty bay to go by steamer, "Kui Kiang," down to Canton, by way of the wide river of the same name, called also the Pearl River. On board this boat I met with one who had made a name as an Australian vocalist and ballad-writer. For years I had missed all mention of him. In his present avocation of a "curio" collector and exporter he is well and profitably employed. Another acquaintance turned up in the tall figure of Chang, the Chinese giant, whom I had met when exhibiting himself around the world many years back. He was now seeking to establish himself in business at one of the Chinese ports, if he could resist some tempting terms to again travel in company with another Chinese giant lately found, and who is even taller than himself. I endeavoured, for the benefit of the world, to turn the scale in favour of the tour of the Celestial giants. Traders are plenty in China—"too plenty," as they express it in their attempts at English—but giants of 8 ft. are scarce, and the world likes wonders.

The Chinese, when they learn any French or German, speak it correctly. Not so with the English language. They mess it about in a comical manner, and make of it new words and phrases. The trouble with a Chinaman is to pronounce the letter R. With the Japanese the same trouble exists with the letter L. "American" is by the Chinese pronounced as "Melican." " Askee Melican man topside" was said to me by a Chinaman. It meant that he would ask an American on deck some question as to the value of a United States dollar that I was paying to him. Anything that implies a higher situation is "topside" in this "pidgin English."

"Pidgeon (or pidgin) English," as this cackle is called, really means "business" English, the word "pidgin" being as near as a Chinaman can bring his tongue to the sound of the word "business." As the Chinese can get no nearer to English language than this childish half-and-half talk, the British trader has to adopt it also, and the result is very whimsical. Grown-up men with grey beards are heard talking to Chinamen as a child might use broken English at three years of age.

On board this steamer that was taking me to Canton I noticed that all approaches to between decks were guarded with iron doors, in front of which one of the crew walked with a loaded gun. On the upper deck plenty of Chinese of a better class were left at their ease, but those taking second-class passage, and they were legion, were placed thus under guard, and within iron gates. I asked of the captain as to this state of things.

"You are walking on a volcano—that's all," was his reply.

"See," he said, drawing a revolver from his breast pocket, "I am never without this on me."

An alarming state of things certainly, which I heard this explanation of:—

"Only two years ago, between here and Canton, a similar lot to what I now carry raised a quarrel among themselves, and brought it upon deck, and ended it by killing the captain, my predecessor, and the crew, and taking the vessel!"

The iron gates at the foot of the stairs were now explained, and so were the men with the guns, and he that walked the quarter-deck with the drawn sword in his hand. "The Volcano" consisted of about a thousand Chinamen lolling about in all attitudes, smoking opium or tobacco, playing cards or dominoes, scraping at stringed instruments, singing ballads in voices like to that of a cat, telling stories to a listening crowd, or sleeping in every conceivable attitude in which humanity can get sleep. I got the iron gates opened, and walked among this crowd of possible pirates, and saw a different scene to that which I had looked upon in the work-a-day city of Shanghai. There all was industry and plodding labour. Here it was the improvement of the leisure hours in that manner most to the taste of each.

Opium-smoking takes first place in the number of Chinese amusements. It is far more general than I had imagined, quite as common as was the chewing of tobacco amongst the folks of Great Britain forty years ago, and more common than snuff-taking is with Europeans at present. A veritable little cabinet of articles has to be carried about by the opium-smoker. It is as large and as full of instruments as a lady's work-box. No. 1 is the buffalo horn box that holds the treacley-looking stuff that is the opium about to be smoked. No. 2 is the steel skewer, with which sufficient of the opium is taken up and wound about the skewer's point. No. 3 is the little lamp now to be lighted, at which the opium will be heated. No. 4 is the bowl of the pipe, covered over all but a small hole in the centre, into which the heated opium is squeezed by the point of the skewer. No. 5 is the pipe-stem, now fixed on to the bowl. All this bother being finished, he that has taken it lies down at half-length, puts the pipe mouthpiece between his lips, and the light to the small hole in the bowl. That ignites the opium within. The smoke is drawn from the bowl and passed into the mouth, and thence into the lungs, whence it is, after a second or two, expelled through the nostrils. After four or five long whiffs the opium is exhausted. The smoker will then lie quietly to enjoy the effects, or, if the dose has not been strong enough to produce them, he will prepare another one. It looks like to taking of great trouble, but "the labour we delight in physics pain."

Usually one pipe suffices, and the smoker passes into half an hour's doze. As I look at him I would give something handsome for his pleasant sensations, and the gorgeous visions that he is now enjoying, but cannot bring myself to buy them at the cost he pays. In a neuralgic attack I once had to take a mild preparation of opium in the shape of a morphia pill, and I recall all the pleasant dreams of that painless night; also the light head and the sick stomach of all the next day. Like other pleasures, it is very nice, but the day after, and its sufferings, counterbalance all the pleasure—counterbalance it until the pleasure in its lightness kicks the beam against the heavy weight of the suffering on the other side.

Beyond the opium-smoking vice, at a long distance, comes the gambling one. Of three average Chinamen caught at a street corner, one will smoke opium for amusement, the second will gamble, and the third will sleep. Cards and dominoes are seen everywhere among the strewn battlefield-like scene that I now am picking my way through. I have to tread on tiptoe between the arms and legs of the sleepers, and am like to a camp-follower that looks for the prize of a dead officer among the mass of dead and dying of the rank and file. The musical instruments and the singing scare me out of the place at last, and I pass through the iron gate and by its guardian, and on to upper deck again, having seen the possible pirates at all their leisurely amusements.

The scenery of the fine river on which I am steaming down to Canton affords equal interest to the scenes between decks. To some it would be more interesting, but Pope was of opinion that the study of mankind is of first moment. Dr. Johnson believed also in what Fleet-street could show him against all other scenes. On either side of the Kui Kiang, and on the islands in its midst, are forts that English guns have destroyed, now lying dismantled and deserted. Stone walls that cross hill and dale at their rear and side still stand. The useless labour and wasted work over these Chinese fortifications is a painful sight, except perhaps to the philosopher, who may regard all the works of men as coming to much the same thing at the end.

Here, too, on the left side of the broad river stands Whampoa, or what remains of that once populous town. It is now a deserted water-side village, with a towering pagoda overhanging it. This building is over 200 ft. high, and has a tree growing from the summit of its tower. It is of the shape of one of the round towers of Ireland, and not of the ornamental style that is brought to mind by the word pagoda. Vegetation is growing also on its window-sills, and wherever a creeper can get foothold or a seed dropped by a bird find mortar and moisture to aid its growth. Whampoa's good time was when no foreign vessels were allowed to pass further onwards to Canton. That state of things is done away with, and the formerly busy port may now write "Ichabod" on its landing-stage, in its deserted streets, on its empty and trembling houses, and its decaying temples and pagodas.

The busy life of the Kui Kiang River begins after Whampoa is passed. Dozens of the native boats (sampans) appear on either side. These increase in number to hundreds. By the time that the anchor is dropped at Canton, the boat-life of the big river is in full view. The surface seems to be covered with water-craft of all sizes, but varying little in shape. From 500 tons down to five, and to half a ton only, these boats are seen everywhere. Those from two tons upwards constitute the dwellings of their owners. In these floating habitations they are born, and in these they marry and live, rear a family, pass on to old age, and sit as grandfathers steering the boats that they sculled as boys.

The Chinese boat-women do all the business work that comes in the way of boat life. The husband's duties appear to be amidships, keeping the boat clear from other craft, and taking orders from his busy and barefooted better half. She picks up the pidgin English more quickly than her dull mate, and for that reason generally gets the boat licensed to herself as the owner. Preference is given to the best educated in China, even down to the boat-folk. I am sitting on board the steamer, getting a friendly Chinese scholar to write me several cards showing name and address in Chinese characters, when my shoulder is tapped, and looking up I find a smart-mannered, bright-looking woman at my side. Two or three others are also around, all desirous to assist me on shore. Says my lady,—

"Come, master, you go shore, you come hotel, my boat."

"What hotel are you going to?" I ask.

"Rosario Hotel. Only one hotel. International Hotel fall down."

Finding from the captain that this is truth, and that there is but one hotel, I take Hobson's choice in the matter, and go with my neat-looking guide. She looks to be about thirty. It is true that she is shoeless, and has on but a blue blouse; but then her fine black hair is elegantly put up and neatly ornamented. That so assists her that she is almost good-looking. She wants to take my heavy travelling-bag, but I have not the conscience to let her do such drudgery. I gallantly take it from her hand, at which the captain laughs. He says,—

"She can carry it better than you can. She will think now that you are afraid to entrust it to her, and take her for a thief."

It was, of course, possible that my politeness might be so misconstrued; but I let her lead the way to her family boat, which she at once pushes out from the landing, and begins to scull across the stream. How herself and her husband ever get through the mass of boats that cover that teeming river is best known to themselves. I sit down under a circular covering of bamboo, roofed with rush-made matting, and find there two little children, sitting quiet as mice, and good as gold.

They have but small room for play or mischief, and are never away from the eyes of their fond papa in the rear, and mamma in the front. At night-time this covered space of 6 ft. long by 3 ft. broad serves, I suppose, for family bedroom. There is more wretchedness and misery to be seen among the Irish cotters and the peasantry of wretched Turk-governed Syria than I have seen in the boat-life of the Chinese rivers.

Susan, for so she called herself, took me to an hotel, the steps of which went down below the water. It had an overhanging balcony of wood, and was wood-built all through. There was ready escape, however, into the river in case of fire. Rosario's Hotel would not suit fastidious folk, but I was well satisfied with it for the time I stayed.

On the river that I look at right and left from the balcony of the hotel, its owner tells me, 50,000 people are living, having their boats for sole residence.

I find that I am now at Honam, and that Canton is on the opposite shore. There, at the left, is Shameen, the foreign settlement, in which neither hotel nor coolie is allowed. The bridges to it are guarded, that the English, French, and German residents may live in a strictly select manner. Shameen is certainly a well-laid-out and nicely-planted place, but a first-class hotel ought certainly to be built there for the convenience of foreign visitors. All travellers have not friends there in whose houses to find a welcome. Rosario is a Portuguese who speaks broken English. At present he enjoys a monopoly which is not to the advantage of travellers.

I engage a guide for the proper exploration of Canton on the following two days. In the evening Susan comes to me of her own free will and wit—as knowing the wants of the friendless traveller.

"You want to see river, master. I come at eight. Take you to boat. Show you wedding party. Take you to tea-boats, and show you lots of things."

"You are a jewel. You come at eight, and I'll go."

Her English was not so plain as I have put it down. In fact, she had to repeat twice or thrice everything that she said, but the truth generally dawned upon me at last, as it does to all of us.

So that evening I am taken on board the family boat, which now in the moonlight, with a pretty paper lantern at stem and stern, looks like to a gay gondola. Susan sculls and talks, and her husband sculls and is silent. His mother, at the helm, steers and looks after her grandchildren. It all looks very novel and pleasing.

In and out among the endless boats, I make way for a mile or two; sitting down under cover is now not to be thought of. The paper lanterns give a gay and carnival look to the river scene that forces one's attention and admiration. It was so very different to anything that I had hitherto seen anywhere —this scene on the Canton river by moonlight. The boat is drawn at last alongside a large one of similar build, into which I am bid to step.

It is a tea or pleasure boat that I am now upon. Music is on hand, and tea and cakes and sweetmeats. Folks tired of the day's tussle on shore come to these boats in the evening to enjoy the river and the breeze, the feast of Chinese raisins, and the flow of the tea-bowl. Of that warm, insipid beverage Susan brings me a basin and a plate of sweetmeats. I endeavour to do as others do, but find that I am not happy at the tea and sweets. The latter make the sugarless tea taste positively bitter. I try to sweeten it with them, but it by no means improves the flavour.

"No saki to be got, Susan?" I said.

She asks for the rice spirit, and gets it. It is but little better than the tea; but it is better, and Susan brings a cigar with it in her happy way of spreading bliss around.

From the pleasure-boat I progress in another direction for a mile or so, until sounds of revelry come upon me in the night and the moonlight. I am drawn up alongside a still larger boat than the last one, and bid step into it.

It is a wedding celebration that I have now got among. The bride is resplendent in dress and hair-dressing, but keeps her face closely covered. One of Susan's sisters is a bridesmaid, I suppose, for she looks almost as fine as the bride. I fear almost to shake hands with her until Susan tells me that I will be allowed that liberty with her, and also with the bride. Thanks to the saki, I suppose, I gather courage to do so. Hat in hand, I return the bows that welcome me under the large awning, and take my seat among sixty or so of wedding guests. Prompted by Susan, my good genius of that evening, the bride uncovers her face, and brings me a tray with tea. The courtesy with which she tendered that tray quite overpowered me. My good breeding was hardly equal to returning it, and, taking the tea and getting upright again, and spilling none of it. The bride looked very nice—but I scarcely ever saw a bride who did not. The tea really tasted better than other tea, because herself had brought it to me. Call it not vain. I do not err in so saying. Longfellow says that Nuremberg looked better, and its sunshine brighter, because Albert Dürer, the artist, had trodden its streets. Said Susan, now again at my side,—

"You thank the bride. You wish them both happy life. You give bride present."

The last suggestion of this good woman was easily complied with; but how to thank the bride and wish happiness to the married pair was a teazer. Not one of them but Susan probably would understand a word I said, however much I might try to "pidgin" my English.

It was really distressing—so much so that Susan, seeing my hesitation, increased it by getting the bride to bring me a cup of hot saki and water. I gained time by asking Susan to put sugar in it, waited until it melted, and then got the bride to stir it around with her fair finger. It did, indeed, taste sweet after that.

I gave Susan the dollars to distribute; but she brought the recipients to me that I might place them in their hands, which I did, Susan dictating what should be given, and managing the whole matter in first-rate diplomatic style—a born politician.

I hoped to sneak out of the speech-making, but that was

not for Susan. Oh, dear, no! I was not to be thus let off. She now spoke decisively about it. The power and influence of women on such occasions is wonderful. They seem to shine then as at no other time. There is amongst them the joy over the captured husband similar to what there must be, I think, among the angels in Heaven over the sinner that repenteth.

Said Susan, "You wish them good luck. You stand up and tell them so. Don't be humbug."

This was not "pidgin," but plain English. The last word was scarcely applicable. If anything, I was the soft party in the business of that strange evening. Susan must have meant "fool," I think, but it mattered not. There was no help for it. Nobody there to understand me but Susan, and none to report the speech. Every speech-maker has had occasion to wish he could get off on as easy terms.

I made the speech in the usual wise way of such addresses, and Susan led off a round of hand-clapping, and got others to follow it. I then got bride and bridegroom to write me their names in pencil on a card, and got Susan to give me the English equivalent sounds, and then she insisted on my shaking hands all round.

I never had so good a guide anywhere in all my travels as that bare-footed boatwoman. She was made for the office of guide, and perhaps philosopher and friend as well. She took an interest in her "pidgin," and anticipated my wants, and not, like to others, left everything to be suggested and asked for. She volunteered her services, and as a volunteer was worth a dozen hirelings.

CHAPTER XI.

A LOOK AT CANTON.

I.

CANTON proved to be a city well worth any trouble taken to see it. The native guide, Ah Kum, who steered me through its network intricacies, was a professional, and none the better as a guide for that reason. It was Hobson's choice, however, as my better boatwoman guide did not undertake land labour. Her domain was the water only. All the zeal that she had voluntarily showed for one's benefit was not to be bought of others, pay how one might for it. The hireling cared not for the sheep, except for fleecing him. Ah Kum was a heathen Chinee in every sense—too much so altogether for the good of any one but himself. Canton was to him a certain number of show-places, to be visited and got through with as quickly as possible, and be done with and paid for. A certain number of shops and stores, at which he had credit, and from which he drew commission, were then to be visited, and purchases there recommended, and there only. To fight against all that sort of thing involved a continual assertion of a freeman's right, and constant squabbles with a guide who was neither philosopher nor friend, as was the zealous boatwoman of the day before.

He would not walk, this guide of mine. His ankle was bad for the same reason that Talleyrand suggested that a certain diplomatist had the gout. Palanquins had, perforce, to be taken, and Canton to be viewed over the naked shoulder of a perspiring Chinaman in front, and out of two small window openings at the sides. These views around were at an elevation of six feet from the ground—not a height to make one giddy, but still higher than one had usually looked at things from, and therefore unnatural. The motion of the palanquin had some resemblance to that of a boat at sea, and made one's stomach feel sickish. As there was nothing but Chinese food to be had at the Canton tea-houses, the latter trouble did not much matter. Appetite was wanting for that day, had even the most tempting dishes offered.

CHINESE PALANQUIN.

How we pushed and squeezed our way through those ten-feet-wide streets, crowded with the millions of China! Jostling here and there, and sometimes coming to a dead-lock altogether, we made our way somehow, but it was all struggling and trouble. The stones of these mercantile alleys were worn smooth and slippery by the ceaseless traffic of the surging crowd, but the barefooted bearers who carried me through it all never slipped or tripped. It would have been delightful to have walked and elbowed one's way on one's own account, as a man should do. Then upward glances might have been given to the countless thousands of flags of oblong shape that served as signs for the shops over which they hung. Then I could have stopped to examine this or that novelty that fixed one's attention, and looked after the curiosities in the way of humanity, past which one was now hurried. A city can only be seen satisfactorily by the pedestrian. The novel industries that here and there cropped up, the singing beggars, and the awful lepers might have had one's full attention, and not been scurried past as they had to be.

Having found out the word for calling a halt when wanted, the first use I made of it was at a shop in which, in a most limited space, three small bullocks were blindfolded, revolving round millstones. This was the process of grinding grain that I saw often repeated elsewhere during the day—a primitive method that had probably been in use some thousands of years. A most extraordinary industry next called one's attention. It was a dyer's workshop, in which a man, supported by his hands between two horizontal bars, such as are seen at a gymnasium, oscillated by his feet an enormous stone of triangular shape. The obtuse apex rested on a roller that was rolling and pressing some silk fabric that had been newly dyed. With his feet on the upturned base, first pressing one end and then the other, he kept the roller in rapid motion—his own motions being equally rapid. Only long practice could have given him the knack of guiding the heavy stone so as to go within hairbreadth of slipping off the roller and never doing so. The roller slipped not from under that foot-and-a-half of stone surface that kept it going, and pressed with five hundredweight upon it. At the end of a quarter of an hour this dancing workman could, with a single movement of his foot, cant the stone on one end, and, descending upon the floor, place a further portion of the silk in position to be similarly treated to that now removed. And yet these Chinamen believe that they do everything more cleverly than the rest of the world! Their conceit is of a most self-satisfactory sort. A rolling-mill of the most simple kind would do the work infinitely quicker and better than this most rudimentary method of doing it. They are, however, satisfied with their way. It suited their forefathers in countless ages past, and must therefore be the proper thing. The Chinese reverence antiquity—its traditions and usages. They are the most conservative of the nations of the world.

Little mobs that were assembled where any space offered for their doing so proved, on inspection, to be around gambling tables. Nothing but copper "cash" appeared to be staked. I suggested to Ah Kum that he should try his fortune with a

A CHINESE HOUSE.

silver coin—that was the smallest currency I had with me. He placed it on the board, but the table-keeper rejected it. He would not take so large a stake.

The crowds of hurrying human beings, all on industry bent, that are to be seen in Canton give one a good idea of the dense population of this over-populated China. Canton is one of its large cities—seemingly as large as Yeddo in Japan, but not covering so much ground. It is a walled city, and space is consequently economized to the utmost. A dozen people are to be seen in Canton in the same space that only one would be visible in at New York. The struggle for existence seems to be very desperate indeed in these Chinese cities. My thoughts about it were interrupted by a blow on the roof of the palanquin that nearly sent it off the bearers' shoulders, and caused me to clutch at its sides. The palanquin-carriers had jostled a stalwart, blind beggar, who, in a frenzied manner, lashed out right and left with a bamboo staff that he carried. He was evidently a semi-lunatic, who elsewhere would have been in confinement. Looking back towards him out of the rear window of my swinging-cage, I perceived a crowd round him, and the bamboo still at work. Save for his blindness and half-nude condition, he might have represented one of the sturdy quarterstaff-carrying beggars of England's bygone days. Police of any sort do not appear to be about in Canton. The preservation of the peace seems to be left to the co-operation of the public. At one place the street was blocked up for five minutes by a mob that listened to the abuse that a furious coolie was hurling at a shop-keeper. The cause of the trouble was that copper cash, equivalent to a penny, but about a handful, nevertheless, had been paid to him for some small service that he considered worth twice that amount. It was not until his indignation and his lungs became exhausted that the stream of traffic could move on. It was rare strong abuse that he vented forth. His features and the hoarse tone of his deep bass voice told that. I saw no street fights.

While listening to and watching that scene, a skinny arm was thrust within the window of my cage. In place of a hand at the end of it, an earthenware cup was strapped thereon. It was the arm of a leper, whose hand had been eaten off by disease—a horrible sight. These poor creatures are not, as in some places, placed in hospitals, but wander about Canton begging—rubbing shoulders, meanwhile, with the jostling crowds.

The heart of the crowded city is now reached. I feel that if left in it I should remain there for all ability of getting out that I possessed. Not a soul had I met that showed a sign of speaking English—not one that I could even think of addressing in the faint hope of his doing so. Not a European costume had met my eyes. All pigtails and shaved polls, and smocks of white or blue, for the richer, and bare shoulders for the poorer class. To get into the city I had progressed for some time through outskirts as crowded as was that part within the walls. That I had reached the walls became known to me by my cage-bearers asking me to get out and scramble up some hundred rugged steps that led to their top. This wall looked very old indeed. It had not kept out the cannon-balls of the English, however—fired into Canton in 1859. Marks of these troublesome things were visible in many places—notably so in one of the temples, in which swings a fine bronze bell of many hundreds—I was told thousands—of tons weight. Out of the side of this bell a ball had knocked a piece 2 ft. wide, and left the ugly ragged gap as evidence of it. The grand bell is thereby quite spoilt. A legend attaches to this bell that, if it ever rang, the city would be lost. The cannon-ball that caused it to ring on that occasion was a wonderful fulfilment of prophecy. Canton did not long stand that bombardment, which was something like throwing hot coals into a beehive.

Brick, of a slaty colour, is the prevailing building material used in Canton, but some walls are visible that are wholly made up of oyster-shells—a novel and not a bad material, as it seemed to me. The city wall is built of a bluish stone, much honeycombed in course of its volcanic manufacture.

A halt is called by Ah Kum at the temple of the Five-hundred Genii. It is an unpretending building of one story only, but contains many halls filled with 500 sitting figures, all gilded. The gilding of the sitting figure of Prince Albert in Hyde Park was probably suggested by this show of 500 such gaudy things. These figures represent different half-length figures, on whose forms and faces the sculptor appears to have exhausted ingenuity to produce variety. No two are alike. In several cases an arm of the figure is upraised and stretched out to 5 ft. in length. None of them, however, look any worse than the Albert Memorial figure. After looking at about two or three hundred of these life-size figures, curiosity about them is satisfied, and the rest postponed. A priest of the temple, who has watched in the distance, then approaches, and I pay him as I should do for visiting a waxwork show. The 500 are carved in wood. They are all supposed to have special influences with the deity. A devotee can take his choice as to which is likely to do best for him. A laughing one, with three children in his lap, and one on each shoulder, looked most domestic of the number. From the temple of the Five Hundred I pass to the gaol of Canton. This place is like, I suppose, what gaols were in Europe before the efforts of Howard had called attention to their disgraceful state. Anything more disgusting than the gaol at Canton cannot be imagined. My squeamish guide refused to go into it. The nasty smells that came betwixt the wind and his gentility made him sick, he said. I might go in if I liked, but was likely to catch gaol fever if I did. As no prophecy was ever fulfilled in me, I regard it not, and passed through a rotten old gate into a dirty courtyard. In this place men were standing about with heavy stones chained to their feet. That, with the greater misery of utter idleness, is one of the punishments. Passing through a narrow filthy passage, I look into what appears to be an old stable, but is an apartment of about 25 ft. square. Through some holes in the wall that admit light, and some iron bars that help to keep it out, I look upon a sight that cannot be forgotten. The smell of the dungeon was very foul, and the sight more so. About fifteen men were here cooped up, each with his head thrust through a heavy wooden collar, made of several pieces of planking nailed on each other. This strange instrument of torture was about 3 ft. square, projecting over the shoulders on each side. With that on, there is no lying down for the wearer, and no rest to be had in any position. Its weight must be considerable, and its torture also. It is worn for a fortnight and three weeks at a time, and is equivalent to the

British punishment of "hard labour" added to short sentences. Hard labour would be no punishment to add to a Chinaman's sentence, if of the lower orders. His whole life is made up of that. The poorer wretches crowded to the bars of this pen with outstretched hands. What good money could do them in that place I could not imagine, but they had what change I possessed. If it made them less miserable for a moment only, it was well given.

In another part of the prison I found other punishments in progress. Culprits were receiving heavy blows on the face, with leathern things made like to the sole of a shoe. The jaw is frequently broken by this punishment; but that matters not. It is left in a broken state. Others were tied in a kneeling position, and one with outstretched arms tightly bound by cords to bars of wood. I did not see the thumbscrew, or the scavenger's daughter, or the iron boot anywhere in use. The Chinaman is too conservative to adopt European customs.

A gaoler sat at a door, which I asked him to open. He did so, and I walked into a quadrangle, in which about twenty men were walking, or sitting and lying about. Their cells were all around. They were not bound or ironed in any way. I thought that it might be the hospital or lunatic ward that I had got into, and went out to inquire from the guide, who was playing with his toothpick outside. I learned that this was the condemned cell. He said, "Those men you see there are not punished beyond imprisonment. They are to have their heads cut off next week; you stop and see it. I take you to the execution ground this afternoon!"

These men were then condemned to die—as we all are—but these knew when 'twas to happen. I went back to see them and took them some tobacco, which Ah Kum suggested as the most likely thing wanted. Though knowing when their lives were to be ended, they all seemed quite careless about the matter. Life is not a very dear thing to a Chinaman—in poor condition. The waiting a week for death was, I think, their chief misery. The tobacco was a rare gift for them. They all seemed ready to die then and there to get a share of it. Walking about among twenty condemned criminals is not an every-day occurrence. Their hands were not, however, stained with murder. People are hanged in China for things which the Insolvent Court clears them from in the Western world. I had no doubt that among these twenty were men as good as any other twenty that I had passed among anywhere.

From the gaol to the temple of horrors was an appropriate progression. It is a temple fitted up to represent the punishments of the wicked—whether here or hereafter I could not well make out. There cannot, however, be much difference. A man was represented as sandwiched between two planks, and being sawn through down the middle. That is a death still in fashion in China. Others were being mangled in their way, and that too horrible to look at. Yet this temple is more crowded with visitors than are any others. It is to be hoped that the moral lesson intended is not lost. Outside this temple a sort of fair is holden. Dentists are there drawing teeth in the open air, and quacks selling their nostrums. Something of that sort is required, no doubt, after the sights within the temple. They are enough to make any one feel unwell. One stall particularly attracted my attention. It was that of an astrologer, who drew horoscopes for a shilling. Ah Kum seemed to sneer at this man and his profession, but then what could a heathen Chinee know about spiritualism? I paid my money, and got the mysterious paper from the mystic man. It looks all the more wonderful and weird from being in Chinese characters. I was offered a translation of it for five shillings—four times its cost, but it is as well not to know one's fate. I shall keep that horoscope. Framed and glazed, it will look like one of the old needlework pieces that used to be so honoured and hung up in every house in our grandfathers' days.

The ten-storied pagoda now came into sight, and its summit afforded a fine sight of the city from a downward point of view. The streets looked at from thence seemed like to cracks in a pavement. Had I not known by rude experience that they were streets, one would not have so thought on seeing, for the first time, Canton from this point of view. It was like to a city all roofed in; the street openings might have been mistaken for roof guttering. Near to this ten-storied pagoda, I passed a tall, old Mahomedan round tower, which has no access to the top. On the top grows a large tree that has sent its roots adown the brick sides of the tower in search of nourishment. A similar thing I had seen at Whampoa. The Temple of the Five Genii differs from that of the Five Hundred in this, that the five goats are shown, on which they flew through the air into Canton, there to remain for its good. The goats, I suppose, had wings; but when their mission was ended, they were turned into five lumps of rough stone that are now deposited in front of the genii. I asked Ah Kum if he believed the legend. He answered, "Not much." He gave no reason for doubting it, and seemed to take the presence of the five stones as no evidence. He seemed to believe only in his dandy British gold watch and pencil-case. A dozen times an hour he would pull out the one or the other, and seemed surprised that I took no notice of them. At last he broke forth, "Best watch in Canton—cost forty guineas. Chinamen can make anything but watches."

It was not true, but still it was something to hear a Chinaman admit that there was something his countrymen could not do. I asked, "How did you keep time in China before you got timekeepers from other countries?" "To-morrow I take you to tower, and show you the great water-clock of Canton—then you see!"

CHAPTER XII.

A LOOK AT CANTON.

II.

AH KUM'S determination to do no walking about Canton was very vexing. I specially thought so when he brought up two palanquins next day, seemingly as a matter of course.

"Is your ankle no better?" I queried.

"No! cannot walk!" He said this with an immediate reference to his gold watch. It was evident that the possession of that article had much to do with his general ideas. He looked at it, not to know the time, but to settle all questions generally. He walk with property like that in his possession, indeed!

Ah Kum wore his finger-nails very long—over an inch. In China that is done to indicate that the possessor of the fingers does no work with his hands, as the small foot indicates that the owner does no walking. When Ah Kum exhibited his watch, he took care also to show his finger-nails to the best advantage. Of this hideous deformity he was most unwarrantably proud. I doubt if any European could get so elevated in mind on uncut finger-nails. They were always, too, a nuisance to him, interfering with all the movements of his hands. He endured it, however, for fashion's sake, as folks do the modern torture of high boot-heels.

"Very well, then—you will ride and I shall walk. I can see nothing when shut up in those palanquins. Send away the one you mean for my use!"

This satire on his vanity did not seem to suit his feelings, but I was strong on the subject, and the second palanquin was sent away. Being on foot, I was master of the situation for the day, and could stay where I pleased, and for long or short time—using Ah Kum in his cupboard merely for reference now and then. In this style we went to see the great water-clock of Canton. It is not relied upon now, as formerly, for time-telling purposes, but it keeps its count of the minutes and hours as accurately as ever. It differed with my time only two minutes. Ah Kum had his watch out at once, and held it now altogether exposed. Such an opportunity of exhibition was not to be lost. With that watch the clock differed nothing. It was no doubt keeping correct Canton time. Its construction seemed simplicity itself. Three large barrels were set on end —two of them at a height of 3 ft. each from the other. From bamboos inserted in the bung-holes, the water from the highest barrel dribbled to the next, and from that to the lower one. The head of that one was removed. In its water floated, uprightly, a graduated metallic scale like to the face of a thermometer on which the twenty-four hours were marked. As the water increased, this indicator marked its progress and the hour next to be reached and covered over. The upper barrel of the three held the exact quantity of water that would dribble out and into the lower one in twenty-four hours. At the expiration the water would cease to run, and the indicator be covered with water. The lower barrel would then be emptied into the upper one, and business begin again. Three patient Chinamen superintend this timekeeper and watch their hours thus dribbling away. In former times it was death to any one of them that was found to be sleeping out of his turn. A graduated sand-glass would have been a much better article than this water-clock, but the hour-glass was not a Chinaman's idea.

Of glass the Chinaman makes much. It appears to be blown in egg-shaped pieces of very large size and very thin quality. At none of the places where I saw glass-working going on were any flat sheets of it to be seen. Out of these large glass bubbles, as they appeared to be, the artisans were cutting pieces of different sizes for purposes, I think, of fan ornamentation and toy mirror making, when the glass should be silvered.

The temple of the laughing Buddha is one of the curios of Canton. I was, however, quite full of this figure, whether with laughing face or not. I had seen Buddhas all through the East everywhere, and could draw the figure on a wooden wall with a red-hot poker with my eyes shut. After the grand Buddha figure seen at Kunakura, in Japan, in its 50 ft. high sublimity, all other Buddhist figures were insipid.

No gold or silver smiths' shops were seen by me anywhere in Canton. They exist, no doubt, somewhere about the city, in places where no wares are shown to the public eye, but kept, as in most Eastern cities, locked up in boxes and drawers, and exhibited only at visitors' request. The Jade market was the personal ornament of Canton. Business is over there at ten o'clock a.m. I reached it at its busiest time, shortly before its closing for the day, and before the beginning of the festival of the Chinese New Year, when every one must look gay, or as near to it as coloured clothes and ornaments will help. Jade is a greeny-white stone of watery appearance, a sort of agate malachite or malachite agate. The Chinese set great value on this stone; all sorts of ornaments are made of it —comb-backs, rings, and earrings. A Chinese woman must be very poor indeed who has not jade earrings. Where want has really reached to that low depth, imitation glass-jade work has to be substituted. The wearer is, however, unhappy with this substitute, which to a Chinese eye is seen at once to be but imitation. A foreigner's eyes do not so soon detect it. Hundreds of shops and stalls were open in this Canton jade market, and trade seemed to be brisk. The articles were, however, in European ideas, all much too expensive. Jade is not by any means so pleasant-looking a stone as the greenstone of New Zealand. It looks a commoner thing altogether. Yet double the price asked for greenstone in New Zealand is asked in Canton for this jade stuff. When Canton was taken by the English in 1869, much of this jade was taken away as loot by the soldiers, but it failed to find favour in any but

Chinese eyes, and brought no fortune—sold, I think, for farthings elsewhere.

In Canton, as throughout India and the East generally, are stalls for the sale of the betel-nut-chewing preparation. It is a compound of nut, green leaf, and a stuff called gambier, with a little lime and tobacco added. This abomination, rolled in the green leaf, is sold in balls at four for a penny, or its equivalent. It makes a red mixture when chewed, and gives to all the men and women who use it—about half the people—the appearance of having a bleeding mouth. It blackens and destroys the teeth. The chewing of this stuff and the smoking of opium are sad vices of the Chinese. Tobacco-chewing, like to snuff-taking, is disappearing in Great Britain, but the Chinaman is not open to reform. He is by religion a fatalist, and would answer "ché sara sara" to all arguments intended for his good. If he did not, he would probably ask for the loan of five dollars as a test of one's interest in his welfare.

At the further side of the city from the river is to be found the five-storied pagoda. It stands on the ramparts, and on the highest ground within Canton. It is a stiff walk to reach it, but the view from the summit, o'er city and suburb, repays the toil. Looking outwards from the city side is to be seen a stretch of green country for miles—all filled with graves. I am looking here at the cemetery of Canton. Ah Kum, with finger and long claw of a nail extended, points out to me the grave of his father—referring to his watch to be quite accurate as to the locality. It cost him, this grave, he said, seventy pounds. These ancestral tombs are often visited by deceased's kith and kin. Hereabout they are shaped like three large horseshoes laid on a slope. In the middle of the second one is the door within which the coffin has been placed. A semicircular courtyard of four feet or so across is thus left in front and below, and also above, and at the rear of the entrance. Tasty stone-work in many instances makes these graves of a very neat appearance. They satisfy one's ideas about tombs. Chinese civilization looks well in all matters connected with death and the tomb, respect to parents, and veneration of ancestry. They are ahead in those matters of all mankind. They are fond of their children, and cling to them until poverty forces them to sell their clothing. The children are not sold until all else is gone. With Ah Kum I go to a Chinese tea-house to have a mid-day meal. He tells me I shall not like it; but I have taken many meals of that sort, more than of any other.

It is tiffin time in Canton. The tea-house I go to is three stories high, and each floor is used as a restaurant. The staircase and walls are in well-carved woods of dark colour. The house evidently has been a costly one. I am, in the

DOMESTIC LIFE (CHINA).

second floor, bid to sit at a little table for two in a room in which thirty or forty are similarly seated. A cup and saucer are brought to me. Tea is thrown into the cup, and hot water poured upon it. The saucer is then placed over it, and the tea left to "draw." A tray full of confectionery and sweetmeats is next brought, and I am left to choose from a dozen plates that are thus set before me. One of them proves to be eatable. "Try all things, and hold fast to that which is good," occurs to me, and I get the plate replenished. The teacup I now find to be half full of tea-leaves. The Chinese can drink their tea scalding hot, but I have to saucer mine, for the weather is too hot to let me hope of its speedy cooling in the cup. No milk or sugar is supplied, but I had learnt in Japan to take tea neat. I had that teacup refilled five times. Canton investigation is thirsty work with the thermometer at 88° of a moist heat. Everybody in the room seemed to be tobacco-smoking with pipe or cigar, eating and drinking at the same time. The repast was a light one, rice cakes and tea. I did a long afternoon's walk upon it, which testified its suitability to the climate.

In these tea-houses, and in the steamboats, pleasure-boats, hotels, and elsewhere, fire-sticks are always to be found with a smouldering end to them. They are made in walking-stick lengths of some pithy matter, and look and feel like to sticks of compressed brown paper. A walking-stick length, broken up into six pieces, provides for a week's want of matches. All cigars and pipes are lighted at these sticks. Rimmel would, of course, add perfume to them, and then incense would seem to burn in all houses. As congreve matches are gradually being introduced in China, these fire-sticks may go out of use. In the flint-and-steel days of Great Britain such sticks, always burning their slow length along, would have been welcome—would have saved much knuckle-knocking and probable profanity.

All day has Ah Kum been anxious to take me to the execution ground, which he evidently regards as something good in the way of sights. I have asked him if any one is to be decapitated there, and he has said, "Not till next week—then twenty—you stop." I have explained to him that the attraction is not great enough; also that an empty execution ground is only a vacant piece of ground, and to me nothing to look at. I explain to him also that I am ignorant of the great and good who may have suffered there with the vile and the bad, and that there are no associations connected with the execution ground that will people it with ghosts and make it enchanted ground to me. He listens and looks at his watch, he tickles his ear with one finger-claw, and says,—

K

"Come and see the heap of skulls and bones; all the hair sticking to some of the skulls yet!"

After that answer, further remarks were unnecessary. It closed the matter. I dropped sentimentalizing, and told Ah Kum to walk on, asking, by the way, what was the time. It so pleased him to pull out that watch that he walked on to do it, and forgot his palanquin. By constantly keeping him pulling out and pocketing the watch I kept him always now at my side. In that glow of happiness he forgot his ankle, or rather what he said had ailed it. He explained that he had been saving up for years to buy that watch and the pencil-case. It was one of the strange instances in which the possession seemed to give the happiness that generally only attends the pursuit. He worshipped his baubles more than his Buddha, for he told me that he never went to worship. "Send my wife and the children instead, and give them the money." After all he perhaps attended substantially to what the priests might have said was the principal part of the business.

We had by this time reached the execution ground, and lo! it was a potter's yard. Space is too valuable to be wasted in Canton. Busy artisans were here working at their wheels and moulding pitchers, jugs, and basins over the blood-stained ground. The skulls and bones of which Ah Kum had spoken were piled against the side wall. The sight of the hair attachments was wanting. The dogs and rats had no doubt accounted for that. "You can take any of the skulls that you fancy," said Ah Kum, for which sarcasm I retorted by asking how the time went. I wanted to see the headsman's block, but was told that the decapitation was done without it, one cut generally sufficing if the kneeling criminal held his neck steady. "They always do that for their own sake," said Ah Kum.

"Have you seen executions here lately?" I asked.

"No, never come to them now. There were thirty executed here a month ago."

It seemed a great sacrifice until one looked at the super-abundance of humanity that exists in crowded China, and thought of the millions that might be well parted with for the benefit of the others. Looked at in that cynical light, this clearing away of the people in batches of thirty seemed almost one of the ways of Providence.

As Chinamen and women advance in years, they become shrivelled and hideous beyond other humanity. Death must, I thought, be afraid to approach some of the ancient beings that I saw, who had for years been plainly flying the blue peter at the fore.

"We will go now to the dog and rat market—English people want to see that," said Ah Kum.

This sneer at the select tastes of the English was not bad, but could not be overlooked. "What time will it take?" I asked, forcing that watch to come out again. Ah Kum could not think of time, I knew, without consulting that oracle.

"Take a quarter of an hour; I show you some good things by the way." The good things consisted of some ornaments made of blue feathers, or the down of some bird of blue plumage. Some shirt-studs, so covered, were neat curios, looking as if made of blue enamel. It was of the delicate filagree work in which the Chinese excel, as also were the inlaying and tracery work on wood that I was next introduced to. The plan is worked out by perforations on paper, which is then laid upon the wood, and the paper sprinkled with a white powder well shaken over it. On the removal of the paper, the white outline of the design is seen, and the wood is then handed over to the workman to be painted in thin but strongly-sticking varnish, over which powdered colours are shaken. To decorate a tray in that style takes a workman days, and yet it sells for about a shilling, wholesale price. Labour counts for nothing in China. The material seems to be that which is only counted in reckoning cost.

I resisted all Ah Kum's attempts to get me into shabby old buildings, that had been only tolerable at their best, where the grandees of the city lived. The viceregal residence, or what was equivalent to it, looked a very tawdry affair, not to say somewhat dirty. Like to the Japanese, the Chinese do not excel in palaces or temples. One must go to India to see what the Eastern world can do in that way.

A trouble had weighed upon Ah Kum's mind all day since the hour that he had seen me purchase some Chinese books. It was the common leathern purse, of English make, out of which I took the necessary cash, that fixed my Chinaman's fancy. His soul thirsted for that purse. It would match the pencil-case and the watch, and his happiness would be then trebled. He had a small, mean-looking English one that he had thought something of before. It had probably cost 6d. when made, while mine might have cost four times that amount.

"I will change purses with you, Ah Kum"—here his face lighted up—"if you will let me cut your nails down as short as mine are." Here it darkened.

"I am a gentleman," he said, "and must look like one."

"But you look like to a bird of prey, or a madman, with those finger-nails. They don't become a man who carries an English watch like to yours. Besides, I want your nail-tops to take away in a lozenge-box as curios."

I could see the mental struggle that was going on until we reached the dog and rat market; but it finished in favour of the finger-nails. He looked at them several times, and decided to keep them.

"You can grow a new lot at any time," I suggested in Mephistophelian manner.

"I have not cut my finger-nails for years. They would take years to grow to this length again."

That was so self-evident that I could not dispute it. There was no chance of doing so, as we were now with the skinned dogs, and the skinned and split rats.

Shakspeare is authority for calling rats and mice "small deer" and articles of food. Here this miniature venison was in plenty. Shops after shops showed tiny carcases hanging up for sale, looking scarcely as nice as chickens and ortolans, but about the same size. The dogs looked lean, but then all the dogs of the East look so. It is very short commons with them all their miserable life long. An Eastern dog is so sharp set at all times that he will devour anything. One of them left the mark of his teeth on my fingers in Shanghai in his eagerness to snap up a crust of bread. The loss of life is but little loss to such, and they revenge it by the poor picking that their bones must furnish to those who starved them thus in their lifetime. The rats are plumper and are classed as barn or vegetable-fed rats, and drain or carrion-fed ditto. The latter have a gamey flavour, I was told, but the former fetch the higher price.

CHAPTER XIII.

IN CHINA.

I TAKE ship at Canton for Macao, and find myself among some 600 passengers of many nationalities, but 580 decidedly Chinese. That large majority, with the exception of about fifty, were kept between decks, as I had seen done on the

MACAO, FROM THE BAY.

voyage from Hong Kong to Canton, and locked out with iron-barred gates from any nearer approach to the upper deck. That upper deck held, besides the fifty Chinese allowed to be there, about twenty men whose native places were widely apart. Two of them were Armenians, three were Greeks, one was from Portugal, and two from the Manillas. These, with Germans, Dutchmen, and Americans, made up the number that were not Mongolians. On board that boat I was the only Englishman. The most agreeable of our number were the two Armenians, polite and intelligent men, who talked English as if born to it. The great attraction of the steamer's company was, however, to be found between decks.

In "Lower Canton," as that portion of the ship was termed, were some very strange sights. Three large vats of some nine feet in diameter and six feet deep were here to be seen, filled with water and large fresh-water fish. I am sure that there was as much of fish as of water in those vats. The fish were to be sold alive at the end of the voyage. The method of keeping them in that state was ingenious for Chinamen, though a European would have perhaps called it clumsy. The water was continually dipped up from the vat in a bucket which was then emptied into a barrel fixed on the vat's edge. From this barrel came a bamboo, of two inches diameter, sloping towards the water in the vat, but stopped up at that end. Two notches, of the size of a florin, cut in the bamboo within three inches of the end, sent the water that came rushing down it into the air for two feet or so. A rude fountain was thus made, and the water kept sufficiently charged with air by that means. Each vat must have held a thousand fish, some of them of ordinary cod and salmon size, and few of them smaller than herrings. Chinese labour is cheap, or three men could not have been allotted to each vat to keep this fish-fountain continually going, which they had to do. The fish were now and then gently stirred up with a long bamboo to bring the overlaid ones below up for a mouthful of fresh air.

It was evidently market morning next day at Macao, for "Lower Canton" was filled with kitchen produce, all very anxiously kept in best order and freshest state. The market gardener had planted the cut celery and lettuces in moist sand, and so with the bundles of asparagus. Plenty of finery and fancy-work for the Chinese New Year was hung all around and above. The whole place looked fair-like and gay, and more like to a stage operatic market-scene than anything in common work-a-day life. Had the men at the vats struck work and broken into a fisherman's chorus, à la Masaniello, I should not have been astonished. I walked about expecting something of the sort, but found that those not obliged to be working or watchful were opium-smoking or sleeping.

Looking at the gambling going on upon deck among the superior sort of Chinese, I wondered if the governing powers there had withheld a currency from the country to help stop it. The want of any circulating medium of a reasonable sort is one of the wonders of China. The copper "cash," of which about 100 pieces make a shilling's value, is a great drawback to business as well as to gaming. It is necessary to have a coolie with you to carry the large strings loaded with this currency. About a sovereign's worth is a good heavy weight. Except for the hole made in the middle of this coin, and through which the string is passed, a large bag would be required, or a good sack, to carry many pounds' worth. I went into this gaming for an hour or two to pass away ship-time, and was nervous at the sight of the pile of money—about sixpennyworth—that I from time to time recklessly staked. It looked like tempting of fortune so to stake such a heap on the hazard of the die. When I did not win I doubled the stake on the number, and then the shilling's worth put down seemed quite a fortune in its size, and fairly frightened me. No luck favouring me, I doubled again, and the over-flowing pile of eight hundred and odd coins brought a good result—it looked so comical that all fright fled, and I could but laugh at it. The luck turned with the odd number. On that third stake I had to take up upwards of 1700 coins. I felt that a competence was made, and that I might then and there retire for a year or two and live at ease. It was impossible, however, to get away from the fascination of such gaming and the new delight of handling such masses of money. As a Rothschild might feel at Monaco, staking his hundreds at roulette, I felt at this Chinese gaming. I gave up such deep "plunging," as racing-men phrase it, and took to smaller stakes. The money then dribbled away in bad luck, and the banker came off the winner in the end. I must have lost as much as 5s. or 6s. value before three hours had quite slipped away. One satisfaction remained. Had I have been a winner to that amount, I must have invested in a portmanteau to carry the coin, and paid porterage at the landing-place. My travelling-bag would not have held a tenth of it. Wealth of that sort brings trouble.

The Hong Kong colony, as before mentioned, started a mint and coined silver and copper currency in value like to the English coins. The Chinese, I suppose, did not take to it. They object, in their conservative nature, to all innovations, whether improvements or not, so the Hong Kong mint was sold to the Japanese Government, who have done what China would not do, coined a national currency for the empire. When the Hong Kong currency now afloat shall be exhausted, travellers in China will find trouble. To carry about the small shoe-shaped lumps of silver weighing a pound or two, or the copper cash of the country, will be a bother that I had not to endure. The Hong Kong coinage is at present taken at all the ports, and so is the Mexican dollar. Previously to the starting of the mint, the latter coin was the circulating medium that the traveller used in the ports, but I was told that in the interior it did not always find favour. The other moneys of the world are rejected altogether. Folks with nothing particular to do and a taste for excitement would find trips in these Chinese port-steamers a pleasant variety—especially in the cheap gaming.

Macao is an old Portuguese settlement, about ten hours' steam from Canton, and something less from Hong Kong. It is an ancient-looking place, and picturesque in appearance. Its day has, however, gone. Trade is for some reason dying out, and decay everywhere appearing. The ruins of a fine old cathedral stand well-exposed upon an eminence in the rear of the town. Macao has, however, one matter of interest to some travellers. It contains the tomb of Camoens, the Portuguese poet—that will keep the old town green in the world's memory when all its other claims on recollection shall be forgotten.

At Macao I was bid wait aboard the steamer to see the landing of the live fish that we had brought down from Canton. Boats half-filled with fresh water came out to us. The ports of our steamer were then opened, and large funnel-shaped nets extended from these to the boats below. The fish were then ladled out from their vats in net-made scoops that held about fifty of the silvery-looking strugglers. These were turned out into the funnel net, and went helter-skelter down into it, and into the water of the boat. A few would stick fast by the fins or gills in the net-work on their way down, and remain struggling until the next flood of fifty other fish drove them along. One of the fish fell overboard from the net opening, but had scarcely reached the water ere an amphibious boat-boy plunged in and captured it. It had, I suppose, become too dazed and stunned by its late treatment to know exactly what it was about in the changed element of salt-water. Its troubles are, however, over by now.

In the market-place I found that fish was the prevailing article for sale—that and vegetables. The big waters of China plentifully supply the fish food of the Chinese nation. It gives them to collect it not a tenth part of the trouble that growing their rice does. Rice may be called semi-aquatic wheat. It is grown in patches of ground that are six inches or more covered with water. To keep this water on the land the fields are divided into sections of all sizes, but generally not less than about the eighth of an acre. Each patch is banked all around with earth or clay a foot and a half high and of the same breadth. That retains the water within its wall. All these rice patches are graded with great care, sloping almost imperceptibly downwards, so that if water drains away from one enclosure it passes into the next one below it. A field of forty acres will contain a hundred or more of these enclosed sloping patches. The rice, when growing, looks like to blades of grass coming up above the water of a pond. It is wet and dirty work indeed for the cultivators. They work in the water and mud all day. Before the rice is sown, the ground is dug up with a spade shaped and used like an adze. At each chop at the ground made with this instrument, a splash of water occurs that bespatters the labourer with mud from head to foot. He weeds the land also with his hands, and altogether does about the dirtiest agricultural work that a labourer can do. Rice is a delicate plant. It is not every field sown that yields a harvest. Three crops can be grown in a year, but not from the same land. Generally only one crop a year can be got from it. When it is no longer rice-producing, the water is drained off, and other crops sown on the dried land.

It gives more trouble than wheat-growing, does this rice cultivation. One field that is sown with the grain brings up enough to transplant into, and fill, four fields. Grown from the grain, it comes up too thickly to thrive, and so is pulled up when a foot high, and tied in little sheaves. The labourers, mostly women, take these sheaves into other fields, and there, standing all day half-leg high in water and mud, they plant the rice, stalk by stalk, at a distance of four inches apart. This rice-planting looks very tedious work indeed, and the stooping attitude in which it is all done must make it irksome. The root of the young rice-plant is stuck down into the muddy bottom of the field beneath the water, and is there left to find holding-ground and flourish, or to droop and die.

Trouble is not over with rice when grown and cut and garnered. It gives about twice the trouble that wheat does to unhusk it. No cereal clings with such tenacity to its shell. I carried several ears of rice about with me, forgotten, in a pocket corner for some weeks, and not one grain had left its covering. The modes of threshing it, so to speak, are many. The flail is not in fashion, but instead is generally used a short pole or club, fixed at a right angle to one end of a lever. That is made to stamp away at a small vat full of grain. The motive power for this machine is a man, who jumps on and off the short end of the lever, and so raises it and lets it fall again. The rice looks very poor, dirty stuff indeed, when this workman has done with it. I could scarcely believe the dirty grey-looking grains to be the rice to which we attach whiteness as chief characteristic. Many are the processes that it has to undergo before it gets to the colour by which the general public know it—perhaps as many processes from its beginning to its finish as are undergone by sugar.

The labourers, male and female, returning of an evening from labour along the foot-and-a-half wide walks that divide the rice patches, are a sight that arrests attention. In Indian file procession, a hundred or two of them walk two or three feet apart, their dark forms looking darker against the setting sun. They generally work unclothed, their scanty attire being carefully stacked on sticks set up on the dividing ridges. The first creek or watercourse affords them the necessary washing after their day's work. The matter of washing is so urgent that necessity really knows no law and no decency. All bathe together, and no attention is paid to the hundreds of passers-by. The hundreds of passers-by pay no attention either. The rude traveller may look once or twice at such a sight, but naked Chinese soon become no more of interest than naked flies, and are regarded much less than the audacious mosquito.

This daring and bloodthirsty thing will in China take no denial. Harried by the heat of the day—the moist heat that so enervates one—a tired traveller will seek mid-day rest, but finds it not. With a flourish of their shrill trumpets, the mosquitoes are upon him by day as by night. Samson disposed of the Philistines that were upon him with ease. He would not have done so with the Chinese mosquitoes. It is strange that Scripture says nothing about these torments of Eastern lands!—this thorn in the flesh and messenger from Satan that buffets one by day and night. They must have plagued the prophets, and added another to Job's many troubles that his potsherd was powerless against. They would care as little for that as they do for mosquito curtains. At these they fairly laugh. After brushing round and round the whole bed enclosure with a long feather whisk, the simple traveller thinks that he has secured a bed to himself. He tucks the curtain in all round and turns down the lamp. Then he performs the acrobatic feat of jumping harlequin fashion through a small opening that he makes between the curtains. The mosquitoes jump after him, however, or lie in wait for him out of the way of the whisk that he has flourished around. Their shrill song of triumph soon sounds loud in the darkness, and slaps, instead of sleep, occupy the sleepless one until morning. Slaps are suspended only for scratchings. The mosquito always raises a mound to its memory. If all that is in this world be for our good, if whatever is, is right, it then requires a great understanding of the ways of Providence to work the mosquito into his proper place in nature. That he was created to keep the tired traveller and weary worker from his necessary sleep is not right and not good—as I at present understand things. Those who would argue the matter must please first experience the ways of the Eastern mosquito. A little of such experience will go a long way.

Hotel charges in China are not too economical, but the traveller must remember to pay his bill when he leaves any place for a trip that he thinks may be short, but which may exceed his idea of the time required. Happening to be away for four days, I found that the charges for food and bed to a leather bag and a walking-stick which I had left behind were the same as those charged to myself when present in the house. Henceforth, when I went abroad, I took those little things with me, and opened a fresh account on my return. One finds soap and lamp duly charged as extras in all Eastern hotel accounts.

My little tour round the Chinese ports had taken me to Shanghai, Foo-chow, Amoy, Hong Kong, Whampoa, Canton, and Macao. I now took steamer from the last-named port to Cochin China, on my way to Singapore. There was great temptation to go to Manilla and see the Philippine Islands and cigar-making, but the steamer had left two hours before I reached Hong Kong, and there was not another for eight days. That nuisance, a passport, too, was an essential which would have taken a day to obtain, and so kept me from going had I been even earlier in port. I had therefore unwillingly to pass by the Philippines.

Their cigars are, however, a prominent feature of this part of the world. Manilla cigars and cheroots are everywhere in Japan and China, and are to be had for a shilling a dozen retail. The consequence of that cheapness seems to be that everybody smokes cigars from morning till night. The bank manager sits smoking in his inner room. He rings the bell, or sends his native boy for the accountant, who comes in also smoking. The ledger-keeper will then appear, book on shoulder, pen in hand, and cigar in mouth. The "shroff" and the "comprador" are the names of the native officials who appear to do all the money-handling work of Eastern banks. What one has to receive is from their hands. The "abacus," or counting-board, is always before them, and so is the fire-stick that lights their cigars. An abstract of what is to be paid to me is handed to one of these officials, and I get what I am told is the current value of the day for my English bank circular note. That value varies daily, and papers and telegrams have to be consulted each morning before it can be determined what I am to have for twenty English pounds paid to a banker by me in London, or Melbourne, or San Francisco.

It was always with me less than the value, and never more. Only in India and Italy did I find English money at a premium. How such a valuable thing as an English 5*l.* bank-note should be worth only 4*l.* 14*s.* to-day, and 1*s.* more or less to-morrow, is, next to the fluctuations in the price of wool, one of the things that the traveller has got to understand.

No one will regret a visit, short as mine had been, to China, if even only what part of it I saw be visited. Canton is a great city, and easy of access from either side of the world. The mail steamers of the Peninsular and Oriental Company run to Hong Kong fortnightly. Alternately with them run the superior French Maritime Messageries vessels. Little Hong Kong has by these means got a weekly mail from Europe.

The British India Steam Navigation Company also have a fleet of steamers running in China and India, calling at twenty or so of intermediate ports each trip. From London to Hong Kong is not more than a five weeks' voyage, and from the latter port to Canton it is a pleasant five hours or so up the fine Pearl River to Canton—a city of exceeding interest to European eyes.

It is not for a mere visitor to vaticinate; yet it is said that the close observer may prophesy of things not come to pass. A mere traveller on his way through the world must see much, and, by practice alone, become ready in discernment. Let me, from what I saw of the busy Chinese, venture on prediction. I had seen their patient industry and great organizing power in Australia. In America I had seen it also, and travelled on that Great Pacific Railway which Americans frankly avow could not have been made but for the cheap and efficient work of the Chinamen, who mainly constructed it. At Foo-chow I had noticed that they have long ago forestalled the Frenchman in oyster cultivation. The bamboo beds there constructed for oyster spat catching and growing are things that Great Britain might advantageously imitate. In industry and patient labour the Chinaman is king, and we know what levers these qualities are in moving men upwards and onwards. What is to keep the Chinaman down, now that the flood-gates of his migration have opened? He is all over the East! In Java he is what the Jew is in all the Western world—the trader and trafficker and money-changer—not the labourer. He is a practical man, the most practical of men—a mud-fish that rises to no fancy flies. The Mormon evangelists utterly failed to make a single convert from among the Chinese. They similarly failed with the Jews. The Chinamen tell the Mormon missionaries that they have no time to spare to "talkee religion." It is perhaps good for them. It would be equally good also for some others that we all know of to imitate them in that matter.

The Chinaman is spreading over the world. He is the laundress and navvy labourer of America, and in both he is the best of workmen. The white laundress who takes your washing from the hotels, and charges you four shillings a dozen for washing handkerchiefs, gets the Chinaman to do the work for her for sixpence. Those folk who prefer so to encourage white labour are quite satisfied with the fraud. He is the best of domestic servants—the finest of all cooks. He will, by the simple laws of demand and supply, spread over the world, and compete with all white labour. In Australia he is the market-gardener, the fisherman and fishmonger combined. He is the great peddler of the country, and is becoming its general cabinet-maker. There he is merchant, banker, and gaming-house keeper. His superior civilization gives him powers of combination unknown in men of other nations. One hundred work as one. He is consequently most successful of all gold-diggers and miners.

What is to stop his progress and his dispersal over the world, now that the Chinese Empire, mainly through the shakings of English assaults, is tumbling to pieces? As the Goths and Huns overran the Old World, so it seems probable that the hundreds of millions of Chinese will flood the present one, and that at no very distant date.

CHAPTER XIV.

IN COCHIN CHINA

By French Messageries steamer "Meikong" I went away from Hong Kong, and, after two days at sea, passed into that great river of Cochin after which the steamer was named. Two hours and a half of progress up its winding waters, between low banks overgrown with jungle, brought me to anchorage at Saigon.

The proper name of Cochin China appears by the map to be Annam. It is the adjoining land to Siam, but in the division has got the lesser-sized share of territory. The natives are called "Klings." All the lands about here are peopled by the Malays. The generic name for this quarter is Malasia. I am now passed from among the Japanese and Chinese and meet with a new people, see new characteristics, and pay in different coinage.

This Saigon is a French settlement. It is about sixteen years old. Louis Napoleon, in 1859-60, wanted to turn the attention of the French from things in France, and to make some stir in the world. That pleases French people. When they brood too long upon their own affairs, they get troublesome and revolutionary, and kick out their ruler as they did peaceful Louis Philippe. Making a raid upon Cochin China and a settlement on its shore were then decided upon. Later on, in his feverish rule, it became necessary to do something else, and then the Emperor came down upon Mexico, and set up Maximilian as deputy emperor there. The Americans were just too busy then, fighting among themselves, to interfere with this French madcap movement. The principle of such doings seems to have been anything to occupy the public mind, and no matter at what cost then or thereafter. That the project would be profitable formed no part of the calculation.

Well, here is the sixteen-years-settled Saigon—the result of the French Cochin China movement. What it is is very soon to be seen. A Frenchified town laid out on a low, dead level flat, formed by a bend of the Meikong River. What benefit the French get by living here in the tropics, instead of in France, is not so apparent. Taking climate for climate, and balancing the loss of all society, and the living here out of the ways of the world, in an unhealthy place, the profits ought to be commensurately large. Here is to be endured a moist heat that is furiously strong at mid-day, and strong enough at all times. The low site on which the town is formed brings to it a greater share of the hot trouble from which it suffers—the confined stifling air of a valley. That compressed, dull, heavy heat, that weighs upon the spirits, makes life languid and lazy, takes the backbone and stiffening out of a body, and leaves folks limp and flabby.

The produce of this French possession near to the line appears to be tigers, rice, peacocks, and monkeys. The peacocks are just the finest in the world. The climate seems to favour the growth of feathers, as witness the legs of the well-known fowls of the country. Peacocks' feathers—even at five feet long—are not so marketable a thing as ostrich feathers. Cut up, they make pretty fans and whisks, but the industry does not appear to be profitably worked. Tiger-skins and claws are made marketable articles. The tiger-skin rug and carriage-mat are well known, but the claws were a novelty. They are here set in gold for earrings. I mistook them then for the semi-transparent eye-teeth of the tiger. Two claws, joined by a gold band in the centre, make a brooch. These ornaments are pretty-looking as novelties, and, while the novelty lasts, may be admired. No great exportation of them, however, seems to be made. Whether the monkeys can be skinned to profit I could not learn. They are plentiful enough and lively in their ways—these undeveloped Darwinian men.

As it is hot all the year round here, the pleasures of wild animal hunting do not look promising. It is impossible to wear more than a smock and trousers of thinnest material, and it is death to go abroad uncovered by an umbrella. No country would be very likely to want Saigon save for looting it. The French are pretty safe there, and likely to keep their possession, and for ever foregather with the Malays. Of the two, I incline to the idea that the latter get the best of the alliance. As to any honour and glory got by a descent upon Cochin China, and the killing of some hundreds of its semi-nude natives, to make a settlement in one corner of the land, all that can be seen only from a distance, say, as far as France. It must be focussed from afar off, as all glory generally is. Hereabout it is not so apparent. The Malays can scarcely understand this French inroad yet. They took it that they were to be killed, and perhaps eaten, as, by other warriors of darker skins, had been their previous experience. Idea they could have none that their new visitors had taken a fancy to their unlovely and malarious grilling and stewing land, and meant to come and build a town and live there, bringing stores, and provisions, and money into the country. The worst that any one could wish to any European would be to send him to Saigon, there to permanently live and to toil for a living. Nature has plainly made the place for penal—almost purgatorial—purposes.

Hotels and cafés in the French style are to be seen in plenty, mostly on the tree-planted and shaded esplanade on the river side. Sitting outside of these, under the shade of the trees, sipping lemonade, and smoking halfpenny manillas, seems to be all that can be reasonably expected from any one in Saigon—of any European at all events. I observed none that were doing anything but that. It was quite hard work enough. It is about enough of labour there to live and breathe, rise up and sit down, smoke, and talk, and sleep, or rather to doze, for sleep is a thing impossible. All these operations are accompanied by constant use of the handkerchief to mop up the perspiration that exudes, whether you do anything or nothing.

The conveyances are covered carriages, like to small broughams, called "gharries" in Hindostan. No palanquins or chairs are carried about by the Malays, as is done by their neighbours, the Japanese and Chinese. I incline to think that the Malay is not willing animal enough for such very hard work. One of these carriages carried me round the flat town and the enclosures of Government House and the Botanical Garden—anything but a pleasant drive, as it proved to be too warm to get out of the vehicle to look even at the rarest flower—a great drawback to collecting specimens of the plentiful flora of this tropical place. The sensitive plant grows well here. I picked off a stem with five leaves on it, that shrivelled to nothing in an instant, and nearly disappeared in my fingers. Also a pommelo—a large shaddock-shaped fruit with inside like to an orange, but bitterish—my first and last pommelo.

The ship was to stay two days at Saigon. It looked a wearisome time, as the place itself could be seen in a few hours, and then nothing for it but to sit about, wiping off the perspiration, and fighting the flies and mosquitoes. For the latter purpose I bought a fan, and soon began to understand why all Chinamen carried this article, as they do, stuck in the back of their necks. I had found how powerful the mosquitoes were in China. In this low-lying Saigon they had improved upon their Chinese form, and were as near as possible to mosquito perfection. American mosquitoes are pretty good in their way, and much stronger in the trumpet, on the wing, and more vicious in their bite than the Australian sort; but these Cochin China ones were as strong in comparison as are the native breed of fowls, and were, I believe, also feathered about the legs. I judged that by their weight. But sitting under a mango-tree, in swampy Saigon, fanning the mosquitoes was no work for a traveller to do. I was not orientalized enough to lounge about the whole day doing nothing, and dozing half the time, and then doing the same thing for the whole night. I found what I wanted at last. I could explore further up country.

A steamer was starting that afternoon to Cambodia, the capital of French Cochin, to return to Saigon the next evening. It is only sixty miles up the Meikong to this city, where lives, under French inspection, a native rajah, prince, or king. A Malay city would be more novel-looking than a low-lying waterside settlement of Frenchmen, Malays, and mosquitoes. Of my fellow-passengers on that journey there was not one who could speak English. That mattered little. It was too hot to talk.

At Cambodia all the elements of a capital city are wanting —save the king's palace. That is a poor affair, and likely to get poorer-looking for lack of repair. The town is not free from French intruders; but I doubt much if they are happy there. Cambodia is so very unlike Paris—about as much so as it is possible to be—a dirty place of Malay huts and dirty dens, called bazaars, for sale of dirty stuff of one sort or another. Unswept streets, tropical trees, and a few lean dogs make up all that is to be seen there, save a temple or two. The Malay language, with its alphabet of twenty queer sounds, is difficult to acquire, and there is nothing to stimulate one to taking the trouble. I never saw Malay man or woman that I felt the least desire to talk to. A Malay has no gratitude, no energy, no industry, no manners of any good kind. His hand is ever extended for more, even if you pay him three times over. He never thanks you. He is thievish also, and lying is no name for the distance he can go from the truth. He is, or seems to be, naturally morose. It is his nature to be "nasty," and he can't help it. His idea of cleaning leathern boots is to rub them over with a rag and steal the laces. He then brings back the boots, and holds out his hand for money. He will swear he knows nothing of the laces, and has no blacking. He has both, but is too lazy to brush the boots, and too much given to appropriation to part with spoil. You acquire a dislike to the Malays more than to any other coloured race, and *you* can't help it.

I have noticed that the fine-grown mosquitoes at Saigon were a feature of the place. They make features also on the visitor. One had raised a bump on my eyelid that kept the eye nearly closed for two days. It might have been worse, both might have been so served, for we become quite at the mercy of these foes at the last. It is too hot at Cochin altogether to go on for ever fighting the flies. I could understand there how it was that the Spartan boy kept quiet with the concealed beast gnawing at his liver. As energy dies out, the strength of endurance arises. To suffer patiently is the next best thing to fighting vigorously. "To suffer and be strong."

As a seeker for artistic novelties I wandered about the Cambodian places of business, seeking to snap up any unconsidered trifles of that sort. The inlaying of mother-of-pearl upon woods and ivory is the speciality of Cochin. A small dark wood box so inlaid, that would have been thought valueless in artistic Japan, was here priced very high. The dealer ultimately parted with it to me for one-third of what he had asked, though he was ready to swear to each price asked being a fair one. Had I stopped longer about the town I might have got it for even less. Another purchase that I made was a ring of white metal having a tablet on it, on which was engraved nine divided and figured compartments, that might be the ten commandments compressed into nine— the omitted one probably that against stealing. The ring, I was told, is a talismanic one—whatever that means. It looks quaint and queer, but wants much rubbing up to keep it bright. It seems to be constructed of the metal that soupladles are commonly made of. Novelties were not plentiful. The cocks and hens of the country could not be so classed.

The palace and gardens of the king could be seen by any one whose curiosity was superior to 110° of the thermometer. Mine fell below it. The name of the monarch was given to me several times; but as I could not get it written down, I failed to pronounce it properly. It was something like to "Chromo-Lithro." All further idea of the visit to the palace was finished up by my being told that I must go in full dress. In my innocence I thought this pleasant, as I felt greatly inclined to go about nearly nude, and that was all I could imagine Malay full dress to be. It was explained to me that it was French evening dress that was required. His Majesty wished to be honoured similarly to the dress-circle of the opera. I had to give up all thoughts of it. I could not have done it in this Cambodian climate for a dozen kings. As I thought this, I knew that I should afterwards regret it. We always regret that which we "jib" at. The regret has, however, not come yet. This mania for European dress suits is spreading over the East. The Japanese Court require it also. Travellers who think a tweed or balbriggan suit, with an Ulster, sufficient outfit, must not expect to walk about palaces much in their travels. Royalty expects to be waited upon in waiter's costume.

From Cambodia, the journey up the Meikong River can be extended any distance. At the farther end of Cochin there is Tonquin (which is the real Annamite capital), but I could not hear of any inducements to go thither, had time and opportunity even allowed such a long exploration. The Tonquin bean is to be had there, but then it is to be had elsewhere, and is used principally for flavouring that old-fashioned form of tobacco called snuff. It wants much temptation, indeed, to go about in Cochin; and Tonquin and the French are at loggerheads, and gunboats. I ought doubtless to have read up all about the land previously, and so been prepared to see it with the light of knowledge, and in the halo that history might have cast around it, or any part of it. The baggy-legged birds that have familiarized Cochin to everybody are not enough to satisfy the traveller. Dorking, equally famous for fowls, is more accessible. As to all the rest, that burnt-up cinder Aden, on the Red Sea, is a very good substitute for Saigon, and much handier to the world generally. Of the two, I think Aden preferable. It stands upon the sea, and is, of a consequence, better placed than Saigon, on the low banks of a river.

I am not sorry when the steamer starts that takes me again to Saigon. If it went across country, and out of the land at once, I should have been better satisfied. What a delightful thing I now think it must be to feel cool—to live among "the thick-ribbed ice" that Shakspeare talks about! A touch of the wind from that quarter upon this river just now would be very acceptable. Heat is scarcely the word for what one feels! The sun burnt through one's coat, and one's skin, and into one's bones. You could feel the marrow of them frizzling.

Returned to Saigon, I was told to go see there the field in which the French killed the Malays in 1859-60. I declined the trouble. A monument has been erected on this spot, bearing only a French inscription. In that manner one side is allowed to tell its own tale. An inscription on the other side of it, penned by the Malays, would give the visitor the views of both parties. That would be more satisfactory. I once remarked to one that looked battered about the head that he appeared to have been much beaten. "Yes," he said, "but you should see the other one—he's got it worse."

Some Château Roux ale attracted my attention at a large café in Saigon market-place—a light ale that reconciled one to the exertion of getting a perspiring hand into one's pocket, and pulling it inside out in one's efforts to get the money to pay for it. That ale was light and good—not bitter, and I made a memo. to remind me to inquire where Château Roux may be.

As I am not likely to see Cochin China again willingly, let me say a grateful word. Though a French settlement, I was not asked at Saigon for a passport, nor bidden to turn out a travelling-bag by a custom-house officer—two things for which I felt grateful. Repacking a bag with the thermometer at 110° would have led to much perspiration, and perhaps profanity. Another blessed remembrance of Cochin is that it is not possible to spend much money there. That is a good thing to remember when the traveller takes a retrospect, and counts up the cost of travel.

The heat of the climate of Cochin has somewhat soured the milk of French human nature. The famous courtesy of the nation is not conspicuous in Saigon. A sort of churlishness, not to give it a stronger term, seemed prevalent. I could both understand and excuse it. Harried by the heat, and tormented by the insects, who could be polite? A man scratching a bump that a mosquito has lately raised is apt to mix up his language, and one gets often some of what is only intended for the insect. In the only boat that was in shore at the time for my departure, a Frenchman was going off to my steamer too, but would not let me set foot thereon, though I explained that I would pay the whole of the cost, and that there was no other boat about. "Wait for one," he said; "I pay for this boat waiting all day. It is my boat." I did not call him a bear, but inwardly pitied him. The climate would no doubt do as much for all of us after a year or two of its liver-drying and spleen-producing effects.

On leaving Saigon for Singapore, I have to pass Labuan and Sarawak. Borneo is, I find, almost an unvisited place by the traveller. It is as little favoured in that way as is its neighbour Sumatra. The Dutch have nearly the whole of both these large islands, and the Dutch do not seem to make their lands popular. I shall see, perhaps, something of the reason why when I reach Java, of which they have had snug possession for 260 years, save for the little break of six years, from 1810 to 1816, when England took possession as protector against the French.

Borneo and Labuan were well-known names to English ears thirty years ago, when Brooke endeavoured to get an English colony settled there in the fashion of Saigon. He got knighted for his good intentions; and it is as well, perhaps, that they were not carried out. Saigon cannot be colonized, nor Labuan, any more than India. Europeans cannot live there. Certainly none of their children could be reared there successfully. As a visitor only for a few years can the emigrant make use of these tropical spots, and even then it is done at the risk of health, and to the certain shortening of life. The Dutch have not been more successful in their attempts to colonize Java and all their other possessions round about here. On board of the steamers hereabout I meet with the clean-shaved English-looking faces of fifty years ago—before the beard and moustache fashion prevailed. These folk are all Dutchmen, and I am coming now down among their Eastern territory. They disappoint me as Englishmen, for whom I am always mistaking them.

CHAPTER XV.

SINGAPORE AND THE STRAITS.

SINGAPORE is reached in two days' steaming from Saigon, and in five from Hong Kong. I am now among the Straits Settlements, made up of this Singapore and of the neighbouring Penang and Malacca. Singapore is head-quarters and Governor's residence. The Governor, at the time of my visit, was Sir William Jervois, in place of Sir Andrew Clarke, removed to India. His domain is scattered hereabout, and not the snug nutshell of a thing that Hong Kong is.

The fine Bay of Singapore is mostly filled with shipping, the crafts there being apparently from all parts of the world. The settlement lies all around the shores of this bay, from which a grand view can be obtained, and an equally good view of the bay and shipping is to be got from the strand when one is on shore, if the sun does not nearly burn one's boots off when stopping, even for five minutes, to admire it.

Singapore is as nearly as possible on the line. It is called an island, and is about twenty-four miles by fourteen in size, and constitutes the point of the Malay peninsula which is sometimes called altogether Malacca. Between it and the neighbouring Sumatra—that large tropical island—run the famous Malacca Straits, about which much was heard at the last election of Britain's Parliament. This Singapore point of Malacca is washed off from the mainland by a stream of a quarter of a mile or so only in width, just as Ceylon has been washed away from the continent of India. It has been only proclaimed as a British colony since April, 1867.

At the other end of the Straits of Malacca is a similar point of Sumatra territory, called Acheen, which, with England's consent, was lately—about five years ago—seized upon by the Dutch, who are desirous to make it another Singapore. It is some consolation to the English traveller, who sees good things thus taken by others, and one gate of these important straits—the highway from England to China—so seized by another power, that the Dutch have got a hornet's nest in this Acheen. For four years the Acheenese have made it very hot indeed for their would-be owners. They would have submitted quietly to the mild, kindly rule of England, that does not enslave for money-making purposes the population of any country that it rules ; but they will not have the Dutch for their masters if fighting can avail them. The stars in their courses fought against Sisera, and climatic influences fight for the plucky Acheenese. Of every hundred Dutch soldiers taken thither from Java, seventy have to be taken back sick before three months are over. Of this seventy, two-thirds die on the voyage. On the steamer that took me away from Singapore they were thrown overboard at the rate of twenty-four a day. Of the remaining thirty soldiers that stay in Acheen, the Acheenese are said to account for fully half in the guerilla warfare that these true patriots carry on. It has lasted now for four years, and cost the Dutch seventy millions of guilders! The end is as far off as ever. There is no going back, or such course would, perhaps, be adopted, for the Dutch clutch their guilders. They have five-sixths of Sumatra already, and want this Acheen to make a complete thing of it as of Java. If beaten there, then all *prestige* would be lost, and the quiet possession of the other part of Sumatra be endangered. A candid Dutch merchant told me that another twenty years might not see the end of it. The Dutch generally are getting to be of the same opinion, but dare not all say so.

Singapore, though nearer upon the line than Saigon, is an English place, and, therefore, more endurable to the English traveller in the way of society and matters of interest. If he knows nothing about the place or its history when he lands there, he soon begins to inform himself. He sees how very often the name of "Raffles" turns up there—as often as the word "lottery" does in a Dutch settlement where these antiquated swindles are still legal. In Singapore are "Rafflesstreet," "Raffles-road," "Raffles Library." "Raffles" this or that is always meeting the eye.

Fifty-seven years ago, Sir Stamford Raffles, then and for six previous years Governor of fair Java, handed over that gem of the east, at the bidding of his Government, again to the Dutch. He then came up to Singapore. Having buried Lady Raffles in Java, he contracted a marriage with the daughter of a rajah of Johore, on the nearest mainland. He then set up the colony of Singapore on his own account, on the land that formed his wife's portion. It was to make a settlement that he could not be required, against his opinion and advice, to give up to the Dutch. He declared the place a free port. The dreary little fishing village and tiger jungle soon increased in population under his care, and grew—like to the Lord of Burleigh's village wife—to noble proportions. It has now 100,000 inhabitants, 5000 of whom are Europeans.

It produces nothing, this Singapore. It owes its trade and prosperity solely to its geographical position at the point of entrance to the Straits of Malacca and the China Sea. In common trade language, it is one of the best "corner stands" in the world—a house of call for the large fleet of steamers and larger number of trading vessels that the busy seas about it abound with. The mail steamers to China and Cochin China of the English and French lines call here. So do the large fleet of steam-ships of the British India Company, and the thirty-six fine steam-vessels of the rich Netherlands-India Steamship Company. A busy place is Singapore, and a nice one only for salamanders. Human life to Europeans is scarcely endurable in it at any time of the twelve months.

Pope sings of something that "lives along the line." Nothing of European growth could do so for long. To common sense it would seem that a cooler atmosphere would come on the sun going down, and taking its fierce, fiery glow with it. It is not so; the nights seem to be, perversely, hotter than the days. About 8 p.m. the heat, which has lulled for two hours previously, seems to get "second wind," and returns to stop for the night. Sleep is out of the question. Artificial warmth may encourage sleep in cold climates, but not so in hot ones. It must be possible to get acclimatized here. Some pale, sickly-looking, full-stomached folks that I saw had existed here for years; so that keeping vitality within one is learnt somehow. Until that is done, however, life becomes a serious matter to a European. The greatest cynic or philosopher would no longer call it a farce. As many handkerchiefs are wanted there a day as are elsewhere required for a bad case of cold in the head. One of them becomes wetted through with perspiration, after about five applications to the forehead, face, hands, and neck. Such applications are made every five minutes. It gets very monotonous work after the first few hours. The novelty wears out more quickly than some others do. The wish of Hamlet that his solid flesh would melt and thaw is here exactly realized. That's just what the said solid flesh does. The climate of Singapore would have brought the Prince of Denmark to his senses in a very short time, if the melting and thawing process would have helped in that way. His soliloquies would have turned on other matters, and had to be spoken sitting, with handkerchief in hand. A Malay boy would have had to hold Yorick's skull for him.

No one who has visited Hindoostan but must see that Singapore has taken all its ideas, examples, and way of life from that land. The private houses are bungalows built within spacious compounds. The houses of business are roomy, thickly-built buildings of two storeys; the ground one is set inwards for 10 ft., and so shaded by the roof and the pillars in front that support the upper storey. Inside the houses also, everything takes Hindoostanee fashions. The bath is a big tub placed in a back building like to a stable, and fed from outside through a bamboo funnel. By the side of the tub stands the little bucket with which the tubber gives to himself douches of water. The large folding-doors to all the rooms have Venetian-blind-like laths, of larger size, throughout their length. The large screen that stands within this door, the bamboo chairs, Indian rush matting, and other *minutiæ* of Hindoostanee life, are all reproduced here at Singapore. The "gharries," or little broughams, that one sees all over British India, are here the common modes of conveyance. No carriage chairs or palanquins are, however, visible. The patient beasts of burden and draught that can be made out of Hindoos, Japanese, and Chinese cannot be made out of the Malay. He does not take to this means of transport, and perhaps it is as well. If he did that work as grumblingly and extortionately as he endeavours to do everything else, it would be unpleasant—at least to the traveller. Everything seems to be unpleasant to the Malay. I suppose it is that fiery sun that turns his wholesome blood to gall. It strokes his hair the wrong way.

At tiffin time and at dinner the native servants appear, as in Hindoostan, each covered with his peculiar head-dress, and look all the better for it. The Europeans are then all dressed in white, the men in linen jackets and trousers, and the women in a sort of linen night-dress, with a coloured table-cover wrapped around below it. These white dresses and their pale faces help to give them a ghastly look, especially to the pale-faced women. At these meals the customs of the aboriginals have eaten into the manners of the whites. They take a "chow-chow," made up of rice and fish and hot curry. The first two are the right sort of thing; but, for the sake of their liver—that torment to them—it were better that they let the last one alone, and also the wines and spirits. In America, where these could with more impunity be taken, only water is drunk at meal-times. In the East—where water only should be taken—the heating wine and the fiery spirits find favour—and victims.

In front of the town-hall at Singapore stands the only monument of note in the place. It is of squared freestone,

and bears a carved marble elephant. The monument records, in the English and Malay languages, this important fact:—
"His Majesty Somdegh Phra Paraminder Mahr Chulaloukorn, the Supreme King of Siam, landed at Singapore 16th March, 1871. The first foreign land visited by a Siamese monarch." Let nothing be said about the folly of Albert memorials after that! As it was considered worth recording upon stone, I am sufficiently excused for copying the record upon paper. It is really funny when you give thought to it.

Omission must not be made of the introduction to the Malay population that every traveller has before he sets foot in Singapore. They come around his ship in their little scallops of boats, and clamour to him in their strange tongue. He wonders what it is all about. They cannot want him to go ashore in their little craft. There is hardly room enough for themselves in it. The truth soon dawns upon one, which means that a ship's servant explains the matter. The mission of these Malays is to dive for voluntary contributions thrown, not to them, but into the sea. Bits of silver are soon going over the ship's side, and the splashes are seen, as also the heels, of half-a-dozen divers that go after each piece. How they settle matters among themselves underneath the waves I could not understand, but one of them always comes up with the sixpence. It never has a chance, I think, to get to the bottom. Throwing silver became too monotonous at last, not to say troublesome; so I resorted to the expedient of wrapping copper in bits of white paper. The wrapper helped to impede the sinking of the coin, so that it was easier got, but did not to the Malays seem so satisfactory. Nothing is satisfactory, as a rule, that we get easily. Perhaps that was the cause. Or they may have looked upon silver as an honourably understood thing, and thought themselves swindled, and that their dives had been obtained under false pretences. They doubtless had divers reasons for the dissatisfied looks the coppers gave them. They spoke about it, too; but that went for nothing in an unknown tongue. When I came to know Malay character better, and saw what a thankless, unpleasant folk they were, I looked back upon this little diving delusion with complaisance. Diving at Singapore should have required no payment. There was not a hot stewing European that watched their splashes into the cool waters but would have gladly gone and done likewise if he could, and been pleased to make a payment for doing it. A Malay always wants more money, and is never satisfied. A Japanee is worth a dozen such, as a good and easily satisfied fellow.

The vegetation all around is of the tropical sort that one sees in Ceylon and India—the cocoanut, bamboo, banana, betelnut, and other varieties of palm. In the native part of the town the streets are tenanted by Malays and Chinese. There are quarters for each, all filled with the dirty, hut-like shops which are dignified as "bazaars," the like of which one sees in every Eastern town. In these streets—Raffles-street, Pekin-street, Calcutta-street, Synagogue-street, Malay-street, Canton-street, Johore-street, and so on—I meet with Parsees in their unmistakable hats, by which they are as well known as are Quakers by their head-coverings. Here, also, are Klings, Arabs, Chinese, Hindoos, Siamese, and natives from all the islands of the Indian Archipelago. All are attired according to their peculiar fashions—as little of attire as possible being that which is most observable. One wishes that one could follow the fashion, but a white skin looks like nakedness; while those that wear only "the livery of the burnished sun" seem in some sort clothed by it. I watch the artistic work of the hair-dressers, or rather face and head shavers, who are here plentifully at work. Eastern folk are fanciful about their way of wearing their hair. The Western world have lately taken to that fashion of skin close-cutting that the Chinese introduced some thousands of years ago. Chinamen are here seen having their pigtails made up and plaited. In this ornament they are no more honest than a modern Western belle. It is lengthened by additions from the horses' tails, eked out by threads of silk, and finished off with a silken tassel. The head and tail work of the barber generally concludes with the

M

operation of ear cleaning. For that he has a little case of instruments, and goes artistically to work. As done by him, the work seems to be so necessary a thing, and so much better done than one can do it oneself, that it seems an oversight by other countries not to add this useful branch to a hairdresser's education. It is at least as much or more needed than the art of the chiropodist. We can all cut our own corns as easily as we can tread upon those of others.

In the bungalow called an hotel that I stay at in Singapore, the house is surrounded by trees that are covered with either red leaves or red flowers. They look all aflame. Another tree, majestically large in size, has roots that will not stay within the earth. They rise up for a foot or two above it, and twist about in ridge-shaped forms. In that way the tree seems to have a mob of gigantic lizards at its foot. The birds fly from the compound, as the garden is called, into the rooms in the most free and easy manner—perching about anywhere out of reach. They wait for a chance of darting down upon what takes their fancy, and then away through the door with it. Lizards run along the walls of the room, and, at night, moths and winged beetles of all sizes are attracted inwards by the lamp, and not easily frightened away. In the East, man comes closer to nature, or nature comes closer to him—not as he lived in the days of the Golden Age, when all created things are supposed to have waited upon him, but just in a way that reminds him of what must have been the unpleasant side of that state of affairs. Created things must then have come for orders, and have sometimes intruded. In the early dawn, each bedroom is noiselessly entered by a native servant, who removes the nightlight and one's boots, and leaves a cup of coffee and a slimmock of dry toast in their place. These are usually quite cold by the time I awake, as, after struggling with the heat and the mosquitoes all night, I fall asleep when the latter are satisfied. Those accustomed to Singapore life wake up when the coffee-cup comes. After eating and drinking, their thoughts turn to the bath and its cooling water, so that a habit of early rising is cultivated, the coolness of the morning taken advantage of, and lazy folks got out of bed betimes.

I learn to get up early, and go and see the markets. There are two large ones in the town, to which the industrious Chinese bring the chief supplies. Strange looking are some of the fish here to be seen. A crab is here to be had shaped like to a long-handled fan. The handle is its tail. The fan-shaped part looks as if carved out of solid bronze-work. It is, however hollow, and filled with green eggs of the size of small peas. The crab itself looks but a small thing in the centre of its elaborately-made shell. Stuffed as curios, these crabs would find buyers among the visitors, but none are to be had in that way; nor of the white bony fish, that is shaped like to an oblong waistcoat pocket snuff-box. Its head and tail protrude at either end of its queer-looking coffin-shaped carcase. Cleaned and polished, it would form a good match-box.

The "nasty" nature of the Malay culminates sometimes in his "running-a-muck," and stabbing, as a mad dog snaps, at everybody he meets. It is a sort of mental *delirium tremens* that has come upon him, the result, not of drinking, but of unrestrained rage and passion. He seems to be always in a state of ill-nature—I never saw one smile. This running-a-muck fit of theirs is the bursting of the pent-up volcano. It is allowable to shoot them when seen in that state, but Europeans generally prefer to get out of their road. At night, in front of the hotel, walks a Malay with a loaded gun. He mounts guard thus to protect the sleepers and their property, all exposed by the wide-opened doors. There they lie in their pajamas, all other ways uncovered, on the mattrasses. The tread of the Malay so keeping guard is mixed up with the shrill whirring of the mosquitoes that are inside the curtain, and the loud flapping wings of the moths and beetles that bump now and again against the outside of it. As I listen to it all, I hope that this particular Malay has nothing on his mind that might cause him to a run-a-muck in the night-time. All his sleeping charges, and those trying to sleep, are then at his mercy. What he stabs with is a "creese"—a dagger of irregular shape, about

18 in. long. He carries this in a sheath at his girdle. That a scratch with it may be effective, it is generally kept well poisoned. Streaks of blood are carefully preserved upon it as honourable marks.

Over the little stream that separates Singapore from the mainland of Malacca, the tigers swim, and wait about in the woodlands of Singapore for the brown-skinned Malays. These are, by the statistics on the subject, found to be thus snapped up at the average of one a day—not a pleasant thought for those who would take their pleasure in the woods. The Malays work there at wood-cutting and collecting of "gambier" for chewing with the betel-nut, to produce the black teeth and red saliva considered here to be so pretty. A European naturalist was nearly caught in this way lately. He was used to tree-climbing, which helped him much on that occasion. He got safely up in time out of the reach of the tiger's spring, reducing the annoyance to a blockade that lasted over thirty hours. The hope, no doubt, was to starve the besieged into a surrender. It was not, however, to be done, as our naturalist's large pocket-book of specimens—grubs, butterflies, spiders, lizards, and beetles—would have all been eaten up before that could happen. The tiger got hungry and tired first, and, in fox and grape fashion, gave up the game. The besieged had been employing his time in collecting insect specimens from about his roosting-place, and had found healthy exercise in the pursuit. At night, fearful of sleep, he had lashed himself by braces and neckerchief to a stout branch. In the morning he had sucked the heavy dew from the leaves, and could look with complacency on the dry, out-hanging tongue of the tiger.

Talking of tigers leads one to think of the lion of Singapore, which is unquestionably "Whampoa's Garden." Every visitor is urged to see it, and it is quite worth the visit. Its owner is a rich, retired Chinese merchant, who has a fine taste for botanical collections and their proper display. The many acres he has had tastefully laid out can be walked over by the astonished visitor, and something surprising seen at every turn. Two lakes have their waters covered with lilies, the leaves of which are as large as open umbrellas. With all respect to Derbyshire Chatsworth and its Duke, as also to Paxton, its gardener, or his successor, they are not much, if at all, ahead of Whampoa. He needs no conservatory or hot-houses, which is greatly in his favour. It is strange that these hot, dry countries should have the finest vegetation—the fierce sun above being seemingly hot enough to frizzle up every leaf in a few minutes, and boil all the sap out of the branches in an hour or so. This botanical celestial gets good and cheap labour in the dozens of Chinamen employed about his grounds. The keeping up such a fine affair in the style he does would otherwise cost a larger sum than most folk would like paying for the support of a hobby.

At Singapore is to be found a choice of steamers for nearly everywhere. One can go from here to any of the thousand islands of the Archipelago—pass to the Philippines and Manilla, or to the Celebes and Macassar, or to Borneo and Sarawak, or to the Moluccas, and there and thereabout gather the nutmegs, peppers, and cinnamon of the Spice Islands, or to Formosa, that island of George Psalmanazar who made himself the talk of the time of our great grandfathers. All these trips are worth taking by any one who can stand a tropical life for months, and is not troubled with liver and loss of sleep. For such Singapore is good head-quarters and starting-point for what I have named, and a long catalogue of other places of interest.

CHAPTER XVI.

IN NETHERLANDS INDIA.

IN haste to get away from stifling Singapore, I went on board the Netherlands India Steam Company's boat fully twelve hours before the anchor was swung. Thereby I gained a clear air and a night's sleep in the sea-breeze, escaping, also, from the attentions of many of the land insects.

The way now is through the Thousand Islands. Calls are made at Rhio, and also at Muntuk, a town on the island of Banca, after which the straits of that name are passed through —islands lying everywhere handy. These "summer isles of Eden, lying in dark purple spheres of sea," remind one of the two days' passage down the inland sea of Japan—for the time that we are threading our way about them. For a yachtsman it would be a pleasant way of passing a few months to visit a few of these little isles—say a hundred or two of them. There are dozens, our captain tells us, upon which a Robinson Crusoe life, which is the ideal life of our youth, might be passed out of the cares of the world, and its rates and taxes.

On one of the larger of these islands a Mr. Ross, a Scotchman, is well established, as were also his father and grandfather. Here, monarch of all he surveys, he, with the help of native aid, cultivates sugar and other tropical produce, and hoists the Union Jack among all the red, white, and blue flags of the Netherlands that fly everywhere hereabout. His father wished to hoist some flag for protection, and asked permission to use the Dutch one, but he was looked upon as having, in mining language, "jumped the claim" in taking possession of this island. Though imitation is said to be the sincerest form of flattery, the Hollanders did not approve of this Scotchman thus following their suit. In default of getting the use of the Dutch flag, he ran up the British one. Protests were made by the Dutch against this proceeding, but the flag still flies.

From Malacca downwards, all the lands here and there and all about are held by the Dutch, and called "Netherlands India." This large property, including Java, is so farmed and philanthropically used by the Mynheers that it is made to yield a large income of about four millions sterling annually to the treasury of Holland. In addition to that, it is made to feed fat and enrich six or seven thousand resident Dutch, who, in a semi-missionary way, attend to the natives, and teach them that labour is worship, and that it is not good for them to have too much money for it.

Netherlands India consists of Sunda, Java, and the neighbouring Madura; the Celebes group—the capital of which is Macassar; seven-eighths of the large island of Sumatra, in which a four years' Christianizing fight has been carried on for possession of Acheen, the remaining eighth; three-fourths of the big land of Borneo, the islands of Rhio, Banca, and Billiton, on the two latter of which are some profitable tin-mines; the Molucca group or Spice Islands—the chief of which is Amboyne—a large share of the island of Timor; also the northern part of New Guinea, called Prince Frederick's Land, and many other islands, smaller or larger, about the prolific seas of this quarter.

None of these lands can the Dutch colonize. The children of Europeans will not thrive here, but must be sent to Europe to be reared. The land cannot be cultivated by white labour. All of Netherlands India is therefore used by the Hollanders for short sojourns.

Liver complaints, fevers, and other ailments terribly shorten the stay of many, forcing them to leave before they have done as much good for the native population as they probably intended.

I had thought the Malays that I met about Singapore and Cochin to be morose, thankless, greedy, and treacherous. This race is largely spread among the other native races of Netherlands India, and requires good examples from the Dutch to improve their character. It is to be hoped that the opposite result will not be obtained. Tennyson has warned one against being "mated with a clown," for "the grossness of his nature will have weight to drag thee down." The Dutch are, doubtless, beyond danger of contracting such an evil effect from their mixture here with the native races—at least I should hope so—but, to use feminine language, we none of us know.

The natives, Malays, Javanese, Sundanese and Madurese, have had some bad example, and have imitated it. Some foreigner has been here, having dull, heavy, phlegmatic ways and manners, a greedy and thankless man, and he has been imitated. He has shown an utter disregard for religion, art, and learning, and hence they are not cultivated hereabout. The grand temples which are to be seen in the interior of Java, that, for architectural design, carvings, decorations, and finish, are worthy of Greece itself, testify to a cultivation of art by the natives in past times that has since been utterly killed. These temples are evidence that religion once held with the natives a large share in their thoughts, yet I never knew when it was the Sabbath in Netherlands India, save by reference to the almanack. Business seemed to proceed on that day just as on the other six. *Laborare est orare* is a profitable maxim—keeping folks at work keeps them out of vanities and mischief, and the labour of the 18,000,000 of natives in Java is worth something for a day. Chapels and churches, as well as schools, are not prominent things there, as they are in that English-governed Java called Ceylon.

In this Dutch India has Holland been doing good, on the quiet, for more than 200 years. To attend to her philanthropic labours here she seems to have forgotten herself altogether,

and is no longer the great selfish Holland of bygone days—
when she was almost in the first rank—when she was foremost
in navigation with her Tasmans and Van Diemens on their far-
away voyages of discovery; in naval warfare also, with her
Van Tromp sailing up the Medway, with a typical broom tied
to his topmast, intended to terrify Charles the Second; in art
also, with her Rubens, Vandyck, Wouvermans, Rembrandt,
Paul Potter, Jan Steen, and Ostade. All that happened
when Holland had not, in her present way, realized the value
of her Eastern possessions. As a good mother, forgetting
herself in her children, so is Holland with her Netherlands
India. The world hears now but little of her former vanities.
No more Tasmans and Van Diemens, nor terrible Van
Tromps, nor artistic competitors for the world's admiration!

Holland and Spain have alike experienced this change, and
from the same cause. This Netherlands India has quieted
Holland, while Cuba and some like islands have done the same
for Spain. The Dutch and the Spanish prefer to encourage
the industry of others—the native races—and to send millions
home to the treasuries of Amsterdam and Madrid as evidence
of the good they are doing. They make no noise about it.
It might be thought, but for the example of these nations to
the contrary, that the wealth we do not earn profits us
nothing, but is really debilitating and destructive to us. We see
in these two examples that all which formerly elevated these
nations, and kept them to the fore in the world, has been
neglected by them, that they might look after and tutor the
heathen, and not live, as some have supposed them to be doing,
a life of luxury on the labours of others. It is a mistake to
suppose that Holland was greater as a nation when poor and
struggling, and that all her greatness has sunk like to that of
Spain, that neither of these nations has now a voice of its
former weight in the world, and that they contribute little to
its noise or news. Both nations have been steady in the
pursuit of money, and if they have obtained it under fewer
difficulties than formerly, it is to their credit; at all events the
money is so, and Holland can show a big bank balance and

lend to her neighbours. Cynics may say that Holland and Spain have forsaken their former aims, forgot their true worth, debased their national spirit, and grovelled for the dross of earth like to Bunyan's man with the muckrake, until they have forgotten how to hold their heads up in the world; but then cynics say nasty things, and often what is untrue. I have sometimes heard, with pain, misinformed people say that these two nations were effete pensioners on the earnings of the tens of millions of wretched toilers whom they held in semi-serfdom.

A facetious Dutchman said to me, "Take Java from the Dutch, and you might wipe out Holland altogether." "But Holland," I said, speaking in ignorance, "was great and powerful before she had possession of Netherlands India; could she not become so again?" "Oh, no; she's forgotten how she lived without that possession, and is past learning old lessons over again."

This was very good humour for a Dutchman, who mostly is a solidly matter-of-fact person. I am, meanwhile, looking about among all the passengers who are on board with me. About a hundred are invalided soldiers from Acheen, for whose people the malarious fever fights sadly against the poor Dutch. The Hollanders want to make of Acheen, at one end of the Malacca Straits, what the English have made of Singapore at the other, and these cantankerous Acheenese won't give it up to them. This holy war—to put the Christians in the land of the heathen—has already cost the Dutch the last five years' profits of Netherlands India, which may be doubled twice over before the trouble is ended.

The number of our passengers lessen by many daily as we pass along the coast of Sumatra. The climate of Acheen has been found so killing to these imported Dutch recruits that but few are likely to recover from the fever that is so reducing their numbers. I hear their dead bodies going overboard, splash after splash, as I lie in my cabin in the grey of the early mornings. It is a most unpleasant sound, and I fancy that it is that, or the sickly air of the ship, that makes me quite content that no breakfast is given to one on board

Dutch vessels. After these sea-burials in batches every morning, one feels dull indeed all day, and glad to get towards the journey's end and out of it.

Before that was reached, however, we met several islands not described in the accounts of these seas, nor named in any map. These are floating patches of land, laden with tropical trees, that had been washed down the rivers of Sumatra and so out to sea. On one of these islands afloat was a cluster of three cocoa-nut trees, with large bunches of nuts, nearly ripe, at their tall tops.

Most Dutchmen talk more or less understandable English. The poor, wretched soldiers were no exception. One of them I talked with knew something of six languages, and was a well favoured and mannered young fellow. The youngest of five sons, he had chosen a soldier's life, and left his mother's home for this distant Dutch war only nine months before. It was sad indeed to see one so young, well educated, and favoured by nature, thus victimized in this persevering war that the Dutch are making for the land of the plucky Acheenese. If he blessed, before he died that night, those who had so brought him to an early death, it was, I hope, with his last breath. I trust also that the blessing went, with his soul, to the presence of the recording angel, and was added to other million similar blessings on the awful record.

The habits of the Malay as regards food have been imitated by the Dutchman in the matter of his meals, but his manner of taking them is here in French fashion. A cup of coffee at 7 a.m. suffices to satisfy nature until 1 p.m., when a chow-chow of rice, fish, and curry is served up for tiffin. Into this chow-chow is put also sausage-meat, potatoes, chopped-up anchovies, and small seasonings from a tray of eight compartments, that contains different seasonings of all colours. A soup-plate full of this nastiness, yellowed over with curry-powder, is the staple of the Dutch tiffin. This meal is wound up with the eating of half a dozen bananas of the size of sausages and the consistence of soap. If I were to be made over again, and had a voice in the matter, I would choose to have a Scotch constitution and a Dutchman's stomach. I should then have the good digestion which Rochefoucauld said made the heart hard and one's life happy.

At 8 p.m. dinner is served, when the tiffin dish reappears, with small, yellow, waxy potatoes, and some sour cabbage, apparently pickled in bad beer; that is called "saurkraut"—a dish adaptable only to Dutch taste. These followed upon soup and fish, and then came beefsteaks three inches thick, and tough beyond all mastication. Pork chops followed as an aid to indigestion, and then slices of seed-cake rubbed over with chocolate jelly. Mangosteens, pine-apples, and bananas followed; and then, as at tiffin-time, came pipes and cigars, smoked at the table while coffee is drunk, and that whether ladies are present or not—and they generally are. As the smell of curry and the sight of the yellow mess is not agreeable to every one, those to whom it is not come off but badly at these Dutch tables.

The Java tobacco here used is about the worst in the world. A hundred cigars made from it are sold by the box for ninepence, and dear at that. The stomach and the nose that can stand the curry and saurkraut can very well endure the tobacco, which might, for the matter of that, be chopped up with the rest in the curry-bowl. The cheapness of this tobacco is easily accounted for—no other white folks will smoke it.

The west monsoon blows in these parts during December, January, February, and March, bringing with it almost daily rain. The east monsoon—a dry wind—blows similarly for some months of the year, so that there are long alternations of wet and of drought. The vegetation seems, however, to thrive particularly well, judging by its luxuriant profuseness and endless variety of beauty. This Netherlands India contains all that the Western world would have imagined as belonging to Eden. Palms of all kind, bread-fruits, bananas, mangoes, and mangosteens, pine-apples, cocoa-nuts, tamarind, and frangipanni trees, with scores of other tropical fruits and spice-plants, are here to be found in profusion. The fruit-bearing trees of the Eastern world are more luxuriant of foliage and graceful in form than are those of the Western. Such trees are the homes of birds of prettiest plumage, and feed butterflies, beetles, and insects that look like animated gems as they sparkle around in their glories of all colours.

Thunderstorms and driving rains in deluging showers are here common. Caught in one of these storms, I found all coverings unavailable, and the umbrella quite useless. A west monsoon wave half filled my cabin one night, entering by the port-hole I had kept open for coolness. Others followed ere I could close it, nearly knocking me over. Battling in the darkness with waves rushing through a port-hole, with the fastenings of which one is unacquainted, is a mild help out of the monotony of sea life. In the morning we are in the Straits of Sunda, and see the Sundanese land very shortly on our side. This land of Sunda is an adjunct of Java, but a distinct language is spoken by its natives. A settlement hereon that we now see is named Bantam, familiar through its fowls to most folk.

The bay, in which we soon anchor, is not a picturesque one, nor is the low-lying shore as seen from it. A few steamers and sailing vessels are at anchor, and the tymbanums, or passengers' boats, soon come around us. In one of these I am taken to the river Tijiliwong (Cheedeewong), and towed by the boatmen, who walk on the bank, for two miles up its narrow, yellow stream, that soon enters between brick embankments, and so runs up to the Custom-house steps. I am there forced to take everything out of my travelling-bag, and even to open a tin of chocolate, which is thought to be opium. A Malay does the examination business. His Dutch superior does duty in smoking and onlooking in a way becoming his dignity.

I am bid to report myself at the police-office if I intend to stay over four days. That caution is given to prevent mistakes, and get folks to give an account of themselves, and what they mean by wandering into other people's country. The Dutch are a slow, quiet-going, thoughtful race, who sleep with one eye partly open. The time spared from sleep is much of it spent in smoking. They don't wish to be disturbed. Like to bees settling on flowers, they have ceased their hum in the world, and are busy here looking after the natives and the guilders—a serious occupation that forbids them to smile much, and they laugh as seldom as do the Malays.

I am next introduced to the Java ponies, a small race of horses little larger than Shetland ponies, and fit companions for the Bantam fowls. In a little *dos-à-dos* car I am dragged by one of these wretched animals, whose driver never ceases beating him, through two miles of road by the brick-embanked, dirty road. The first mile of the road takes me through the "Calli Bazaar," an insignificant Chinese and Malay settlement. I then emerge into a tropical forest, with white one-storey houses here and there among the tall trees for two miles onwards. A few bungalow buildings, called hotels, are scattered about. At one of them, named Hôtel des Indes, I find quarters in a dark room on one side of a courtyard. I find that I am the only Englishman staying there. Not many travellers visit Java. My room has a red-tiled floor, a red wood sofa with cane seat, a bamboo chair, a rickety table, a screen with three pegs at the top, a wretched washstand with a water-jug that holds a pint, an earthenware water-bottle, no soap, and a towel of the size of a pocket-handkerchief, and seemingly made of similar material. That is my bed-room accommodation. I am supposed to bring the bamboo chair outside the door, and sit under the verandah and smoke until the bell rings for tiffin; then to sleep for three hours, and then take a two-pony carriage, at three guilders and a half pay, for two hours' drive; then to come back to dinner, after which to sit and smoke until bed-time. Such is Netherlands India life, such the end, hereabout, of every Dutchman's desire—a semi-sleepy and smoking existence for philanthropic objects, in a Turkish-bath atmosphere, tempered by guilders.

The guilder—value 1*s.* 8*d.*—is to this part of the world

what the rupee is to the East Indies. The one I give to my Malay driver for the two-mile drive from the custom-house does not satisfy him. He would not be contented if I gave him two. Although his language is foreign, his meaning is plain. Unlike the Chinese and Japanese, the Malays never learn a word of English. He talks to me in his tongue, and I reply in mine. I know from whom he learnt his greedy ways, and I pity him for the bad example he has had, instead of giving him more money.

About my all-but-unfurnished room flies of all sizes are numerous. In the evening the moths will come, and the jubilant mosquito. The moths put the candle out and go out themselves afterwards, but the faithful mosquito remains. By-and-by others come, for I am landed on a low, flat shore by the side of a river—a condition that ensures a plentiful supply of these things. The room gradually fills with them, and is alive with their music. For the Dutch settlers in these hot nights, so filled with such trouble, I have no pity; they can smoke the mosquitoes away with tobacco that would choke anything, but I am sorry for myself—the keenest of sorrow.

CHAPTER XVII.

THE SUNDANESE CAPITAL.

I FIND myself wondering what other place it is that the aspect of Batavia—chief city of the land of Sunda and its straits—recalls to my memory. It is, I find, more like to that other Dutch-made place, Cape Town, Cape of Good Hope, than any other that I have visited. Except in the native and the Chinese parts, called now the old town, there is but little of a town look about Batavia. White villa-like houses of a ground-floor only, with spacious verandahs, standing two hundred feet or more apart, set back from the roadway, and shaded by trees, are the characteristics of nine-tenths of Batavia. Such houses do not look very like shops, stores, or offices, yet they are the places of business, with but a small exception, where an attempt has been made at a street of shops that has stopped at the eighth one. It was all like to this in Cape Town when I was there. An English settler in the main street there told me that he had been three years in business, and hoped to get in a shop-front, in place of the parlour window one, in another year. There is no hurry about anything in Dutch settlements, nor where, as in Cape Town, the Hollanders are ground landlords.

In the evenings the verandahs of these houses show very brightly. A large lamp or two is placed upon the tables there, around which sit Mynheer and family. The Tijiliwong River runs between its brick embankments through half the town. Therein the natives are ever washing themselves or their linen. The city has been laid out on a large scale, not as yet filled in, so that distances, to an unpleasant extent, exist between public places. One must take a *dos-à-dos* car to go two miles to the British Consul's office. From there it is another two in a different direction to the post-office. Riding in these vehicles is nasty and not cheap. The horse will not go without incessant whipping; the Malay that drives cannot understand a word that I say, and worries always for an exorbitant charge, which he never gets. A primitive tramway has been laid down from the old town to the centre of the new one; but it is such a shabby affair that only the natives seem to patronize its dirty, ugly carriages. These are raised three feet or more from the ground—for some unknown cause. Their height from the tram-rail renders the appearance of the three ponies harnessed to these cars especially ridiculous. Small enough in any vehicle, they look but three cats in size in the front of these ugly van-like cars.

In the centre of Batavia is the club-house. Over the front entrance is written "Harmonie." In Samarang it reads as "Concordia," and in Soerabaya as "Amicitie." These club-houses combine reading-rooms, billiard and coffee rooms, and a large concert-hall. They are floored with marble, and well built and kept. The Dutch, when tired of smoking in the family circle of the verandah, come hither to sit and smoke for the rest of the evening. The reading-room is furnished with papers and magazines that appear to be as little used as is a bright poker. I look in vain for English, American, or Australian literature. Not a paper from those countries, save the *Illustrated News* of three months back, is to be seen. Each of the three leading towns of Java—Batavia, Samarang, and Soerabaya—publish two newspapers in the Dutch language —wretched-looking prints to English eyes.

Batavia is altogether a roomy place. The elbow-room that is given by the house-builders is extended also to the streets, which are of great width and mostly macadamized. Space is nowhere economized. Such a liberal spirit in dealing with town allotments as is here shown is not seen in many Eastern places. It is easy, however, to be liberal with that which we take from others. William the Norman was similarly liberal with the land of the Saxons. "To the victors the spoils."

Street-lamps are to be seen—at the rate of three to a mile—and some stunted-looking natives are about on police duties. The attire of such functionaries ill-becomes Malay figures. At long intervals apart are watch-boxes for the use of these men, and there a gong is sounded at certain hours of the night.

Opposite to the Harmonic Club-house is that attempt at

JAVANESE CARRIAGE-CHAIR.

an ordinary city street to which I have alluded. Its eight white-fronted shops are half of them kept by French proprietors, and all are for the sale of drapery, perfumery, and other feminine fancies. No attempt at walking exercise is ever made here by European residents, and therefore the straggling character of the town is not so inconvenient. Time also is of no consequence in Eastern places. Folks there object to be bustled.

Two attempts are made at theatres, but they are poor things. A French opera company was performing at one; the other was closed. The place is theatrically visited from Singapore on the one side and from Australia on the other. An English company from Melbourne had lately left Batavia, and left one of their number behind, who had altered his mind as to his proper vocation and seen his way to hotel-keeping.

In one of the prominent places or squares, here called plains, is erected a similar monument to the one I had seen at Singapore, surmounted by a bronze elephant. It is to commemorate the same important event—the visit of the supreme King of Siam on the first effort at travel that a King of Siam ever made. I begin now to have a proper respect for his Majesty. When at Cambodia, near to his own land, I thought but little of him, in that unreflected light in which I could but regard him. Admired so, and so honoured by others, he now became of dazzling brightness in one's eyes. What is admired of others is most admired by ourselves. It is the unreflected light that but seldom dazzles the vision human.

Near to this plain is another called the King's Plain, on one side of which is something very creditable to Batavia or to any other city. It has written upon it "Museum of the Netherlands Indies," and is just what a museum should be. There is not too much of it, and little or nothing that one has seen elsewhere. Here are the products of Sunda and Java and all the surrounding islands, and that is all. For that good reason, this collection is, to any European, the best of its kind, and can be only uninteresting to the natives. The labour of the plantations is for them, however, and not museums—taking a Dutch view of the matter. All that one sees is novel, and much of it very interesting. Here are some strange things as musical instruments. One of them is made up of half a dozen pieces of bamboo, like to small organ-pipes, and, like to them, of different lengths. These are notched with holes here and there, and are all strung upon a frame. When shaken, they emit most musical sounds; but native talent is needed to bring out the proper music. Pieces of wood of different lengths and thickness are here also arranged on framework, like to a rock-harmonicon, and can be played upon by sticks with goodly effect. Altogether, a day can be well spent in this place, to which a fine library is attached, and also a splendid collection of photographs, that have the advantage of not reminding one of pictures seen elsewhere.

In a book in this library, written by Sir Stamford Raffles, for five years English Governor of Java, I find these words:— "The interior of Java contains temples that, as works of labour and art, dwarf to nothing all our wonder and admiration at the Pyramids of Egypt." Nothing more should be needed to determine a traveller upon seeing such wonders, so certified.

JAVANESE MUSICAL INSTRUMENTS.

The Zoological Gardens claim the next visit, but turn out to be unsatisfactory—a disappointment after the surprise of the museum. It is the fauna only of distant lands that may be seen there, and not that of Netherlands India, which is probably too near to be thought rare. I look with no astonished eyes at English rabbits, cats, fowls, hedgehogs, foxes, pheasants, and grouse. I wanted to see again that finest of birds, the Java pigeon—a bird of heavenly-blue plumage, bedecked on the head with eight small pillars, each crowned with a glittering jewel or something like it, such as I had once seen in a zoological garden elsewhere. Not one was to be seen here, nor even one of the pretty Java sparrows that I had expected to see flying about in Batavia, but didn't. A Ceylon elephant was here, but not a Java tiger or leopard, nor any zoological surprises.

The notes that one makes of things noticeable are better set down as they occur. They might be grouped and arranged under different headings, as in the book on Iceland, which contains that famous chapter on the non-existent snakes that alone is remembered by the world. Acquiring knowledge by observation and information only, it was necessarily of a miscellaneous character, but none the less valued for that reason—to me all the more interesting, and so I set it down.

The Dutchmen that I meet here are like in appearance to the English of forty years ago—the shaved and neat-whiskered men that our fathers and grandfathers were. In the early morning they are seen in their white smocks and wide trousers of Turkish cut and Manchester print pattern. It is not cotton print, however, but stuff called "batuck," or so pronounced, woven by the Malays, and the pattern painted in by some indelible pigments. The Malay men and women wear these batucks folded round their heads in turban fashion, and also around their legs, as one might similarly pin around one a printed table-cover. It is, when thus used, called a *sarong*. When this batuck is not twisted round the head, a bamboo hat of the size and shape of a colander, or kitchen strainer, and painted like to a Chinese wooden coffee-bowl, is worn by the Malays. It makes a sunshade and small umbrella combined. The wearer seems to have a huge painted toadstool upon his head. It is tied under the chin by a band as broad as an ordinary horse-girth. The Dutch ladies seem to wear all the day long a white smock like to a short night-dress, and the batuck continuation—not a dress calculated to show the figure to advantage, but decidedly comfortable for the climate —which the "pin-back" dress of modern fashion would certainly not be in Java. The children wear but one article—the white children I mean—for the children of the natives, up to six years of age, appear to wear nothing—that is a short smock, with shorter leggings that reach to the knee. Shoes and stockings are never thought of for any children. A heelless slipper and sockless feet are the fashion for everybody, male and female, native and European. The white children are given in care to Malay nurses, and thus, to the annoyance of their parents, learn the Malay language long before they do the Dutch. At ten years of age they are generally sent away

WEAVING THE "BATUCK."

to Holland to be educated and reared, and to acquire colour in their complexions and strength in their limp-looking limbs. Reared in Java they would look something of the colour of putty, and appear to be about as soft.

At tiffin time I reject the mess of curry and co. that others take, and attend to the fruits. These are mangosteens, custard apples, dorians, bananas, dukkos, rambutangs, pappiyas, and a roasted root called katellapotion. With bread and iced water these make a satisfactory lunch, and one quite proper to the climate. If I want more, there is rice and milk—the proper food for the country. The mangosteen is the king of Java fruits. It has a dark brown, soft, and thick rind, of a turpentiny smell, that encloses five, six, or seven creamy-white pieces of ice-cream-like fruit, which also has a pleasantly nice savour of turpentine. For that reason some object to it—say, one out of a hundred. The other ninety-nine can eat and enjoy mangosteens as we elsewhere eat peaches. The custard apple has a green and rugged exterior of artichoke-look. It is full of sweet white custard and large black pips. The dorian is as large as a melon, with a prickly rind, and not generally liked, though I found it an enjoyable fruit. Folks particular about perfumes say that it smells like to a rotten onion. It is peculiar that way. Its heavy and thick rind contains four compartments, in each of which is a large amber-coloured stone, enclosed in a sort of whitish birdlime, that sticks much about one's fingers. It is, however, very good eating—barring the smell of it—and as nourishing as the South Sea "taro" or "poi"—the staple food of the Maoris and Sandwich Islanders. The dukko has a smooth shell, enclosing a pleasant-eating, whitish, jelly-like substance, that must be nibbled or sucked off the stones it covers. The rambutang might be mistaken for a nettle-top in appearance. Its bristles are, however, softer, and, when peeled, the fruit is found to be a kind of minor mangosteen in appearance and flavour. The pappiya is a veritable melon. The katellapotion, or sago potato-root, tastes, when roasted, like the best of roasted chestnuts. With these novelties in the way of fruit, the traveller can steer clear of curry and its concomitants very satisfactorily, likewise of the detestable sourkrout.

The Batavians ignore blacking altogether. It soils the white trousers they wear in the after-part of the day. The traveller finds his leather boots getting browner every day, and no help for it but to buy varnished leather shoes, which exclude the air and heat the feet. Sending blacking to Java would be as profitable as exporting thither warming-pans or skates.

After tiffin I take a *dos-à-dos* car for a long drive through and around the city. All the city is, I now find, like to the suburbs of any other town—white; ground-floor villas peeping from among thick and tall tropical trees. I see the Waterloo Plain, on which stands a tall granite monument on a green, surrounded by barracks. In front of the officers' quarters is a grand-looking colossal figure in bronze, which, in the distance, in hat and feather and general dress, looks like to the pictures of Sir Walter Raleigh. At the risk of a sunstroke I emerge from the shelter of the covered carriage and inspect it. Its inscriptions tell me that it is the figure of one Jan Peterzohn Coen, Governor-General of the East Indies from 1618 to 1625, and again from 1627 to 1629; that he was born in Hoorn; that he died in Batavia on 21st September, 1629; and that he was the settler and first Governor of Java. The Dutch at one time ignored British India altogether, and called their settlements round about here the East Indies. On their old coins of 1796 the letters O.C., for "Ost-Indie Company," appear instead of the crown of Holland. A company, similar to the British East India Company, had then the management of affairs in what is now called Netherlands India, and were made to pay handsomely to the Exchequer of Holland for their privileges.

On the occasion of a probable French invasion of Holland, the Dutch once threatened to submerge that country, as Russia burnt Moscow and all the towns on the march thither of Napoleon's army, and to bodily emigrate to these eastern possessions of theirs. It reads very Spartan-like and patriotic until one comes here to see what pleasant possessions they have in this Garden of Eden and earthly paradise. The threat then has a very different look.

To leave damp, foggy, ditch-enclosed Holland for Java, the spicy Celebes and Moluccas, and the Thousand Islands, was not giving up much—not a sacrifice like to that of the Pilgrim Fathers when they left England to settle in America, there to live upon their own labour. The good that Holland has done the world since then makes one glad that the sad threat was not carried out, and humanity thereby deprived of its best gin.

Looking around here, it does not appear that the Dutch would have lost anything by it. They thrive well in this land, and on the care they take of its labourers. Like to Jeshurun, they have here "waxed fat," but his other characteristic appears to be taken out of them. They are quiet as mice at work on a rich cheese.

The other side of the Waterloo Plain to that on which is the statue of the founder of the city and first governor of the country contains a monument that records on its four sides the great fighting deeds of one Michiels, who seems to have been the Joab of the time in this part of the world. His battles were no doubt something like to the robber raids of buccaneers, but they all counted up to the good of civilization as represented by Holland. The monument is perhaps as well deserved as many of such things.

While in this neighbourhood I again visit the museum—a thing that may be done many times. There is a room full of gods and goddesses in stone, more or less damaged, brought down from interior temples. Most prominent is the elephant-nosed god. Next to that is a goddess who appears to be counting her fingers. Here also is a wooden figure of incalculable age, and in that respect like to one I saw in the museum at Cairo, which was labelled as being 6000 years old—the effigy of the chief of the household of some king who reigned about the time of Adam—going by the time of Jewish records. "About this time Adam appeared," might be written in the histories of Egypt, China, and other lands. These wooden images appear to endure time's wear and tear equally well with stone. The features can be rubbed away scarcely more easily on the one than on the other. The great toe of Jupiter's stone effigy—now called St. Peter—in the cathedral at Rome, is nearly kissed away. An old wooden figure of a god in a Canton temple had, similarly, its nose entirely kissed off by those who believed that kissing it was good for their eyesight. Some strange carvings of monstrosities are here on show, cut in wood, and indelibly painted—one of them remarkably like to the figure of our own familiar Punch. From Siam are shown some figures cut in cardboard, well painted, and jointed with cocoa-nut string, after the manner in which cardboard figures are put together in the Western world. Cups of metal, of different thicknesses and material, are set here in a dish. When half-filled with water, and rubbed around the rims with wetted fingers, the musical-glass music, somewhat improved, can be produced from them. All of our novelties are not so novel as we think for. Inventions seem but to travel in larger circles than fashions.

It is evening, and therefore dark when I get towards the Hôtel des Indes. There is no twilight in Java. One bungalow is so like another that I mistake a neighbouring one for the hotel, and tap at my driver's back that he may stop there. I can ask him no questions, nor he tell me anything, so that there is no chance of his correcting any error. Dinner is spread, and I, without a thought, leave my pith helmet and umbrella on a chair in the verandah, and take a seat at the table among the twelve or fifteen seated there. I do not notice that they are not the folks I saw at tiffin. They seem to smile among themselves; but I take it to be at some Dutch pleasantry that is going round, and so go on with dinner. The dishes are passed around by the Malay attendants as at the hotel. I can see no difference. There are several ladies dressed in white, as usual. All the gentlemen are in white apparel. I am conspicuous by wearing a thin black alpaca jacket. Ignorance was bliss on this occasion, and I dined well and satisfactorily, taking water and tea only as drink, and refusing the wine that I knew I had not ordered and considered as passed to me by the Malay servants in error. When dinner was over, and the cigars were lighted up, I went out upon the verandah and took a chair there, as one who might enjoy his ease at his inn. A tall, elderly gentleman took a seat beside me. I had observed him at the head of the table, and took him, rightly enough, for the host. He spoke a little English, and addressed me as of that nationality. He hoped I liked the dinner. I told him that I did. Had I been long in Batavia? Only two days. Was

I going further? Yes, to Samarang and Soerabaya. By what means? By the first steamer next week. By which way had I come? By way of Japan, China, Cochin China, and Singapore. Where was I staying in Batavia? Why here; at the Hôtel des Indes, room No. 7! Oh, then, that accounted for it; the Hôtel des Indes was half a dozen houses—a quarter of a mile—further on! I had intruded upon the private table of a hospitable, gentlemanly planter, who had humoured the mistake. I was glad of it, for he gave me endless odds and ends of information that were useful. If Dutchmen had any faults, the behaviour of this one had atoned for all.

A curious thing is on the beds here nightly, which I now learn is called "a Dutch wife." This abuse of a good name is applied to a bolster of about half the thickness and twice the length of an ordinary British one. This article, that I have hitherto kicked off the bare mattress, which is all that serves for bed, should, I am now told, be kept through the night between one's ankles and arms, and so provide space and promote coolness. The idea, I believe, has not been patented. With all people it is not a success at first. It was not much so with me. I always found my Dutch wife rolled off on to the floor by the morning.

CHAPTER XVIII.

BUITENZORG AND THE HILLS (SUNDA).

No less than six languages are common in Sunda and Java. These are the Malay, Javanese, Sundanese, Madurese, Chinese, and Dutch. Madura I have mentioned as a large island, of one hundred miles by sixty, very near to the mainland of Java, and in constant communication with it. The Dutch bank-notes of Java and Sunda are endorsed with notices printed in four languages, which for that reason may be taken to be those most required—Malay, Javanese, Chinese, and Dutch. These notes, with the guilders and half and quarter guilders in silver and cents in copper, make up the currency. One hundred cents go to the guilder. The coinage has a pretty appearance. On one side is the Dutch crown, and on the other an inscription in Malay script, surrounded by another in Javanese character—something like to the shorthand of Gurney in its look.

Only Dutch maps of Sunda and Java are to be found here. From one of these I get ideas of the islands. Their combined length is near about seven hundred miles from Bantam to Banjoewangie. The greatest breadth is in the middle, in the neighbourhood of Samarang; there it is nearly a hundred miles. The population, other than European, is about twenty millions. The Europeans number some five thousand. The Chinese are over a million, of whom the majority are traders. The Javanese, Sundanese, and most of the Malays are the toilers, the tillers of the soil, the wealth producers. These eighteen or so of millions are a sort of semi-serfs, who cultivate coffee, sugar, rice, tobacco, and other produce on the Government lands, out of which the millions are made annually for the spread of civilization in Holland. The coffee has to be delivered by its native growers at thirteen guilders a picul. Up to 1874 only nine were grudgingly given for it. A picul is 125 lbs., and fetches from forty-five to fifty-five guilders when sold by the Dutch in that open market to which the native grower is not allowed to bring it. His position is consequently definable by a very plain word. When I have added that the Pasoeroewan district, near Soerabaya, produced last year five hundred thousand piculs of coffee, the profits made on this product alone can be easily estimated for that part of Java. Every opposition is placed by the Government in the way of private individuals obtaining land in Sunda and Java for purposes of cultivation. Some have been waiting for years in vain. The private grower decreases the profits of the state monopolizer. Salt is made a state monopoly altogether, and a large revenue is obtained from it as from other monopolized things.

This magnificent, highly-productive, and profitable Sunda and its adjunct Java are divided into twenty-five districts of nearly equal size. These are named Bantam, Batavia, Buitenzorg, and Praenger, which constitute Sunda, or that portion of the island in which the Sundanese language is spoken by the natives. Then come Krawang, Cheribon, Regentschappen, Tagal, Banjoemaas, Pekalongan, Bagelen, Kadoe, Samarang, Japara, Soerakajarta, Djockjakarta, Putjitan, Madiven, Rembang, Kediric, Pasoeroewan, Soerabaya, Probolingo, Bezoeki, and Banjoewangie. At this last place the telegraphic cable from Australia is landed. The names of these places need not be all remembered except by those who fancy their euphony.

Each of these districts has a superintendent, whose house is called the "residency." Native princes are kept in puppet state, and are ludicrously designated sultans and emperors. They receive pensions from the Dutch, and a guard of thirty or so of Dutch soldiers. Their palaces, I observed, were generally opposite to a Dutch-built fort, which ornamental thing occupies the centre of every town in which a sultan keeps his state—or is kept in it.

Sunda and Java have many fine mountains, some rising, I am told, to nearly twelve thousand feet, which are, as in India and Ceylon, sought as a sanatorium. Several of these are volcanic, accounting for the occasional slight shocks of earthquake experienced here. The hill-sides are the coffee lands. The low lands grow the sugar and the rice. Higher up than the coffee, tea is cultivated, but coffee is the staple of the country. It is to Sunda and Java what wool is to Australia. Java coffee is the great rival to that of Ceylon. Mocha, on the Arabian coast, grows the favourite berry, and much of Java coffee is shipped there, and properly, or improperly, branded, and then transhipped as "real Mocha." Ceylon has only three millions of inhabitants. Its produce is, therefore, very small compared with Sunda and Java, where the Dutch grind the coffee out of the natives in a more profitable manner than the British have yet practised.

The mountain ranges give a plentiful supply of water, the streams running into rivulets and rivers of useful length and breadth, equally plentiful all the year round. Three of the prominent ones are the Tjidami, the Tjitarum, and the Tjiliwong, to which may be added the Callimass, or golden river, of Soerabaya, that floats the cargoes of coffee from far inland to the seaport. Some of the scenery on these rivers is the loveliest that imagination can picture. The eye never tires in gazing at it. The beauties of Sundanese and Javanese scenery would make poets out of many men; but the Dutchman inclines only to be a philosopher and philanthropist.

This country appears to have but few sheep. Mutton is a rarity at the table. Pork takes its place at dinner-time. That seems to be plentiful. Bullocks and cows are seen but rarely, and I saw nothing of grass lands. The buffalo is the common animal—a huge beast that has a hide like to a dark-coloured pig, and but as little covered with hair. It is, however, timid and easily managed. A small, naked Malay boy of six or seven may be seen driving half a dozen of them home from the fields, astride, as far as his little legs will reach, on the rearmost one. Nothing in nature can look more wretched than the general run of dogs here. In all Eastern countries the dog seems to come off very badly. His bones can be counted in most cases, and his life appears to be altogether a mistake. If the Indian idea be correct, that he bears his master company in the next world, it is to be hoped that his fate will be bettered there. It can scarcely be made worse. He is positively obliged to drag out existence in the East on mainly a vegetable diet that evidently does not agree with him.

The Dutch ladies seem to be a fair-haired race. Most of those just arrived at womanhood remind me of Faust's Marguerite in their appearance. They develope in after-life to a bulbous form that does not look so graceful, but which their style of dress—white smock (*camisa*)—and their *sarong* much favours. Neither ladies nor gentlemen wear head-coverings after the sun goes down. Then comes the time for the evening drive. The hood of the carriage is thrown back, and its bare-headed occupants take their much-wanted airing. As for exercise, they get none. Cricket and croquet, horse-racing and hunting, are not the fashion of things in Sunda and Java. Occasionally a ball is held at the club-house, and the birthdays of the King and Queen of Holland are honoured in that way. Dancing does not, however, seem to be the most desirable thing in a climate where it is perspiring exercise even to fan oneself.

Now that so much is known of the world, now that Nineveh has been unearthed, and Dr. Schliemann's discoveries have settled all questions as to the localities of the Homeric battles, it is strange that the locality of the Garden of Eden has not been agreed upon. In Ceylon I was shown Adam's Peak, upon which is to be seen his footstep, though unanimous belief does not appear to confirm that statement. Ceylon is nice enough for Paradise, but this land is more beautiful, and as such more likely to have been the Eastern Eden. There is nothing paradise-like to be seen in Palestine—that stony, bare, and barren country. Taking Eden, then, to have been in one of these favoured gardens of nature, one can well understand, feeling what the climate is, that orginally man was not intended to labour. I am supposing the first man to have been a white one. His creation, in such a country, on that condition, does not square with one's reason and notions of the fitness of things. The curse that he should live by the sweat of his brow can be understood only in the fulness of its punishment in Eastern lands.

I go from Batavia to Buitenzorg, forty miles, by a primitive-looking, slow-going railway that runs American-fashioned cars. I am glad that it is a slow pace, for the scenery is something so delicious that one would like to go but a mile an hour through it—or stop in it altogether. There may be better places in the world, or may not. I don't think that there can be, but this satisfies one to the full in the way of Nature's most lavish loveliness. All along the road the eye rests upon and revels in a wealth of verdure that seems almost that of another and a better world—the world of the yellow meads of asphodel, the amaranthine bowers, and the delectable mountains. They are all here, and much more also than poet ever dreamed or painter depicted. Nothing in the imagination of man can equal the works of Nature. Truth is ever stranger than fiction, and reason tells us that it must be so.

The bamboo-built huts of the natives, rush-mat covered, peep out from among the palms and bananas and other full-foliaged trees that the Western world sees only growing under glass. Love in such cottages would seem to have its proper home. Copper-coloured cupids play about the doorways. Cocoa-nuts, breadfruit, bananas, and custard apples can be had for reaching up for them. The purest of water runs everywhere from mountain rills. Cold and hunger seem distant and impossible things. All around the eye sees but the clearest of blue skies, verdure-clothed hills and heaven-kissing mountains, with eternal summer, lapped in flowers, smiling ever rosily at their feet. An Eastern dream of delight! Glimpses are obtained here and there of the most delightful of little valleys. It is an upward journey all the way, and gets sensibly cooler and pleasanter every mile. Buitenzorg is among the hills, and for that much favoured by the stewing Batavians. The palace of the Governor, Van Lansberger is here situated—a sort of ground-floor Versailles—a tastily-built white palace in an immense garden of finest trees. For living in this pleasant place he draws a larger salary than any British colonial governor. He has besides, I am told, the opportunity to double his handsome pay by private speculation, of which some governors largely availed themselves. A goodly honey-pot to Dutch flies are these fair lands of Sunda and Java. What a pity, one cannot help thinking, that Sir Stamford Raffles did not continue their Governor! He saw the way somehow to England's continuing to retain them, and so advised in a despatch that was, strangely, never shown to the Prime Minister of the time until too late. It had remained unopened for long after its receipt, but by whose fault has never been explained. By such mere threads as that hang the fate of nations!

England took charge of Sunda and Java from 1810 to 1816 during that general scrimmage caused by Bonaparte, in which nothing was considered safe. In the final re-settlement of things that took place at the latter date, after Bonaparte had been put away in a corner for wanting the world as a plaything, these fair lands of Java and Sunda were handed back by England to Holland. Very few indeed of the English have been to visit them since that. It is too saddening to do so, and they also lie out of the world's way. Even the Torres Straits mail-steamers do not call there, though their way-bills so promise. Every Englishman who sees these lands may think that England might have done with them somewhat differently to the Dutch—perhaps have improved them. Nature has done all for them certainly, for

O

which reason it is, perhaps, that the Dutch for over 200 years have not done much more than they could help. They have made them pay, however, which is more than England might have done. In that way she is not Holland's equal, and may never be so.

Here in the gardens of the Palace of Buitenzorg I find the tomb of Lady Stamford Raffles, wife of the one English Governor that Sunda and Java have had,—

> "Her part in all the scene that fills
> The circuit of the sunny hills
> Is that her grave is green."

Yet one might wish to die to have one's long sleep in so sweet a place. The inscription merely records her name, Olivia Marianne, and her death at Buitenzorg 26th November, 1814.

I find quarters at an hotel that appears almost overhung by a huge mountain, called Salahk, eight thousand feet high, largely infested with the tiger and rhinoceros. On its sides are many tea and coffee plantations. I get the sleep at Buitenzorg that failed me in Batavia, and duly appreciate it. The upper part of the Tjiliwong River, that runs through Batavia, is here to be seen. Its waters are now clear as crystal. On its banks are many pretty falls. The scenery about Buitenzorg is altogether such as might tempt any man, Dutch or otherwise, to make his residence there. My host talks every modern language, and takes an interest in his visitors. He has been a sea captain, and is now settled here, his rovings over, with a Malay wife, and several pretty-looking half-caste children. He smokes everlastingly, and his wife chews the teeth-blackening, mouth-reddening stuff that is made up of betel-nut, gambier, lime, and tobacco. He says, in excuse of it, that every Malay woman does likewise. It does not look ornamental to feminine lips.

"If you would see the beauties of our scenery," said my host, "take a carriage to-morrow, and go up forty miles to

Sandanglaya; you will then know more of what we have to show."

I do as he suggests, and start early in a low-built carriage, with four rats of ponies, harnessed mainly by ropes. My Malay driver knows where he has to go, and I am to supply him with money as he wants it for horse-changes and buffalo-hiring. I ask what the buffaloes will be wanted for, and am told that they are necessary to draw the vehicle over the mountain—which sounds sensational. I wish that I could talk to my driver and learn particulars as I pass along, but that cannot be, and I have all the more opportunity for looking around. By this time I have got pretty well used to dispensing with language, and find how well one can get along and through the world without it.

At every six miles the ponies are changed. An archway across the road indicates these post-houses. It is all up-hill work, and through delightful scenery. Cooler and cooler it gets every mile of the way. The mountains around attract the clouds, and they presently distil gentle rain upon us. The vegetation varies, and coffee instead of rice appears upon the uplands. Tall fern-trees, or tree-ferns, such as one sees in the mountain gullies of Australia and Tasmania, now appear in profusion, and add additional charms to the scene, as do new flowers and flowering plants. Waterfalls and rushing streams make music all around.

We stop at mid-day at a post-station called Toegoe, where I get some boiled rice and water for a meal, mixed with sugar. They satisfy hunger and thirst, and no one gets anything better among those around me. A rajah, or some native prince, is driving downwards in a handsome carriage, and makes also a stay here. He is sitting smoking a chibouque, or water-pipe, in Turkish fashion, and looks grandly in his silk turban and sash, long petticoats, and embroidered slippers. He knocks down one of his Malay servants for not doing something rightly, or quickly enough, and kicks an inquisitive dog clear across the road. Altogether, he is evidently some great man in his small way.

At the next six-mile stage ten Malays come out and harness themselves to the carriage with ropes. My driver then leaves his seat and delivers the vehicle and horses to their care. The cause is soon apparent. We have to go down a steep incline, cross a mountain stream, and ascend a stiff hill. Altogether, I think it looks best to walk, and get out accordingly, and join my Malay driver in the rear. Quite as quick progress is made in that way, and one gets better opportunity to look around and admire the panorama on every side—mountain, loch, and glen.

When difficulties are got over on this stage of the journey, other ones begin, and buffaloes take the place of the horses and the ten Malays. A mountain of between two and three thousand feet has to be crossed—some parts of which are very steep indeed. Getting to Sandanglaya is not ordinary road work—very far from it. It is now quite cool, and I put on an overcoat that I had the forethought to bring with me. Its weight, however, tells on the toil of getting up that hill of difficulty, and one feels quite winded by the time the top is reached, and the buffaloes detached. The scene from this elevated position is glorious indeed. A little Scotch whisky at the bothie-like hut by the wayside would not be out of place, but, worse luck, is not in the place. Travellers must be content, so I have to feast on the views around, and instead of the whisky to drink in the beauties of the scene. They are, fortunately, very satisfying. Nevertheless, I feel that the ascent of the mountain has taken much out of one who has had nothing since the early morning but rice and sugared water.

The mountain has now to be partly descended to get to Sandanglaya and its hotel. Here, at the top, is a gate and a sign-post, on which is inscribed "Tussaroa-Praenger," indicating that I am entering into a new district—that of Praenger. Such gates mark the divisions of the districts throughout the land. It is easier work getting down hill, and my umbrella now becomes of service to shield me, not from the sun, but from a mountain shower. I am, in fact, among the mists.

In an hour's time I reach lower land, and the hostelry of a retired doctor, who has established a sanatorium and hotel combined in this inviting but not easily accessible spot. He cannot speak English, nor can his wife. I am glad of that, for his eldest daughter, whose appearance compels admiration, is called into requisition, and we exchange ideas in English and German-English. It sounds very pretty, though, from her lips—anything would have sounded so from them. I am not surprised to find that she is engaged to a coffee-planter with a horrible Dutch name. I might have known, by looking at her, that she would be engaged to somebody. There may be "flowers blushing unseen and wasting their sweetness" all unadmired, but they are never to be discovered. Those that I thought were so situated were, I soon found, like to Swiveller's dear Gazelle, engaged to planters, graziers, or squatters, or something of the sort. Even one that I met with in a Maori "pah" called Arawanui, in New Zealand, a glory of a Maori girl, named Kiti Kohoota, was engaged three or four deep. Poets sit at ease at home, and imagine fine things—making "the thing that is not seem as though it were." The unfortunate traveller, at his toil and cost, discovers the plain prose of the world. It is the poet, however, that oft incites him to the travel. As that gives him more sense than he previously had, and further knowledge, he has for that much to thank the poet after all.

CHAPTER XIX.

SANDANGLAYA TO SAMARANG (SUNDA-JAVA).

SANDANGLAYA, as a hill-country sanatorium, has the usual characteristics of invalids and hypochondriacs. I find at dinner-time an assemblage of its visitors, of whom I was about the only one who did not think that anything was the matter with him. The company was made up of those who were really sick, and those who go about imagining some ailment —as an excuse for travelling, idling, or loafing. Here was a young Englishman, smoking all day like to a factory chimney, and playing billiards, who said that he was not strong enough to take a journey to visit the great temples in the interior. I noticed that he ate like to a farmer, and drank equally well. He would have felt, if possible, all the stronger had he walked all over Sunda and Java, which he looked quite able to do. Monetary plethora and laziness were his only ailments. A tropical thunderstorm set in with great violence on that evening. I had gone, after dinner, to visit a fine lake in the neighbourhood—nearly as fine as that other lake, Tahoe, that I saw among the American Nevada hills, and got caught in the downpour ere I returned. The lightning and thunder were grandly terrific. Up at that height in the mountains they seemed to be, as I suppose they were, all around, and not above, one. The torrents of rain nearly washed me off my legs, and, helped by the wind, made a wretched wreck of my umbrella, and subsequently of myself.

The journey down from the mountains to Buitenzorg was

made in much quicker time than the ascent. It was enlivened also by the incidents of an upset and of as troublesome a team, on one of the stages, as were ever harnessed together. In Sunda and Java, as elsewhere in the East, only stallions are driven, and they seem to be more recalcitrant and pugnacious as they get smaller in size—"little pots are soon hot," says Shakspeare. At one part of the journey the off-leader appeared to think that he was doing more than his fair share of the work, and came to a dead stop to express that opinion to his three partners. He talked to the two wheelers, with his heels, in a most emphatic manner. I thought that he would have kicked their heads off. They replied by backing hastily, and then rearing up and striking out with their fore-feet in a creditable manner of self-defence and resentment. The carriage was thus backed over into a dry ditch, and myself and the driver thrown out. On recovering my legs, I found the offending off-leader now at war with the near one, whom he was biting in a way that caused the bitten one to shriek and scream. He then kicked them all round as a final thing, and afterwards took to grazing on the adjoining hedge—in the coolest possible way ignoring the whole lot, and turning his rear to them.

After mending the harness and getting things straight again, the journey was resumed, and completed satisfactorily. For the rest of that "post" in which the upset occurred, I noticed that the driver applied his whip to three only of the four horses. That off-leader was now treated with much consideration—those who behave worst in this world too often are.

After another cool night of sleep at Buitenzorg, I am taken by my kind host around his garden, and shown, among other things, a flower, a red orchid, that catches and feeds upon live flies. It seized upon a butterfly while I was present, and enclosed it in its pretty but deadly leaves, as a spider would have enveloped it in network. The sensitive plant also grew here. Its leaves shrunk from a touch, and shrivelled up to nothing when plucked. That flower and this plant must have a nervous system closely allied to that of animals. The orchid to which I have referred has a delicate discrimination in the matter of its food. It must, in the fashion of an Eastern faith, kill its own meat—rejecting any dead fly that may fall upon its leaves.

From Buitenzorg I make unwilling way to low-lying, hot Batavia. Not wishing to stay longer there, I make inquiries for a steamer going to Samarang—a central seaport, from which I can get to the interior. I meet with general opposition to this intention, not only from the hotel-keeper, from whom I might naturally expect it, but from the banker who exchanged money for me, and the agents of the steamer by which I was proposing to start on the next day.

Samarang, it appeared by their statements, was as treacherous a place as the butterfly had found the orchid to be. The west monsoon was blowing, and would blow for another month. During that time Samarang was a highly dangerous port. I might go, and go there again, and still find the blue or "danger" flag flying. To try to land then was forbidden to ship passengers, and by the state of the rolling billows on the bar. If I landed, as I might be at my own risk in other boats than the ship's, I might not get away when I wanted, and might see weekly steamer after steamer come and go away again while I was left lamenting. Dozens of folks, I was told, had found things so at Samarang. Why should I hope for better luck?

To me it was, above all things, necessary to get away from Samarang to Soerabaya by boat of the following week, there to catch the outgoing steamer. If I lost that, I must wait about two months for the next one. Two months' detention in this climate sounded like to two years. He that regards the winds and clouds, however, shall neither sow nor reap, and the traveller who regards all the dangers he is threatened with will miss seeing some of the things best worth seeing. I had received, at different times and places, so many warnings that I had got quite callous to them. I was not to venture upon landing through the surf at Madras—but I did. I was not to leave the steamer off Suez in the Red Sea, and land by a boat, until next day—but I did, and got to Cairo by next train, at the expense of only a wet jacket in both cases. I was not to go into the Great Pyramid, after the fatigue of going up and down it—but I did; nor under the Falls of Niagara, a really dangerous excursion—but I did that also. I certainly should do neither again, but that I learnt for myself. It had so often been "nearly" with me, and never "quite," that I felt bound to trust the fortune that hitherto I had always found at flood.

One companion had been stricken by dysentery in Calcutta, and another by small-pox at Bombay, a third by sciatica in China, and others by ague in America, and fever at Naples. They each had to stay behind for those good reasons, while I had to go on. I had nearly been shipwrecked off Nagasaki, in Japan, and nearly got dislocated limbs by falling off a camel in Syria, and slipping over an elephant in India. But then we all nearly get run over in the great cities every day of our lives; and take some risk, however little, when we venture abroad. I nearly came off the perpendicular sailors' ladder by which one climbs into the ball and cross of St. Paul's, and tripped, and nearly fell, in the descent of the lofty Kootub Minar Pillar on the plains near to Delhi. It was always, however, "nearly," and never "quite." In life it is all like that. I therefore took my ticket for Samarang, per the "Koningen Sophia"—spite of the monsoon and all monitory advisings.

For the rest of the day I made another round of Batavia, and discovered a town wall built of blocks of lava from the up-country volcanoes; also churches of the Lutheran and Roman Catholic faiths, and two Chinese temples. My journey extended to the fort or citadel of Batavia called Ryswik. Here labour and ingenuity and money have not been spared. If such things as forts be of any good, then Ryswik is the right thing. It will hold upwards of 4000 people, though what good they would do by being shut up there is not so perceptible. It were better that they stopped outside and fought their besiegers, who could surround the place and starve it quickly into a surrender. For water supply a splendid artesian well has been sunk in this fort, ensuring the besieged from thirst. Sunda and Java are such fat places among the world's good things, that this fort will likely be wanted some day, when the world shall next, in Malay fashion, "run a muck" at no very distant date.

I find the "Koningen Sophia," like the steamer of the same company that brought me down from Singapore, crowded to excess. The Netherlands India Steamboat Company must, I now think, be a well-paying affair, and I am told really is so. It has its head office in Austin Friars, London, and its larger number of shareholders among the English. It is, in fact, an English company, with a Scotchman for chairman. Like to a Turk, they will "bear no brother near the throne." Trading among the Dutch, they perceive how profitable it is to monopolize, and they do here as the Dutch do—exclude all others from a share in the plunder. Other vessels that have tried to get some of their overflowing loads of cargoes and passengers have been run off the line by the Netherlands Company reducing their fares below paying price. They are rich enough, with their twenty-five and thirty per cent. dividends, to stand that for a long time. That state of things explains why the Torres Straits Mail Company's boats no longer call at any port in Sunda or Java. They got nothing but loss of time by so doing.

It is, for the thirty hours that I am on board this steamer, very difficult work to move about. A dozen of the passengers have no berths, and sleep on the deck chairs. The deck is further thronged with soldiers from Acheen going to Samarang barracks, and with half-naked natives. They lie about so thickly on the deck at nights, that it is quite an acrobatic performance to walk a yard. A dancing-master only might accomplish it. I am glad next day to come to Samarang, where the vessel is to stop, or more, to unload cargo, ere proceeding on the voyage to Soerabaya, to which place I have, as remarked, yet to go, to join the outgoing steamer. Meantime the business is to get on shore here. The terrible blue flag is seen through the glass to be flying at the masthead of the flagship, and all countenances look blank, and faces lengthen at that news. The vessel, too, begins to rock in a very unpleasant manner, and the rolling waves can be seen breaking on the bar in the distance. Boats nevertheless come round the vessel, and there dance about like to corks on the heaving waters. It does not, however, look worse than Madras. The boats are smaller here than those used there, and worked by three men instead of ten. For five guilders I am offered a boat passage. It will be lowered to three if another goes with me to share the expense. That desirable other one cannot be got. One, an Australian from Port Darwin, volunteers, but he "jibs," after he has stood for ten minutes on the steps, trying to get into the boat. He returns to the deck and gives it up. I must go alone if I go, and one generally has to get through one's troubles that way. I am suddenly an object of much regard to the other passengers, and the ship's officers smile pityingly upon me as upon one going into danger. I have seen a daring bridegroom going into church similarly smiled upon.

I get my travelling-bag into the boat, and wait for the next billow to lift it up high enough that I may get in also. It lifts it too high that time. I look at it so going up, and retreat upwards also on the steps. It appears amusing to those on deck, who are taking now a greater interest in the matter. Longfellow's young man, who would go up the mountain with his flag on his shoulder against all warnings, was scarcely begged by more people not to do so. The next attempt was not more successful, but the luck of odd numbers held out, and the third effort saw me in, and trying to get off from the ship's side. It was just like to the business of shore-going at Madras, except for the smallness of the boat. The waves took great liberties in the way of wetting one, and I soon began to envy the half-stripped boatmen. The water ran off them, but hung about with me in plenty in coat and vest.

My pith helmet—that useful hat for this climate—was knocked off very soon, and floated away on the crest of a billow. All this was seen by the two or three hundred passengers left behind, who wanted to get on shore, but did not fancy the sensation. The worst part of the passage came in twenty minutes' time, when the bar was crossed. A rolling billow came over me, as I bent nearly double to receive it, and knocked the stroke oarsman on to his back in the bottom of the boat, causing it to rock and stagger with the shock, half filling it with water, and making a wet mess of me. It was very exciting—amusing perhaps to those who, in safety, looked at it; but the worst was now over. I got into smoother water, and soon to the landing-place at Samarang. I have left Sunda behind, and am now in Java.

This necessity for thus hurrying on shore was caused by that which drives many folks onward—want of time to take it easily. I had only five days in which to do my journey there and back from Samarang to the temples in the interior—of which I have quoted what great things Sir Stamford Raffles wrote. To miss seeing those was to miss the gem of Java—almost the gem of a fifteen months' incessant travelling—judging by the language of that quotation, " that these temples dwarfed to nothing all one's wonder and admiration at the labour bestowed upon the pyramids." That was surely enough to tempt any one to a little trouble and the risk of a wetting or two.

Not a soul, I found on my return, left the steamer that day or the next, nor until the morning of the third day. The trouble that they had lying there, in sight of shore, and so awfully crowded, in that now rolling and rocking vessel, for two days and nights, was something greater than all I experienced in my half-hour's boat voyage. They all seemed of that opinion also. By landing as I did I saved two days of precious time, and that alone enabled me to do the intended journey. There is generally some trouble attending getting anything, sights or otherwise, that is valuable. The trouble which I had had was, in that light, an earnest that it would not be found to have been wasted.

I found that the train, on the railway that would take me more than half the journey, started in an hour's time. I looked at the clock at the hotel at which I got lunch, and saw that it agreed with my watch. Both proved to be wrong. The train started by Samarang time, which was twenty minutes, or nearly so, in advance of that of Batavia. I had therefore to wait for next train, early in the morning, and to spend the afternoon in looking about a Java seaport town.

The Samarang Hotel has a strange name. It is called "Heeren Logement," which, I find, means "gentlemen's lodgings." It was full of guests and mosquitoes, and as close and hot as an Australian theatre on Boxing night. Several sea captains are stopping here—against their will. The weather is such that they cannot discharge cargo, and see little hopes of doing so for some time. They smoke, and drink schnapps, and they sleep—which is as much as one can expect from a Dutchman in Java. I want to get a companion to go with me in the morning, and propound the subject to several of those about me who have nothing wherewith to fill up their time. I am evidently altogether ignorant of the Dutch mercantile mind. They look on me with as much curiosity and astonishment as can be shown in a Hollander's face. They do not seemingly appreciate works of art, nor the idea of going one hundred and thirty miles up country to see any. I do not think, on further talk to them, that any of them would go a hundred yards to see St. Peter's or Cologne Cathedral. How men like these can learn to talk English as they mostly do, and acquire nothing of English tastes, is a subject I may meditate upon at leisure.

That I may not be left behind weather-bound when I come down again, I inquire as to the chances of getting away from this trap of a place. If I cannot go on board the next steamer due from Batavia *en route* for Soerabaya, I shall be fixed, indeed, and that may very likely happen. Is there no help for it? Yes, there is! Pope says that—

> "The mouse that has but one poor little hole
> Can never be a mouse of any soul."

The other hole or outlet that I discover is that of the mail-cart to Soerabaya. It is over a rough road, in a jolting conveyance, and the distance is two hundred and seven miles. I must bespeak a passage twenty-four hours before starting, and interview the postmaster that he may see I am a proper character to be let go through Dutch territory. These sleek, quiet, philanthropic Dutch are so careful of this Java! They seem as timid about it as a thief would be about stolen property. I took down the names of the seven townships that I shall have to pass through, if I take that journey, and inquire particulars about each. That trouble is not thrown away, for I find that, half way, I shall come upon the Valley of Death, wherein grows that upas-tree that all the world has heard of.

I don't care, now, whether the winds and waves are adverse or not. Let the west monsoon blow its worst, and the thunder and lightning and rain come with it, and do their best. I am safe! I can get to Soerabaya overland, and there is that sight midway—that valley and that upas-tree—which will make all the trouble of the journey feather-light. Who has seen the upas-tree? What writer has written about it—that upas-tree of Java? I had put the upas-tree away along with the phœnix and the unicorn, and other known things that belong to an unknown world. No wonder that it is trouble to get to Samarang! Wonders such as these grand old temples and that upas-tree would naturally not be easy of access.

If I should fail to see that upas-tree, I know that I have seen already plenty of sprigs and leaves and cuttings from it. I have been for days and days among those who for between two and three hundred years have been a dead-weight upon the life and progress of this fairest of all lands that be—who have killed all art, literature, and learning in the whole of its length and breadth—who have oppressed its people and monopolized all their labour and its profits, treating them as brutes and serfs—who have crushed all their efforts to attain to the better state of their forefathers, and have kept the gem of the Eastern world in a state of dulness, darkness, and torpidity. In all that I have already seen the typical but true upas-tree of Java.

CHAPTER XX.

SOLO AND JOCKIO (JAVA).

THE above names, which look like those of monkeys, are the titles of two towns, in one of which resides an emperor and in the other a sultan. They are the strange abbreviations adopted by the Dutch of the more euphonious Soerakajarta and Djockjakarta, interior towns of fair Java. It is said that the great names of this world are not upon the scroll of fame; and though I visited Solo and Jockio, I cannot name the potentates that dwell there. I had trusted to that German almanack of Gotha, as a kingly *Court Guide*, to supply the information, but it failed me—as also do such books as *Men of the Time*. So much for the scrolls of fame!

A railway of 120 miles in length runs from seaside Samarang to these two towns—cities I ought to call them, perhaps, seeing whom they contain. The emperor and the sultan are natives of Java, and descendants of a long line of royalty. Born in the purple, they retain still the names and abodes of their ancestors, and from their palace windows look upon the fair lands over which they reign, but do not govern. Their power is impalpable—so superfine, in fact, as scarcely to be felt. It has been taken from them, and appropriated by the Dutch, who in return allow them princely pensions. They have, in addition, an allowance of an army of thirty soldiers each, which is about as large as that of the reigning power in Monaco. These soldiers are paid by the Dutch Government, and so perform the difficult matter of serving two masters—Mammon and Gammon, or the Dutch and the emperor. Perhaps the absence of kingly cares compensates for the loss of power, and makes easier to lie the heads that wear such crowns. At all events, the monthly-paid pension does so. By early train of next morning I am *en route* to the old temples of Prambanan, on which route are Solo and Jockio—a five hours' journey by this slow-going line. The temples I go to see first are in ruins. Of that sort I shall see three in Prambanan. Further afield, at Moendoet, two more will be visible in better state, and then further on, at Boer Buddha, and in best condition, will be seen the crowning architectural wonder of this part of the world, or any other, if Sir Stamford Raffles wrote rightly about it.

The journey is all the way through a long and broad plain, flanked in the distance by high mountains. The peaks of the lofty Japara and loftier Marapia can be seen throughout the day's travel. For companions I have two young Dutchmen, really natives of Java, returned from Holland and education there but a few months. They had been for some days in London, and looked on that and its memories as the great events of their lives. For further information that I could give them about that smoky, foggy, sloppy, chilly, and east-windy city, they reciprocated with much that I wanted to learn about Holland and its Java—about Dutchmen and Javanese. The young Dutchmen were of an English poet's opinion, that "Better fifty years of Europe than a cycle of Cathay." Distance lent all its enchantments to their youthful views. In this Garden of Eden—this enchanting Java—they could see nothing worth living for, nor understood that

> "A man's best things are nearest him,
>   Lie close about his feet,
>   Though 'tis the distant and the dim
>   He ever strives to greet."

Such wisdom would come to them only with later years, when the judgment is less green and the blood much cooler.

Along the road were to be seen the fields on either side, in which the produce of the lowlands of Java were in course of cultivation. The natives were everywhere busy at their daily toils. Some were ploughing the rice swamps, seated on buffaloes to keep out of the knee-deep slush, or standing in it, gathering up the weeds that the primitive-looking plough had turned up; others were planting the shoots of young rice in the mud from the bundles of it carried under their arms. Rice-planting here, and reaping there, were going on for mile after mile of the way. Then came the indigo fields with their gooseberry-bush-looking plants. Then came the fields of katjang, an oil-producing shrub. Acres of tobacco came next, and then stacks of it in sheaves, drying in the sun, near to the tobacco mills, the chimney-shafts of which could be seen in the distance. Fields of sago and tapioca were now to be seen, and then a wide expanse of sugar-cane, two, three, four, or five feet in height, according to its age. Not a foot of land seemed left out of cultivation. Where the food for the buffaloes came from I could not see. They were, I supposed, fed upon the rice straw after the tops had been gathered. Nothing else seemed to be left for them.

With tobacco factories, the rice and sugar factories alternated: not a church or a school was visible anywhere on that long ride of five hours. Industry, for the enrichment of the foreigner, was the uniform order of things here noticeable.

Petty stations called "haltes" were stopped at for a few minutes here and there. They were for the taking up and setting down the natives, who, in their red and white holiday dresses, were waiting at these "halte" stations, or travelling in the third-class waggon-like carriages in the rear of the train. It looked—to European eyes—terrible work, toiling in the open fields under that sultry sky; but I suppose that the brown skin feels the heat less than the white. Here, in the carriage, under shelter, I found it work enough to sit still and perspire, and wipe off the moisture every five minutes. A shirt collar soon became soppy in Java. The fig-leaf attire of forefather Adam was the proper thing for the place.

In the fields hereabout, it, or something like it, is the only attire adopted. Looking at the warm and sloppy work doing among the rice-fields, it was certainly quite sufficient.

At the stations of Kadongati, and again at Socrakajarta, ten-minute stoppages were made. My young friends kindly warned me against the imposition of two guilders and a half (four shillings and twopence) charged there for a lunch. I contented myself, therefore, with a biscuit and some schnapps and water for half a guilder, which was stiff charge enough. My friends had, of course, never seen the temples of Prambanan that I was bound for, nor those of Moendoet and the grand Boer Buddha. Nor could I persuade them to come on and visit these wonders of their future home. Oh, no! They were going to the ball given at Solo that evening by the native emperor. His Imperial Highness gave this ball in honour of the King of Holland's birthday. I might have asked, "What's Hecuba to him, or he to Hecuba," that he should do honour to the birthday of a king who was but the chief of those who had taken from him the inheritance of his ancestors? I feared, however, that my Dutch friends might misunderstand me, and so said nothing. Probably to such prudence it was due that I got them to include me in that night's visit to the palace—to an introduction to an emperor who was such by right of birth and a long line of ancestry, and not bearing a mere gingerbread-gilt title of yesterday's making. I should also there see a nautch-dance by the native women, and other high jinks of such festivities. All that I could take in the way back from the sight of the solemn temples of Prambanan—much as the mourners at a soldier's funeral go home to the tunes of merry music.

It was a "halte" station only at Prambanan. A young Dutchman, who officiated as *factotum* here, took especial interest in me when I stated my mission. What did I want to see the temples for? "Did I mean to say that I had come all the way from Batavia to do so? Did I think that there were any buried treasures under their stones?" He could nohow understand it, I plainly saw, but he got me a guide, and gave him full instructions, a part of which was, no doubt, to cry "halves" for him in any treasure I might turn up. He was a true Dutchman.

Accompanied by my silent guide, who only spoke Javanese, I started under umbrella covering for the long walk. No conveyance was to be had. In the little villages passed through, in which I stopped to buy cocoa-nuts and drink their contents, I saw that Europeans were not every-day sights. Without these cocoa-nut drinks I could not have got on. Relays of them were carried onwards for further use. No foresight was wanted to do that. About a cocoa-nut full of moisture seemed to exude from one every ten minutes. I had not previously noticed that cocoa-nut water was so very nice.

My guide carried, in his girdle, or in the cloth wrapper round his middle that formed his only attire, the "creese" or short dagger-sword that all the natives seemed to have with them who can afford to buy it. It had a tastily-shaped yellow wood sheath, and a well-carved red wood handle to the dagger. That was of steel, and shaped in three curves. It looked ancient and curio-like, so much so that I bargained for its purchase. Our negotiation was carried on in dumb motions, but satisfactory at last to both of us. I afterwards learned that the five guilders paid for it was not over the market value. With that on hand, I was ready to "run a muck" at any time in Malay fashion, should the climate, or other cause, so influence me. I now became more than ever an object of interest to the natives. With an umbrella hoisted, a Malay creese in one's hand, and walking about on the plains in the heat of the day, when all Europeans in Java are usually sleeping for three hours, I was exceptional, to say the least of it.

The first of the two temples was reached at last. I had been prepared for it by seeing carved stones used in the villages for domestic purposes, and noticing others supporting gate-posts at the entrances to some of the fields. Thus are the works of the past utilized in the present! A man that

sat at a wayside village turning, having some native produce
for sale, supported his stall upon a stone of four feet high, on
which was excellently carved a full-length feminine figure,
that an antiquary would have rejoiced over, and any museum
been glad to get.

This first of the Prambanan temples is a huge ruin of many
tens of thousands of carved stones, all having bas-relief
figures, or parts of figures, on them. These are now lying in
a heap of fifty feet in height, and some three hundred in circumference. An old native, who dwelt in a neighbouring

AT PRAMBANAN.

hut, took me a winding and scrambling journey over this
heap, and to the top of it. Among the stones were five
small throne-like canopies or cells, each having in it the
figure of the Buddha. At the summit is the larger and
crowning cell, having in it a larger Buddha figure. Worship
is still made at this old heap of ruins. Before the figures
that are still here were flowers in fresh condition—left recently
by devotees.

This temple was once, in ages past, of pyramidal shape,
and had distributed, around its ascending terraces, a hundred

of such shrines or cells as the five that I had seen. Every stone had on it bas-relief carvings. These were continued on those above and below, if one stone did not suffice, the joints being scarcely perceptible. Temples like to this, having no interior, were certainly novelties in architectural art. These had been produced by an artistic and art-loving people of a highly devotional order of mind—a race that had not Dutchmen for masters, and, if the ancestors of those that now constitute the eighteen millions of this teeming land, then superior men altogether. Perhaps not so, but only a race allowed and encouraged to cultivate their tastes, and to leave evidence thereof for the world's wonder.

The second of these temples of Prambanan is a mile further onwards. The ruins of a smaller third one, scarcely noticeable, are passed on the way. This plain, covered with rice-fields, that I am now crossing, was, in its bygone and better days, the site of a large city, the builders of which have passed away, and left their labours to follow them.

Two colossal figures in good preservation guard what was once one of the four entrances to the courtyard of this fine temple—a far larger one to that first seen, and one that must have been nearly half a mile in circumference. By the little that is left one can guess at that which has been. These figures at the entrance are each carved from a solid block of granite. They represent a male and a female, who are hugely stout, and, by general appearance, of mature age. Each of them is represented as sitting, and they have a broad smile of welcome on their pudding-like faces—a fat old grandfather and grandmother welcoming their guests at the hall-door. Their height, of ten feet, and their immense weight, ensure their stability. Dutch enterprise will not go to the expense of removing them to the Batavian Museum, which appears to have been done with all the other figures of this ruined temple. These two will probably sit here for thousands of years, though enveloped by the prolific vegetation of the tropics.

That tropical vegetation is doing its work here, as I saw it doing at Baalbec and elsewhere—overthrowing and overgrowing everything. It is curious to notice how Nature reclaims and draws again within the earth all that man takes thereout, and leaves upon its surface. Seeds are dropped by the birds, or blown by the winds, between the joints of the stones. Moistened by rain, and fed by dust, they germinate, spread their roots, and grow, forcing the stones asunder, and toppling them down upon the earth. There vegetation soon covers them up, until the antiquary shall appear and unearth them as wonders. The Egyptians knew this process of decay, and of Nature's work, when they coated the pyramids with their enduring cement, harder than the stones it covers. That alone can preserve monuments for all time, if thousands of years can be so called. Building on the sands of the desert was another instance of their foresight. No vegetation there grows to help the winds and the rains and the sun in their several labours of destruction of man's masonry.

About the remains of this second temple of Prambanan one may wander for hours, looking always at something of interest. Twenty, or more, tall piles of stones, of various heights, are still standing, fifty or more feet apart. All are richly carved in bas-relief, all enclose empty cells from which the figures have been removed. The centres of the other three sides each show figures in bas-relief, from which arms here, and legs there, have been knocked away. On the tallest pile a large tree is growing and spreading its huge roots throughout the stones—throwing them down all around. It must have a lizard-like nature to find nourishment among them. In its progress downwards, it will, in a few years, stretch its roots into the earth, and scatter thereon all the building through which it has made its way.

I sit upon the piles of fallen stones—none of them broken—that are around me, and break a cocoa-nut upon one of them. As I raise it, to get a drink from its interior, I find myself facing an exquisitely carved female figure in dancing attitude in the centre of the standing pile of stone that is opposite to me. As I look upon the beauty of it, a huge lizard runs up and rests upon this figure's face. It is more in its place there, I think, than I am here. It is doing its work in this world.

I again take the sultry walk to the railway station, and feel baked, or stewed, by the time I reach it. The sight of what is left of Prambanan's temples does but further stimulate me to see those of Moendoet and Boer Buddha, that still are nearly perfect, and not as those that I have now seen. If the ruins are so grand, what, I think, must be such temples in their entirety?

I wait for the train that is to take me to Soerakajarta, and to the imperial ball given by the emperor there. Next day I am to see a sultan at Djockjakarta, on my road to the greater temples. I shall surfeit with grandeur at the courts of these great ones of the earth! The station-master does not seem to to think so. He has but insignificant ideas about emperors and sultans, and smiles at the mention of their courts. But then he is a Java Dutchman, whose thoughts are only of coffee-growing and guilders.

I have got cooler by the time the train arrives, and, after paying my guide for his services and his creese, I go away to Solo, and there find an hotel and my young Dutch friends, and get a Dutchman's dinner. The emperor's ball is given in a ground-floor building, having marble steps and floor, in the centre of the city. The place has a population of one hundred thousand, nearly all of the native race. I walk about its broad right-angled streets and shaded avenues, and look at the walls of the Dutch fort, which is sure to be in its centre. That is mounted with heavy artillery which warns the emperor to keep himself and the people quiet. The house of the Dutch resident looks quite as fine as the emperor's palace, and its occupant must necessarily think himself the greater man, though he is but plain Mynheer van something. Of the two, I would rather be in his place. Titles without honour are very empty things, though many who take them by inheritance only get along very well with them elsewhere.

All the king's army and all the king's men are arranged in full dress, squatting on the marble steps of the pavilion and along its broad landing-place. They must have numbered fully a hundred. Their uniform was very fine. The Dutch supply these puppets for attendants upon the greater puppet. They gild the one and give gold to the other. This emperor gets an allowance of 30,000 guilders a month, with permission to make as much more as he can grind out of the natives who live and work upon such estate as the Dutch allow. Land is too valuable in Java for any one but the Crown of Holland to have more than a small share—and that grudgingly given and well accounted for.

EMPEROR'S RESIDENCE.

The emperor, on this occasion, sat upon a throne in the centre of this marble pavilion. The Government officials were in European evening dress, seated, with their wives and families all around them. I see Dutch ladies here in full attire for the first time. They look better now than they did in their white smocks and tablecover-like wraps. The emperor has something like a Windsor court-dress upon him, and a star, the size of a cheese-plate, upon his breast. He sits bolt upright in an attitude of no end of dignity. In front of him a dozen Japanese girls are squatting down who are waiting to give their nautch-dance. They are dressed in close-fitting bodices, and are painted and powdered in a very gay fashion. I fear for the paint and powder if the dance is to be what I understand by dancing. The perspiration is ready enough, I find, without any exertion to promote it.

The nautch-dance is, however, no violent effort. It is about the tamest thing in dancing I ever saw. The Court minuets through which our forefathers walked are the nearest approach to it. It consisted of a girl rising and then slowly moving herself around and about, throwing herself, meanwhile, into as many attitudes as the human figure is capable of—while upon its two legs. One could look at such movements for hours without a feeling of excitement—if one could only keep awake after the first fifteen minutes. What kept me lively was the expectation of something more lively to come—which never came. The one girl was joined shortly by a second, and the two performed the same movements as the first. Then the third arose, and after an hour the whole ten were afoot. The effect was then something like to the movements of the ballet girls in an opera, who do dumb motions and attitudes, and group themselves about, while the pet of the ballet has gone off for a rest—and a drink at the wings. The premier *danseuse* never came bounding upon the stage in this nautch-dance which thus looked like to a ballet by the members of the corps only. I almost expected the stage manager to come forward and apologize for the absence of Mademoiselle Zepherini, but he came not. The movements of the girls got a little more rapid towards the end, but it was never exciting. An excuse for their lifelessness was to be found in the music, which was entirely native. Those who have heard Chinese music have heard something like it. It was better than that, but of the same order of harmony, and always in one tune.

I got some supper at a side-table in an anteroom, and then, being very tired, and having to get up early next morning, I retreated from the place backwards, as others did, and by so doing fell over a native soldier who was squatting down behind me. Neither of us was hurt, and it was a good warning that going backwards in the world is to be avoided.

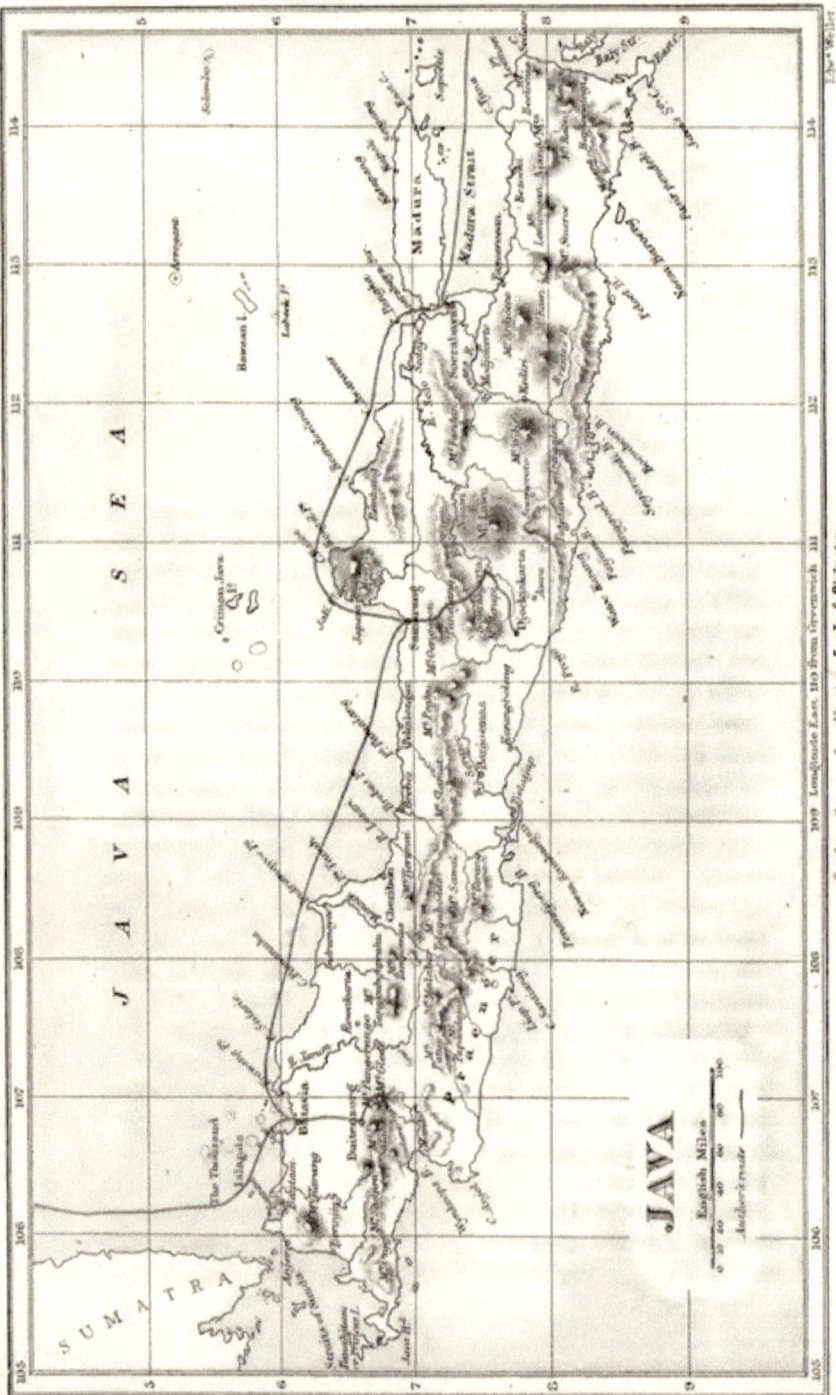

CHAPTER XXI.

THE JAVANESE UPAS.

OF the lions of Java that I could make time for visiting, there remained to be seen the upas-tree and the temples of Moendoet and Boer Buddha as up-country sights. On the way to these attractions lies the city of the sultan—that Djockjakarta that the Dutch have vulgarized, as they have dealt with everything in Java, to Jockio.

By the slow-travelling trains it was a distance of three hours' journey from Solo to Jockio. Some use was made of this space of time by my despatching a telegram to an hotel-keeper at the latter town to have a conveyance in readiness for the journey to the temples—thirty-five miles beyond railways.

The city of the sultan is reached about 9 a.m., and at that hour has a quiet provincial look about it. It always has that look, I believe. The usual Dutch-built fort occupies the centre of the city, and faces the sultan's palace. The presence of these forts at Solo and Jockio is like to that of a cathedral in an English provincial city. Everything is dulled and deadened by the incubus. Who ever saw a cathedral city that had not slowness, dulness, and heaviness as chief characteristics? The exceptions to that do but illustrate the rule.

Facing the fort stands the customary Dutch club-house, with "Concordia" lettered on its front. Between that and the fort is a rotunda, in which the military band played on fine evenings. Native singers and musicians were, however, about. To listen to their strains, and look at the strange shapes of their old-fashioned instruments, was more amusing than listening to the band. These folks supplied what I may call the music of the past, in contradistinction to Wagner's music of the future.

Jockio seemed to be as large a place as Solo, and better built. Its streets were broad, and shaded by tall trees. In the central and business part of the city were narrower streets, crowded with native traders and dealers. These things having

NATIVE MUSICIANS (JAVA).

been observed, there were yet the palace and gardens of the sultan to be seen, as also an ancient temple in the city's centre, that was thickly surrounded by native dwellings, and embedded in tropical vegetation. I was warned not to go to this ancient affair, as a matter involving much trouble. Good advice is, however, mostly disregarded.

The sultan's surroundings lay on the road, and were, therefore, first visited. In the large courtyards about his dwelling he has shown fantastic taste in dealing with the tall and thickly-leaved trees. Huge ones, of a hundred feet high, with wide-spreading branches and foliage, are here cut into the shapes of vases, balloons, globes, and square and oblong boxes. Two trees that stand at the entrance of the grounds are disfigured into the appearance of big butter-tubs set upon thick scaffold-poles. The sultan has a fine family of young princesses, who must be costly for dress, judging by their appearance. These young ladies were accomplished musicians, and played the Javanese pianoforte, called a "gamelong," while seated on the floor. It was far from displeasing as music, and very different from that given at the nautch of the

THE "GAMELONG."

emperor at Solo the day before. The native Javanese women have the freedom of those of Japan—their faces are not covered by yashmaks, nor are the ladies secluded in zenanas, as in some Eastern countries.

The sultana had a card-party in one of the palace apartments. She was not the only sultana by very many, but, what was perhaps as good, was the favourite one—the mother also, I believe, of the four young ladies I had seen at the music.

In one of the anterooms of this palace were things more

noticeable than sultans, and quite rival attractions, in an old bachelor's eyes, to the ladies. These were two fine puppies, as I took them to be, of some large breed of dogs—Mont St. Bernard or Newfoundland. I was quickly undeceived, and told that they were really young lions—whelps of a deceased mother, and believed to be orphans. Both parents had been, it was thought, killed by hunters, " butchered to make a Javan holiday." The little ones were being brought up by hand, and were most interesting creatures. The young of all animals are so, but these were additionally so from their kingly character and their rarity. There was nothing frisky about them—indeed, their countenances bespoke a settled melancholy—but the absence of friskiness was caused, perhaps, by their great weight. Though not larger than a tom-cat or a Newfoundland pup, they were heavy as lead—ever so much weightier than it was possible to imagine from their appearance. I might have had one as a present if I could well have lugged it about, but the taking of it under one's arm, as is done with a puppy, was out of the question.

In considering the extraordinary weight of these young lions, one could well understand how the adult animal can break the back of a horse by a blow of its paw. The fibre of a lion's muscles lies close and compact as that of lignum-vitæ or other weighty wood. There was nothing of fatness about these whelps; their great heaviness lay wholly in bone and muscle of much density. I left the ponderous puppy so offered me with great regret then, and more now. I had similarly, but for different reasons, to decline a cobra-di-capello offered to me at Lucknow—a snake that was as well trained as any poodle, and danced to the tunes of a wooden whistle in a fashion that reminded me much of the famous one-legged dancer, Donato.

Like to the native ex-King of Oude, who is kept in a prison-palace near to the landing-place at Calcutta, this sultan here has a similar fancy for keeping caged tigers. They illustrate, perhaps, the state of their owners, and a fellow-feeling and sympathy may thus exist between the pampered tigers and their puppet proprietors. Here, at Djockjakarta, eight of these pretty creatures are imprisoned in one huge wooden cage. It is difficult to imagine how they can be peacefully fed, and each satisfied with its allotted bones. I was led to that thought by the way they growled at me—tearing at their wooden bars and thrusting forth their paws in what, but for their growls, looked like an effort to shake hands with one. I seemed to see all the way down their fearful throats, so widely did their mouths open. They would have been happier, I thought, stretching their limbs on the side of the lofty Merapia, that is here to be seen smoking from its eight thousand feet elevated crater.

This Sultan of Djockjakarta has a pension of thirty-five thousand guilders a month, but not the reputation for private wealth that attaches to the native emperor at Socrakajarta. There seem, to a European, to be such very limited means of spending a large income at these places that I wondered how the money was made useful. The Japanese Government have taken to cutting down the allowances of the daimios every year. They get now only about a tenth of the income they had when, ten years ago, they held their landed possessions. Java may very likely take a leaf out of the Japanese book in that way. It would bring more guilders to the treasury of Holland, and that is the end and aim of Dutch government in Java and Netherlands India generally. "The greatest good to the greatest number" is read that way.

The old temple at Djockjakarta is difficult indeed to get at. I think that I went through the private houses and back-yards of a half a dozen Javanese before I got into the jungle that surrounds what remains of the building. To get through that thick vegetation—tall grass and creepers and brambles, neck high—was to get well wetted with the heavy dew, and much scratched. The walls of a building, very different to either of those at Prambanan, are here partly standing—enclosing court-yards and tanks that altogether cover a space of 400 feet by 200. More like the remains of an old palace than an old temple is what it appears to be. There are rich carvings over the doorways, and evidence of some one having built this place and lived in it who ruled in a different way to the emperor and sultan of my late acquaintance. In the centre of the busy, bustling city, this quiet old ruin, with its broad and silent courtyards paved with marble, now stained and time-eaten, was a curious solitude. Open all to the skies, the rain kept the tanks in the centre of the two courts well filled. The lizards ran upon mouldering, tumbling walls, and everywhere the aggressive and destroying vegetation was feeding upon, throwing down, and covering up the ruins. Up its tottering stones I scrambled to the topmost ones, and there obtained a view of the flat-lying town and surrounding scenery—so far as the trees permitted. Difficult, dirty, and scrambling work was this visit to Djockjakarta's antiquities; but an antiquary would pay a dozen such visits to it, and think as little of the discomfort attending it as a German doctor does of experimenting upon himself with new drugs, and making novel surgical operations on his limbs.

The horses and vehicle bespoken at the posting-house were waiting for me when I got back to it, as also was a young Englishman, who seemed fallen from the clouds, to go with me and halve expenses. He had been three days in the town, intending to go the thirty-five miles to Moendoet and Boer Buddha at some time, and this time seemed to him the best. A Cambridge University student, whose studies had broken his health, he was travelling to recruit it, and was very welcome company indeed in this land of Dutchmen and Javanese—in this unvisited island of Eastern beauty, white masters, and brown-skinned serfs.

The four ponies took us stages of six miles each, and were then exchanged, and a different driver also taken. Those that we left behind we were to take up again on the return journey. The road was pretty good, except at the crossing of rivers where no bridge had been built, and there twenty natives joined us, and helped the ponies over their difficulties. I thought that things were going on too well to last. A betting-man said once that "What's the odds, so long as you are happy?" were ten to one that you did not continue so. Three miles from the journey's end an important bridge over a broad stream had broken down. There was nothing for it now but to walk. Three miles or more in the heat of the day in the interior of Java, far removed from sea-breezes, is about equal to twenty miles of walking when and where the thermometer stands at 60° or less. How we broiled and stewed and panted and gasped over that longest of short walks! Two rivers had to be crossed in baskets slung upon bamboos, and pulled across by Javanese. In Java the bamboo is everything. All around, in forests, on the hill-sides, the famous teak, equal to the oak for ship-building, grows in plenty indigenous to Java; but the strong, lighter, and handier bamboo is the favourite of the Javanese. If the carriage broke down altogether, I think they would have made a new one by the wayside out of bamboos there growing. They supplied a splinter-bar in that way in a few minutes, when a new one became necessary on one of the stages.

Small temples fortunately preceded the great one, as in the Prambanan district. We had got now again into the region of temples. The first seen was a small gem that might be restored or removed, stone by stone, and set up elsewhere. A huge tree—one of those with lizard-like roots—is growing into and utterly destroying it. Every stone of it is beautifully cut and carved. Some of the bas-reliefs represent figures that are feminine in the upper part, and bird-like in the form of the lower—a variation of the mermaid idea. This little beauty of a temple is only thirty feet high by twelve feet broad. The enterprising Americans who wished to purchase Shakspeare's house, the Japanese Dai Butsa, and other antiquities for the embellishment of New York, might advantageously buy this elegant little temple, and set it up in their central park. Here it will, in two years' time, be scattered over the earth in loose stones, and in another three years be quite covered up by vegetation. Not a stone of it at present seems to be wanting, but all are tottering. In the interior, up seven marble steps, is a conically-shaped cell, in which sits a female figure—some goddess, gracefully enshrined.

Moendoet Temple is half a mile further on. It is of square shape, but finished with a conical top, and encloses a hall—twenty-eight feet by eighteen—in which sit three figures, all seemingly feminine. The central figure is eighteen feet high, though in a sitting attitude. She is represented in the ungoddess-like occupation of counting her fingers—seemingly trying to solve a like difficulty to that which troubled Dundreary over his digits. Carved out of one block of stone, by some cunning native Canova, this exquisite figure challenges comparison with the labours of all sculptors, ancient or modern. There is a fascination about its stone face and features that bids one sit and look at it, and keep one's gaze fixed as the Ancient Mariner's stony eyes did that of the traveller whom he bade to listen. One stops, similarly, here to listen to what will come of the finger-counting. The half-smile upon the pleasant face of this figure tells one that it will be pleasant news when it comes. Like Marguerite in the garden, plucking the rose-leaves to learn if she is loved or not, this figure, for like reason, seems to be consulting the tapering fingers of its delicately-carved hands. The other two figures are apparently seated attendants that wait and watch upon the words and movements of their mistress. They are richly bejewelled in carved representations of rings and necklaces. Some devout Javanese has laid bouquets, from time to time, at the feet of the central figure. One such had been apparently, by its freshness, left that morning. Such devotion is easily excused. We felt inclined to follow suit, as one would present a bouquet to a living beauty—or what one thought to be so.

The exterior of this temple shows sides that are each seventy feet in length, and all of richly-carved stones. It is surrounded by a sort of dry moat and low stone wall. On the eastern side, a flight of fifteen marble steps leads up to the hall in which sits the goddess or feminine figure I have referred to. The height of Moendoet Temple is about seventy feet. Any guide-book as to what it was, when built, by whom and to whom dedicated, would have spoilt all its charm. It was pleasant indeed to find such a temple there among the trees, and to look at it and at all its novelties, and to leave it there in all its beauty and seclusion—a thing of mystery, a puzzling surprise, and to be the longer remembered for those reasons. The things of beauty that are joys for ever are mostly those about which we are the least learned, and therefore the less bored.

We thought that the end and aim of the journey—the great Boer Buddha—never would be reached. With steps that were slow, but not weary, we plodded along to it, carrying on our arms all clothing that could be well taken off. We had soon to transfer even that to the arms of our native guides, and travel on with umbrellas alone. The carrying those seemed a trouble. It is in the East that the grasshopper is spoken of as a burden. It is quite burden enough for a European in the tropics to carry himself. It is dire necessity only that can force him to do even that.

Our guide had, in fact, gone out of the usual road, and lengthened the journey to avoid some further obstruction. It proved a profitable divergence, however, introducing us to another and a great novelty of this land of Java.

Mention has been made of the volcanic Merapia that was in our neighbourhood all day. It has a similar effect upon the surrounding country to that of Vesuvius around Naples. I am shown a depression in the earth here, in which it is said to be death to lie down and sleep. A tree is growing on it, however, in an apparently good state, which I am told is the upas-tree. Here, then, was the meaning of the story of "the deadly upas-tree of Java." The tree had nothing deadly about it, but the earth in that depressed part emitted fumes of carbonic acid gas, that hovered over the ground for about three feet upwards, as in the "Cave of the Dog," near to Naples, suffocating those who might lie down on the earth there.

How wind-bags shrivel and bubbles burst when squeezed!

The Javanese natives believed that the evil influence found here and in some other similar places was due to the properties of the tree. Those who slept under its branches did not awake, therefore the tree caused their deaths. That was told to the first-coming Dutch, who told it to all travellers, who told it to the world—which believed it.

Finding that my Javanese friends believed also in this delusion, I—as I had seen done in the Cave of the Dog—to explain the chemical nature of the phenomenon, lit a match, and, holding it near to the earth, showed that the fumes exhaling therefrom instantly extinguished it. A dozen lighted matches were so put out; but when held three feet or more above the earth, they continued burning. The mephitic nature of the vapour did not ascend that height. Standing in the midst of it, I was all right. Had I lain down, I should have got asphixiated, and, unless promptly pulled away, have died. The upas-trees of Java have, therefore, no distinctive character. The gas that exhales about their neighbourhood is fatal only to animal life. It is questionable whether in any two of these poisonous places the same species of tree would be found to be growing. Any tree is an "upas" that grows on these spots.

We are loth to part with cherished beliefs, of which the upas-tree is one, and, as a belief, equal to any reality. We knew from boyhood all about this tree and its miraculous qualities—that its pestilential influence dealt desolation all around, so that no herb, flower, or animal could live within a mile of it—that poison was gathered from it by criminals, who were sent to that work on the do or die principle, and that they mostly died.

I had seen the upas-tree lately upon the stage in one of the newest operas, but that proved nothing, as I had similarly seen there the "Flying Dutchman," and afterwards found that the people at the Cape—Caffres, Zulus, and Dutch—knew nothing of the phantom ship that is believed to flit for ever about their coast. Clinging still to the firm faith of childhood, I read here, down at Samarang, what the plain matter-of-fact Hollanders have to say about the upas. It is in a semi-official volume, entitled *Batavian Transactions*, edited by a learned doctor, whose name has a halo of letters about it, giving one that respect for him which the aureole about their heads does for the figures of the saints.

This great authority says that all that has been related of the upas-tree is fabulous. There is, he says, a tree in Java called the "anchar," from which a milky juice is obtained, whence poison can be distilled or extracted. Beneath this tree, however, herbs and flowers may grow, and men and animals sleep in safety. It is but another species of that vegetable production from which the Macoushi Indian prepares his *wourali* poison. The anchar and the wourali poisons are, however, more manufactures than are any of our spirits. The art of preparing them is handed down in families. The native "creese," or dagger, that I had bought was, I was told, smeared with this vegetable poison. I now give up the upas-tree, though parting with it is like almost to losing a tooth.

On the mephitic spot to which I have referred, near to Naples, a dog is always introduced to the visitor, who is expected to pay five shillings, or more, to see the poor animal killed by the noxious gas. This case of cruelty to animals is allowed to go on week after week unchecked. Several dogs per day must be, in the travelling season, sacrificed in this shabby way. The extinguishment of the match and a candle was quite sufficient for me, and should be so for any one that knows that what supports the flame keeps also flickering the vital spark.

CHAPTER XXII.

THE BOER BUDDHA TEMPLE.

EXPECTATION rose very high indeed as myself and fellow-traveller neared the locality of the great Temple of Boer Buddha. The long journey by rail, and then by road, had something to do with it; so had the little troubles in the way of the river to be crossed, and then the broken bridge near to the journey's end; so had the long walk in the still, tropically sultry afternoon that followed; so had the sights of the elegant little temple at the roadside, and subsequently of the larger and finer Temple of Moendoet; so had the lengthening of the walk by the unexpected finding of further obstruction to the road; so had, and chiefly, the words of Sir Stamford Raffles, Governor of Java, in the time that England had that island. Of this temple district and of Boer Buddha he wrote, as before quoted :—" In the interior of Java are temples that, as works of labour and of art, dwarf to nothing all our wonder and admiration at the Pyramids of Egypt."

My inquiries in Sunda and Java, at Batavia and Samarang, had failed me in finding any account, in English language, of these works of ancient art in Java. A learned Hollander had, I was told, published such a work, that could be had only on personal application to him at some distant place up-country. As it was in the Dutch language, it would have done me no service.

From a fellow-traveller, at one stage of my travels in Java, I had been told the wondrous

Legend of Boer Buddha.

Nearly 2000 years ago—no accuracy could be got as to date—the then inhabitants of Java had determined upon the building of this temple. Its present site was selected as the best in the island for that purpose. The architects, and the artificers in stone-work, quarrymen, masons, sculptors, and carvers, to the number of many thousands, laboured for years upon the work. The designs for it had tested the whole talent of the people, and that which Boer Buddha now shows was selected by a large majority of votes. Like to Solomon's Temple, no sound of hammer or chisel was to be heard when the time came for placing the many hundreds of thousands of numbered stones in their proper places. No mortar or cement was to be used. Each stone was to fit upon its fellow-stone so evenly and closely that cement could not be admitted to distend, ever so little, the closeness of the joint. All these stones were to be brought to the ground, and laid in order for those who were finally to place them one upon another. That time arrived, and 100,000 chosen men went to the task of laying these cut, carved, and sculptured stones, and placing and fixing the sculptured figures of Buddha that were to fill the hundreds of temples then and there to be built up to form together the great Temple of Boer Buddha.

The time came at last for the building, and the solitude of Brodjo-alang, and the banks of the Calli-Progo that runs through it, were enlivened by the presence of that great multitude of workmen collected from out the many millions of all Java—a multitude such as only the greatest national event of the land could call together—the building of its grandest temple!

It was decreed that three days only should be given to the great work—that every stone should be laid, every terrace formed and finished, every one of the hundreds of minor temples built up, and every sculptured figure placed and fixed in that short time—including the final and crowning temple that should be the shrine of the greatest of all its figures. A miracle was thus to be worked in so doing the apparently impossible. All the long labours of the designers, architects, artificers, carvers, and sculptors were to be crowned by the wondrous work of these swiftly-working workmen and masons who, thick as clouds of bees, were to work as busily upon the large mound already raised and levelled for the reception and support of the stones of this many-hundred-templed temple.

High holiday was then proclaimed throughout the length and breadth of Java. The population pilgrimaged to see the wonder-work performed. The immense amphitheatre in which Boer Buddha stands was filled with the myriad-multitudes that came to see this greatest of all the works of Java, and to watch its progress. It was a multitude such as the land never before or since saw gathered together, for the fairest of Eastern islands was then a devoutly religious nation—one also that loved art, encouraged its culture, and gave liberally money, labour, and time to the aid of that which they loved.

Before these assembled millions day by day, of the three days, arose this Temple of Boer Buddha. Not a sound of tools was heard. Magically, and as silently as are done the works of Nature, the majestic pile arose in all its white wonder of colour and artistic perfection of form. Its workmen laboured with inspired ardour, carrying out swiftly, but unmistakingly, the plans that had been long studied by them elsewhere.

So was the great Boer Buddha built! The sunset of the third evening saw the fulfilment of the promise of its then completion. Illuminated by the rays of the gorgeous Eastern sunset, the crowning figure was then placed in this temple of temples. It was then, at this given signal, that the assembled myriads bowed to the earth in adoration. Never had those we call pagans and worshippers of images so goodly a cause for worship. If *Laborare est orare* be truth, then would the building of this Boer Buddha be but one great act of worship. He is bold and rash, regardless of justice and of judgment to come, who, in these latter and grovelling days, shall say that our time and labours are any better expended.

Turning the corner of an avenue of trees, at the end of our long trudge, the great temple now came into full view, enthroned upon a raised mound in the grandest of natural amphitheatres that one could wish to see. No other building is near to it, nor any within sight from all points. Only hill and valley and flowing water, as features of Nature, and that great temple on its central mound as the one work of art.

Boer Buddha, or Boro Boudo, as it is sometimes written, is not a ruin. It stands to-day as a complete pyramid-temple touched here and there by the crumbling hand of time, but as complete as is the pyramid of Cheops. Of that pyramid the cement casing has long since dropped, and piles of stones are to be seen, fallen from one of the four corners. No one calls the pyramid a ruin for those reasons. The stones of majestic and beautiful Boer Buddha are there as the builders left them, still showing, mostly, the delicate carvings and sharp cuttings of the thousands of sculptors and masons who for years laboured at their artistic work. As a crown of glory of the land, and a work of art, this temple may dispute precedence with all the Eastern temples. Its construction was fully as laborious as that of the great pyramid, the stones of which are but roughly hewn, while those of Boer Buddha have a dozen figures artistically grouped on each. It is as graceful as is the elegant Taj Mahal of Agra, and, when of the age of that comparatively young temple-tomb, must have been as bright-looking and equally beautiful. I shall always cleave to the picture of it, made by a native artist of Djockjakarta, that I may convince myself that I have seen it, and that it is not all a dream of the traveller.

It redounds to the glory of England that it was in the time of its five years' occupation of Java that this splendid temple was cleared of its o'ergrowing vegetation and restored to the world's sight as it is now to be seen. The Dutch, for two hundred and more years, had been too busily engaged on coffee, guilders, and the labours of the population, to care aught for the wonders of art in the land they look upon but as a workshop. Even now, the care of a mason or two, necessary to protect the structure against the effects of time and wind and rain, is required. The heads of the figures that have been knocked off, or have fallen, are allowed so to remain in dozens, though a trowel-full of cement here and there applied would replace and fix them for another hundred years or two. The rains and the dust running between the mortarless stones displace them to the extent of many inches, in numerous instances that an artisan's care and skill could remedy, and so save by timely aid the ruin that such neglect will lead to. All one's thoughts about the Dutch and the way in which they treat Java culminate at Boer Buddha temple. At Agra, in Hindostan, I had seen an expensive scaffolding erected to repair the guttering of one part of the roof of the Taj Mahal, and a crowd of masons rubbing and removing the discolourations caused by water to some parts of the exterior marble. All honour to England for such care of native art in a conquered land! Ashamed am I to mention England—enterprising and art-encouraging England—and its doings as matter of comparison in such connexion. Comparisons are indeed odious in some cases, and in this case the odium is all so much on one side.

One can look long and gaze gratified at Boer Buddha before the eye begins to take in details. The full view of it, in all its ample fulness, is so pleasant, so novel, so utterly different to anything that one has seen elsewhere or looked upon anywhere in pictures or paintings, that it is impossible almost to tire in gazing at it, and bring oneself to think of its measurements, the number of its terraces, or the smaller temples of which it is the great embodiment. It is such a surprise altogether that one has a long and pleasant time of silent admiration before activity of mind asserts itself, and investigation of details can commence.

Boer Buddha, then, is a pyramid of something under 200 ft. in height. It might be higher for its great breadth, but its magnificence is not in size, vast though it is, but in the artistic labour shown upon every stone of it. By pyramid is meant a solid mound of masonry, with no interior space. The largest of its many cell temples, which contains the greatest of its seated figures, is that which crowns the building. Each of the sides of Boer Buddha measures at the base 350 ft., a total of 1400 ft. all round. The terraces, up to which steps lead on each side, decrease in height, one from the other, as they go upwards. They are eight in number. The first five are of square form; the three upper ones are of circular shape. Mounting up the steep mound of earth that forms the groundwork, I come upon the first terrace. On that I walk around the four sides of the building, and look upon the carved stones on each side of me, for the terraces are walled in to the height of 5 ft. Here are figures and groups of figures standing out upon each stone, or upon several stones that mostly unite so evenly that they seem but one. They all did so when first placed here, but the rains have worn away the fine edges in many places. At the foot of each of the four flights of steps that lead from bottom to top of this temple are two well-carved stone lions. All around the building, on the surrounding mound, are cell-shaped temples, each holding a sitting figure of Buddha about 3 ft. in height. These ground-seated cells were, in number, when complete, 116.

The floor of each terrace of the eight is 4 ft. in width. The stones used in the building are of a uniform size—about 2 ft. square. In this limited space the artist has often grouped as many as a dozen figures. They are mostly as clear and well defined to-day as they were long ages ago, on leaving the artificers' hands. In colour they have only deteriorated. At the four corners of all the square terraces stands a three-celled temple, each cell fronting differently, and holding its sitting figure of Buddha. The single-celled temples are repeated about 10 ft. or 12 ft. all round the structure. Counting the treble-celled temples at the corners as one only, there are no less than ninety-six temples on this second of the terraces. Over each flight of steps, as we ascend from terrace to terrace, is an arch surmounted by a cell holding a figure. The third terrace is a smaller reproduction of the second. All the figures in bas-relief are of different subjects, and ingenuity seems to have been quite inexhaustible in producing these groups. The antiquary can perhaps discover what they illustrate, and read the stories thus told in stone. The mere traveller only looks on, admires, and makes note of what he sees. Eighty temples are upon the third terrace. The fourth, to which we now ascend, is smaller than the third, and has only sixty-four temples. The fifth of the square terraces shows forty-eight of them. A decrease of sixteen temples will be noticed on each terrace as we have ascended.

The circular terraces are now reached, of which there are three. A different order of things altogether here comes upon one's notice. The carved groups upon the walls disappear, and the celled temples assume the shape of cages, or like to the exterior one of a set of carved Chinese concentric balls. All the temples of the lower terrace had open fronts to them, in which the sitting figure of the Buddha could be fully seen and touched. Here the figure is enclosed all around by broad bands of stone-work, through the interspaces of which it can alone be seen. Of these strange-looking cages, so to call them, there are thirty-two on the first of the circular terraces, twenty-four on the second, and sixteen upon the third. No more steps have to be mounted now, as in the centre of this third circular terrace stands the crowning temple. The Buddha of all the Buddhas is here seated—a figure three or four times the size of those seen below. On the exterior of that crowning temple a passage has been cut to the top of it, from which a view of the gorgeous mass of masonry beneath can be seen in another aspect. The country all around is a minor thing just now, but it is a truly magnificent sight when the eye can be detached from art, and let roam around over the beauties of Nature that are there to be seen.

The smaller temples on the terraces, it will be noticed, number no less than 472. Truly, this Boer Buddha may be called a temple of temples—one artistic, harmonious whole, built up of many! The world has no like to show to this work of a great people who have passed from earth, but left a record fair behind them.

Each of the cell-temples is surmounted by a square-shaped, tapering stone, or spire, of a foot and a half high. It is only on the ground terrace and on the square ones that any of the figures are headless. The cages have protected those on the circular terraces. The heads are placed in a pile below, and every traveller will wish to spend time and money, as the Government should do, in restoring them to the shoulders of the figures. It was real desecration to injure such a magnificent work of the highest art, and it is gross and disgraceful neglect to leave the vandalism unrepaired and uncared for as it is now.

At the corners of each terrace, and by the sides of the stairs, are gurgoyles, as in Gothic architecture. These are shaped as elephants' heads, having the trunk turned upwards and over the forehead. There are endless details, to be further noticed, interesting to the lovers of art and architecture, as well as to the antiquary. Boer Buddha offers to the sculptor, the artist, the architect, the poet, the *dilettante*, and all who have taste or the love of art within them, full repayment for all trouble taken in getting thither. Such a painter as Turner would have revelled in the sight, and have depicted it as what it really is—a *Dream in Stone*.

That time may be taken in the study of this great congress of temples, a kindly man has built a decent sort of bamboo hotel near to the foot of it. Good accommodation can be had there, and fully a week might be given to the study of this strange building—the real wonder of Java, and quite substantiating that which Sir Stamford Raffles wrote of it.

Shakspeare wrote of "sermons in stones," the full meaning of which is fully understood when looking upon the wondrous piles that the giant architects of the past have left for our astonishment ere they, like to the gods of old, went from the earth. Though the day of architecture is done, its great works yet speak. In Shakspeare's day, sermons were sermons, and not the dry rot that too often gets from the woodwork into the words of the pulpit. They had the eloquence, power, and life with which these piled stones that have been left to us still speak. But all the eloquence of all the tongues that were ever attuned to speech could not give one the sensations experienced when gazing upon the Agra Taj, the Delhi Kootub Minar, and this Temple of Boer Buddha—labours to which those of the modern architect are as the squeak of a rat to the roar of a lion. The age cannot develope great builders. It is an age of utilities and makeshifts—of electro-plating, gilding, and lacquering—of French polish, varnish, and veneer. We build to last our time, and not for all time, as did those of old. The race of giant-builders has left a cut stone, dressed and finished, in a quarry at Baalbec, as a sort of challenge to their degenerate successors. This trifle is 75 ft. long and 14 ft. broad and thick. With such stones they built in the bygone days.

Sydney Smith's recommendation to a narrow-minded man to live near to a cathedral, that he might expand his intellect by gazing at a great object, had much sense in it. An American well expressed his ideas—as Americans mostly do—whom I met looking long at Milan cathedral. I asked what he thought of that many hundred years' progressing work. He said, "Speech won't run to it."

Respect for Buddhists and Buddhism gradually grows upon one. Effects must spring from causes, and they must have had "an inner beauty in their lives" who have left in this Temple of Boer Buddha such outward and visible signs of it. "By their fruits ye shall know them." Since landing in Japan, and journeying down thither, I have been all along, through China and Malasia, among those of this faith, and shall be with them as I go further eastward.

The followers of Buddha are numbered at 400,000,000—a full third of all the people of this world. It will be noticed that they are not the majority, and cannot therefore be classified as the fools said by Carlyle to constitute that part. At Ceylon, I shall be at the fountain-head of this faith, whence its stream has permeated the East, and where its doctrines were written and disseminated before the Christian Era. I may there better understand it, but have found already that it has many merits—that it is the worship of one power, whose earthly exponent was this Buddha, the figure of whom has been lately so often before me. Many of his doctrines and moral teachings were, I learn, in certain points identical with those afterwards taught by Christianity.

Although Boer Buddha, once seen, will remain prominently in the picture-gallery of the mind while life lasts, yet I intend to get a native artist to go there, and bring me down a picture of it. My object is to get that effort extended by a water-colour drawing, if I can find some one with artistic zeal, taste, and talent enough to undertake a task worthy of Turner himself.

CHAPTER XXIII.

SAMARANG TO SOERABAYA.

The journey back from Boer Buddha was made by a long night-drive, darkened by a tropical thunderstorm, and electrically lighted up now and then by the most brilliant of lightning. The result was a very welcome coolness of air and refreshed spirits. The fireflies were now abroad everywhere over the fields and roadway—veritable little lumps of light. By one of them that blew into the carriage, and whose egress I arrested, I could see the hour on a watch-face. A dozen of them, put into a phial, would seem to be a good substitute for a candle, enabling one at least to read ordinary letter-press. The light is in the tail of the fly, which is in appearance like to a small working bee. A cunning work of creation is this firefly, with its phosphorescent tail.

On the way down to Samarang, I am among a number of Hollanders, not one of whom seems interested in the grand works of art in this usurped Java that I have lately visited. It is from one of them that I learn that it is due to the labours of the English, during their short but well-spent time in the land, that I have had the chance of seeing them even as they now are. There is no money to be made out of these temples, and they are, furthermore, not the work of Dutch hands. They cannot, therefore, reasonably be expected to interest many Hollanders, who are mostly what is termed practical men. We find such folks everywhere. A lady, a European, fond of visiting the theatre, once replied to my question of what she thought of a particular representation of " Richard the Third," "Do you think I ever pay any attention to the rubbish on the stage?" She should have been a Dutchman's wife.

The tramway that I had seen disfiguring Batavia was, I now found, the enterprise of a foreign company. I had wrongly given the Dutch credit for it. "The fault of the Dutch is giving too little and asking too much," said Canning, who compressed thus his words and meanings in the days of the fourth George. They still keep that character, are proud of their monetary plethora, and took care to remind me that Holland and England—which they place as I have written—are the only two nations that can at present lend money to others. They said nothing about the two nations not getting it in the same way! Their greatness as a European Power has now taken an altered form to what it was in the days of the second Charles. The world can value the Dutch now for their wealth. They are worth so many millions annually—mostly ground out of these Eastern possessions. I will not say that that is all they are worth, but there are those who will.

The Germans have a saying, perpetuated in a public stone inscription which I saw in their land, that poverty begets enterprise, industry, and invention; that these beget wealth and power; that from these spring ease and indolence; and that weakness and poverty then follow—completing thus the round of fortune's wheel. Taking the German reckoning as right, the Dutch are now on the last but one of that wheel's spokes.

All the islands around Java and the Eastern Archipelago have been explored by the Hollanders. They have a treaty with England about their ownership. One nation is not to encroach without the other's assent, and other nations are to be, jointly, kept at bay. Four years ago or so the Dutch began war with neighbouring Acheen, giving up to England, at the same time, that Gold Coast about which Great Britain got into the Coomassie war. Any island of the Archipelago, not claimed by the Dutch, may be considered as little worth, as may also that part of New Guinea which they have not included in what they have there taken. New Britain and New Ireland, which are near to New Guinea, are islands that the Dutchmen do not want—there is no money to be made out of them.

To give the Dutchman his due, he has been worth much praise as an explorer. The Thousand Islands have been to him a diggings that he has well "prospected." He thought to find another Java in large Sumatra, but has been disgusted to find only about four millions of natives there instead of the expected twenty; and only a portion of that limited number can be got to labour for others' benefit, like to the Javanese. The Acheenese, who, as respects Sumatra, are the counterpart, in geographical position, to the Sundanese in Java, know the Dutchman well, and will not have him. They value liberty more than life—thorough Britons to a man, these plucky men of Acheen, whom I would I could help.

Taking it all "by and large," as sailors say, one understands why the Dutchmen gave up the Cape of Good Hope, and did nothing with Australia—which, I see by all the Dutch maps here, they still teach young Dutchee to call "New Holland." Also, it is to be well understood why they so readily gave way in America, and never tackled New Zealand. The natives of those places could not be got to labour for the Dutchman's profit, as do the eighteen millions of Java. The Caffres, Australian aboriginals, Red Indians, and Maoris were no good to the Dutch, and so were left to the British. The discussion of these things and the like with my Dutch fellow-travellers takes up the time that brings me down to Samarang. A steamer is going away to Soerabaya that day, but no money will tempt the boatmen to take me off to it. It looks smooth enough in the river, but the blue flag of danger is flapping vigorously in the strong wind, and the surf on the bar is, they say, impassable. Another boat will be there in thirty hours, which may have better luck. There is time, I find, to wait for it.

The waiting brings better luck with it, and I get away from Samarang and its treacherous, trap-like bay at the expense of only a wet jacket. It is not without difficulty, however, that I can get on board. The steps cannot be reached in safety. I get, therefore, into a sling, and the boat runs along the ship's side until I feel the cord tightening under my arms, and I am hauled on board in horse fashion—glad to be there in any way.

Soerabaya is reached in thirty hours. It is the third of the large seaports of Java, and at the other end of the island to Batavia. It is said to contain less inhabitants, but looks quite as large, or larger, to the eye of the visitor. There is no difficulty in landing at this port, as at Samarang. I pass from the bay into a walled river, as at Batavia, and so up to the Custom-house and its trouble. This walled river—the Callimass, or Golden Water—is full of craft that, like to my tymbanum, or Malay boat, are being towed by natives up its yellow stream. Many come from Madura, a large island that lies near to Soerabaya, whose people are constantly trafficking with the mainland. Their produce is what I see filling the larger boats upon the Callimass. Those boats that I meet coming down are laden with the inland produce of Java, brought many miles down this river. All is bustle and business at this port of Soerabaya. I pass along up the canal-like river, and am landed at some steps that lead me into a dirty, wharf-like landing-place, amid the smells of decaying sugar and other water-side nuisances. Near to this is the Soerabaya Hotel—on the banks of the dirty-looking Callimass, and in the midst of its wharf warehouses. It is in about as bad a position as it could be placed.

The verandah is full of Malay, Chinese, and Javanese dealers, who have unrolled their wares in its wide expanse, and there await customers. Javanese cigars are here offered at half a guilder the box of 100, but I do not see that they find any purchasers among the whites. The native population, possibly, have a taste for them. Walking-sticks, slippers, ready-made clothing, and basket-ware are of the other merchandise offered for sale, after which came the goodly native fruits.

A lively young native planter, from Sumatra, and a

chubby officer, from a Dutch man-of-war in port, take special interest in me as an Englishman, of which I am glad. They have nothing especial to do with their time, and I am excuse enough for bringing out and airing the little English that each of them knows. By them I am initiated in the ways of the house and those about the town, and informed of the manners and customs of the Soerabayans. I find that more English are located at this port than at any other in Java, numbering, I am told, over 300. The town is flat and low-lying, and largely infested by Chinese. Our friends the

THE HOTEL VERANDAH.

Jews make no show in Java that I could see or hear of. With the Dutchmen and Chinamen as traders, they could hardly squeeze in here as in other places. If they did, they would be in the position usually known as " between the devil and the deep sea." The two nations mentioned leave but little pickings indeed in Java. What trade they leave others to do can scarcely be worth doing, and is sure to be of the unprofitable sort.

My young friend the Sumatrian coffee planter is very hospitable in his ways. His curly, and always uncovered head and dark West Indian-looking face is often appearing at my door to propose this or that excursion, which he thinks may interest me, or to show me some native wonder or other. Before the day is over I might become his biographer—so much has he told me about himself and his belongings. He is a sort of very young St. Clair that we read about in "Uncle Tom's Cabin," and has a veritable Uncle Tom, a real good old man, with him as body servant. Only twenty-one years of age, he has but just come into the property of a coffee estate in the mountain land of Sumatra that produces, or is to produce, an annual income of 40,000 guilders. Uncle Tom is an old family retainer—a kindly, white-bearded, black-skinned old fellow, who looks after his handsome young master as a nurse would. This lively and generous youth has but two years ago returned from Europe, whither he was sent for education. He has learnt something of French, German, and English. What is of more use to him, he knows all the dialects of the Malays, Sumatrians, and Javanese, and is withal as canny in business as the cold northern Scot. He is now here on a holiday trip, visiting his factors in Java, who will buy the piculs of coffee from him that are ripening now at Singkarah, on the west coast of Sumatra. I am to go to that estate some time. I must promise *that*, and stop a month among the hills and the coffee when I go. He will then show me a planter's life upon the line, and all the wonders of that tropical island. I can only promise to do the same kindness by him when he shall come my way in the world. The likelihood is probably as great on either side, and is what some one once described as "Nicks."

Accompanied by this young St. Clair, and him of the gunboat, I am driven around the outskirts, and shown the white villas of the notabilities of the place and their green gardens. The banks of the river, I perceive, get very pretty the further one leaves the town behind. I come at last to a bridge from which the view up and down the stream and all around is well worth coming a long way to see. The further I go upwards, the better I am told I shall like it. The Callimass, in that case, must be well worth sailing up. A visit is then made to some sugar-mills, and I see much simpler modes of making sugar than the Greenock refineries make use of. Much of the sugar exported from Java in its rough state is sent to the refineries at Melbourne and Sydney. Six vessels were loading with it at the Java ports I had called at, and as many, I am told, are generally doing so. The cargo that passes me coming down the Callimass I shall probably taste of, in an improved state, in Sydney, Melbourne, or Adelaide in days to come.

Maize is also growing much about Java, but neither that nor the coffee seems yet to have found an Australian market. As this coffee stands high in its character, and Java is near to Australia, the opening up the market for such produce will probably take place now that the South Australians have induced the Dutch to place a line of steamers between the two countries. That line is to run every two months only at present. A subsidy is paid by the South Australian Government for the carriage of mails to that unprofitable part of its possessions—the Northern Territory. It is to be hoped that this effort to open communication may be successful, as otherwise Australians have no other means of visiting Java, now that the Torres Straits mail line no longer calls at any of its ports. And Java is worth seeing—well worth seeing indeed—and no place more so.

My excursion round about Soerabaya is brought to a close by a visit to the club-house. Here a goodly orchestral band, in a rotunda in a nice garden, are playing a fine selection of music. The house and gardens are well lighted. The white attire of the frequenters of the place looks well at night-time. Coloured servants are about everywhere handing cups of coffee and glasses of schnapps, or carrying firesticks for the use of the never-ceasing smokers. My old friend, the Southern Cross, is in view again above me. For many a month have I missed it. Here, for coolness and respect, I uncover in its presence, and feel glad indeed to look upon it again. The "plough" that I saw so long in the other hemispheres was well enough there, but this southern substitute looks better and brighter. At least so it seems in these Java skies, where it looks nearer to one than in Australia.

Not much disposition is shown by folks here to visit that Australian land by the fine steamer that is shortly about to start. I find plenty of cabins disengaged. That is a blessing in one way, as it is really so warm here, and will be so all the way through Torres Straits, that a cabin to oneself is almost a necessity. The vessel proves to be a finer one than any of the boats of the Torres Straits line that I had seen, and her captain looks all over the right man. Two Germans who have tried their fortunes in Java for seven years, and only got liver complaint by so doing, are going to the more temperate air of Victoria. A sugar-planter, with his wife and little son, is taking a trip for change of air, and he looks as if he wanted it. He is also a German. The crew are Malays and the stewards Chinese. The vessel is nearly a new one, of Clyde-side build. For the first three days on our voyage we had nothing to do but to note the many islands that are always coming into view and being left behind hourly. Some of these look very inviting places, seen as we see them. Off Sandalwood Island a sensational event occurs. A case of kerosene explodes, and the flames burn the skin, in patches, of the face, neck, arms, and shoulders of a Malay seaman. It sets fire also to the little house on the lower deck in which it occurs, and finds its way among the loose sacks of coal thereabout. These add to the blaze and smoke, and general fright that seizes upon us. For a time it is a case of ship on fire; and I am glad of the sight of pleasant-looking Sandalwood Island, that is well in view. In going all over the world one expects to have a share of all sea dangers. In this fire on shipboard the second of the series had come. The first one came in the shape of running on the rocks on the Japanese coast. The third was yet to come, and came further along the road in a collision with another vessel that ran into ours whilst we waited a pilot-boat's arrival. It knocked all our boats off the davits, brought the deck's awnings down on the top of us, and generally upset all our views and arrangements for the day.

New Guinea is now to our left, and some natives come on board in the early morning with birds of paradise—stuffed ones—for sale. These are eagerly caught up by the passengers, who would have bought any quantity that offered of these lumps of feathered beauty. New Guinea is the native home of this bird, and would seem to be its chief, if not only, article of merchandise. The natives brought nothing else, and, what was very strange, wanted no money for their wares. Tobacco in any shape was the equivalent. A simple handful of the odious Javanese cigars bought me a bird of paradise that looked really deserving of its title, though New Guinea hardly comes up to one's idea of heaven. It rather tends to remind one of the hereafter in its other aspect—it is so dreadfully hot. The idea of white men ever digging there successfully for gold, or digging for anything else, is ridiculous. Labour for the white-skinned is out of the question altogether in New Guinea. To lift a shovel and carry it along would bring a shower of perspiration about one. The peculiar heat of the country is of the moist kind that indisposes the most energetic to any exertion. It is also a swampy and miasmatic land for the most part of it, and greatly productive of fever and other sicknesses to most Europeans. Hospitality might be obtained from the natives if they had wherewith to show it, but it is a poor land in that respect, and its inhabitants seem mostly to live in a state of want. Nature puts lines and bounds within which the white man may successfully labour. He fails outside of these, and New Guinea is a long way on the outside. One thing, to my mind, settled all questions about the value of New Guinea as a settlement for a white population. The Dutch have for years had possession of the northern part of it—"Prince Frederick's Land." Had their possession proved profitable—and none know better how to make profit of other folks' land and labour than the Dutch—they would long since have got possession of the whole island. Their not having done so tells, to any one who knows the Dutchman, all that I want to know about New Guinea, and all that any one needs to know.

In Java and its adjuncts I leave a country which, if it cannot be called "a dark land" equally with Africa, is due to no fault of the Dutch. They have omitted nothing calculated to "keep it dark," in all senses in which the term can be applied. It is strange, when thought is given to it, that the notion of "flying" should have ever become connected with the name of a Dutchman. He is most unlikely among men for winged flights here, and the probability of his becoming one of the cherubim hereafter is preposterous. Among humanity he takes that position for physical and intellectual heaviness that is among quadrupeds allotted to that Dutch-stomached one which, if it can be taught anything whatever, is called "learned," and is shown as a rarity, and is said also to be the least likely animal to fly.

When Peter the Hermit visited Palestine and saw its condition under the grinding, robbing rule of the Turks, into which it has again fallen, he returned to Europe, telling of the wrongs of the oppressed people, and preaching up that crusade which, 800 years ago, helped to free for a time the best part of Syria from the Turkish incubus. Another crusade is as much wanted in the same land now, and more wanted, as it seemed lately to me. There are other lands the condition of which would move to action Peter the Hermit, or any who have hearts like his. "Ten thousand of those men in England that do no work to-day," of whom Westmoreland spoke to Henry the Fifth at Agincourt, may yet find work, and renown too, in the world, if led on by such as Peter, or his more modern prototype, Garibaldi. It is disgusting to any manly mind to see the strong oppressing the weak, and living upon their labours! The disgusting sight of slavery no longer offends the eye in America, and should not be permitted under any flimsy disguise to do so in Cuba or Java. It would be better for Spain and Holland to live upon their own labours, as men and nations should do. They would thus earn the respect of the rest of the world, and that place in it which they lost when they descended to a position more disgraced by the ill-gotten wealth it brings than is that of poor pimps, pensioners, and panders.

CHAPTER XXIV.

SOERABAYA TO SOMERSET (TORRES STRAITS).

THE scenery about Torres Straits, in the neighbourhood of Port Darwin and Cape York, is a pleasant surprise to the traveller who has only previously visited the Australian shores

PORT DARWIN.

on the south, and seen their dreary appearance from seaward. What Victoria and South Australia have to show in the way of sea-shore vegetation and attractiveness to sea-weary eyes is not much to look at, and less to speak of, but on the little-visited northern shores it is all another and finer sight.

Palmerston and Somerset, the two settlements on the northern Australian coast, are nice-looking places indeed, as seen from the sea. There is a wealth of verdure about them in tropical plants and flowers down to the water's edge—a generous fulness of greenness that answers all expectation. Pretty outlying islands, about which are anchored the boats of the pearl-fishers and others, add to the charm of the scene. It is all, however, like to fine things generally, best seen at a distance. Than Somerset it would not be easy to pick out a prettier spot for a settlement, nestling, as it does, in a little bay in a narrow sea-passage, among a network of pocket-islands. If the climate did but allow it, one might reasonably wish to stay thereabout out of the way of the world and its news, adding one more to the very sparse population of this primitive-looking part of the earth.

Palmerston was settled as a substitute for Port Essington, which was then deserted. It just now looks as if the same fate awaited the new township. It had 300 of inhabitants at the time that its territory had 3000, and has now little more than 100, and the territory not more than 300. Of these the majority seem to be Government officials. There is a paid Resident, in his white residency on the cliff, and a Government harbour-master and a health officer. There are two telegraph-stations, and a staff of officials, one for the overland or local line, and the other for the English company's cable branch. A law-court and police lock-up, a post-office, and other appurtenances of a bigger town are here to be seen. Two streets, east and west, and two at right angles to them, in no particular way reclaimed from the bush roundabout, constitute about the whole of the township. Stores are set up here and there, as also several drinking-shops. All the houses are of wood, and roughly made, with six or seven stone exceptions. A printer issues a weekly half-sheet as a newspaper, but he has no news to tell. The telegraph folks will not give him any, will not give any one a single item of news, though he be, as I was, dying for it.

Palmerston, with two telegraph stations, is three months

behind Melbourne, Sydney, and Adelaide, in learning any
intelligence. Its inhabitants will be praying for the Queen's
health for that time after her decease, when that undesirable
event shall happen. In the second week of March I could
not learn which side had won the great cricket-match between
All England and Victoria on the 31st of December, nor what
horse had won the Champion Race on the Melbourne course
on the following day to that. The telegraph officials must

AN ABORIGINAL.

have known it all, but considered their lips as officially sealed
on all matters. So Port Darwin remains in darkness. The
latest newspapers to be got there—I mean those of Sydney,
Melbourne, and Adelaide—are nearly three months old. In
the United States outside towns, items of public news are
affixed daily on the exterior of the telegraph offices. So
doing can harm only the newspaper interest, and that in Port
Darwin is nothing. The Palmerston weekly print does not

publish much in the way of telegrams. It seems only to serve the purpose of publishing Government advertisements. Without that support the paper would most likely collapse.

Walking about, but more often sitting or lolling, appear everywhere the gaunt-looking natives in nearly their primeval state. They are a tall, thin, upright race, and seem mostly

A NATIVE KING.

half-starved. Nowhere had I seen such tall, skeleton-looking women. Their black faces, painted in bands of white, give a disgusting death's-head look to many of them. These natives know nothing of throwing the boomerang, and are a different kind of folk altogether to what one sees about Melbourne, Sydney, and Adelaide. They are taller and straighter, having also—the men at least—better-featured faces.

An ugly fashion of these natives is cutting across the flesh of their arms, legs, and chests, in a way that, helped by some medicating aid, leaves raised bands or ridges when the wound heals. I thought that I had seen elsewhere every fashion of disfiguring nature, but this idea of corrugating the skin was a novelty. These ridges are half an inch thick, and of the like breadth. Beauty or utility does not seem to be in any way

A NATIVE QUEEN.

served by this rudimentary attempt at tattooing. It gives one a correct idea of the position of these aboriginals as compared with that of the New Zealand Maories, who carry tattooing to the perfection of the art. These people merely disfigure themselves, but some Maori faces are made quite picturesque in their many colours. Between the savage idea of putting the colour under the skin, and the civilized one of putting it on the surface, the choice, in all reason, must be in favour of the first. Nice ruby cheeks, and coral lips, fixed in pigments by the tattooer's art at twenty-one, preserve a fresh appearance for all the time of the wearer, who is thus made beautiful for ever—or what to him or her passes for beautiful.

About the streets of Palmerston these aboriginals saunter in plenty, establishing themselves comfortably about the back-yards and dunghills of the whites. I saw a king here sitting on a dust-heap, and only knew of his regal character by the tin badge that recorded it hanging round his neck by a string. In bygone times I suppose that the native element was as conspicuous as it is here in Melbourne, Sydney, and Adelaide, where an aboriginal is never now to be seen. The fate of the man of colour to die out everywhere on the coming of the white man seems exceptional only in Africa, where the Kaffirs and Zulus give one plenteous evidence of their presence, increasing and multiplying much as they ever did.

They come to me, these lath-like, corrugated men, offering to show their skill in spear-throwing for my edification—and spare coppers. Their aspirations never rise to silver. A tree trunk is usually selected for the target, and at the distance of 200 yards is generally hit once out of three trials. A native boy officiates as runner for the arrow, which is thrown from a notched stick, on which it is for a moment balanced. As far as practicable, these natives are used by the whites as servants. In that capacity they get the name of "niggers," and learn to make an attempt at broken English. Their heads are woolly, and their skins black, in which respects alone are they like negroes. For ornaments they cut a very slender bamboo, or thick straw, into bugles of an eighth of an inch long. These pieces are strung together, and worn by men and women alike as necklets and armlets, showing in their whiteness with good effect on their wearer's blackness.

As house-servants the natives get often to be valued. For that reason they must be, I take it, a superior race to their black brethren of the southern coast, whom I had never seen so utilized. In addition to their strange tattooing they have a novel fashion of mourning for the dead. It is by cutting off a joint of the mother's finger to mark the loss of each child of hers that dies. A woman with a large family has the bad look-out before her of coming down to her stumps if her family should not be fortunate. It must be a great incentive

NATIVE MIA-MIA.

to her taking care of them, as also to her not marrying too early. Another custom permits of their killing weakly children, in place of rearing them. That practical way of illustrating the doctrine of "the survival of the fittest" is very appropriate for a district named Darwin. The women, as I have said, are miserable, scraggy beings, that look unlikely

s

to make home happy. As wives they are not, however, more ill-used than wives are too often by whiter savages.

Palmerston is the port for the up-country townships of Southport, Union, Pine Creek, and other digging grounds. Small in number as are its people, and young as it is, this Northern Territory has its history, which is something like to that detailed of himself by Dogberry—it has seen better days, and had losses. Since 1870 it has had its rise, its hey-day of success, and is now in the doleful state of finding itself daily deserted—that is to say, it would be so if there existed any means of getting away from it daily. Its rise was too fast and too artificial altogether to be sustained. The quartz reefs here are good—some very good indeed, but could not be developed so soon as shareholders expected, and so were abandoned, and the machinery, that cost thousands, sold for a few pounds. Some of the purchasers have done well. One, who bought a claim and its machinery for 700*l.*, let it to eight tributers, and has, in six months, got back his outlay, and will now look on each crushing as yielding net profits. He expressed himself as only wanting capital to enable him to make more such paying purchases. Sellers, he said, were plenty; the shareholders in Adelaide would no longer contribute funds. The mines were too far off to be inspected, and the promises held out when shares were issued had not been realized. The result of the outlay of ten, twenty, thirty, forty, fifty thousand pounds or more was thus abandoned, and its costly machinery left to rust and rot. The reefs have yielded crushings of many ounces to the ton in numerous instances.

The difficulties in the way of getting to and from Port Darwin are formidable indeed. Not only is nearly a month's time required for the voyage, but it is the most dangerous voyage that can be taken anywhere. Night after night, for a week and longer, the vessel has to come to anchor at sun-down, and so remain until sunrise. Danger from rocks and shoals is all around for three-fourths of the journey. Few vessels choose these waters for their trade. So many that have gone have suffered long delays, or total loss, that Port Darwin seemed destined to remain almost unvisited until the contract made by the South Australians with the Netherlands India Company brought a steamer to it, going or returning monthly.

By such means Palmerston and Somerset will obtain news of the busy other end of their own Australian land by way of Ceylon, Singapore, and Java, of a much later date than before —say, only two months old. A sad accident on this treacherous coast put an end to the strange farce of making Palmerston an assize town of South Australia, and sending a judge and his staff round here from Adelaide periodically. The shipwreck of the steamer, and the loss of the judge, Crown prosecutor, and other officials, ended a senseless proceeding that has not since been revived. It was in that instance senseless in all ways, as, of the two prisoners to be tried, one had been called away to appear before a higher tribunal, and the other, a Chinaman, had freed himself by "leg-bail." Port Darwin now deals with its own prisoners. One of them disposed of himself by getting on board our steamer as a stowaway.

It is useless for all sailing vessels to attempt the voyage round from Port Darwin. One unfortunate storekeeper there told me that he had started on such a voyage in the brig "Springbok" two years before, and was five months in getting round to Sydney. His partner concluded him to be lost, and so proceeded to administer to his estate by realizing the value of the stores and business, and clearing out with the proceeds to some place where money could be spent to better advantage than in Palmerston. The Great Barrier Reef is, and always will be, the trouble to navigation on this route, on which it is what Giant Despair's Doubting Castle was on Christian's road. As that was strewn around with skulls and bones, so is this with wrecks. It begins near to Cape York, where Somerset is situate, winding away down, like to a large snake in its appearance on the map, nearly to Rockhampton. Steamers that dare to go between this reef and the shore after nightfall run the risk of wreck. Two per twelvemonth is about the average rate at which they come to an end on this treacherous coast.

The pearl-fishers are of those few folks who make calls at Palmerston and Somerset. Their fishing-ground is all around about the coast here, and their neat little vessels dot the small bays that one can see from the steamer's deck, here and there, among the lovely-looking islets of the straits. A pearl-fisher, who is on shore at Somerset, shows me two small phials of pearls, that look nothing worth in my eyes, but are to him the value of 50*l.* He has a boatload of shells in the bay, for which 150*l.* or more per ton will be obtained at Melbourne. They are large shells of the size of cheese-plates, coated inside with what is called mother-of-pearl. These shells are his profit; the pearls will, he considers, pay the wages of divers, and seamen, and of provisions. For the divers the pearl-fisher has to go to some of the islands that besprinkle the seas between here and Java. The Australian native is of no use to him in that industry. When pearl-fishing was an Australian rage, three or four years ago, Palmerston and Somerset had these visitors more often and in larger numbers, but, like the gold diggings, the pearl-fishing has declined, though some boats are still engaged at it. It did not prove that certain road to a quick fortune which the world has been so long vainly endeavouring to find, and still expects.

We are received hospitably by the Palmerstonians—a likely event, as they so seldom see fresh faces. The news of the world and of their own Australian land that we had learnt two long months after date was yet all news to them. All the *élite*, "the upper ten," or perhaps fifteen, which would be about the number in Palmerston, came to tiffin on board our handsome vessel—the largest and finest ever yet in that port, and they brought their wives to an evening dance on deck, and subsequent supper provided by our liberal captain.

The Resident had unfortunately lost his wife and family recently on their voyage round to Sydney. The Great Barrier Reef, like to an octopus, caught their vessel in one of its unseen but great spreading coral arms, and there an end to it, as to so many other good vessels.

All tropical plants seem to thrive at Port Darwin. As it is in latitude 12° or thereabouts, such would necessarily be the case. Bananas are growing to a goodly size, and so are cocoa-nut-trees. It has been sensibly suggested to plant all the islands round here with cocoa-nuts, that the tall tops of these palms may be the means of more easily marking their locality to the mariner. A cocoa-nut-tree thrives best in sand and salt water, so that only the trouble of planting it is required.

After bidding adieu to the Palmerstonians, and taking about twenty-five of their sparse population away with us, we discovered that one more had included himself, unasked and unpaid for, in the number. After anger at his intrusion had passed off, amongst those innocents who had paid their passage, he was *not* put upon the nearest desert island, as first proposed, but set to work, and brought on along with the rest. It was told us that he was a criminal who had not served all of his sentence. His prison work was probably quite as easy as what we set him to do in the ship. He was not the only criminal on board, I dare say, who had not suffered all punishment that was his due.

Booby Island was the stopping-place for the night after leaving Palmerston, where, with several others, I went on shore. It is a small hill of an island, thickly covered with the sea-birds which give it its name, and which one can knock down with a stick. These and their eggs would afford plenteous food to a shipwrecked crew, as would the numerous fish that can be had thereabout for putting a line into the water. Caves abound that afford good shelter. Fresh water and wood are in plenty. Many a ship's crew would like to stay to get fresh provisions and water at this desolate island. English grass grows there in patches, and so does a sort of wild cabbage. With its caverns, wood, water, fish, and endless boobies to eat up, this Booby Island would be just the place for a hermit.

The clump of pretty islands, "summer isles of Eden," that surrounds Somerset now comes into view. We are soon threading our way through their beauties, and find an anchorage in the charming little bay around which is that sweetly-situated settlement. About fifteen houses seem to constitute the whole of it. Climbing up from the yellow-sanded shore to the rising ground upon which the houses stand, I take in the view all around, and think that the verdure-covered islands, with their yellow sands and calm bright-green waters and well-wooded shores, compose a scene of loveliness. The residents are tired of it, however, and complain of dulness. They do not appear to understand that Adam and Eve were no better off in paradise, in the way of company, and could not have had a much better garden than what Nature has here provided. In their dissatisfaction at having to stay behind while we went onwards, they spoke even disrespectfully, not to say profanely, of our first parents, to whom I so made reference. It is impossible to find folks anywhere in the world, out of Japan, who are satisfied with all their circumstances. To better them, the township of Somerset is shortly to be removed altogether to Thursday Island, about four hours' steaming off, and now preparing for that event.

An instance of aboriginal manners is afforded to us as we lie at anchor in the early morning off the mainland between Howick Island and Cape Flattery, in latitude 15°. We had to drop anchor at sundown, and lie there, sweltering in the heat of our then still air, until next morning, when I am awoke by strange noises under the cabin port-hole, and, looking out, find a canoe with four natives in it, all talking at me at once. The canoe is the primitive affair of the hollowed trunk of a tree. It has an outrigging arrangement at each side of two projecting poles, that support a third one laid transversely at their ends, and dipping into the water. That steadies the frail craft, and renders its upset not so easy. Our black-skinned visitors are tall, shapely men, tattooed in the raised ridges of flesh across their chests and arms. They do not come empty-handed, but show commercial instincts in bringing half a dozen pieces of tortoiseshell and some large finely-marked fish-shells that have mother-of-pearl lining. They have learnt sufficient English to say that they want "pipe" and " bacco " in exchange. The desired barter is satisfactorily effected. A large shell brought by the natives, that would hold nearly a bucketful of water, is filled by us with bread and tobacco, to which is added a short pipe and some Javanese cigars. The one pipe was all that we could spare. The cigars were given with that liberality with which we part with what is of no use to us. Their flavour was too strong for our taste. The aboriginal stomach is stronger, and we saw our friends begin to chew them in their raw state as we might have done with sticks of chocolate. These men were of a better appearance than the aboriginals I had seen in the more southern parts of Australia. I did not meet there with many who had such ideas of trade, or of what things would be acceptable to their white visitors.

The Northern Territory has had occasionally overland travellers. Five or six, in as many years, have been found to get safely through that terrible four months' tramp. How many others that have started on it, and not got through, will never be known—until all things are known. Those who have got to Palmerston from Adelaide in that way have carried a gun in self-defence, and had the essential aid of a faithful dog. They alone know of what real value to man is that best of all friends of his. The dog has watched by night while the man slept. At any footfall of natives heard by the dog, or known to him by instinct, in the far distance, its master has been at once awakened and put on guard against danger. By day the dog has slept while the man has watched. This mutual reliance, this sharing of danger and this companionship, has alone enabled man to overcome the difficulties that the desert and the dangers that the natives together threatened. Visitors by that overland route are not likely to do much in the way of increasing emigration, though occasionally a group have come from Adelaide or Queensland by waggon-track. The Northern Territory expects some day to have its overland railway, after the fashion of the great one in America. Such a thing looks now an impossibility, but may look differently in days to come.

Port Darwin, named after the celebrated author of the theory of man's development from the monkey, is progressing not much more successfully than the doctrines of its namesake. Its one bank thrives on extravagant percentages and discounts, of which all its customers complain. One evidence of the decline of the district was very painful to contemplate: the last of its lawyers came away in our vessel. A sailor made a remark on that circumstance that I did not quite understand. He said that it was a bad sign when the rats left the ship.

Care has been taken to mark with buoys and red-coloured boats, there anchored, all the dangerous passage from Port Darwin down to the end of the Barrier Reef, near to Port Bowen. It is on this part of the voyage that steamers have to anchor at nightfall until next morning. As full speed cannot be made always during the day, but little more than a hundred miles are ever run in the twenty-four hours. The compensation for this wearying delay is to be found in the calmness of the seas and the picturesque character of the endless islands dotting the whole length of the passage. The monotonous appearance of a wide expanse of objectless water, so productive of *ennui* to the voyager, is thus escaped on this route.

With this chapter is concluded the notes of places of interest visited on the Torres Straits route. They may have served to give some ideas of what there is to be seen by taking this route from Australia to Japan, from the ports of which latter place steamers run to San Francisco. What is to be seen anywhere depends, however, altogether on the opportunities the traveller may have or may make for himself as he goes along, as also on his observing faculties. There are those, says Sterne, " who go from Dan to Beersheba and find all barren "—which, by the way, they may very well do if that Palestine part of

Syria has always been as sterile as I saw it. There are others who, again to quote Sterne, find "that a large volume of adventure may be grasped within a little span by one who interests the heart in everything, and who, having eyes to see what time and chance are perpetually holding out on the journey, misses nothing that can be fairly appropriated." I hope to bear that in mind in the chapters on another route which a traveller between the ends of the earth may profitably take.

CHAPTER XXV.

NEW SOUTH WALES.

Sydney.

EVERY English-speaking person has heard of Botany Bay, and the remembrance of its name leaves one vague general association, and that is, with the punishment of the evil-doer. The place was never put to such purpose, but that does not matter. When popular error becomes popular belief, to eradicate it is impossible. We have no doubt that the footman would watch the coats and hats in the hall, and the butler the plate on the table, were any one within the house— a well-ordered English home—who handed in his visiting-card with this address. In our case, Botany Bay was visited as a reward for doing well—and over-doing it, and getting fatigued with application to business. To remedy this we took to the sea and its sickness, and to a voyage southward to Sydney.

The man who from the masthead of a vessel was first to see the opening in the wall of rocks that lets the sea-sick soul into Port Jackson well deserves having that haven named after him. For haven, one might interpolate a letter and write heaven, and that without subjecting oneself to correction. Sea-tossed, sick, and weary, with ocean rising up before us, dim and dark with flood and foam, and skies o'ercast with clouds and gloom, we lay on shipboard, wishing the dark night were over and that morning would come. Sickness by daylight is more tolerable than by darkness. That

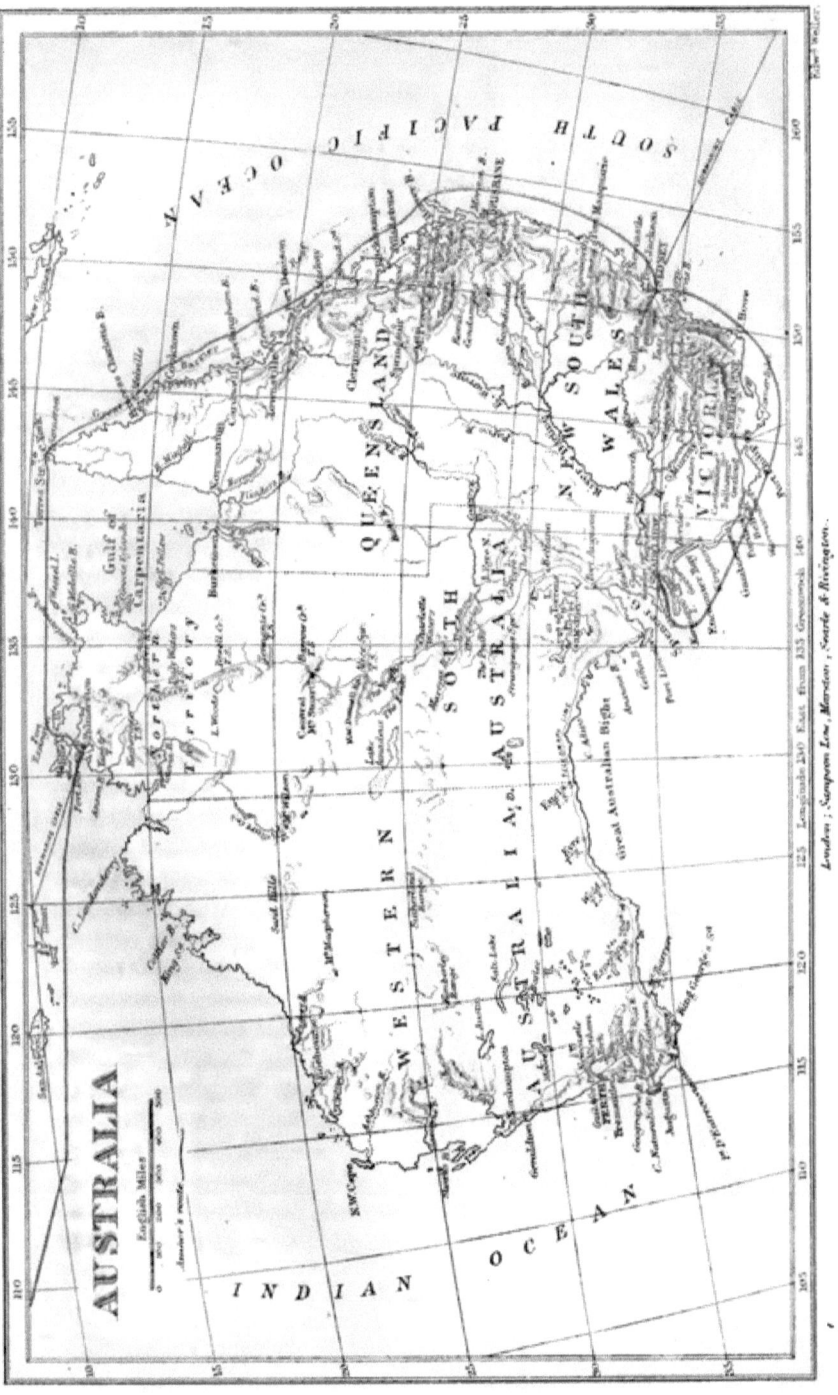

was why we wished for the morning. Not that its coming would steady the rolling and pitching vessel, and enable us to keep a steady stomach, for we had lost the idea of eating and drinking. To see others do it was nauseating to us, and we despised our fellow-man who had appetite when we had none. Our bones had begun to ache with three days and two nights' lying upon a hard mattress and rolling against the harder ship-side, or the sharp edge-side of that little shelf upon which they put away a passenger at sea. We never look at those little enclosures of six feet by two without a thought of that other six feet by two, made a little deeper, that will hold what shall be left of us yet, if we die upon dry land. There are stages of sea misery in which death loses its terrors. We talked very often in Melbourne to one of the survivors of the wreck of the "London," on board which ill-fated steamer we could count a score of friends. Our wish was to know how the death that came at the end of three days of sea-suffering in the Bay of Biscay was looked at by those who had to face it. We found that the king of terrors ceased to be terrible as, hour by hour, day by day, and night by night, cold, wet, hunger, and general wretchedness and misery had done their work upon the miserable sea-sick company. Starting as they did in wintry weather, but a few days before, they had encountered rough seas that had laid them down with sickness. These seas increased, and with them came o'erwashing waters, dark days, and bitter cold and stormy times. Fires were extinguished, and cooking and fire-comfort were at an end. All were wet and cold, and sick of stomach and of heart. The captain's forewarning of their fate had gone forth, and hope—that sheet-anchor of the mind—was lost to all. They met their doom with gladness and not with fear; for cold and hardship such work had done that none seemed sorry as death drew near. Those who have been to sea in stormy weather will know the picture that we wish to portray by this digression, and understand that we use it as a dark background to light up the bright morning that shone forth as we entered and anchored within the portals of Port Jackson.

We left dark ocean and dark-frowning rock-bound coast outside, and entered into sunshine and Sydney Harbour. We glided into smooth water also, and could keep on our feet and feel that it was as well to be alive—a thing that we had for two or three days and nights past been quite careless about. Had Sydney Harbour been nothing but a sheet of smooth and land-locked water, it would have been welcome only as such; but being what it is—a wonder of beauty—it looked to us as paradise regained. We know nothing of the Miltonian "paradise regained," any more than any one else who has never read it, and that is nearly everybody; but Sydney Harbour, on the occasion we write of, stands, to us, as the realized idea of that unread book. If we remember our Bunyan aright, we enter the land of Beulah before we get to the city Beautiful. Sydney Harbour suggests that idea. Sydney stands amid that harbour as a "fair vestal throned in the south," as a Venus risen from the sea, a sort of golden city washed by silvery waters, fringed in all their little bays and inlets and windings and turnings with an emerald verdure. Little islands dot the waters everywhere. The entrance we have passed through has been hidden from us; a turn of the wheel and we are—in fairy land. A great deal of all this feeling is no doubt owing to the escape into sunshine and smooth water from outer stormy waves and sickness; but, discounting that much from the total effect produced, what is left will support all our statement, and a little more that we will leave to the poet and the painter. The painter should certainly be Turner, and the poet Tennyson. He that wrote the "Lotus Eaters" and talked of "The land in which it seemed always afternoon," and who penned the scenery of the "Palace of Art," might do justice here to what is real, and not of the imagination. We appealed quietly to the captain of our steamer, "Anything to beat this in the way of harbours that you have come across?" "Oh, nothing that I have seen. I am told that Rio comes up to it, and that the inland sea of Japan excels it, but I have seen neither," he replied.

We think, as we look about us, that nothing but a forcible exportation would make any one wish to leave the place. That is all that we can conjecture as a reason why folks have gone to cold and leaden-clouded England when they could have stayed here. We wish, for a moment, that we had committed some early misdemeanour, or been found out in those that we perhaps have committed, and been sent out here a quarter of a century ago. We suppose we should have acted as others did, and gone back again. The Gordon rioters opened Newgate, and let loose the prisoners, but the majority of them voluntarily returned. It is human nature to be obstinate and pigheaded, and not to know when we are well off. But we are beginning to feel hungry, and will get on shore, which we do by stepping from the boat-side on to dry land by the help of a short plank. It is deep water to the land's edge all around and about Sydney Harbour; no sandy or shingled shelving shore, or mass of mud-bank at low water. A merchant can almost with his walking-stick touch the mast of his ship from his drawing-room window.

All sides and angles of Sydney, but one, run to the water's edge. The city is built upon a many-bayed peninsula, that makes a site for a city that cannot be improved upon. Nature has given a groundwork there on which no labour and toil needed to be spent, and which no amount of it can better. A yellow building-stone, that looks golden in the sunshine, is to hand everywhere, and of this all houses are now being built, or re-built, as also are all public buildings. Our idea of the golden city will be realized in a few years to every eye that shall then see it. The natural slope of the land to the bay supplies the best of drainage, and the moist exhalations of the surrounding waters keep the greenness of a well-kept and watered garden everywhere around and about. We try hard to find faults, and look for things that Nature might have bettered, but find the search a vain one. All that has been mismanaged about Sydney has been done by the works of man. The coming years, and the men to be in them, will correct all that, and the mental vision looking into the future

sees but a queenly city on Sydney site. In its nearly a
century of existence, Sydney city has grown gradually, month
by month, to what it now is. Each one of the citizens did in
the building-line that which was right in his own eyes.
Building acts and the duties of a city surveyor were unknown
to the early Sydneyites. Scarcely two houses are built after
one design or of the same materials. That would not be so
much to speak of if they had been kept to one frontage-line.
It is not altogether pleasant walking on a footway six-feet
wide in some places and only two in others, or to have to
cross a flight of steps to regain the continuation of the pathway on the other side of them. All these objections are of
those that touch upon "vested interests," and wait upon time
and Acts of Parliament to be set aright. Many of the shops
that abut upon the chief streets are built upon what a while
ago was a front garden to a private residence, and the whole
streets have grown into what they are as from time to time
traffic led to the turning of the domestic dwelling into a shop
or store. Scarcely a building in Sydney seems to have been
built originally for what it now serves. The pavement is
similarly varied in character—bits of good pathway here and
there, flagstones for a few yards, then cobble stones, then
wood planking, and then plain mud and gravel. There is
this good about it all that we see that the place is not over-
built. No rows of buildings appear to have been put up by
speculative builders. Bad as many of the buildings appear
to be in condition and exterior appearance, we can well
believe that they have all, long ago, well paid the builder,
and that what cost tens is now worth hundreds, and that
costing hundreds is now saleable for thousands. Sydney city
appears to have been never properly laid out by a surveyor.
The land was sold in large blocks, and the purchasers seem
to have sold pieces, of any shape or size, to sub-purchasers,
and to have left much to chance as to the boundaries and
measurements. The large centre of commerce that Sydney
has now grown to be was not foreseen in that dim past when
the lovely spot was used but as a convict depôt.

George-street.

No more characteristic street exists than George-street, Sydney—the main artery of the city. In shape it is very like to a dog's hind leg cut off close to the body and laid down sideways. It has the same turn of form, and widens out towards one end in much the same way. Yet it is a noble street, and a busy one, and a crowded one, and a market one, and a very wealthy one. It is two miles and a half long; seventy feet broad in some places, and a hundred and seventy and two hundred and seventy and twice that again in others. It is thickly packed with shops the whole of the way, and that on both sides—five good miles of shops! These shops are mostly like to shops in a market—with much of their goods outside the doors, and nearly all under verandahs that cover the footpath. The footpaths always seem to be crowded, and the roadway is as busy as Cheapside in London city itself. Only omnibuses and hansom cabs are used as public vehicles, and of these there appear to be an endless quantity. The strange names painted on the side panels are all that tell the wayfarer that he is not in London,—"Woolhara," "Woolloomooloo," and "Coogee," and a score of other inscriptions, bring back the wandering mind of the Londoner to his whereabouts. The market-place is in George-street, the Post Office is there, and there are the Town Hall and the railway-station, as also most of the bank buildings. It is an o'ercrowded street—a congested thoroughfare, that will one day suffer from the effects of plethora, and find its life-blood diverted to another channel. The value of land in some parts of this wonderful street must be equal to that of land in any of the busiest streets in London, Paris, or New York. Those who object to the narrowness of some parts of George-street forget that Sydney is a city in a sunny southern clime, and that in similar climates in Europe it is not the thing to have wide streets. The narrow streets and the tall houses give shade to the shop windows and their goods, and to the street passengers too, and keep house-fronts, goods, and faces cooler than wider streets would do. George-street, Sydney, is not likely to be forgotten by any who have ever seen it. We have to go up George-street to get out, seven miles or so, to Botany Bay, and we have only chatted, as we have done on our way up the street, as we talked of the harbour when coming up it. A nice green-sided country road leads to Botany Bay, and prepares us well for the green-grassed and prettily-wooded shore of the bay on which we now come. Nothing has been done to this bay since its discoverers landed on its shores a century or so ago, and made their way overland to where Sydney now stands, and saw the port and harbour, and then came back to shallow Botany Bay—to bid it adieu. The wild flowers that Sir Joseph Banks so admired, and the verdure that greeted and pleased his eyes after a long sea voyage, are there now, and so are an hotel named after him, and stone busts of himself and Captain Cook over the gateway to the hotel garden. Botany Bay is a pleasure-suburb, and was never used for any other purpose—a tea-garden, picnicking, honeymoon-spending sort of place, with a house kept in good style, where a few friends may dine together and spend an afternoon and evening, or to which one might, in early years, drive one's sweetheart, and by-and-by one's wife and family. On holidays, "high jinks" are held in the hotel grounds, and balloons go up, and the amusements of a fair are instituted, and the Sydneyites make it a day's "outing" to go to Botany Bay and back. "And this quiet, innocent, rural spot, with its Sir Joseph Banks Hotel, is Botany Bay," we said to ourselves; "this milch cow is the roaring lion with the bad name that is given to it in England; this is the quiet sheep that wears the wolf's clothing to English ears." How things are misrepresented sometimes in this world! No convict settlement was made here or within many miles of it. Tom Hood tells of a deaf woman so greatly relieved by a patent ear-trumpet that "the very next day she heard from her husband in Botany Bay." We know that that is where the laugh comes in, and we know why, and we know now how Hood was misled, and how he misled us, and how maligned that poor woman's husband was and is by those verses—in their popular sense.

"Always where least expected," we exclaimed, as we got into the chat with the then keeper of the Botany hotel, and found him to have passed his youth alongside of us in the same little street of large London. Gradually remembrances of the past grew upon each of us. Names of folks long forgotten creamed up again to the surface, and for half an hour or more we lived our boyhood o'er again, and felt about forty years or so younger. We seemed to have now a part and lot in Botany Bay, and shall consider it henceforth as of our neighbourhood. We shall, after that, expect to find a schoolfellow waiting for us on the landing-place at Yokohama or Shanghai, and an old sweetheart keeping a boarding-house at Medina or Mecca, or some other least likely place.

On the way back from Botany we passed through the Domain and Botanical Gardens of Sydney, situated quite within the city. The place is easy of access, but very difficult to leave, and impossible ever to forget—quite "a secret nook in a pleasant land, whose groves the frolic fairies planned." Nothing in the way of "parks and ordered gardens stately" —nothing of the beauty of botanical treasures from all climes in this the finest clime, and in this the fairest garden, greenly sloping, shaded to the sea—can excel these gardens of Sydney city. That tropical birds of grandest plumage are added to the scene is merely saying that nothing is omitted that could adorn the exquisite retreat from the surrounding circuit of busy care, restless crime and strife, and squabble for riches and honours. "What are they all in their high conceit, when man in the garden with God may meet?"

As we go on board the steamer that is to bring us away from Sydney's shores and sights, we notice the large number of steamers and vessels of all kinds that fill the port. A fine sight for the lovers of commerce is that. The mail steamers of the overland route from Southampton, and the mail steamers of the American San Francisco overland route are lying here—offering the choice of two enticing ways of leaving this fine scene. Steamers for other places, intercolonial ones, are everywhere, and here also are lying men-of-war steamers from England, France, and Russia. In this magnificent harbour, every country seems to be represented by its ship, and it seems right that it should be so. That is not all. Business is well represented, as we have said, and so are the great navies of the world, but here also is wealth and its pleasures represented. The fine yachts of two English noblemen have found their way hither also, for the days are now come when men paddle their own canoe to the ends of the earth.

CHAPTER XXVI.

NEW SOUTH WALES.

The Blue Mountains.

THE scene is in long, busy, winding, and shop-thronged George-street, Sydney. The time, the eve of Christmas. The *dramatis personæ* are four visitors from Melbourne, casually met. Their dialogue follows:—

"What are you going to do with yourself to-morrow, White?"

"I have thought of nothing as yet, Black; how with yourself?"

"Well, I was thinking of calling upon Brown, here, at the Royal, to ask him to come with me up the Zigzag Railway, over the Blue Mountains and back, to fill up the day."

"I'd thought of going there when leaving Melbourne, but it had gone from my mind. Now I think of it, I shall go also."

"We'll see Brown, then, and ask him. Oh, here he is! What do you say, Brown, to going with us up the Zigzag rail to-morrow, and over the mountains to Bowenfells and back?"

"Can that be done in a day?" said Brown.

"Oh, yes; look at Bradshaw—there is one in the office, I daresay."

And to Bradshaw we referred, and that was confirmatory of our idea, which was that we could start from Sydney at nine in the morning, get to Bowenfells, and see the wonderful descending terraces of zigzags there; get something to eat there, and drink toasts in honour of Christmas Day and all friends far away, and then return at night by the train—set down in Bradshaw as starting at twelve—and sleep all the way back to Sydney. The excursion was desirable on several grounds. The Zigzag Railway, beginning its ascent of the Blue Mountains at Lapstone Hill, was an engineering wonder. Nothing can be shown to equal it in Europe, nor on the huge railway across the American continent, though two ranges of mountains have to be passed in its course. That was one reason; another was, that the air of the Blue Mountains was a good change from that of Sydney, and the scenery the finest that the eye could delight in; and, further still, there was the greater reason of the journey affording something to do on a day when it is most miserable to be shut up in a city where one knew nobody, and to think that every one was enjoying the Christmas festival of friendship save and except one's own isolated self.

Fine and fair broke the morning, and punctually we all met at the railway-station. To save any after remorse, extra care was taken by us to inquire as to the return train to Bowenfells at twelve that night. Bradshaw might be wrong. He had not erred, we were told, and no further care remained. A very pleasant feeling that!

The carriages were large and the seats broad, well adapted for sleeping, we said, on our night journey back. The windows, too, were of the right height and size for our having a long look around at all which was to come in our way. It came very soon, too, for we were quickly whisked up to the foot of the ascent, and our train began to go up stairs. We will pause for a moment—though our train did not—just to breathe. The Blue Mountains of New South Wales stretch away from within a short distance of Sydney to the neighbourhood of Bathurst, a good day's journey right through. The trouble to reach the far-away summit, up the steep side, is only the beginning of trouble. When the top of one mountain is gained, the tops of all the others have to be crossed; for it is a huge jumble of mountains that has to be traversed, with dark wooded and rocky valleys everywhere between and around. Through the whole long length of that line there is scarcely a straight hundred yards of road. It is zigzag up the sides, zigzag on the top, and zigzag to the bottom, when the ride is over. When it is over, it is not a ride that will be forgotten.

We remember ascending a staircase in a square tower in a Belgian town, up which we went some twenty-five steps forward to a landing, and then faced about to go twenty-five more steps to another landing, and then right about again, and so on to the top. That is the way that the Zigzag is ascended on Lapstone Hill, with this little difference, that in ascending the tower staircase, we faced about at each turn, which the train does not. The engine pulls up for half a mile or so, and then pushes for another half mile, and then another pull, and a repeated push, and so lugged and pushed, the level earth is left quickly far away beneath us. All heads are out of the windows now, looking over at the staircase-like road down away below us, and up which we were dragging a few minutes past. The feeling is decidedly new and sensational. The landscape, too, lights up, as it were, differently as each further ascent is made, and larger views around obtained. The head gets giddy at some stages of the journey, where but a little projection of earth or stone seems to be between the roadside and all that lies so very far away down there. We think that if our iron horse were but to bolt, or to become restive and upset the coach, how little talk about it we should be likely to have after the accident. It is seen, however, that the engine is of the strongest and largest, the gauge of the line of the broadest, and, though but a single line of rails, we see plainly that the traffic on this wonderful line is not such as to lead to any fear of other trains running into us before or behind. The idea that there is but one train a day—and that probably the same engine takes it back again—allays all nervousness on that score. The Blue Mountains line was not constructed, we believe, with any idea of its being a paying concern. The country it "opens up" must be a long way ahead, for the mountain tops we have now reached, and the dark valleys all around us can be only dwelling-places for opossums, wild cats, and eagle-hawks, now and for ever. The tops of the mountains afford payment in scenery for all the trouble in getting thither. Our train now and henceforward takes to a serpentine movement, and that unceasingly. On looking out of the window—and all heads are outside—we see either the engine or the last carriage of the train about broadside on to us, always one or the other. In and out, and winding about everywhere, did the makers of this difficult road go to find their way. How they ever found it and made any road whatever is all the astonishment. Cuttings through here and there in short tunnels—cuttings down on this side and on that, and now and again on both sides—filling up of great gaps, and making winding viaducts over others—was of the work to be done everywhere. We never tire of looking out of the windows. The trouble is that we cannot look out on both sides at once. The scenery varies at every turn, and the turn is every minute, and the views are of the finest on both sides—wild ravines of torn and upheaved rock, with no speck of vegetation or trace of life of any kind—darkly-wooded valleys of all depths and variety of characteristics, on which the sun and the driving fleecy clouds make picturesque effects of light and shade—are to be seen from one side or another in endless profusion. Little stations are reached every now and then and stopped at, apparently for form's sake. The idea of taking up passengers from the population hereabouts never enters the mind. We have got beyond passengers and taxes. A man might dwell here and never get into the census. In times gone by a monastery would have been perched upon one of the lonely peaks, or on the side of one of these inaccessible valleys, after some holy hermit had chosen such place for his peculiar life, and got sainted for so doing. It may happen so yet, for that which has been will be. An oasis comes at last, when One Tree Hill, or Mount Victoria, is reached. A most delightful spot is this, as it naturally would be, considering all the difficulty in getting to it. From here the Weatherboard Falls can be seen, which Von Guerard has so well painted. Here, also, is a huge valley, which has been bridged with evidently great labour and expense. On the one side of this bridge the view is into the wildest of rocky and craggy depths, and on the other into a long, cultivated valley of green fields and farms. It is as if this bridge parted the goats and their rocky residence upon the left hand from the sheep and their green pastures upon the right. There are two good hotels at One Tree, and a road that leads on to Hartley, distant some few miles, and connected with kerosene produce and coals. A week could be very well spent about here by those wishing for that time's breath of mountain air. We got on by the rail after this towards Bowenfells, through similar scenery of mount and valley to that which we had seen all the morning. Towards three o'clock we came to the descending zigzag—the downstairs-going business—and to our journey's end. This descending zigzag far exceeds, in every novelty, the ascending one. It is a stupendously grand affair. Slopes and turnings, turnings and tunnels, viaducts and sweeping descents, each down many hundreds of feet, that go as near to danger as practicable, and no further. All heads are looking out and downwards during these descents, and when it is over and done, all heads are turned upwards, and so remain for some time with the fixed stare of astonishment. This point was as far as the rail then reached. At the Bowenfells station we said to the porter,—

"The train starts at twelve punctually, does it not?" We don't know why we should have said so, for we had made quite sure about that at the beginning of the journey.

"No," he said; "no train to-night, and none back to Sydney until twelve to-morrow night!"

Open-mouthed dismay was all the answer we could show. Porter did not know nor care what had been said at the other end; he was right. We were in for it at Bowenfells for the rest of that day—that night—the next day and the next night —until that long twelve o'clock came. Company we could have in plenty, if we fancied any of the angry-looking faces around us. We whispered the porter, "How far off to the village—to Bowenfells?" "Three miles" was the answer. "How do you get there?" we said. "That 'bus will start presently," he said, pointing to a little affair that would hold about ten of the thirty or more that were waiting its departure. "A good hotel at Bowenfells?" we queried of our porter. "One house," he said, "and not of much account." Words were now raised between the 'busman and the passengers who "rushed" his vehicle. They must come off. He would only take so-and-so, for whom he had expressly come. They, however, would not get down, asserting the nine points of possession ; and so out came the horses from the traces to settle the question on the 'busman's part. Our necessities sharpened us. We said, "If that lot gets to the hotel before us, they will make a famine for those that follow." It was really a case of the devil taking the hindmost. Strolling carelessly away, as if waiting for a vehicle, as the others were, we got ahead, and then put on a good pace, which we increased as we warmed to the work. Fortune favoured us for trusting to her as we did. We reached the hotel, and quietly spoke of dinner. We could have it. It was just ready—turkey, beef, plum pudding, and mince pies. We could have that room at the end, looking out into the pretty garden, too. All right. We took that room at once, and as we were strangers we thought it best to prepay for our dinners—to landlord's surprise. After that, Brown got the table-cloth and spread it. White fetched in the turkey and the beef, and Black got hold of the pudding, some beer, and two bottles of wine—saving the astonished handmaiden nearly all trouble—and then the blinds were pulled down, and the door locked. It was only done just in time. We heard the tramp of horses and of feet, and the sound of voices, and knew that the Philistines were upon the landlord. We had bagged the dinner. A photograph is very commonly known, in which a cat is shown complacently grinning out that "it has eaten the canary." Our faces must have had a similar expression to that cat's. We should have been dealt with as we had dealt had we come late. We agreed that what we had got was due to our very superfine intelligence—to which we mutually drank in the good wine that we had nabbed. All due honour was done to Christmas, and all friends properly remembered —including the thirty just outside. When all was over, and the dinner finished that we had so grabbed, we went out through the window into the garden, not wishing to arouse any feelings that the turning of keys might agitate. We came gradually round at last upon the landlord, and in the most commonplace manner introduced the subject of beds. He was not in a good temper. Neither was his wife nor the servant-girl—the latter being particularly waspish, as if she now understood why so much help had been shown her in dressing our table and getting in the dinner. She really looked as if she had been taken advantage of in some way.

A stroll about pretty little quiet Bowenfells—a happy valley of Rasselas embosomed in the mountains—opened our eyes to the fact that we had to stay there for some time yet, unless our wits devised a way thereout. In the yard of a baker and storekeeper we saw a dog-cart and came to council at once. Thirty miles further on across the mountains, by a good coach road, lay Bathurst—second of the cities of New South Wales. If we could get that dog-cart we could start when the moon rose —about eight—take a moonlight drive to Bathurst, stop there a day and get back to the station in time for next night's train. The same thought would of course occur to others, so now to seize the opportunity. The door of the store was open, and in the parlour was seated an idiotic, gibbering youth, who only bawled at us in reply to our questions. His father was asleep in a back room, and on our rousing him and quietly putting the business before him, he agreed to let us have the cart and a horse for so much. We at once counted it out to him and took a receipt—we felt as if we had eaten another canary! At all events we were independent of beds and landlords in Bowenfells, and had something now to well occupy our time, and make memorable our hitherto remarkable Christmas Day.

In the calm summer's evening, with a big bright silver moon o'erhead, we three thankful children of tact went away over the Blue Mountains, with a good horse before us and that feeling of happiness that comes from reflection on well-spent time—an especially happy feeling after a good dinner. The silver clouds were sleeping about everywhere in the hollows of the mountains—a very curious effect, seen in the bright moonlight, against the backgrounds of dark verdure everywhere around. The fresh rarefied air, at the height we then were, had a champagney effect upon the spirits; and had any one, short of a bushranger, wanted to get money from us, it might have been had for the civil asking. We were glad that we could not have gone back to Sydney. There would have been nothing in the way of business to do on the next day—Boxing-day—and here we were trying to realize Disraeli's aphorism that "adventures are to the adventurous."

CHAPTER XXVII.

SOUTH AUSTRALIA.

Adelaide.

IN 1852 I first saw Adelaide, two days before arriving at Melbourne. In 1876, twenty-four years after, I saw it for the second time, two days after leaving Melbourne. The intervening time had been passed in that mill-horse round of business that habit alone relieves from irksomeness. "The labour we delight in physics pain," says Shakspeare, and much of the delight we have in labour is from habit—that second nature that accustoms us, thank Providence, to all things. When I saw Adelaide in 1852, it was at the end of a long sea voyage from England. We had to approach it by passing Kangaroo Island, and going up the river, the Yatala, something like to the Yarra at Saltwater River, and dropping anchor at an outlet called the North Arm, about two miles or so from the port. Thither some of us went, at the cost of 10s., on the deck of an empty water-tank, and of our little number three were fated to meet with a watery grave. Something attracted attention to one side, and the rush thither caused our unballasted craft to turn over, leaving us all struggling in the water. In sight of the shores that they had travelled 16,000 miles to see, three of us struggled in vain. A Cornish clergyman and his daughter, and a young and promising actor, were the victims—a sad slip between the cup and the lip, and a sorrowful introduction of the wet survivors to their long-sought land. That land looked all the worse for it, and felt as badly as it looked. The day was broiling hot, and the dust, heat, and flies had all the special annoyance of novelty in their several ways of misery. We intended to have got up some feeling appropriate to the occasion of landing in Eldorado, but our bodies and our spirits had been too damped to permit of any enthusiastic warmth showing itself. The landscape looked barren and yellow, hot and thirsty. The first hot wind we had felt kissed us with the breath of an oven, and dirtied and blackened us with dust and grit. We had dressed in our nicest to come on shore, too, which intensified the grief felt at seeing what wretched scarecrows we all then looked.

Port Adelaide was then a sort of primitive Sandridge, containing a few buildings, mostly of wood. It was eight miles from Adelaide proper, the way to which was along a half-made road, with cottages here and there, deserted mostly by dwellers who had gone to the diggings. There was no conveyance to be had. Half our number were for paying another half-sovereign to return to the ship, which now seemed to us a haven of refuge indeed. Stouter hearts were owned by the others, who, having landed to see Adelaide, would see it. A long drink, of some stuff or other, was obtained at a long price—I remember its deliciousness to our dusty tongues and thirsty throats—and we then set out on our walk to Adelaide, crossing the Torrens River, unknowingly, by the way. It was, of course, dried up, as it often is. Our clothes had dried upon us, but got soaked again in perspiration on that walk. All that "half-way houses" could supply us with did not seem to quench the thirst of that day and that walk. We looked at the deserted cottages, and envied the absentees. Wherever they were, they could not, we thought, but be better off.

Adelaide I had heard spoken of in London as a desirable place for emigrants, and it had, indeed, obtained a hold as such upon the female imagination. It was looked upon as something between Paris and Paradise. We thought of all that as we neared the township, and looked at the reality of that ideal. We grimly smiled, spite of our many miseries, at the idea of any one in womanly shape wanting to come to such a place. Remember that this was in 1852. Adelaide, as a town, looked then, to the eyes of a Londoner, about as wretched as could be imagined. Two streets, partly built upon, and half a dozen ones diverging therefrom and but just commenced, constituted all of it. Wooden buildings, "wattle and dab" huts, of about 8 ft. or so high, were the prevailing buildings. A brick house would be visible here and there, a brick tavern or two, and a roughly-built stone church, and a primitive post-office. Roads and side-walks and gutters were all rudimentary. Creeks and chasms ran down the sides of the streets, serving drainage purposes. The few oil lamps lighted at night were of no service to the pedestrian, save to guide his stumbling feet to the taverns that might show them. Adelaide was then about seven years old. As seen by us then, and under the circumstances mentioned, we did not fall in love with it. I left the Lord Admiral, in Hindley-street, then the leading hotel, without any regrets. I had not taken my ease in my inn—the mosquitoes prevented that; my first night in Australia had been a sleepless one, spite of the miseries and fatigue of the day. For twenty-four years I never went back to Adelaide, so prone are we to think that things remain as we leave them.

They have changed altogether, however, as far as Adelaide is concerned, in that time. The scrubby little village is now a pretty little city. The Lord Admiral is not now the first hotel. In fact, it is very far, indeed, from being the first hotel, and its owner, no doubt, will readily admit as much. When Rip Van Winkle came down from the mountains, he saw similar changes to what astonished my eyes. Is it possible that this is the miserable little hole that I left in 1852—yesterday, as it seemed to my vivid memory? Dear me! what a long sleep I must have had, and how things have been improving whilst I have been sleeping and working! Let me take a look around.

No more of the port and the long dusty road of eight miles thence to the city. *Nous avons changé tout cela.* The landing is now at Glenelg, a place like as Brighton is to Melbourne, and of about the same distance. A jetty, somewhat longer than the Brighton one, and wood-built, there receives passengers from the little steam launches that bring them from the anchorage in the roadstead. Glenelg has no harbour or breakwater. The landing is like what it is on the West Coast of New Zealand, and, in rough weather, is, perhaps, attended with sea difficulties. The steam launch imposes a shilling tax, that may some day be relieved by a longer jetty and a breakwater; such are of the things that are to be in another twenty-four years. Glenelg has a nice hotel, some well-built waterside residences, some dozen or so of stores, a post and telegraph office, and a line of rails down the centre of the street, or chief street of the place. We take our tickets at the office, a wooden shed, superintended by a lady, and wait for the train to Adelaide. All very nice, indeed, and a great improvement on my landing, in the fashion described, twenty-four years ago. The post and telegraph department are, like to the railway shed, superintended by a lady. Femininely named, Adelaide patronizes feminine labour, we perceive, and we don't object to it. The sending of two or three telegrams, and the posting of as many letters, takes up the time while waiting for the train, which now comes up the centre of the street. It seems a modification of the tramway system, this running a train down the centre of a street, for we soon perceive that the terminus at Adelaide is in the centre, or nearly so, of its principal thoroughfare—broad, well-built, and handsome King William-street. It is a primitive sort of railway, with roughly-built and large-carrying-capacity carriages, but answering its purposes admirably.

The country looks nice and undulating to our right, and the range of hills in front of us smile in the sunshine. Adelaide lies at their feet, and we now draw up in its chief street, separated only by a planted enclosure, called Victoria-square, from the busy part of the city. King William-street is about as long as Collins-street, with a sky-line at both ends—a great improvement upon Melbourne's plan of building up the ends of her chief street with a Treasury and a railway station. The towered Post Office stands on one side, and the towered Town Hall on the other side of this fine street, and have a highly pleasing effect as seen from the railway carriages, or from any other part of the city or its outskirts. The Post Office is admirably built; the public are admitted to a covered hall, around which are all the postal and telegraphic offices. In Melbourne they are kept on the outside of the building, and the effect altogether is in favour of the accommodation afforded by the Adelaide office. It is a finished affair, which is more than can be said for the Melbourne Post Office. Finished, indeed, are all the public buildings of Adelaide that meet my view, and seemingly more adapted in size to the city than are those of Melbourne to its size. The Supreme Court buildings are just what they should be, and are there and finished, and not in the far future, and likely to be unfinished then, as some nearer home. Nothing so disgraceful to a city as the unfinished Parliament Houses of Melbourne meets the eye in Adelaide. What is done appears to be well done, and to be finished and done with.

Our old friend, the dusty road from the port to the city, across the River Torrens, is now supplanted by a railway over its course. Merchandise and intercolonial steamer and sailing traffic are taken to and fro by this line, and not by that of Glenelg. The port stands in the relation of the Queen's Wharf at Melbourne. The city is well supplied with water, and passably well paved, and, as to the roads, satisfactorily metalled. The absence of the blue-stone, that gives such a dingy appearance to parts of Melbourne, is supplied by a brownish-coloured freestone, or sandstone, which appears to take the place of both blue-stone and brick, and has a better general effect than either of them, or of both combined. The banks and their buildings crop up everywhere in the leading street, as they do in Collins-street, Melbourne, with the same well-known names on them. The Bank of Adelaide, a most successful local enterprise, of some ten or twelve years old, is now paying 10 per cent. dividends, and is about to build for itself the regulation banking palace that successful banks affect. The Exchange is well situated and attended—an improvement on the Melbourne institution in that line. The names of well-known Melbourne merchants appear here and there on branch establishments, equal in appearance to those owned by them in Melbourne.

The hospital is nicely situated next to the gardens, and is altogether a well-built and well-cared-for place, differing pleasantly from that affair in Macquarie-street, Sydney, which is still tolerated as the leading hospital of New South Wales. Adelaide does not rejoice in the suburbs that go to make up the greatness of Melbourne, and has no such reserves and parks as Carlton and Fitzroy Gardens and Albert Park. North Adelaide is, however, a sort of East Melbourne and South Yarra to the city, and is well studded with the villas and goodly houses of very kind and hospitable folks. No special folk beyond the English appear to have chosen Adelaide. Ireland did not seem to be better represented than Israel, and the latter is well represented wherever there is business to be done and money to be made. Adelaide offers both opportunities, in its slow and sure sort of way.

Very distinctive in Adelaide, Melbourne, and Sydney are the street conveyances. In Sydney, the hansom cab is the most conspicuous; in Melbourne, the one-horsed Albert car is the peculiarity; and in Adelaide, a four-wheeled, heavy-looking wagonette, drawn by two horses, is the most seen among the means of conveyance. Next to the lumbering, brougham-like vehicle with two horses, seen in Hobart Town, it appears to the least advantage. A few omnibuses, drawn by four horses, are also visible, and are presumably only used for long stages. In the matter of road traffic and its means, Melbourne appears to most advantage of all the Australian colonies.

As handy to the city centre as they are in Sydney are the Botanical Gardens of Adelaide, and better kept than are those of Melbourne. The zoological element is also, as at Sydney, combined with them. All that a city needs seems to be well supplied to Adelaide, except in the matter of theatres and amusements. In such there is a woful deficiency, and Melbourne stands immeasurably superior. Nothing like a theatre can anywhere be seen. The inquirer for it is directed to a tavern in Hindley-street, of plain two-storey appearance, at the rear of which he is told there is a theatre, opened now and then in the course of the year. The word "stalls" is seen over a side-door, that confirms the truth of the apparently incredible statement that this paltry apology is the only theatre of this fine city. A concert-room, like our Hockin's Rooms, called White's, stands in King William-street, and is also occasionally opened. The visitor thinks of Melbourne's grand theatre and Opera House, open all the year round, with its St. George's and other halls, and thinks, too, that Adelaide must be somewhat sleepy, to say nothing more of the matter.

The streets might be better lighted, too, after dark. They are well provided with police, and these officials look after their business sufficiently well to prevent the visitors' eyes being shocked by night-sights that are to be seen in Melbourne streets. Beauty, in silks, satins, and jewellery, is not to be seen and heard in those drinking, fighting, and abusive states that are too common to Melbourne eyes. Adelaide, as becomes its queenly, feminine name, is highly proper and well-behaved. Churches and chapels abound. Not a dancing-room is to be seen, nor did I see there the crowds of ragged children that run about Melbourne streets, apparently as unowned as the dogs in Constantinople. The dirty, demoralizing Chinese element, too, is pleasingly absent. A well-to-do, thriving, sound, healthy, industrious, but rather quakerish city is the Adelaide of 1876—a place that I should feel safe in owning property in, and which only owns to one want—that of labour, and seems able to employ profitably all that it may obtain.

CHAPTER XXVIII.

NEW ZEALAND.

West Coasting and Landing.

NEW ZEALAND, it is usual to say, as everybody knows, is long from south to north, and short from west to east. There is much more, ever so much more, of the short than of the long about it. In shape it is something like to a long stocking—one that garters above the knee. Cutting off the foot at the instep, the toe part will well represent the third or southernmost island, called Stewart's—the name of some whaler who has managed to stick his name on it. The whole of the three islands might with better grace be called "Cook's," after the famous captain who, in the last century, five times visited them, surveyed them, and introduced to their shores pigs and potatoes—blessings that have thereabout increased, multiplied, and replenished the earth. A cut made at another part of the stocking—through the upper part of the calf—will represent Cook's Straits, that divides the middle from the north island. A very tight garter above the knee will stand for that isthmus part of the north island that joins the harbour of Manakau on the west coast to that of Auckland on the east. The whole length of the three islands is about 1100 miles, a week's unpleasant journey in the coasting-steamers. Our business just now will be with the west coast only. New Zealand of the future will be paradise to yachtsmen. Lying as it does, surrounded on all sides by the Pacific Ocean, and indented here and there with the loveliest of bays,

channels, and sounds, it is the place, of all others, for those who love to navigate their own canoe. On the southern end of the western coast there are about nine inlets of great prettiness. You sail into lovely little bays, and sail out again—unable to land anywhere. High mountain walls oppose any aggression, and discharge at your head here and there, through their dense verdure-covered fronts, rushing cascades of melted mountain snow. Everywhere these waterfalls are rushing down—making the only music in the stillness of those birdless and lifeless woods. When you *can* land on the west coast, there is no pretty bay, or bay of any sort, to receive you. An open ocean roadstead lies fronting the flat land that the traveller seeks to set foot upon. His steamer comes to a stop a mile away from shore, from which another and smaller steamer comes away, through the surf, to fetch him to the strand. On that strand the long rolling waves of the Pacific break, break, break, in a high-swelling surf. "The long wash of Australasian seas" that Tennyson sings about, can be seen to perfection at Hokitika and Taranaki—both on the west coast of New Zealand. The small steamer that comes to fetch you from the large one comes not too near to it, but sends a whale-boat off to you that she has had in tow. The whale-boat comes alongside with four seamen in it. One steers it clear of your steamer's side, another holds on to the steps with a boat-hook, and two stand at the fore-part to grab hold of you when a wave raises their boat to a level with the gangway on which you are standing—and trembling and shuddering. It is a very odd sensation, seeing this boat and these men rise some twelve or sixteen feet on a wave, and feeling them lay hold of you, anyhow, and down with you in their arms. You lose your hat generally, and have a faint idea that your head has gone also. Put on one side in the boat, you have to wait until the other passengers, destined like to yourself, are similarly caught and lodged alongside of you. Rising again and again on the tops of these waves to catch passengers is very sensational. It would make even Sir Charles Coldstream's pulse beat quicker.

The little game is repeated when the boat has got alongside the smaller steamer that has to carry you in to shore through the surf. You are then caught by two seamen, standing at the gangway, when the wave raises the boat to the level of their deck. Babies are landed first. The anxious mother in the boat has to surrender her charge to the arms of the boatman, who, when the wave pleases, delivers it to the seaman above. When there are several babies, mistakes will occur. Anxious mother, on reaching the deck and rushing for her baby, will get the wrong one given to her. Her terrified appeal on that matter is answered this way:—"The number is all right, mum; some babies are down below; you can go down to the cabin and change it." Danger sometimes begins before one gets into the surf, for on our little steamer drawing up anchor to start for the shore, a wave carried her against the sides of the large steamer, and crash—like to breaking a match-box—went the small boat that hung upon the davits at her side. That was another sensation. The next wave might have smashed the smaller steamer, had it not managed to steam away. And then you go through the surf, and are told how lucky you are to get through it so well, and how it often welcomes you to the west coast with its salt, wet kisses, and now and again takes you bodily in its cold, moist embrace, and drenches you and half drowns you in its green and white, foamy caress. So you land on the shores of the Te Wai Pounuma (the water of the green-stone), the middle island of New Zealand, half-way south and north on which stands Hokitika. You cannot always land there when you will, but must wait and wait until weather and tide permit.

The distinguishing characteristics of the west coast of New Zealand are high mountains with snow-covered tops, and a thickly-wooded country. The forests are of the densest, most impenetrable kind. Tall trees struggle up to thirty, fifty, and eighty feet high, very close together. The life of these trees, equally with their growth, is a great struggle. A Dorsetshire labourer, rearing a family of twelve on eight shillings a week, is the nearest approach that we can think of to the troubles of these trees—they have such encumbrances. Each one looks like to the figures in the sculptured group of the Laocoon. Thick, ropy vines, and other clinging things called Supple Jacks, encircle the trunks and branches like to so much wire-made rope. Having reached the tree-top, these clinging, snake-like parasites descend on all sides, hanging down like to so many loose ropes, until the branch or trunk of a neighbouring tree can be seized by them. Some of these clinging encumbrances have a peculiar arrangement of outer prickles that catch hold of everything that they touch, and never let go. The New Zealanders funnily, but with a leaning to sarcasm, call them Lawyers. These down-hanging and out-spreading affairs make quite a net-work, and to get through most part of the west coast forest is tremendous work. With the aid of a tomahawk and reaping-hook, perhaps half a mile a day might be cleared, and a passage two feet wide to that extent be effected. After seeing the park-like lands of Australia, the New Zealand bush on the west coast presents a great contrast—for the worse. Cattle sent into this bush can only be got out again by trained dogs sent into it for that purpose.

Hokitika is Ballarat East brought down to the sea-side. Its long, fine Revel-street represents the Ballarat East Plank road; and it has a wooden road also, in the shape of a tram-way, running the length of it, on which cars go to diggings fourteen miles away. Tramways are specialities in Hokitika, another one running for five miles or more inland to the Kanieri (Canary) diggings. At these diggings, and at the others at Piper's Flat, Staffordtown, Waimea, and Rosstown, we could not but notice the use made of flumes—long gutters of wood, supported on sticks twenty feet or more in height, bringing and taking away water for dozens and dozens of miles. Hokitika is of the wood—wooden. The site of the town was cut out of the wood—the stumps of the trees stand thickly everywhere—the houses are all cut out of wood also—wood strews the beach, and an eternity of fire-wood is ever before one's eyes. From wood to water, and water to wood, all the streets run. It is a grand sight in the morning to see the sun upon the snow-covered tops of the thickly-wooded mountains that make the majestic background to Hokitika. They are so near and yet so far, these mountains. In the matter of fresh water, there is pretty Maihinaipau (Mayheenaypaw) river, and its prettier lake, to supply all desires. The row on this delightful river to the lovely lake at its source, some twelve miles up, is a very great treat. It took a day—a fine sunshiny and balmy day it was—to do it in, and that day was well spent. The lake is of large extent—miles across—of clearest, purest water, fringed with trees and pretty vegetation, with the grandest of backgrounds of hill and mountain scenery. Those who get no gold at Hokitika are well repaid for their labour in going there and back if they but see the surrounding beauties of the place—the grand scenery of the coach-ride to the east coast, the beauty of Lake Maihinaipau, the Fern Tree gullies and gulches of Kanieri, and the delightful scenery on and beyond the tramway-ride to Waimea. Hokitika—like to Dunedin, to the Otago gold-fields, and to the famous Thames—has made large drafts upon the population of Victoria. The Irish are said to look with contempt upon Scotland as a country that they had peopled; a special legend assigning the little job as one of the many wonderful things that St. Patrick took in hand. The Victorian can look in the same spirit upon all the New Zealand gold-field townships and their inhabitants. He sees old friends and well-known faces everywhere, and, where he least expects it, has to answer to his name. At wild Waimea, seventeen miles to the north of Hokitika, and in mountain Rosstown, as many miles on the south, we came upon long-forgotten folks, people that we had supposed to be dead years ago. We speculated seriously on this matter of recognition and identification of ourselves in out-of-the-way places, and came to the conclusion that New Zealand is no place to go to for any one who wishes to travel under a name not got by fair christening.

Melbourne banks and Victorian industries are well represented all about the town. The names over most of the stores are names that we remembered elsewhere some time back. Cobb's coach is there of course, and Cobb's drivers too, one of them keeping the best hotel in the place. The theatre was in full play with Melbourne supplies. The diggers at Kanieri and Waimea and Rosstown had mostly come thither by way of Victoria, and gratefully remembered whence they came. Not a few of them intended returning, but colonists and emigrants are always going to go somewhere or other. We know several who have been "going home," as they call it, for ten years past. Of course they are going home daily—we all are, and that is the only home (and may be the best one) that the majority will ever see.

A long trudge on a heavy sandy beach takes the traveller to Rosstown road. It opens on the Pacific Ocean, and runs up in a straight level line for about two miles back to the foot of distant dark mountains. This road is something like to the long middle walk in Windsor Park; a long tramp it is, so straight and level. At the foot of the mountains lies the town of Ross—an affair of stores and diggers' huts. In every sense of the word, digging seemed to be very uphill work here. One noticeable feature was that six of our fellow-passengers by the steamer were all located together in one store. They were six pretty girls who had been selected in Melbourne for that qualification, and taken down, on liberal terms, to be grog-shop attractions, and to supplement the afternoon's drinking with the night's dancing. They had looked so scrubby in their sea-sickness that we scarcely knew them when that beauty, which was truly but skin deep, had returned to their faces. Their landlord proprietor had, with a fine taste for the romantic, re-christened them all in a pretty way. He evidently thought that there was something in a name, whatever Shakspeare might have said about it. Blanche, Christine, Cora, Stella, Amy, and Constance were names that we could only hope their new owners would always recollect and reply to. They did not do it when we were there, for Maggie and Polly answered as naturally as possible to those names as if Blanche and Constance were not within earshot. Their term of servitude had been fixed for six months, and a promissory note, representing a twenty-pound penalty, had been taken from each, to be enforced if they sought a change before the end of that time. The husband taking one of them would have to take up that note as well. The speculation, on the landlord's part, we looked upon as a tolerably good one—as the world went at Rosstown.

All about our road everywhere grew the native flax. The New Zealand flax has yet to have its day. It will be heard of, and that very profitably. A wonderful plant is this flax. Growing in the sands, growing everywhere, is this strong, hardy, useful flax. Seen at first, it may be taken for a very large and flourishing fleur-de-lys. Its leaves are so shaped, and the whole plant resembles that garden favourite. These leaves, scraped with a knife, show an inner layer of fibrous thread, of great strength and silky appearance. A resinous gum has to be carefully scraped off these threads, and they are then fit for all flax purposes. To get this gum off economically, and to leave the white silky thread unencumbered, is all the problem. We could do it easily enough with a penknife and comb, but such treatment of wholesale quantities is not the way. It won't pay. The four thousand pounds reward offered by the Government of New Zealand for a better way will be claimed some day, and then the wild flax will go to the front with a rush. Meanwhile it is used by the Maories for making rugs, satchels, ropes, and shoes, and by the settlers for harness and other purposes where tenacity and flexibility are required. Every roadside broken trace is mended with it. Rope, cordage, and twine grow in that way all around the traveller.

The boatman that took us to Lake Maihinaipau we had met before under very different circumstances. On the first occasion he was going from Melbourne to England on board the ship "General Grant." He was one of the fourteen survivors of that wrecked vessel who some two years afterwards were found, all ragged and starving, upon one of the Auckland Islands.

Brought to Melbourne, he became of much use there in making affidavits, legally required, as to those of his fellow-passengers who had gone down with the ship's golden treasure. A fine upstanding man was James Teer. His two years' Robinson Crusoe life did not seem to have hurt him. He had been also sought after at Melbourne to join a speculative expedition to the cave into which the "General Grant" had been thrown by the waves, and down into which she had gone. The expedition had been fitted out by some Melbourne adventurers, who looked to the recovery of the gold on board for their repayment. That had brought Teer down to this quarter. The expedition had failed, for no weather was found, for some six weeks, fine enough to permit of the diving business being entered upon. Teer still believes that it is practicable, and that the twenty-thousand pounds boxed up on board the "General Grant" will not remain in the wreck until the deeps shall give up all their treasures. No expedition to get it will do any good without him. He knows that, and patiently bides his time. He will go some day himself—if not taken. Cheerily enough, Teer told us of life on the Auckland Islands. One of the fourteen washed on shore there had two dry matches. The fire that they lighted was sacred. Tended day and night by its allotted watch, it never ceased to burn. Something dreadful was agreed upon as the penalty for letting that fire fade out. Some drinking-cups were scooped out of roots, and ropes were made of native flax. Oysters and seals were food for a long time, and, to help in fishing, a seal-skin boat was constructed by some genius of the company. There was a greater genius than he there in the person of Teer, who discovered the life preserver for the whole lot. Running about the islands were wild pigs, which were doubtless the progeny of a pair that had been landed there by Captain Cook, who has similarly pigged the whole of New Zealand—blessings on him! The wild pigs might have run there, and folks starved in their sight, but for Teer. No horses or guns had they, and no dogs. He was equal to the occasion. With the circumstances necessitating him, the fitting man arose here. Teer fashioned a strong barbed hook, and fastened it to the end of a native flax rope, the other end of which he fastened round himself. The hook was baited with a piece of cooked seal, and laid out to catch piggy. It did so—hooking the pig in the mouth like to a fish. The noise was awful and the rush terrific. It was all that Teer could do to hold on to a tree and shout for assistance. Pig on the rush was too strong for him. He escaped, much bruised, and tied the rope in future to something else. That pig—a magnificent specimen—was carried to the fire in triumph, and sucking-pig, pork, bacon, and smoked hams were never more wanting in that Auckland Island encampment. Such is genius! It often nearly destroys the possessor of it, sometimes quite killing him, but it benefits mankind. He that so benefits his fellows is always forgotten in the day when the world gives its rewards. In this case he is left to row a boat for a living on a Maihinaipau lake.

We had rightly imagined, from the difficulty in landing at Hokitika, that it was a good place to get to. So it was, and the people there were good fellows to us. We felt that we could have stopped amongst them ever so long, and we thought that they would have gladly kept us there. We left it with many pleasant memories of its fine climate, its pretty scenery, and the good time that we had of it there.

Our next landing on the west coast was at Taranaki, a town famous for wars and not for diggings. The surf-boats are there worked with rope and pulley from the shore to buoys anchored in the open roadstead. Having got us on board in a similar manner as at Hokitika, the boat is rowed under this floating rope, which is then carried on to wheels running between uprights fixed to the boat fore and aft. Three or four boatmen pull at this rope, and so tow us through the surf to the shore. A thick, wet rope running along the middle of the boat, wetting our knees and splashing our faces, was something of a novelty—something to remember Taranaki by; and about the only thing, apart from its war troubles and its central raised barracks and fort, that we ever shall recall it by. We shall remember Manakau harbour, further northwards, however, and by a very painful circumstance. As we steamed between walls of rock into its waters, the captain pointed to one part of it with this remark: "Three years ago the man-of-war steamer 'Orpheus' went down there with all hands on board."

CHAPTER XXIX.

EASTWARD HO! ON WHEELS.

THERE may be better rides in the world than that from the west coast to the eastern of the Middle Island, but that ride is enough to satisfy one. It gives a fulness of content, does that two-day drive across the breadth of New Zealand. The coach used is one of the American pattern, and of the strongest build. It need be so. A wheel coming off on many parts of that journey would leave no one to tell the story. The coroner's inquest, if any ever sat upon the remains of coach and passengers, would have to return an open verdict of "found dead." The road is equally divided between the west and east sides of the dividing range of mountains. Its 150 miles of length has seventy-five on the west coast side, and the like on the east. There is a wonderful difference between the aspects of the two. The seventy-five miles on the western slope of this mountain range is all of the wildest beauty; woods and waters, rocks and cascades, hills and valleys, and verdure-covered mountain sides comparing favourably, travelled people say, with any that Switzerland can show in that line of beauty. The eastern half of the journey shows an entire absence of trees on the hill-sides, no cascades, nor anything of the wild wonders of the sublime western half of the journey. How one side of a mountain range can be so different from the other in all its scenery is what every traveller that way will unfailingly wonder at.

We leave Hokitika in the early morning with a driver

between six and seven feet high, a jolly old sea-captain beside him on the box, and myself inside. Besides myself in that department were two Maori ladies, one of whom, I learned from our driver, was a queen. For two very long days we three had to keep company. Folks who have been on shipboard know how intimately that sort of life brings them into acquaintance with the peculiarities of their fellow-travellers. It is so in a coach; when I parted with those two Maories I seemed to have known them for months, years. The first part of our journey and its acquaintanceship, and all its talk, seemed ever so long ago. There seemed to be nothing that we had not talked about, and I felt quite competent to write a biography of my two interesting New Zealanders, with remarks on their manners, which were very amiable, and their customs, which, including smoking, were all that could be expected.

My surprise at their paying five pounds apiece for coach-fare was modified when I learned that their relatives owned half the land on which the seaside township of Greymouth stands, on the west coast. These children of nature have got quite European notions of the value of freehold estate, and draw good rents from that which they lease out, and high prices for what they can be persuaded to sell. My dark friends not only belonged to the aristocracy of their race, but to the capitalists also—an alliance not always found amongst Europeans. Yet had they no pride; they took cigars from me without hesitation, and smoked them, one after the other, in the most friendly manner. It was something, I thought to supply cigars to a queen—we all have a little of the toady in our nature. Not but what I got full value in return. The amount of Maori knowledge I acquired is not to be found in books. I got invited to the Maori village of Kaipoi at the other end of the drive, whither my ladies were bound, and got information of another native village further on, with an introduction to the chief, and to a probable Christmas dinner there, which, a week afterwards, I was fortunate enough to realize.

The first sensation in this coach-drive was that of going through a river and finding its waters covering the coach-floor. This sensation, repeated some thirty times during the two days' journey, became quite a matter of course at last. It does not seem the thing to a stranger in New Zealand to go through rivers. The said stranger has mostly been accustomed to going over them in other lands; but here, through all these mountain streams, and over their boulder bottoms, the coach has to go. Only twice during the journey was it otherwise. Across the Taipo (Devil) River two bridges have been made. They are pathways for passengers only, and of a singular construction—little wonders of wire-work—with one narrow plank down the middle for the feet, and a thin one-wire railing (so to speak) on each side for the hands. Crossing a raging river on a narrow plank twenty feet from the water, with a hand clutching a small wire on each side to steady oneself, seems to be a sort of good practice for learning the "tight-rope business." To look down is to get nervous at the sight of the dashing waters beneath, and to look otherwise is to endanger one's footing on the narrow plank. It is not perhaps so unpleasant a "walking the plank" as that by which a sailor goes to his doom, but it is a modification of that feeling, and a little of the sensation quite suffices for all purposes. It is nasty going through the rivers, but it is worse to go over them in that way.

The mountain range before us soon gets to be around us, and we are travelling over cuttings that wind around its precipitous sides. Everywhere are waterfalls; silver streams descending hundreds upon hundreds of feet down steep mountain sides, and through the dense, dark wood, in which they have cut a channel. These cascades are of peculiar beauty and sweet sound, enlivening the solitude of these eternal hills—these snow-covered mountains, and making a delight to the eye and the ear from and for all time. "This road must have cost a trifle, driver?" to which we are answered that it did so—its construction consuming a quarter of a million sterling. "You are now two thousand feet high," we are told, and hardly need to be so informed, as we look down into the valley far below us. Only a few inches off is the way down to it. Let the narrow knife-board road that we are rolling along upon give way on the off side; let one of the four horses before us take a fit of any kind—kicking or epilepsy—let a wheel come off, or a trace break, and the

WATERFALL, OTIRA GORGE.

chances are to be calculated. The road—the western side of it—is all like that. Round the mountains, through the rivers, now ascending, now descending, but always in scenes of beauty that charm to delirium, and scenes of danger that bring on the tremens. One is so gladly sorry and sorrily glad when it is over. "This is the 'Saddle;' you must get down and walk for two miles here; the coach can't get up this pass with any one in it." So speaks our driver, and out we get, and trudge upwards, round and round the sides of a steep mountain that seems ten miles, instead of two, to get to the top of. What a clear, good, strong head it wanted to look down the side of our knife-board roadway on most of that journey! You were glad to rub along against the mountain side, and keep as far away from the edge as possible. The Maori women did not seem to like it any better than we did, and were decidedly lazy walkers. It occurred to me then that these people did not believe in any exertion. I afterwards found that it was so, and that hard work and Maori notions were far apart. In this respect there can be no question that they are wiser in their generation than the children of light—that is, their lighter-coloured brethren. We burst ourselves with needless labour; wear and tear ourselves out with needless exertion. A Maori at fifty is as young and strong, or stronger than a European at thirty. They die at about ninety, of old age, the only natural disease, and they keep thick heads of hair even up to that date, whitened though it be.

"That is Mount Cook that you see there through the clouds. It is over thirteen thousand feet high, and always snow-covered as you see it. You don't always see it; the clouds mostly cover it as well as the snow." So far our driver. This Mount Cook is the highest peak of the range over which we are crossing. We should have taken its top to be a cloud amongst the clouds but for the information given us. Thirteen thousand feet is a very respectable height for a mountain. We agreed that Mount Cook was likely to remain unvisited—about the top, at all events—until the French had brought balloon navigation to the pitch of perfection. "What the deuce did the colony go to the great expense of this road for? The passenger traffic by this coach can never pay interest on it!" Thus we asked, and thus were answered: "They thought, when the west coast diggings opened up, that another way of getting to them must be made than the tedious one of going all round by sea, and that it would open a good market for stock and sheep for the east coast squatters; besides, the coach takes the mail, and it all helps to pay." A good deal of help, it occurred to us, was wanted in that way, and we began to perceive that other countries besides our own and new ones too, can incur national debts. We began to understand how the taxation of New Zealand amounted to six pounds per head per annum.

"This is the Cass River Hotel, and we stop here for the night," said our driver, as he drew up to a one-story wooden-cottage-looking building in a valley of some stretch around it. All alone there in the valley, that house had a very curious look. There were curious people in it too. The coach-load from the other side, going the way we had come, had got there a few minutes before us. The assembled passengers had all to sleep at Cass River Hotel that night. One amongst them nearly kept us awake till midnight by a superb performance on a tin penny whistle that happened to turn up. I noticed that his music, which nearly set all our weary legs dancing, had no effect whatever upon the Maori ladies. Thinking over it, I do not believe that Orpheus did make the trees dance. These women were not vegetables, and yet they could not be charmed by the most exquisite piping that I ever heard. We had "toiled all day in eye of Phœbus," and we "slept in Elysium."

CHAPTER XXX.

CLOSE QUARTERS WITH ROYALTY.

WITH good fortune, which comes generally to those who trust to it, we fell in with some excellent specimens of the feminine

A MAORI LADY.

Maori. Our wish to see all good things when we thought of visiting New Zealand was fully gratified as to that particular. On the grand coach-ride across the breadth of New Zealand

—which took two very long days to make out—we had the company of Amelia Tanui Arahura and her cousin, Victoria Jawgpetur Kanieri, names that, look long and awkward as they may, we shall never forget. Their owners were the first feminine Maories we had met.

At the native pah, or village, of Arowainui, near to Timaroo, in the middle island, we had a vision of loveliness that compelled us to rub our eyes to be sure that we slept not. This dream of beauty, in burnished copper colour, was Kiti Kohoota, and it is up to this day, and will be for all days to come, our delight to shut our eyes to all common outward sights, and see again this brightest of young womankind.

Victoria Jawgpetur Kanieri, when at home, was a queen in her husband's right. She was journeying to her queendom— the native village of Kaipoi, on the east coast, 150 miles from the town of Hokitika, on the west shore of New Zealand. Amelia Tanui Arahura was nothing in the royal way, but had a rich relative on the west coast, who fortunately owned much of the land on which the township is there built, a street in it being named after him. It will strike the considerate reader that Amelia Tanui Arahura was monetary, or likely to be so. We did not know so much until our two days' journey had come nearly to an end, but we were none the less polite to her, for Amelia was pleasant to look upon and to talk to. Fortune had denied her royal honours, but Nature had compensated her with something better. Her cousin Victoria —the Queen Kanieri—was mean-looking compared to Amelia, who was about twenty-two in years, and had a round, smiling face, not disfigured with tattoo. She had wondrously expressive eyes and mouth. The eyes were dark and restless, with a glitter about them that had something of the fascinating power ascribed to the eyes of the rattlesnake. If those eyes had fascinated us, in the rattlesnake way, we were certain that the mouth beneath them could eat us. It looked so powerful, did that mouth. The thought would come strongly on us that nothing which such a mouth laid hold of would ever be let go. We remembered reading of a brigand chief in

Italy, who, on being pushed over a precipice, had seized in his mouth the coat-tail of his conqueror, and hung in that way successfully on it. In the distribution of such mouths, one had come to our Amelia, and when she put a cigar in the middle of it, and smiled 'midst the smoke, it seemed as if there was an ordinary-sized mouth on both sides of that cigar. Had she attempted to screw up those pulpy lips of hers, to

AMELIA TANUI ARAHURA.

make what is called a "cherry" of them, we considered that the cherry would have been of extraordinary dimensions—about the size of a turnip, perhaps. This mouth was not to be reckoned as a feature of the face. It had features of its own, and might be described as a distinct affair from the rest of the face. Its principal aspect was power, consciousness of power, potentiality in repose, the sort of look that impresses us about the listless lion in the Zoological Gardens. The lips were protrusive, pulpy, flexible, stiff, and strong. Carlyle would have praised such a mouth, as he praises everything that is strong by nature and successful by fortune or by force. It was useless to oppose the owner of such a mouth. Had angry words been uttered by it, the ordinary sharpness of woman's angry tongue would have been terribly intensified to the ear, while to the eye the look of that mouth when in anger, those writhing lips, and those gleaming teeth, must have annihilated to utter silence all opposition. Had Amelia Tannewhee Arrahhoora (for so her name was sounded) spoken to us angrily, we should have been quiet. Had she chosen to kiss us, we should have closed our eyes and submitted as to fate itself—we yield naturally to the superior forces of nature.

Queen Victoria George Peter Canary (for so her Majesty's name was pronounced) was a mother, and had with her a small prince about five or six years old. Whether the care shown to that boy was only the natural fondness of a Maori mother, we know not, but he was cared for immensely. Though old enough to be let alone, he was never scarcely out of his mother's arms, and when out of the coach was always slung round on her back, his arms around her neck. He was well able to walk and run, but was not urged to do so, and, like all Maories, old or young, would make no exertion that could be avoided—and he avoided that. In going up some of the toilsome mountain ascents, it seemed cruel for a great boy like that so to overweight his mamma—but he did it, and both mother and son, queen and prince, seemed to like it. Spoilt children we had hitherto thought to be products of high civilization, but the error seemed to be here corrected.

Both Victoria and Amelia looked at their best when sitting. They were long in the back and short in the legs—sitting the higher for that reason, as all Maories do. Their walk, from the same cause, was anything but the poetry of motion. Amelia's headgear was novel and strikingly graceful. It consisted of the wing or feathers of some bird of fine plumage, brought from behind one ear and carried to the other across the forehead. The feathers appeared to have a natural curve that fitted them to their office, and the effect was very good. We saw nothing better in the way of feather ornaments until we got to the northern island, where we met with a gentle Maori who had a feather run through the cartilage between the nostrils. A feather across the face has a very peculiar effect as an ornament. The ring through the nose is nothing to it in that way. As a rival to the moustache that men now so generally adopt, it is very formidable, and can be stroked and curled by the fair wearer much in the same manner. If the ex-Empress of the French, or some other leader of fashion who must now take her place, would only lead off with a little dark and curled feather through the nose, what a success it would be! The ears have had their time. Ear-rings have been long played out. Let the nose have its day. Fine feathers make fine birds, especially when the feathers are put through the nose. Let some one patent it. The rest of Amelia's dress, after the forehead-feather, does not merit mention. It was a simple shawl and petticoat, but the shawl had an opening made in it for one arm to come through and have full play—a fashion in shawl-wearing that might yet be turned to advantage. The petticoat was secured round the waist by a girdle of native flax woven in two colours. The feet of both ladies were covered, or half-covered, with shoes, also of native flax. The shoes were more of the sandal shape than the shape of a shoe, and entirely adapted to the wearer's comfort. They were consequently without high heels, and we will wager that the wearers had no corns.

Queen Victoria smoked a pipe; Amelia preferred cigars. The pipe was of royal size—the largest pipe we had seen, as to size of bowl, in any mouth. She said it only wanted filling once a day, and we believed her. Victoria was not so communicative as Amelia. She was older and staid. It may be that years, maternity, or the prince, oppressed her, or that dignity did; but we did not get that ready response to our efforts to exchange ideas that Amelia accorded to us. Whilst

Amelia talked to us, Victoria smoked, and seemed to reckon us up. We guessed at her thoughts, which were, perhaps, something of this sort. We were a pakeha (the Maori for white man), and had another Queen Victoria to respect, and that above herself. We were a pakeha, one of those that had come to invade that Maori land that herself and her ancestors had enjoyed for 500 years, when her kindred had left the Malay Islands for Maori land. We were a pakeha and an intruder, an interloper, an alien, a foreigner—one who had come there for no good to her and to hers. Victoria, like all Maories, could have no idea that any one came to her country merely to see it, go through it, and go away from it. The Maories are a practical people, and believe in no travel for travel's sake, nor any nonsense of that or any other kind. No romance or fanciful sentiment is at all comprehensible by them. It would require a surgical operation to get such things into their heads. And yet she might have thought that we were one of the pakehas that have brought to her and to her country some very good things. She was enjoying one of them in the very coach-ride at the tails of four good horses that she was then having. That pipe that she was pulling at, and that cigar that Amelia was puffing by her side, they enjoyed thanks to the pakehas. The potatoes they are so fond of were the gift of the white men, and that famous pakeha —Captain James Cook—at whose name we always took off our hat, all through this New Zealand land of his—planted in Maori land the first pigs, whose progeny the natives now so hunt down, eat up, and relish. The pakeha brought there the corn, too, which these Maories now make into cakes, and won't learn to leaven and make any more eatable to pakehas than is a door-mat; and still more, the pakeha brought the pots, and kettles, and pans, which the Maories had to muddle on without before these unspeakable blessings came into their huts. As we looked at Victoria's searching eye we thought that we had an even account with her, and that but for the pakehas she had never borne the splendid first name that she had borrowed, nor had any of the blessings we have enumerated, and a lot of others we have thought of but not set down here.

In her bosom Amelia had a book! It was an unexpected thing to be found in such company, for Amelia looked the least literary of womankind. Her ways, and those of her cousin the Queen, were not the ways of the literary. There was, it is true, something Dr. Johnsonish about the manners of the queen, as when she ended a conversation, at any time she liked, by dictatorially saying to us, "too much jaw." She would then subside into silence or brief slumber, and we felt quite shut up for the time. Amelia had another way of "giving us pause." She would fill that majestic mouth of hers with smoke, and emit it directly in our face, thus finishing all talk for ten minutes at least on our part. Our wounded feelings, smarting eyes, and coughing lungs, could not always be brought to resume talk again in a hurry. Yet in her bosom Amelia carried a book. We got to see it at last, and found it to be the New Testament in the Maori language. It had been the gift of some missionary, and was carried about by Amelia as a sort of charm, much in the same way as she carried in her ears a shark's tooth set in sealing-wax. To our offer of five shillings for the book she was about to agree, on which we declared off the bargain, until the journey's end. We omitted to state that in the matter of ear ornaments, the Queen and Amelia were peculiar. Amelia favoured a shark's tooth—very white it was—stuck into red sealing-wax, and thereby fixed to a thin ribbon, which was passed through a hole in the ear, the said hole being pierced somewhat larger than such holes usually are with us. This red and white decoration was not at all unsightly against the dark skin of the wearer. We thought of Romeo's comparison of the beauty of Juliet when seen at night, to a rich jewel in an Ethiop's ear, and saw that Shakspeare had taken notice even of such small matters as the effect of coloured folks' ornaments. Victoria wore an adornment in one ear only. That was a piece of the green stone for which the Middle Island of New Zealand is peculiar, and from which it takes its Maori name—

"Te wai pounuma" (the water of the green stone). This green stone has, from being only an ornament in Maori ears, become the same to the ears and to the watch-chains of many Europeans.

We could not get Victoria or Amelia to come to table at any of the road-side stopping-places. They clave to the kitchen and to their own company, and would in no way show us their table manners. When we dined with seventy of their number some time afterwards on Christmas Day, we partly understood why the ceremonies of the table were irksome to these fellow-travellers of ours. We have mentioned that we were talkative on the journey, and we certainly did show great interest in our company, and evidenced much of the inquiring mind. We were as willing, however, to impart as to receive information, and not only information, but anything that the wild road-side could afford in the way of refreshment. Tea and water, however, were the only drinks our friends would take. Their love of tobacco, which was something remarkable, did not appear to lead, as it often does with us, to any liking for strong liquors. In fact, our friends were teetotallers, and not to be in any way brought to taste fermented drinks—a matter that greatly surprised us, all other things being considered.

At the conclusion of two days' ride we had acquired a large amount of New Zealand knowledge, and got acquainted with a whole string of very useful Maori words, that we were always making an after-use of through the country. When we afterwards bought a dictionary and phrase-book, we could not recognize therein half the phrases that we had learnt by ear—the spelling and the pronunciation were, of course, quite distinct matters.

Our friends had their friends awaiting them at the journey's end, and we suppose spoke a good word for us, as two tattooed Maories came to offer the hand of friendship, and invited us to visit the Maori party at their village of Kaipoi, of which invitation we promised to avail ourselves.

We have made no mention of Kiti Kohoota—that queen of beauties. She belonged to another event—our Christmas dinner with the Maories, and must appear in that event only, being, as she was, not the least memorable part of that most memorable event.

CHAPTER XXXI.

THE "SQUARE" CITY—AND PEOPLE.

A MILE, four-square, on the long, level, green plains of the province of Canterbury, lies the city of Christchurch. It is about half-way on the eastern shore of the Middle Island. For contrast there can be nothing greater than that presented by the two towns of Hokitika on the west, and Christchurch on the east, that are joined by the great Otira road across the mountains—a road of 150 miles in length, going through no other towns, and costing a quarter of a million sterling. Hokitika is all diggings and diggers—a population of all sorts, brought together anyhow, with a rush from everywhere. Christchurch is the most symmetrically laid out, and systematically settled, of all the cities that British colonists have made their dwelling-place. When we say that it is the most select and thoroughly correct and respectable of all the cities that be, we write with a consciousness of what we are saying, and with a full recollection of Bath and Cheltenham, and Leamington, and such-like places of decent folk. Christchurch is in our memory the "square" city in all senses of the word. It is a mile square to begin with, and stands surrounded by a huge square of trees, called the City Belt—a sort of band or belt like that which we see in another form surrounding the planet Saturn. Its right-angled streets are all named after the sees of British bishops, except one street that is not on the square, and for that reason, we suppose, not called by a name recalling ecclesiastical people or places. The two squares of

Christchurch are named after the martyr bishops, Cranmer and Latimer. The city calls itself a church, and names its surrounding country after the diocese of the Primate of all England. Towards the end of the forties—about twenty-two years ago—we went down to Gravesend, there to see off the first batch of emigrants then outward bound to settle this city. The settlement had been taken in hand by the high church party of the time, with Lord Lyttelton as a foremost promoter. We heard his lordship address these new Canterbury pilgrims on that occasion, and the concluding words of his speech made as much impression upon us as upon any of the departing pilgrim fathers. "Leave," said his lordship, "your Bible to your parson, stick to your Prayer-book and your bishop, and you'll never go wrong." We were young at that time, and, youth-like, were unsettled, but inquiring of mind, on many matters. That speech of his lordship's much decided us. When a peer undertakes to preach, it is to be expected that his words will have weight. They had with us. We went about for many days repeating to ourselves the formula, "Stick to your Prayer-book and your bishop, and you'll never go wrong." We began inquiring, for the first time, where our bishop—he of London—was to be heard, that we might adhere to him. With the zeal of a new convert, we went about preaching the way of salvation from this point of view. It then occurred to us that a nation's ballads make the leading impression on the national mind, and are the most popular way of conveying facts that one would wish to be ever remembered. To reduce the new formula of faith to verse was, for the time, our great ambition, hoping thus, through the great gateway of song, to communicate it to the general mind. The song, we thought, the song's the thing by which we'll touch the conscience of the—people. Such was our aspiration. We penned the "little psalm of life," as Longfellow would phrase it, and well remember to this day its refrain—"Attend to my song—you'll never go wrong, if you do as directed by Lord Lyttelton." Some difficulty as to the tune, and also as to the terms of its publication, kept it out of print, and spoilt a promising success; but there was still the good intention. Twenty-two years afterwards we were now looking at the city these people, so admonished at Gravesend, had builded, and, to ourselves, we owned that they had never gone wrong. Whether they had "kept their square" before we knew not, but here "all had been done by rule." We involuntarily bowed our head at the city's title, but we took off our hat as we stood on the banks of its river, and heard that river's name.

Who shall guess by what name these high-church settlers —these bishop's people—have called their river? There are sacred and ecclesiastical rivers in plenty. There is that one of Coleridge's, "Alph, the sacred river, ran," and there is the Jordan and the sacred Ganges, and then there are Abana and Pharphar—rivers of Damascus, and "that ancient river, the river Kishon," and then, sanctified by the halo cast around them by the touch of time, there are the Tiber and the Nile. At Kentish Canterbury itself there is the Stour, and at Cambridge is the Cam, and at high-church Oxford the Isis. None of these, nor of a host of other waters, that claim kindred with religious thoughts, have stood as sponsor for the river of Christchurch. That river is named in honour of the Archbishop of Warwickshire Stratford—he that is primate of all the world, and metropolitan of all English-speaking towns and cities—the archbishop ecclesiastical, and master of the ceremonies in worldly matters to all mankind—Shakspeare himself! It is called the Avon! We would we knew in what manner this name was given, that we might honourably mention its proposer. There must have been a splutter over it in committee of management. Who was it that proposed it there, and had to hear it condemned, no doubt, as a name connected with theatricals, play-actors, and other low things? And who was he that afterwards answered these and all other objections, and powerfully, in a speech of praise of Shakspeare and of his great book of life, carried everything before him, and thus ennobled Christchurch for all time? Ennobled it, too, in a manner that all its bishop-named streets and squares

will for ever fail of doing. May we not, parodying Longfellow's lines on Nuremberg and its Albert Durer, say that—
'Fairer seems that Christchurch city, and its sunshine seems more fair, since through it runs the Avon river, and brings its train of memories there"?

We looked for a swan upon that river, and trod gently as we crossed its bridge. Our old friend, the captain, was with us, and we saved him from committing a sort of sacrilege by turning his head aside as he removed the cigar from his mouth to expectorate over the railings. No expectorating in a river of that name, if we could help it.

Whilst upon the subject of rivers, we must mention the great Waimakariri River that runs down from the mountains to Christchurch. This long name means only "cold water," and has a pretty sound—Why-mak-a-rai-ree—when you can get the tongue properly round the word. That river, like to almost all the rivers in the Middle Island, is a great nuisance. It is strong language perhaps to apply to a river, but it is merely sober, straightforward fact as respects the mountain streams. The source of most of the rivers here, perhaps of all of them, is melted snow from the mountain ranges. If this would run in one channel always, and make thereof a decently deep river-like course, there would be no more to say. But do that these rivers never will. They splash and roll over a wide shallow bed of stones, from which they have washed all the alluvial soil. Next season of snow-melting and rains they will take only one side of this course, and so make another wide bed of shallow, desert-looking, stony surface. The year following, the other side of the first river bed is most likely served the same way, and thus a mountain stream that would run in a channel of 25 or 30 ft. by 10 or 12 ft. deep, works out for its fitful self, beds of half a mile, a mile, two miles, and, in the case of the Rangitata, three miles wide. The stream answers no useful purpose—holds no fish, carries no traffic, and supplies no want, but devastates the land, washing away cornfields and grass meadows all along its course. Near to Christchurch the ruin caused by the Waimakariri is very sad. You look down from a bank of alluvial fine black soil to where, 15 or 20 ft. below, all is stones and sterility. A similar blank is visible on the other side, two miles off, and somewhere between is rolling the troublesome stream that has made all this ruin, and left it all so uncovered and unsightly. It will now be understood what "going through" the New Zealand rivers means. It means driving over their rough, stony beds, and through their shallow, rushing waters, when reached. Bridges, when put up, have to be an awful length. Two that we crossed, over the Waimakariri and the Rakaia, were more than a mile long, with water at that time under about only one twelfth part of that length. These bridges are constructed chiefly with gas-pipes, on an economical principle, devised by one White, of Christchurch, who, like to that other inventor, Arkwright, was once a weaver. The Molyneux in the South, and the Waikato in the North Island, are, however, very respectable rivers—and behave as such.

The road from Hokitika, that cost a quarter of a million, is not the only expensively-made road to Christchurch. The city is separated from the sea by a lofty mountain range, on the other side of which is the sugar-basin-shaped port called—after his high-church lordship—Lyttelton. The sea in most places in New Zealand leaves but small spaces between itself and the mountain base. It is so at Lyttelton. The port shows but little land available for port or township purposes —all the rest is but mountain side. For years the Christchurch folks toiled up this steep and down the other side. To get from port to town and back was a good day's work. They have now pierced the mountain with a small Mont Cenis tunnel, and a train runs every hour from town to port on a railway that has at present about twenty-five miles of length from the port inland. That tunnel and rail cost another quarter million. From the top of the mountain range is the best view to be had of flat-lying Christchurch, and its sixty odd miles of level green plains. The staple of the country is supplied by the squatter and the farmer. The earth-slab hedges of the latter, with their green tops, begin fully twenty miles from the city, and the roads and lanes have a very green and English-like look. Everything is green-looking and English-like in and around Christchurch. Green hedges, green fields, and lofty green poplar-trees, with artesian wells here and there, are the features of Christchurch. To that add the best hotels in the colonies—old English-looking houses, well built, and cosy and comfortable, with the best of beds, and nicest-kept stables. The houses are mostly wood built, the streets clean and well-kept. So are all the people. It is easy to see that they are well-selected first-class emigrants—related, no doubt, many of them to good families in England. The tradesmen and mechanics have the same appearance. Every one looks as if he had paid a liberal passage-money, and only came hither to oblige others. We noticed men about in alpine suits, with knee-breeches, that had apparently been worn in Switzerland. They were here, no doubt, on visits to their well-to-do squatting relatives. The Irish element, so marked in most British colonies, seems to be entirely absent in Christchurch. We looked about for Irish names in vain. The most noticeable name, from its repetition, is Oram. That family must be large. Here and there, over shops, one sees this mysterious inscription, "Cookham Boots"—only that, and nothing more. Its repeated appearance forced our attention to it, and we found that a peculiar boot supplied by a particular place in England was best appreciated in this southern city of the saints. There is nothing anywhere about to show that one is out of England save a rare-occurring native name to an outlying suburb, such as Papanui, Kaipoi, and Opawa.

In square-built Christchurch, the central building appeared to be the square four-fronted Bank of New Zealand. We were always coming upon one of its fronts, and they were all alike. By one of its four sides stands a very handsome street bronze drinking-fountain, the best that we ever saw. It is surmounted by a handsome square canopy, on which stands a bronze one-legged heron. Under the canopy is a smaller square one, from the four corners of which hang four bells. These being turned up make the drinking-cups, and are so always turned down when done with. These drinking-bells ring together when set in motion, and the four sounds they rang out seemed to our ears to chime "Act on the square." It may be that only ourselves perceived this, and yet it must be owned that all bells say something, if you have but the ear to hear it. Tintagel bells, on the Cornish coast, are well known to ring out this rhyme, "Come, come to thy God in time; thy youth, manhood, and old age past, come, come to thy God at last," which we take to be as good a sermon as was ever preached beneath a bell-tower. We all know what meanings Edgar Poe has extracted from the language of bells, and if anything further in that way be wanted, there is, in the memory of everybody, what the bells said to Dick Whittington when they told him of threefold dignities as plainly as the witches did his thrice-told honours to Macbeth—perhaps more plainly.

We have mentioned a suburb called Kaipoi, near to Christchurch. It is the native village to which were going our royal lady Maories of the coach journey overland. This word "Kaipoi" is pronounced like to "Carpoy," and means, in the Maori language, "good." It is a word of great use among the Maories, answering also to our use of "very well." We heard it in the first hour of our being in Maori land, and ever and again until the hour that we quitted it. We used it too until we got to like it, and have since so christened a dog in hope that he will justify our choice of name.

Port Lyttelton has a very cosy harbour, reached by a smooth channel, well protected by precipitous hill-sides. As we afterwards went into the port from the sea side of it, we had a good view of the harbour and the way up to it. On a knifeboard-like road on one side of the channel we saw horses and vehicles, which looked, at that height, like to flies on a wall. The railway and tunnel have ruined the value of

Y

property in the port. Nothing and no one stops there now; all are taken at once right through by the rail to Christchurch. A fire had just burnt down one half of the buildings at Lyttelton, and if the owners can so arrange with the insurance companies, it occurred to us that there would not be much rebuilding. The leading journal of Christchurch still bears the name of the *Lyttelton Times*, which points to what the port was in bygone days. It is now, of course, with the *Christchurch Free Press*, published in the city. The meanest thing that we saw in Christchurch was the theatre; but that was to be expected. We did not expect to find any theatre whatever there, and were therefore thankful for little in that way—and very little it was.

Rip Van Winkle, when he came down from his long sleep in the mountains, was in much the same position that we were in Christchurch. On the coach-ride thither we had noted down from memory those whom we knew to have gone to settle there—some of the pilgrim fathers that we saw off at Gravesend included. To us it seemed but yesterday that they had migrated. It was more than twenty years, in truth; but twenty years to those with sponge-like memories and pigeon-holed heads are but as twenty months. We could remember nine or ten, but of all the whole number we failed to find one. "Dead years ago,"—"Gone home three years back," "five years ago," "ten years ago,"—"Gone to here or there so long back"—were the sort of answers we got to our inquiries. Colonists will never call their settlements their "home." That sweet word is reserved for their fatherland, and, all things considered, we would not alter the custom, though one emigrant did write over his doorway, in some colonial settlement—"To him to whom God is a father, every land is a fatherland." The balance of belief is against him; and there are the vivid lines of Scott and Goldsmith as to fatherland and mother country first to be effaced from one's mind. Though we did not find any of our pilgrim fathers, we found a pilgrim mother who had emigrated in the first flight—that Gravesend hegira. Her husband had died within a month of landing, and left the widow and six daughters to manage for themselves in that new land. All had gone well with them—very well indeed. The widow had remained a widow, and had now five families of grandchildren to amuse her. The house of business of herself and daughter was her own freehold, and a valuable one too. If her husband could come back as Rip Winkle did, he would find more comfortable quarters than awaited the poor Dutchman.

A nice, clean, well-ordered, comfortable square city is Christchurch—unlike in its characteristics to the other Australasian colonial cities that we have seen. It might have satisfied the aspiration of Keats for some place away from "the weariness, the fever, and the fret" of sitting but to "hear each other groan." All feverish bustle, frets, and groans are things that will not connect themselves in our minds with this green-belted, green-treed place. We did not look for the prison or the poorhouse, and it occurred to us afterwards that we had failed to observe them, which we did not remember omitting to do in any other town or city. We took our best coat out of the trunk and our neatest linen during the days we stopped there. After that, what more need be said?

A fine high road runs from Christchurch to Dunedin—a three-days' cruise upon wheels. It was either that or waiting for a coasting steamer, and coasting steamers are not worth waiting for. We will not say anything against New Zealand coasting steamers; but if others stand up against them, we can sympathize with their complaints. So it was the three-days' coach-ride that we decided on, with its two nights' stoppages on the road. At six o'clock on a gloriously fine morning in midsummer December, we got a seat beside the driver on a fine old English stage-coach—a real old stage, with four fine horses. It was Christmas time; and, what with that and the stage-coach, we thought that time had travelled backwards for once, and that we were boys again and going home for the Christmas holidays. It says something for the place we were leaving that we could leave it with such feelings. There is something of the school and of all its proprieties about Christchurch; but if we ever turn Quaker we shall, of all the places that we know, go back to live there as to a large Society of Friends.

CHAPTER XXXII.

THE MAORI-LAND BIRD—THE MOA.

AT Christchurch we, for the first time, saw the bones of the moa.

"Maori" means "native," or "aboriginal," as applied to man, and "moa" has the same meaning as to bird. The Maori is not, however, an aboriginal. He acknowledges the emigration of his race to the New Zealand islands from the Malays some four hundred years back, and his language justifies his statement. There may have been no men in New Zealand before him, but the moa was there—had been there for some thousands of years, perhaps, and was no emigrant. When Maori land emerged from ocean, with its wondrous volcanoes of coloured and boiling waters, and of fire, and its vast mountains piled upon mountains, the moa came with it. The land and the bird were kith and kin. We had written "New Zealand's bird" as our head-line hereto, but could not let that stand. New Zealand knew nothing of the moa, nor the moa of it. He may have seen a Maori, but he never saw a white man. It was Maori land, or some other land, before the migration thither of the Maories, when the moa had that country to itself. It was a bird that wanted a country to itself—a backwoodsman of a bird, that would feel crowded if any one came within fifty or a hundred miles of it. As the backwoodsman of the Far West of America retires and retires as this crowding comes upon him, so did the moa, until it could retire no further. There was then left for it but some large cave, whither it retired to die, and to leave there those bones that are now sought for as a great ornithological wonder of the world. What the ostrich or the emu is to the tomtit, what the elephant is to the pig, is, or was, the moa to all other birds. The words of the old book, "There were giants on the earth in those days," will be better understood by those who look at the skeleton of this titanic bird. In the museum of one of the southern cities stands its completed skeleton, more wondrous and more awe-striking than all else in that collection of the curious. There stands the lofty moa, and as we looked at him we shrank before his majesty, and sank—to a seat. As we did so, our eyes caught sight of a bust of Shakspeare, standing on a cabinet in the rear. The heads of the two came into the line of sight, and there seemed to us something proper in that association. Both seemed equally to look down upon us, and upon all around. The solitary lonely genius of the intellectual giant, and the solitary lonely species of the giant bird, came upon our mind as things of proper comparison. To the skeleton form, and to the long arching neck of the moa, some student of natural history had fitted a well-conceived head, finished to a beak, eyes, and feathers. The effect was good—the furnished head to the unfurnished bones. It brought a sense of half-life to the bird's form—vitality to the dry bones. The eyes were well chosen, too, far-seeing and piercing of look, taking cognizance of something, as the natural ones doubtless could do, that was miles and miles away, for that head stood from the ground 16 ft. high at the least. What the bird must have looked like when the huge, bony framework was covered with layers of feathers, we had to imagine for ourselves, and we have not realized the live moa yet. To some minds that have known it only through books, it is represented as a gigantic ostrich or emu, and is the bird of which a leg-bone only was brought to England some thirty-five years ago, and from which one bone a celebrated comparative anatomist constructed the whole bird, not as Eve was made from a rib, but by making all the other bones of the bird to correspond to the size of that one. When finished, the result astonished him as much as the monster of the story did Frankenstein, who made it; but that result was a scientifically correct one. How the world of London, that so petted the hippopotamus when he came there, would go mad about a live moa, the lecturer—say Professor Owen—standing between its legs as showman! He could easily do that. He would like to do so, too, for he built up much of his fame upon the bones of that bird. But that will never be. The moa is gone, so he cannot show now; but we will not let grief for him shadow our brow. His time was up; he belonged to an order of nature that has passed away, and taken with it the mastodon, the dodo, and the moa, and all the Titans that were on the earth in those days. Its skeleton is useful for one purpose—it enlarges one's ideas to look at it. The moa's place, dead as he is, in all the scene that fills the circuit of the sunny hills, is still definable. Its bony skeleton is the best lecturer upon natural history—more impressive than all lecturers that ever opened mouth and laboured away for hours to tell us what these dry bones say in their grand silent language. You take off your hat in the presence of the skeleton of this bird, and sit down and look at it for a good hour, and are desirous to be quiet and let your thoughts have free run. It is the same feeling, I am told, that comes over you at Niagara—the feeling of labour and gestation of mind as new ideas are born within you. It was natural, you perceive, that such as the moa must retire before man and his works. It would run over and destroy them. They or it must go. That feathered giraffe upon two legs—such legs for power!—was wingless and tailless. Its feet and legs were of the earth, on which they ran, strong and heavy, and its head of the air, into which it stretched, light and airy. That king of living birds of flight, the frigate-bird, Audubon tells us, can breakfast at the Cape of Good Hope and dine in New York, so powerful are its large rowing wings. The moa never left the earth in its flight; but, shades of Flying Childers and Eclipse! how he must have "cleared" that earth!

As we looked at its remains, we said to our companion, "What should we back against him for speed, captain?" "You could back nothing but an express train," he replied. "And not many carriages to follow it," we suggested. "Nothing but the engine and the tender if you wanted a show in the race." "If the race could come off, which would you rather ride—the engine or the moa?" "I'd stick to what I'd back—the moa. What a grip one could get round that neck, with both arms!" "But your weight would tell against your chances in the race." "Just as a few more feathers would—a mere feather-weight to that bird. Eh, what a race that would be! London to Birmingham under three hours!" "Could the moa run that time at a stretch, think you?" "Yes, easily, never drawing a thick breath, or turning a hair—no—nor a feather either"—the captain warmed with the greatness of his subject. "Supposing that race to be now—how about going under the bridges and through the tunnels?" "Oh, we'd leave the line to your engine and take on outside the fencing—the country for us." "What about the obstructions there—the hedges, ditches, gates, fences, rails, palings, and the brick and stone walls?" "Clear them all in our stride; never be thrown out of it, and feel no jerk." "What about the waters?" "Nothing in that way between London and Birmingham would stop us. The sea might—clear all the rest with a running leap as a fat barn-door fowl jumps." "No obstructions, then, to that courser, you think?" "Not that I can think of. Obstructions! that bird had a leaping power which, measured by that of the ostrich and other like birds, could have lifted him over everything." "His long jump and his high leap were what do you think?" "Don't mention it; something awful, and yet as light as a fairy's." "He must have gone down from side to side in his run, as a dromedary does—how would you have stuck on?" "Easy enough with arms and legs round that neck, getting into the swing in time; chief trouble would be to catch one's breath." "Suppose yourselves hard pressed by the engine, could you let out?" "Equal at least to double speed." "How so?" "Like to the ostrich and the emu, the moa must have had rudimentary wings; there are none alive to deny it. He would stretch these stumps, and then skim along, touching earth with a toe just now and then." "He could be extended, then, if you had to call on him?" "To any extent, and he'd leave the engine nowhere in the race when he liked. The works of art are but weak imitations of nature. I'd back the moa to run against the locomotive." "How about food and drink," we said, "to keep up the steam?" "Oh, he wanted but little of that. Look at his small head and fine beak—like to the ostrich, he wanted but little, and that little went a great way." "It had to do so, looking at the length of that throat," we said. "He would not want feeding and watering one fiftieth as often as the steam-engine did." "If the moa, as a bird, ever roosted, what then?" "He must have had the strongest scaffold-pole for the purpose." "About the moa's egg, now—don't go away from the subject—what size would that be?" "Big enough to fill a slop-pail, at the very least." "If eatable now, as emus' eggs are, a meal for how many?" "Food for a family for a fortnight at least, perhaps for a month." "You know how hard the emu's egg is—how difficult to break—what about this bird's egg?" "There you beat me; how the young moa ever got out of it, if after the emu fashion, I can't imagine."

The captain's conclusions were roughly made, but no doubt rightly. If the frigate-bird can do the breakfasting in New York and the dinner at the Cape of Good Hope, as Audubon tells us, there is little doubt but that the moa could breakfast on the eastern shore of Maori-land, and have taken a constitutional run of about 150 miles in four hours or so to get an appetite and its dinner on the western coast. We wanted a moa-bone as a relic, and a tattooed Maori's head also, if they could be got; but no such good fortune happened to us. Other folks had wanted such, and gone without them. Like to the relics of Waterloo's battle-field, they should be manufactured somewhere and sent out on spec. As the dense forests, mountain ranges, and untrodden places come to be explored, further remains of the moa will doubtless be found, but that will be in the days far onwards, when our remains shall be like to the moa's, except as to value. Why did the moa retire before man? Do not the large always retire from the company of the little? Gulliver could not have lived in Lilliput! The leviathan squatter retires when the smaller ones—the farmers—come upon his run. They push him backwards, and he retires further from civilization. It was so with the ante-Methuselah giants. Even Cain felt crowded, though men were very scarce in his day, and he sought out a country for himself. The superior know of the jealousy of the inferior, and do not stay to put up with petty annoyances. Like to Landor, they say they "will strive with none, for none are worth their strife." The moa was before man, and was, by the law of his being, to retire when man came—as the gods of old left the earth for Olympus. If the law of development be the law of life, the men we see around us, before whom the black, the red, and the brown man retires, as did the moa before the Maori, will retire before a superior man yet to be developed. By the way, it is time that he came. The native flax of New Zealand—the strongest and hardiest of such plants—retires before the common little creeping clover. That tame little imported growth of the field, by some inscrutable means, kills out the wild, strong, aboriginal plant. It is a sad thing that it does so, for the flax is as useful as the clover, every bit; but there is the fact for reflection that the flax of New Zealand, like to the moa of Maori-land, retires before a puny invader. We may say this in its behalf, that the moa could not have been extirpated by man. Its retirement was voluntary, and not like to that of a dog who leaves the apartment that his instinct tells him he will soon be kicked out of. The Maori had no horses, dogs, or firearms with which to hunt the moa—if such things had been of any use for that purpose. In such a chase the bird might have been seen once, and that would have been all—always supposing that the moa would condescend to run before enemies that one stroke of its foot could have crushed and scattered. Nothing but fire-arms could have touched it, and the Maori, we have said, had none. The Maories know no more of the moa than does the white man, and have no particulars to tell about it. As an article of food it could have been no more palatable than shark or whale. It was not intended to be for man's time in any way—either as enemy or friend, for his service or his food.

There is another bird of New Zealand whose time is nearly up—a wingless and tailless bird of the earth also. It is a fiftieth cousin to the moa, and has decreased in size far more than to that extent in the course of its consanguineous removal. It is the apteryx—a little barn-door fowl of a moa —shy, and retiring of habit, and very difficult indeed to be found. It was supposed to be as extinct as the moa, and is so set down in some books on ornithology, but an occasional one now and then comes to the front. Ten years ago a live specimen of the apteryx was on show in Melbourne as the last of its race—price so much. We never passed but we looked at it, stopping the pathway and staring the little stranger out of countenance. Who could do otherwise? Suppose that the last one of a race of men was on show, the last Jew or the last gipsy, is there one amongst us who would be ever tired of "seeing off" such an emigrant as that? How often we go to see a last appearance of this or that departing star, and flock more to do so when it is the positive last appearance in public! With that bird it was thought to be the last appearance previous to the departure for London and for life of the last apteryx in this world—Campbell's "Last man" in feathers.

CHAPTER XXXIII.

THE MAORIES "AT HOME"—TO DINNER.

WE had always liked to dine out of the routine on Christmas Day, and have accomplished some very out-of-the-common-way Christmas dinners in our time—notably that one amongst the Blue Mountains of New South Wales, whither we had gone by a train that had to bring us back the same day, but broke down and did not. Yet dinner was achieved amongst the rugged peaks of those wild mountains, and as a Christmas dinner it ate all the better from the trouble we had in getting it, and our intense surprise in getting any dinner whatever under the circumstances. The story of that dinner has already been told. When the steamship "Omeo" took us away from Victoria to Hokitika, in the beginning of December, we had promised to ourselves a Christmas dinner with the Maories in one of their wharries, or native huts, at one of their pahs, or Maori villages. We had no clear idea how it was to be done, but done it was to be—and was. We had got some notion of Maori ways and manners from the two days' enclosure in a coach with the two Maori ladies, one of them "of quality," crossing the Middle Island, and had picked up a few words and phrases, which, as we used them, showed in what esteem we held the language, making so much of a very little of it. For all the rest we trusted to fortune, and tobacco, which we had found to be, like to the old English snuff-box, very good as an introduction. On the 24th December, we started at six in the morning from Christchurch for Timaru, a coast settlement about 100 miles to the south of the Middle Island. We were *en route* overland to Dunedin. We had a good four-horse coach and a very amiable driver, who had been at that occupation for several years. Few people travel for whole days on stage-coaches in these latter-day railway times, but all who have done so must have noticed how a long day's ride, from six in the morning to eight in the evening, is like to a lifetime. At starting, in the early youth of the journey, how lively, chatty, and pleasant, how buoyant and youthful everybody is! How much quieter they have got towards the middle age—midday we mean—and how staid and sober, and sleepy they get as afternoon wears away and evening—old age—comes on! The last hour or so of the journey is all quietness, save an occasional yawn or snore, and we weary of ourselves and our company, and wait impatiently that change which "comes when it will come" alike to the stage traveller of the one day and of the longer journey of the day of life. Towards the end of the afternoon our driver pointed out to us the native village of Arowainui, about fourteen miles from Timaru. "Are there plenty of Maories there?" we asked. "Oh, lots of them," was the answer, although we found that our driver had been for some years too near the place to have had any curiosity to go into it for pleasure, and his business had never taken him within more than a mile of it. To-morrow was Christmas Day, and no coach started from Timaru until the day afterwards. Here was luck, and here our Maori village and our Christmas dinner! We fairly crowed at our good fortune, though no one that we mentioned it to on the coach seemed to see it in the same light. Our sea-captain companion—a fine old "salt"—thought it only too absurd to be treated as a serious intention. Our driver would, if we liked, bring a two-horse buggy, and drive us out to Arowainui next morning, but he too thought it a strange caper, and, like to the captain, opined that the hotel at Timaru would furnish a better Christmas dinner by far. We explained that no doubt the hotel would supply the best dinner, but a dinner like to that was to be got at any time and anywhere, by paying for it; but what we wanted was this, that being in Maori land, and at Christmas time, we should have our Christmas dinner with our hosts, the fathers of the country, and be received into the family circle, and be treated as guests, and have a memorable time of it. "Oh, if you can do it, well enough, but the chances are all against it," was the encouraging answer we got. "You can stay away if you don't like the venture," we replied, for go we would, whether or no, and so we arranged for the buggy at nine in the morning, and for stores of cigars and bottled ale. With this bottled ale another idea had come into our mind. We would not only dine with the Maories, but they should, after dinner, drink the health of our mother, an old lady far away in old England, and who was, we were quite sure, drinking our health on that Christmas Day in very different company. That last notion of ours was treated as the wildest of impracticabilities, "And so," we replied, "was the siege of Paris six months ago, and yet it had come to pass!" Such bold comparison silenced all opposition, and the grumblers took their seats in the buggy after all, half hoping for the failure they had prophesied. People are so disinclined sometimes to assist in carrying out projects not of their own conception.

On a lovely breezy morning we started from Timaru for Arowainui on a cruise for a Christmas dinner. Those who had doubted our success now seemed to have referred the matter to their previous experience, and to have gone into the business on the faith of our preceding luck in other business in which we had trusted to fortune. How delightful was that Christmas morning's drive on that fine New Zealand day! We did not then know that our English friends at their firesides in the old country were then shrinking from cold at twenty degrees below freezing point—the only English winter for twenty-one years—or we should have pitied them more than we did. We never go into any happiness but we wish to have our friends with us, and that was our real wish on that exhilarating morning—a fitting wish for Christmas Day.

Arowainui, the native village, was reached about mid-day, and in its midst we called a halt, and got out of our vehicle to take stock of the place. There were some twenty or thirty of wooden huts stuck about here and there, at a distance of about one or two hundred feet or more from each other. They looked outside, as they afterwards proved to be on inspection inside, of one enclosure only—one-roomed huts—of about twenty feet square. These are the Maori "wharries." None seemed better or worse than another, and none had chimneys, kitchens, or out-buildings of any sort. These were the homes of our intended hosts. In a long wharry of some sixty feet by twenty, a large number of villagers had been attending morning service at that their native church. Saying good-morning ("Tenakoe") to every one we met, we went in as they came out, and found ourselves inside this Maori church—a building very like to an old and rickety barn. Only a portion of the congregation had left. A large number were squatting in little groups along both sides of the building. A pathway of about a yard or so wide was left from end to end, along the middle, and ridged off by thin poles laid along the ground—there was no flooring. This pathway and the side squatting places were covered with green stuff of some sort—native flax or rushes. Service was over, and we presumed that family affairs, or the nature of the sermon, were being discussed by the various groups. Naturally, on entering church, we took off our hats, and assumed as respectful a demeanour as possible, whilst looking out for a Maori who could talk English. We thought the native preacher to be the most likely, but found that his acquirements in that way were very small. On different sides of this Maori temple we discovered a young man and a girl who were able to talk to us. They quite understood the importance of that day, and we learnt that some ceremonies were to take place in special honour of it. They showed no inclination, however, to take us round the village, nor assist our efforts towards dinner in any way. We left church somewhat disappointed, but still with a good heart in the matter we had come about. We saw now faces at doors that had been closed, and from one we heard a cheery attempt at saying in English, "Good morning" to us. That was what we wanted. We shook hands with that man, and got him into tow up to where our buggy stood. His eyes glistened at the sight of a cigar, and we found that he would drink our ale, and took care that he did so. He went with us round the village, and things now began to open up wonderfully well. We had a prescience of good things to come. Doubt and fear died, and standing o'er their graves we smelt the aroma of dinner. In one wharry we found a live European, and he was not there to be killed and cooked, as might once have been his fate. How we hailed him—that one of our kindred! and how we curiously smiled when we found that he was on the same errand bent—dinner-hunting also. We took him into our confidence, or he took us, and we agreed to combine—we four whites, ourself, the captain, the driver, and the squatter, for such our new friend was, and down from his neighbouring run in search of a Christmas sensation. The news he told us was of the most encouraging kind. In the church barn buildings, that we had lately left, a great Maori feast was to take place in the afternoon, and he was bidden to that and to all the ceremonies and fakes that accompanied it, and he would take us. In our delight we turned to the captain and the driver, and asked if they did not think it would be best for them to take the trap back to Timaru, and dine at the hotel? They had been such good prophets, and it was so evident that none but a madman would have thought of getting a dinner at Arowainui, except ourself and our new-found friend the squatter, whom we supposed they would call mad too. It was delightful to nag them thus after all that they had made us endure. They were now the enthusiasts, and were full of suggestions for all sorts of things, in which we would take no part—sticking to our original programme of the dinner, and that one toast afterwards. Our simple dinner was now to be a feast, and there were all the Maori rites and ceremonies to be thrown in! As a prelude, we visited, with the squatter, the huts of most of the villagers. One of these "wharries" was just like to another. In them were always one, or two, or three Maories sleeping, another peeling potatoes, and one or two children. A fire would be burning in a hole, sunk generally in the centre of the hut, to which fireplace there was—can one believe it?—no chimney! As there were no windows, the doorway supplied all purposes. When that was shut, all would be darkness, or firelight and smoke. We thought that it might be truth that there was no place like home, however humble, and also that habit must be a wonderful disinfectant to let folks live such a life—and like it! Such intelligent people, and such fine-looking people too! and so healthy and strong, and such artists as they were—witness their wonderfully-tattooed faces, and their flax-made mats and bags. Why! one-twentieth part of the time and talent bestowed on that tattooing would, if bestowed on their dwellings, have made their huts habitable and comfortable—to European tastes.

Perched up twelve or fifteen feet, on three or four poles, were to be seen square, box-like structures, which we found to be provision stores, kept at that height out of harm's way. Dried fish were kept there, and potatoes, and corn, and roots of all sorts for Maori meals. We envied the Maori stomach and digestion as we looked at the stuff, and thought of the coming dinner, at which we were to taste of the Christmas cheer. In wandering about in and out of these wharries, we feared that we might take company away from some of them, but were assured by our squatter friend that annoying insects are unknown in these Maori houses. That was some compensation for their apparent wretchedness. There was in one hut a very fine Maori and his wife, asleep on separate sides of the fire-hole, wrapped each in prettily-woven native flax mats. They arose from their slumbers, and sat up to welcome us. Mahumitti, the man, and Annui, the woman, were as fine-looking human animals as the eye could wish to dwell upon. Properly attired, this pair would have forced all attention to themselves had they walked through the Row in Hyde Park

z

at the hour of promenade. Really good and great things had often come out of these pigsty-like huts. Heki, the great Maori warrior, had come from such an one, and in one of these wharries we found Kiti Kohoota!

We had not visited New Zealand in vain. Had we seen nothing but Kiti in that two months' journey, we were well repaid. We must prelude that her pretty name was sounded as Kitty. She had two sisters, Aomi and Koi, but of the

THE MAORI TYPE (MALE).

Kohoota family Kiti was the only flower. Beautiful vision, flee not away! Thou dark-browed Venus, thou Moorish-looking Desdemona—" the cunningest work of an all-excelling nature"!—we know not where is that Promethean power that can photograph thee as thou art, or bring thee to life—on paper. Thou flower of "a sunny isle, where summer skies and summer women smile," would that we could romance about thee, or were poetical enough to sing thy praises! We can but write the poorest words of thee, and say common-place praises in thy behalf. Books and poems would we write, and call them by thy name. Music should be set to our verses in thy praise, and Kiti Kohoota be synonymous with all that is womanly-lovely for the rest of the nineteenth century at least. Do we exceed bounds in telling of thy charms? Let the three who were with us bear witness! Long they looked at thee, Kiti, and again and again they

THE MAORI TYPE (FEMALE).

returned to look. The captain would be missing, and then driver, and then squatter, and they were, one and all, apart or together, to be found with thee on that Christmas Day. What queer excuses they had for being there! Captain had left his stick, driver wanted a light, squatter wanted this, that, or the other; but we wanted only to look at thee, that was all—and to annihilate them. What was written of one dark beauty might be appropriated entirely to Kiti. She was a beauty "like the night of sunny climes and starry skies, and all that was best of dark and bright met in her aspect and her eyes." Oh, those eyes! Not forgetting our share in the life hereafter, we wished only to live in those eyes, or, to be plain, in sight of them, and to dwell in the heaven of their smile for all eternity. What a smile Kiti had! a smile that would bring any one to her feet, and leave him there—on his knees. The head of this beauty was a wonder of hair, and eyes, and lips, and pearly teeth. The hair was of a peculiarly

THE MAORI TYPE (FEMALE).

dark shade, wavy and curly, and abundant to profusion. She was tall and most graceful in figure, with hands and feet to match her peerless face. No trouble was there in seeing those feet, for Kiti wore neither shoe nor stocking, and looked all the better for it. Nothing that you could have put upon Kiti would have improved her. It would have been like to dressing the bird of paradise. Hers was the beauty unadorned, and that which any attempt to ornament would but disfigure.

Graceful Kiti Kohoota! light of our New Zealand Christmas Day, and of all nature's beauties that we then saw, how weak is all attempt to tell of thy power—the power of loveliness! Did not we want thee to come to Europe, to be a model to all sculptors and a subject for all painters, and did not the driver say that thou wouldst be worth a thousand a year as—oh, what desecration!—barmaid at any town hotel? Driver thought but little of sculptors and painters, and his ideas, so expressed, told of the highest estimation—in his way. Kiti, "a ministering angel shalt thou be when he lies"—wherever he may lie; but never mayst thou help to intoxicate us other than by thy bright smiles, the music of thy voice, and the merriment of thy bubbling laugh!

We must get on to dinner, though that meal had lost much of its attractions since we had lost our hearts. What are dinners to the love-sick? Wandering down to the hall of the intended feast, we found all in preparation outside. We perceived then that our dinner was to be cold and our drink hot. We would have reversed that arrangement if we had our will in the matter. The drink was contained in ten large, wide-mouthed boiling pots, and was the very coarsest attempt at tea that we had ever tasted—and we have tasted some queer tea in our time. In '52, we had tea in Fryer's Creek, in Victoria, that was made with clayey water, that coloured it to the same extent that milk would have done, and in it there floated curious remains of vegetables that were called "posts and rails." We had tasted tea on ship-board also, that had been made with water from rusted tanks, and was of a strange reddish colour; and we had tasted tea that had been made from tank water that had been too long preserved, and that smelt of anything but a rich pekoe bouquet. This Maori tea of Arowainui was, however, a thing by itself. It seemed to have been made long since, and to have got stale, and to have been warmed up again and again, and sweetened with treacle or some other nastiness. We have heard poor drink damned with the faint praise of being "warm and wet." This tea was all that, and was, in addition, sweet and nasty. Whenever we grumbled about anything in our school-days, we were told that it was to be hoped that we might never get worse. We echo that hope with regard to the Maori tea, with the full belief that we could never drink it if we did. Of course, with this Maori tea there was no milk, nor any substitute for it. We have had some substitutes for milk to tea in our days, and among them have been eggs, butter, and gin, but these were in centres of civilization—not in wharries.

Heads had been counted, and the dishes were being set apart for each of the little groups inside, and this seemed to be a troublesome business to settle. So much dried fish, so much of the dried mashed potato, cold, very high in flavour, and dreadfully hard, much like to stinking Portland cement; so much cake, made without leaven or eggs, and as tasteless and uneatable as an old door-mat; and so much cold mutton and a stuff intended to represent Christmas pudding, which was only the aforesaid cake in another shape, with plums here and there. We broke our nails in the first attempt to tear it, as the fingers do all duties—that of knives, forks, and spoons—at Maori meals. That was a pudding of Christmas puddings! When masticated a little, it stuck to the mouth in a most provoking manner, and could neither be ejected nor swallowed. We brought a piece of it away as a souvenir, as also some of the dried fish and a piece of the cake and the cement-like potato. They are preserved in a native flax shoe, which we found in the wharry of Kiti's mother, and which we prize above all the viands it contains.

The groups inside the grand dining-hall had to be counted again and again, and the "messes" for each to be arranged and rearranged. We got tired of lolloping about to see it done, and thought we could have set it right and square in a tithe of the time. We generally think that way of the difficulties of other people—'tis human nature. An old chief, Kohoo by name, a grandfather of Kiti's, we believe, and the middle-aged preacher at the morning service, seemed to have the arrangement of everything, and pottered and muddled over it just as men will do in these domestic matters. Women sat about—tailor-fashion—outside; some nursing their babies on their backs. Looking at the fashion attentively, there is much to be said in favour of back-nursing. It is easier altogether, and avoids compression of the lungs, and all the pains and weariness of constant bending of the head and shoulders. A swaying movement from side to side seemed to rock the child to sleep as easily as the backward and forward rocking of the white mother. Inside the building the utmost patience prevailed. Maories are not fidgety, and wait with the patience of people to whom it is not a usual matter to dine every day.

We found occupation for spare time with an intelligent Maori named Mohe Tehike. He knew a little English and was of a tractable nature. We got a bottle of beer and our tumbler, and getting him away to ourselves—behind a distant wharry—we drilled him into his intended duty of drinking our mother's health at the coming dinner. He got to perfection at last, and would have done for a Lord Mayor's toastmaster. That he did not know the meaning of the ceremony or of the words he uttered made it all the funnier and better. To see him grasping the glass in outstretched hand and roaring out, "To te hent of Arar Hinkton!"—for that was as near as the fourteen letters in the Maori language would let him get—was a sublime sight to us, who had tutored the savage.

We went in to dinner at last, introduced by Mohe Tchike into his family party—two middle-aged women and an old man. We occupied a central position in the place, and counted twelve groups on each side, and four at one end. The other end was appropriated to a large fireplace, in which, on some dead ashes, part of the feast was piled up. We four whites got distributed somehow each into a different group. That arrangement was quite accidental, and was just as well as not, since we had more time for looking about us, instead of talking. Our Maori friends were quite useless to us, and we to them in the way of language, so that we could not communicate ideas, even supposing that either of us happened to have any. Squatting in tailor-fashion is very irksome to the novice, and we were beginning to tire of it when a walk round was called by the chief who stood fronting the fireplace. He chanted, or intoned something or other, on which every one started to their legs. Now the provisions had been spread on the ground down the middle avenue, a complete mess, kettle of tea and all, opposite to each group. We had to walk by the side of the fare, and all round the building several times, walking in single file, ourself being sandwiched between the two Maori women of our group. It was necessary to pick our steps carefully, and yet it was an irresistible necessity to look up occasionally to see captain, driver, and squatter revolving around in this queer procession. Seats were then resumed, or, rather, we again squatted on the ground, and kept silence whilst the chief read something from a book, to which a chorus or something of the sort was responded at intervals by the company. There was then another chant and another procession, this time the reverse way to the previous one. We began to notice that the effect of these walkings around was to well dust the intended dinner spread at our feet. On this occasion it was five times go round and then another squatting, and another reading and more responses. It occurred to us now that all this was an imitation "high church" service, and that, instead of standing up during the singing-part, we walked round instead—a very great improvement, and to be recommended for adoption by those who are bursting to make innovations in their church service arrangements. There were three more to come of these walks around, and it began to be a hard matter to keep from laughing at the looks of captain, driver, and squatter, as they, in turn, came opposite to us in this most monotonous "breakdown." As for the cake and fish, and potatoes and mutton and tea, they got nicely dusted, quite browned by the time that the order came to fall upon them. It came at last, and we tore away at the fish first, and then at the mutton, and then tried the pounded potatoes, the sawdust cake and the stickjaw pudding. We tried occasionally to suck our fingers, in order to be in the fashion, but we felt that we did not play our part well. What with love-sickness and the processions and other fakes, we had not appetite enough to do as others did. On looking round, we found that the three other guests, driver, captain, and squatter, had got together in the fireplace at the top, now that the provisions had been removed thence. They were comparing ideas, I could see, and taking stock of ourself in a very critical manner. Taking a partly-eaten chop in one hand, and a piece of cake in the other, we arose and joined them in the ashes. They were each gnawing away at something, and had got a kettle of the tea to themselves. They had to lift up this kettle and drink from out it, lip to rim. Somehow we seemed to get dirtier than the Maories did at this sort of business. We can easily understand why. We were not used to it. Every one has noticed how those unused to the pen will ink and smear their fingers in their efforts with it. All novices mess themselves in their attempts—so did we. We wanted well washing after that dinner, and well brushing too, and—oh, vanity!—we could not face Kiti Kohoota again in that plight.

We disappeared from the group to give the signal to Mohe Tehike, and then resumed squatting. He did his part well. Shifting himself to the end of the building, he arose, and, holding out his tumbler, which, by the way, he stuck to afterwards, he shouted, "To te hent of Arar Hinkton!" and then, emptying the glass, sat down. To say that we felt proud of our doings after that is but feebly to express our feelings. We distributed cigars all around, and ale to those that would drink it, and listened to many imitations of Mohe Tehike's toast. After that we gathered up some fragments of the feast as memorials of it, and shook hands with everybody.

When we were all seated in the buggy for our start, the natives came trooping out to see the departure, and we went on our way, waving hats and handkerchiefs, in a general and joyous manner, quite satisfied with our Christmas Day amongst the Maories.

CHAPTER XXXIV.

EAST COASTING, AND COACHING.

A THREE days' continuous coaching is not a thing to be done without knowing it. It leaves its mark behind. It leaves its mark in front too, if the time be summer and the days sunny. How the sun came down upon one about noon, in the three days of that drive! It burnt all the skin off our nose, lips, and cheeks, and made our eyes redden and smart. The jolting about is lively enough in the fore-part of the day, but irksome towards the end—when you have pretty well got tired of such play and would wish to rest. With all its drawbacks of sun and shaking, coasting by coach will be preferred by landsmen, as it was by us, as we went southwards from Christchurch. From that place the first port is Akaroa, a small seaport—mostly of French settlers. It has a pretty harbour, and a pretty story attached to it. The story is really of greatest interest to Englishmen and New Zealanders. It is relative to three powers that at the same time struck for the dominion of New Zealand. They were England, France, and Baron de Thierry—on his own hook. "Three up" for a kingdom—to speak in sporting language. Akaroa is the little spot that represents the Frenchman's share in New Zealand. A few acres in the Northern Island, and, latterly, an additional six feet by two there, represent all that De Thierry, that baron bold, got out of the fire. The rest of New Zealand is divided between the claims of the English and the Maories. England's title-deed to New Zealand is a parchment called the "Treaty of Waitangi"—about the largest deed of conveyance, or a conveyance of more land than is contained in any other title-deed that exists. That deed is signed by New Zealand chieftains. Such part of the land as England has not taken by that or by other purchases from the Maories, the latter hold, and their title is that of occupation for the required legal time—fifteen years and upwards—especially the upwards.

The names of great men should not be forgotten, nor should the names of those who attempt to do great things. Success, which is fortune, makes all the difference. The Baron de Thierry shall have a name in our story as one who fully understood the force of the maxim, "Nothing venture nothing have." He proclaimed himself King of New Zealand, and made a bold stroke, like Louis Napoleon's of Boulogne and Strasburg, at attaining the title. The one kept his title a few hours, the other a few years. We feel equally for both, as we do for all those who have done anything to enliven the commonplace of life.

In the year 1840, Captain Hobson, of the Royal Navy, formally hoisted the British flag upon the North Island of New Zealand, after having obtained from the natives, on England's behalf, that deed of cession of territory and sovereignty before mentioned. He chose Auckland for his capital, and was not a day too soon in taking possession, as a French man-of-war arrived very shortly afterwards to do that for the French which Hobson had but just done on behalf of the British. The English Colonial Office had dallied almost too long in taking possession of this New Zealand jewel of the British Crown. The French commander then sailed for the Middle Island, and landed at Akaroa, but some idea of such intention had got wind, and Captain Hobson despatched an English war-sloop thither, which arrived and planted the British flag but a few hours before the Frenchman came. There is no doubt but that the latter said something equivalent in French to "sold again!" but that is for the dry pages of history, and not for us to repeat. The French settlers, however, landed, and formed a small friendly settlement, which New Caledonia and other French attractions have since frittered away to almost nothing. The Baron de Thierry's part in the story is equally interesting—perhaps more so. He was the son of a French emigrant, resident in London, a good musician, and a teacher of music, of polished manners and unbounded self-confidence—to call it by any other name would be, perhaps, too rough on so smooth a man. We will not question his title, because we know that continental barons are as common as native Australian kings, two of whom may be found at a time seated on one doorstep. When young, the baron had eloped with a lady pupil of his of a good family, taking advantage of the confidence reposed in him as her music teacher. He became afterwards a travelling tutor, and got attached in some way to a foreign embassy. While thus occupied, he met with Hongi, one of the chiefs of the Northern Island of New Zealand, who had been taken to England on a visit. That was some years before England took formal possession of New Zealand. With some scheming ideas in his head he thought to buy some 50,000 acres of the Northern Island from Chief Hongi for the price of thirty-six axes, or tomahawks, and drew up some paper for Hongi's signature to that effect. Whether the thirty-six axes, worth about five pounds, were paid in kind or paid for at all, does not clearly appear; but in 1835 this enterprising schemer forwarded letters to the Governments of England, France, and the United States, announcing his modest intention, not of taking possession of his wonderful purchase, but, his ideas having enlarged meanwhile, to establish himself in sovereignty in New Zealand. He, no doubt, announced the name that he intended to call his kingdom, but that has not appeared. He dated his letter from some neutral ground to which he had gone for the purpose, and signed himself "Charles Baron de Thierry, Sovereign Chief of New Zealand." We are writing sober facts, which we wonder that no novelist has yet worked up as the basis of a fiction. There can be no doubt that this incredibly confident schemer had raised funds from some poor dupes on the strength, or rather weakness, of his extravagant pretensions. He must have done so, for he found means to get a ship to take him to Sydney, and called at Tahiti on the way. He left his mark at Tahiti by making a declaration of his "rights" and intentions there. The ship that carried this Cæsar and his strange fortunes arrived in Sydney towards the middle of 1837, and here De Thierry began great operations. He induced ninety-three Europeans—loafers picked up from bars and street corners—to join his expedition—form the nucleus of the De Thierry court—and gave them all their titles and dignities. The captain of the ship that took away this riff-raff was to be admiral of the fleet of the future kingdom. We see now that he must have had money, or these ninety-three Sydney loafers would have had nought to do with him. They were men, no doubt, of ruined blood and prospects, but Tennyson tells us that such men are wise, and from their mud to no fancy flies will rise. The money we may be quite sure was not De Thierry's. Early in 1838, this king, court, and high admiral landed at Hokianga in the Northern Island. He proclaimed his kingdom at once—unfurled his flag, and ordered the court to stand back from his presence and to do him royal honours. The ninety-three and the admiral we can believe readily did so, but the few British settlers there and the natives laughed at him. There were settlers there who had bought their land with better payments than he had, and, indeed, he was told that he had made no payment whatever, the thirty-six axes being only in the nature of a deposit. He collapsed at once. At the slightest pressure the De Thierry bubble burst. His kingdom died without a kick. On his promising to behave himself properly, he was, in pity, allowed some small allotment of land to squat upon, for which he was to make after-payment in blankets, when he should get them. He started a saw-mill with some of the Sydney men who would work, but hard work and his majesty were not friendly, and he sought afterwards to live by teaching the harp and giving lessons in music. So went the glory of De Thierry! He never went back to Europe, but hung about Auckland until his death, which happened but lately. He remained true to his tricky character to the last, however, and about 1864 induced some fools to invest thousands of pounds in putting up large buildings to work out a wonderful method that he led them to believe he had found for cleaning the native flax. It was as great a failure as was his kingly fiasco. Why his dupes never had his theory tested before losing their money, they no doubt asked of themselves when too late. Such is usually the case. Such men as De Thierry are of the peculiarities of humanity. They are not to be accounted for. Looking to his swindling meanness on the one hand, and his mighty aspirations on the other, we can imagine that such as he might have been the offspring, had Count Cagliostro married Joan of Arc, or if Jeremy Diddler had wedded Joanna Southcote.

A stage beyond Akaroa is Timara, an east-coast township; and a further day's stage from that is the white-stoned township of Oamaru, from whence came the stone that the town-hall of Melbourne has been faced with. These are both townships supported by a squatting back country, and will progress with the slow steps of such-like places. Before entering upon Oamaru, we make the passage of the Waitangi —a water that separates the province of Canterbury from that of Otago. The passage of the Waitangi is not a matter to be forgotten. It has to be done upon the zigzag principle, like to the wonderful ascent of the Blue Mountains in New South Wales by the zigzag railway. The Waitangi river has a wide, shallow bed of about a mile in extent, down which, however, run several rushing mountain streams, or, perhaps, one mountain stream which divides into several channels. To go straight across this the four boatmen find to be impossible, so that your boat passage is done on the principle of tacking, as done by a sailing vessel. Half a mile up that way, and half a mile down the other, and that again and again, and then when the pinch comes, over into the water go all the boatmen, and, standing therein up to their shoulders, give all their propelling strength to the passage of the particular rapid that stops the way. It is a long, troublesome job, this passage of the Waitangi, and the boatmen will earn the silver reward which they claim when it is over.

Wandering about the little sea-side township of Oamaru in the evening, we came upon a tent pitched in a field. A poor tent it was, consisting only of a canvas hanging from a stick fixed to the trunk of a tree, the sides only, neither the back nor the front, being covered. We thought it to belong to some road-side stone-breaker, not given to providing too comfortably for his sleeping accommodation, but satisfied with the luxurious couch that a day's hard work in the sun provides anywhere when he seeks sleep. To our surprise it proved to be the residence of a travelling showman, with his wife and two small children. We had no thought that an acrobat, with a wife both vocally and instrumentally musical, could come to such very hard lines as these. They were young people, and their two poor little barefooted children were pretty things of about four and two years of age. These strolling players had made very bad times of it indeed. They had been going through New Zealand from village to village, and township to township, for five months, and bad luck, lately, had quite broken them down. Their travelling waggon had tumbled to pieces on the rough roads, and their horse gone incurably lame and worthless. A little pile of dirty spangled finery was on one side of the wretched tent, and the poor infant sleeping thereon. The elder girl was fetching water, a can at a time, from some distance, and looked more cold and wet and wretched than we remembered ever seeing child look. This poor half-clothed pair had seemingly lost all heart and energy in their struggle with hard fortune. A few handbills in the tent told us of their line of "entertainment," but that word seemed very out-of-place, contemplating as we did the utterly miserable condition of those who were to entertain others. "We performed there two days ago," said they, alluding to the place named on the bill, "but only four people came, and that would not pay for the room. Similar bad luck at the last three places—never saw such times. Regularly stumped up now, and had to raise this loaf, this sheep's pluck, and these potatoes on loan." "Raising on loan" we supposed to be professional language for plain begging, for that seemed to be the real state of things. We stopped an hour or more with these people, devising ways and means of doing something to mend this state of affairs. They had got to such low water, however, that this was not easily to be done, but we think that we left these representatives of the stage in New Zealand better off than we found them. We were not altogether in the best of moods when we happened on them—one of our fellow-passengers on the coach had much annoyed us; but all our little troubles went to the wind at the sight of such tribulation as theirs, and we felt that we knew not what real trouble was, and so went very philosophically to bed. These people furnished a striking example of mental phenomena. The desert traveller, dying for water, sees the mirage of a distant lake before him that exists only in his fevered imagination; and these broken-down strollers were similarly affected. Dying for what pence would buy, they could talk of nothing but thousands of pounds. I never heard capital so lightly spoken of. So-and-so had cleared thousands on a similar trip to theirs. What's-his-name, who began like to themselves, was clearing thousands yearly. With a new waggon and a fresh start they would soon be worth a thousand or two. But for this, or that, or the other happening from time to time, they would then have been worth—thousands. These "thousands" were always before the starving couple like as the lake of water to the desert traveller, and we thought that one would be as likely to be reached as the other. Their ladder had gone up beyond reach—they were a long way from the lowest round of it. It stood on a bank—that ladder did—and they were, metaphorically, down in a deep ditch below it, with very steep sides up to vantage ground.

New Zealand is the land of long distances. What there is of population is but few and far between. We rolled along day after day, with long stretches of mountains on the one side, and the Pacific Ocean on the other—and got very tired of it. The coaches, too, dwindled very much in size and accommodation, and the drivers deteriorated, and so did the horses. We started with a fine coach, driver, and team of four; but stage after stage we got a worse coach, meaner-looking drivers, and meaner cattle. At last we came to a shandry-dan sort of waggon, two scrubbers of animals, and a lout of a boy. Things at the worst will mend. Next morning was to introduce us to the last stage, and it did so, and to a splendidly six-horsed coach, and a driver to match. That was a good finish, and, to make it better, the road and scenery improved greatly, the last thirty miles into Dunedin being almost a pretty copy of the grand first seventy-five miles out from Hokitika. This fine scenery begins shortly after we left Waikiouati (Wyker-white), and culminates in Horse Range, Trotter's Gorge, Kilmog, and Blueskin. The views from the summit of some of the hills were of the grandest, and seen from the main top of a stage coach—fifteen feet from the ground—were of very exciting character. From Blueskin Hill the first glimpse of Dunedin, in the far distance, is obtained, and a very fine view it is all around from thence down hill into the city. A turn of the road reveals Port Chalmers, the pretty port of Dunedin, with islands dotting the harbour like to a miniature Port Jackson. With that, all resemblance to Port Jackson ends, as the waters of Port Chalmers will not admit vessels of any draught within many miles of the city.

CHAPTER XXXV.

NORTH AND SOUTH CONTRASTS—AUCKLAND—DUNEDIN.

CHARACTERISTIC cities in every way are Dunedin in the south of the south island, and Auckland in the north of the north one. They are a week's steam voyage distant from each other, and are not likely to be assimilated in their peculiarities from too much mixture of their inhabitants. The capital of New Zealand, in which its high parliament meets, was, until lately, Auckland. To accommodate the representatives of the southern provinces, the seat of government has been removed to Wellington, which is situate midway between Auckland and Dunedin. At this change the people of Auckland are too indignant as yet to speak fully their feelings. What they think about it is something that finds vent in one word only at present, and that is, "separation." Dunedin is a little Melbourne, and has been brought to what it is mainly by Melbourne men, their money and their enterprise. Auckland is a lesser Sydney, partaking in every way of the characteristic of that city and the people of it, with whom it has most frequent communication. What Melbourne and its people did for Dunedin, Sydney and its folks have done for Auckland. Melbourne has done best. In the works of man, Dunedin, as a city built, is far before Auckland, though only about one-fourth of Auckland's age. The climates, too, of the places are in difference like to the differences in the climates of their prototypes. Sydney and Auckland have much of the same sort of weather, and Dunedin is as much cooler than Auckland as Melbourne is cooler than Sydney. The well-built and paved streets, and the shops, with all their goods inside, which characterize Melbourne, are also features of Dunedin. The unpaved streets, and badly-built and unpainted houses of Auckland, with the shop goods all exposed outside, are all Sydney-like in their nature. Prince's Street, Dunedin, is like to a smaller Collins Street, Melbourne, and Queen Street, Auckland, is a veritable little edition of that characteristic street—George Street, Sydney. Dunedin is like to Melbourne also in its harbour, its shipping having to anchor at a port some distance from the city; while at Auckland, as at Sydney, in a magnificent harbour at each place, the navies of the world might bring their masts beneath the windows of the city houses. In Dunedin, as in Melbourne, one sees no aboriginals, but in Auckland they are a feature of the city, as they used to be in Sydney. Auckland has grown, in some thirty-five years or so, since its settlement, house by house at a time, and presents, like to Sydney, the singularity of such gradual growth, in no two houses scarcely looking alike in architecture or in age, or in choice of line of frontage. Dunedin, like to Melbourne, has had no growth, but came to city shape all at once, fully grown, as Richard the Third came into the world with all his teeth cut, or as Minerva came a grown woman from the brain of Jove. Each way of producing a city has its advantages. The poet and the painter and others with an eye to the picturesque will prefer the gradual growth-like appearance of Sydney and Auckland, with all their drawbacks of pigsty and palace side by side—a footway two feet wide in some places, and six feet in others, flagged here, wood-paved there, cobble stone-covered further on, with mud and puddle intersections. That is natural, but not nice for walking, nor pleasant to the eye for those who like things to look orderly. Those that do so will prefer Melbourne and Dunedin, with their well-paved streets and newly-built stone and brick buildings.

Both Auckland and Dunedin have had to contend with

unlevel sites for building cities. Both are all hill and dale. Prince's Street, in the latter city, is a long cutting, with the rising ground left on both sides. To turn into many of the side streets is to begin a toilsome up-hill trudge, not at all agreeable. It is the same at Auckland, and very trying are both towns to the asthmatic visitor. At Dunedin said visitor will, in other respects, not know that he is out of England. We tried to find something by which we could realize to ourselves that we were as far distant from Great Britain as we ever could be on this globe, but utterly failed to do so. The town looks like to a slice of London, and the people like to Londoners, if we except, of course, the beggars. Of that curse of old countries there is a conspicuous absence, so to speak, all through the Australias. Dunedin is, like to Melbourne, far away from the gold diggings, to which it is the port of landing, and which have made it what it is. They are some eighty or a hundred miles in the interior, similarly as Ballarat and Bendigo are situated with regard to Melbourne. It is the same with Auckland. The Thames goldfield, to which it is the city of supply, is a six-hours' steamer's journey off, but of that more anon. We speak now of the cities only.

Dunedin is permeated by the Scotch element, its founders, in 1848, being ninety colonists of the Free Kirk of Scotland, who arrived there per the "John Wickliffe," and who, as it has since turned out, could not have done a better thing; for though Dunedin—the ancient name of Edinburgh—was nothing until 1862, the discovery of gold in the neighbourhood at that time sent shoals of folks thither, and built Dunedin as we see it now. In Auckland the old colonial element is most prominent, the majority of the settlers being from New South Wales. Mails to Auckland are taken thither *via* Sydney, and sent thence from Auckland. That city has far more communication with Sydney, which is five days' steaming away from it, than with any part of the south island of New Zealand. The south island communicates chiefly with Melbourne. The approach to Dunedin, both by land and water, is equally fine. We have, in our chapter on "East Coasting and Coaching," referred to the prettiness of the coach-road into it. The hour's steaming from Port Chalmers to Dunedin is prettily panoramic in respect to scenery. The approaches to Auckland are by its fine harbour on the eastern coast, and by a delightful drive of six miles overland from Onehunga, on the western coast. Onehunga is a small settlement at the head of Manakau harbour. The road thence to Auckland is well made all the way into Auckland, and shows farms, villas, and homesteads everywhere. To enter Auckland by the west coast and leave it by the east, or *vice versâ*, is equally pleasant. Auckland from its longer time of settlement and the character of its settlers, is more self-supporting in its character than Dunedin; there is much native produce brought to market, and not a little of it—fish and oysters especially—brought in by the Maories. The chief local product that we shall remember seeing in Dunedin is its manufactory of walking-sticks at the corner of Prince's and High Streets. The country is a splendid one for producing the raw material for these sticks. Some branches are found with the native vine curled round them, and so adhesive thereto that, when scraped and polished, the caduceus of Mercury—the snake round the wand—is exactly reproduced. A connoisseur in walking-sticks of the last century would be in ecstasies at the stick show that we saw in Dunedin. Auckland has many people of advanced years amongst her population, but it is difficult to meet with whitened heads in Dunedin. The young, the vigorous, and the enterprising were those that went thither, and there most of them remain. Victoria sent thither two provincial newspaper editors who are men of mark now, and will leave their names in the story, to be, of New Zealand. Mr. Vogel and Mr. Farjeon, who were partners in the *Otago Daily Times*, have left that position, the first to be Treasurer-General of New Zealand, and the other to establish a name in literature in the London literary market. Mr. (now Sir Julius) Vogel, while we write, is in England endeavouring to carry out a crotchet of his in the raising of a ten million loan for public works in New Zealand.

Speaking of New Zealand's governmental and financial troubles, we may say that it is the most expensively, and consequently the worst, managed of lands. Objection may be raised on behalf of Tasmania as claiming that honour, with its upper and lower houses of Council and Assembly, and its thousand and ten paid officials to govern only about 40,000 able-bodied adults, the rest of Tasmania's sparse population being in either their first or second childhood. New Zealand has, to each of its nine provinces, a separate Governor or Superintendent, an Executive Council and Provincial Legislature, and for the whole a House of Representatives and Legislative Council, to which deputies journey from the Provincial Legislatures, and at which they spend their time—at a pound a day's expense to the country—for many months out of the twelve. It is, in fact, the cumbrous governmental system of the United States of America, with its thirty-eight millions of inhabitants, applied to a country that has but a poor quarter of a million only in all its length and breadth. This much-governed people groan with the burden of this misapplied system, and feel it severely in a taxation that amounts to between six and seven pounds per head annually, and in an increasing national debt. What a miserable sort of government it is, the state of Auckland amply testifies. With a municipality to look after its local interests, that city would be paved and channelled as to its footpaths, and levelled as to its streets, and long ago have been made shapely and citylike, and not left with the eyesores that afflict it now.

Queen Street, Auckland, is the chief avenue for traffic of a city that is growing gradually into greatness. It has a day and night life of bustle and commerce that are, as it were, the pulsations of a large leading artery. It is the termination of the long six-mile road from Onehunga, and its finishing point is the jetty that runs into Auckland's splendid harbour. To cross that harbour to the north shore—a sort of Sydney Manly beach—and to ascend the flagstaff hill there, is to get a sight of land and water views worth the going for. It is impossible to look around upon the grand scene of land and sea, and to question that this land of New Zealand will be a great home for the English race—and a goodly one too. What the country will produce in the way of humanity is worth a thought or two. We gave it many thoughts. As the climate and the country, so is the man. We see that the American of four or five generations' descent approximates closely to the characteristics of the Red Indian, whom he succeeds. We know that the ancient Britons were much what the Maories are now; and we see that Britain produces a white race equal to the aboriginal. We do not like the future of Australia viewed in the same light. Its aboriginals are of the lowest in the scale. Will the land that produces such as they are produce a better type of white man? or will he not deteriorate also, and be as low in the scale of humanity as the aboriginal whom he displaces? No fear have we for the future white man of five generations hence in New Zealand. The Malay race that migrated thither five hundred years ago have by climatic influences become a finer, stronger, braver, and better race than any of their kindred in the Southern Sea Islands—than any dark-skinned race that the world produces. Climatic influences that have worked such goodly change from the Malay to the Maori will be ever at work in the change from generation to generation of the Englishman into the New Zealander. He will be a better man then, in the days far onward, than he is now, and will make a grand new England of great New Zealand.

A Maori who was civilized enough to wear a paper shirt collar, and to write his name in our pocket-book, and whimsically addicted to winding up his remarks with the words, " And no mistake," took us to several extinct volcanic hills in the neighbourhood of Auckland, and of its suburb, Parnell. There are some half-dozen of these dumpling volcanoes within a circle of as many miles or less from Auckland. Within memory they have been silent, and it is questionable whether it was fire or water that they "played" when active.

Up the Waikato river, a few miles distant, little geysers, or water volcanoes, are common features of the scenery. New Zealand is very earthquaky. Nature seems hardly to have finished the work of creation in many parts of it. Sea margins are altering, and beaches widening or contracting in many places. The new land gives new vigour to its people, however. They partake of its freshness and youthfulness. The mighty Pacific that so washes their shores all around seems to love the young country that reposes on its broad bosom, and the roar of its perpetual shore-beating rollers are the trumpet notes that tell of that country's rapid march onward.

CHAPTER XXXVI.

COOK'S STRAITS—"THE MIDDLE PASSAGE."

THE channel called Cook's Straits divides the south or middle from the north island of New Zealand. On the south shore of the latter island is situated Wellington, and on the north shore of the south island is Nelson. They do not face each other, Nelson being much to the westward. The memories of three great men are thus preserved in these names, for New Zealanders who shall be further off than we are from the days and doings of Captain Cook, Lord Nelson, and Duke Wellington. The town named after the duke, as already stated, has lately been made the seat of government for New Zealand generally in place of Auckland, to the latter city's great disgust. The reason for the change lies only in the central situation of Wellington, for the place is not, for city purposes, to be compared to Auckland. It has only a fine harbour, round the head of which, in a semicircular form on the beach, stands the town. It will have to stand there. It can move neither backwards nor forwards. The mountain range behind it descends to the back doors of the houses, and the waters of the bay wash the entrances. Except round the circular bay it is difficult to see how Wellington can spread. Terraces might be cut in the hill-sides, and "lifts" used like to those in the Limited Company's hotels in Europe. Art might thus triumph over the difficulties that nature has put in the way, and Wellington might thus go up in the world. Something of the same sort of difficulty occurs at Quebec, and what is Quebec?

It is so hard to make the silken purse out of the porcine auricle. If we called Christchurch "the square city," Wellington might be called the circular one, as far as shape goes. Earthquakes have helped it onwards in one way, which is rather an odd thing for earthquakes to do. Since the city was settled in 1839, the bay has receded, and the decreasing waters have left a wider margin for building frontages. The bay did this on both occasions of earthquakes occurring, for there have been two since the date of settlement. Those who study the law of compensation—the good that is to be found in all things—regard this addition to the level land of the township as a make-up for the evil done by the shakings given by these earthquakes to the people and their dwellings. Some can foresee trouble to the Wellingtonians, in time to come, in this earthquake movement. Earthquakes that come twice in thirty years will come again, and, it is reasonable to suppose, will do as they have done before—give Wellington a severe shaking, and leave it more dry land for bay frontage. The occupiers of the present bay frontages will then find themselves situated in back streets, for anything that the water leaves dry in level land the builders will certainly eagerly clutch at. Wellington is no place for waste lands, save in perpendicular shape, and of that sort any quantity. This settlement is the first place that was founded by the company formed in 1837 in London, by Wakefield, for colonizing New Zealand. Wakefield was to colonization what Cook was to discovery. Australia, equally with New Zealand, is indebted to both of them. When people's merits are fully recognized in this world, what Wakefield did in colonizing British possessions will be properly rewarded, as it should be. Wakefield was to Cook what Stephenson was to Watt in the utilization of the steam-engine. Statues to both should stand not far apart. They will do so some time in the day to come, when this world shall make up its jewels.

The river Hutt comes down into Wellington harbour, some miles from the town, through a valley of most fertile soil that farmers have eagerly sought to settle upon. They are seeking to get out of it now, as that same Hutt is washing them out, and their land also, in the most aggravating manner. The river takes a different channel to itself, or makes a new one, nearly every year, and no man feels safe in a dwelling that is near to it. The land that he has ploughed and planted one year may be river bed the year following. Then, again, he cannot be always shifting his house, which, in the neighbourhood of the Hutt, becomes more like to a boat than a castle to the Englishman that may own it. If it were possible to limit this river to any bounds, a Hutt River Company (Limited) would, we thought, be a good speculation. A little walking about Wellington goes a long way, if it be extended to any place beyond the quay. We trudged up hill to the Houses of Parliament, and are of opinion that the members of Assembly, who are paid a pound sterling per day to come from level places and attend the Legislature at Wellington, deserve what they get. Wellington is not the best place to live in. The ambition of all good citizens to keep carriages cannot be well indulged there. We know several better places for wheeled vehicles—and for horses too. It has taken now to call itself "the Empire City," since its acquisition of the Government business, and we are not of those who grudge it the title, or anything else that will make it feel itself of importance. It wants that. Eight or ten years ago a company was projected in England for making a route for steamers to New Zealand *viâ* Panama, and that company made Wellington their starting-place. A fleet of fine steamers then graced its spacious port. They had fine mellifluous names, these vessels, all of New Zealand origin—the Kaikoura, the Ruahine, the Rakaia, the Rangitoto, the Tararua, and others—all scattered now with the failure of the company that started them. The Panama route from Australasia, *viâ* America, to Europe was a failure, and as such was abandoned. Wellington hopes to get a return of those days by-and-by, when some vessels of the San Francisco route shall get a mail contract, and make head-quarters there. The central position of Wellington between everything north and south ensures its importance, and its spacious and well-sheltered harbour makes it a most desirable bourne for shipping. Its buildings are, and always will be, of wood, and be mostly only one story of that. Wood is good against earthquakes.

Cook's Straits are twenty miles wide at the narrowest points, and at some places many times told that distance. Westward down these waters for sixteen hours we went to Nelson, the other celebrity of this middle passage. Nelson owes its existence to two causes—Wakefield and his New Zealand colonization company in the first place, and, in the second, its excellent position for the forming of a settlement. It does not possess a land-locked harbour, like to those of Dunedin, Akaroa, Wellington, and Auckland; but Nature has provided a boulder-banked basin here, that, though not so sightly to look at, answers all harbour purposes. It is something like the English Portland breakwater, that cost so many years, so much prison labour, and so much money to construct. A ring of low rocks run out from the shore, spread out in bow shape and return inwards, just sufficiently far to leave a good passage for shipping between their termination and the shore. The boulder bank, as it is called, rises but little above the water, but it is sufficient to provide for harbourage. At its furthest point from the shore stands the lighthouse.

Nelson is a great contrast to Wellington in every respect—and all for the best. It is all green gardens and trees and verdure, with level land in abundance. To distinguish it in our memory, we have associated it with the general characteristics that we observed, and it stands with us as Garden Nelson—a green English village of a place that has slowly grown, and will always slowly grow, and never become too much of a smoky, hurrying, factory-like city. It is the seaside depôt of a large pastoral country—and looks like it—looks like to the head-quarters of a population that live upon the products of nature, and not on those of arts and manufactures.

There are many pretty rides and drives out of Nelson, one

being to a suburb named Wakapuaka, which is euphoniously sounded as Walk-uppa-walker, and, as an exercise for the tongue, can be put alongside of the river Waimakarari, spoken of in the Christchurch chapter. We landed here a family that had come from the Cape to settle, selecting New Zealand of all other places for that purpose, and this spot of all others there. Much can be said in Nelson's favour. Its climate is of the best in New Zealand, and so is its land. There is less of rain there than in other New Zealand towns, and not so much of wind. The people of the place, we noticed, never thought of leaving it to go elsewhere. They had intended Nelson for their home when they went to it, and were well satisfied to think as much of it the more years that they stayed in it. Trafalgar Street, Nelson, is not to be counted as one of " the streets of the World " as yet, and the Englishman walking it will not know himself to be out of England, and think probably that he is in one of its Wiltshire towns as he walks the pathways of Nelson.

A long sea stretch of a night and a day took us from Nelson to Taranaki, which the settlers will not, and we very much applaud them for it, call " New Plymouth," the intended commonplace name for their well natively-named settlement. We had several Maories for fellow-passengers on this stage, and two particularly intelligent half-castes, Martin-te Whi-whi, a man, and Koi Raiphaina, a very promising young lady. We were enabled to get into a conversation with both, when we, as a deputation, waited upon them to get their signatures to an address to the captain. What will not passengers on board ship do in order to do something? The "address to the captain" is about the summit of sea-silliness—its culminating point—and shows to what the mind and intellect may be brought by a surfeit of what Shakspeare rightly enough calls " sea sorrow." All sorts of ship excitement had been exhausted before that was arrived at, and we wondered not at the difficulty we found in making it understandable to the Maori mind. The address itself, afterwards used up for pipe-lights, was such as was never seen on sea or shore—like to the light of the poet's mind. It says much for the Maori intellect that it is capable of comprehending humour, which it is said all English-speaking people are not, and we succeeded in getting six *bonâ fide* Maori signatures to our address. They would all know the why and wherefore of the matter before signing, and we much improved in explanation as we progressed. When it came to the half-castes, we were perfect, and felt that we could have compelled, by sheer persuasion, a signature from anything that could hold a pen. Fine fruit, indeed, is the produce of the grafting of the white upon the aboriginal. We wished that our father had been an Englishman, and our mother a Maori! What troubles we should have escaped then! We should have been goodlooking to begin with. Our complexion would have been clear brown; our eyes large and dark—and dangerous. Our hair had been glossy, curly, dark; and as for quantity, saleable every two months or so for chignons and back hair. Our mouths had been shaped like to Cupid's bow, and our lips— had served all purposes of lips. We cannot encumber our pages with an enumeration of the uses of a mouth, and the mouth of a half-caste is all that a mouth should be. We should have had the strength of an athlete as a gift of nature—the stomach of a Scotchman and German combined, and been strangers to dyspepsia for the longest lifetime. We should have known nothing of nerves, nor of headache, nor toothache—and may be nothing of heartache either. We should never have caught cold, never wanted our head wrapped up, or our throat swathed in bandages, nor hot water to our feet, and tallow to our nose at night. A chemist's shop would have been a curiosity to us, and the doctor but a dim imagination. We ne'er had wanted eartrumpets, spectacles, or wigs. We should, in that mixture of blood, the English with the Maori, have renewed primeval man, and have gone through life feeling nothing of the burdens that afflict the too-much-civilized man, and dying with nothing in the world but old age to trouble us. We should have slept at will, and that soundly, and have had no thought for to-morrow, or nervous, vapourish fears of aught here or hereafter. Of such were our ideas on seeing the specimens we did of the half-caste race, and what they looked like will be pretty well discerned by our detail of the thoughts that their looks gave rise to. It is only necessary to look at these half-castes in New Zealand to believe in the virtue and value of mixing blood—"miscegenation." If we wanted any further proof of that value we have it, and that but lately, well brought to our understanding in the notices of the death of the recently deceased Alexandre Dumas, that king of novelists, from whose large heart and brain came "Monte Christo," and scores of other fine creations. Dumas, the son of a Frenchman and a negress, should stand as an answer to all doubts on the question of the half-castes and their physical and intellectual endowments.

CHAPTER XXXVII.

PICTON AND THE "FRENCH PASS."

On the route from Wellington to Nelson there is Picton—Picton the peculiar to get at ; Picton the pretty, or Paradise Picton if you gush. If the weather be fine, and the skies blue and sunshiny, and yourself young and not bilious, and on good terms with yourself and everybody around you, we know not which of the above terms will be used in describing Picton. If you have an eye for the picturesque, and a soul for beauty, we then know all about what will be said. You will be told that this place was chosen by Captain Cook for winter quarters, and you will think that none could be better, and wonder how he could ever have left it. However it was that he found it will have first caused much wonderment. How, having found it, he could let any one else know of such a snuggery, will cause more astonishment to the selfish mind. What a home, you will say, for mermaids and dryads, fauns, satyrs, syrens, and pirates! Shut out from all the world and its troubles, and from the winds and the waves of the ocean, here is seclusion, beauty, hill and dale, wood and water, fish and fowl, and lasting sunshine—everything that the soul thirsts for, except the city soul of cashbooks and ledgers, restless to live other than in the paradise in which God put man, and intended him to stop.

We were sleeping peaceably in our narrow bunk on board the coasting steamer that took us from Wellington when our slumbers were disturbed, at 7 a.m., by a gentle shaking of the shoulder. It came from a good soul who had gone the road before, and who wished us to share in the surprise that was in store. "Come on deck at once; ask no questions now, but come, and you shall see something." We that good behest obeyed, and were soon by his side.

"You see that wall of green mountains in front of us?" he said. We did so, and saw that the sun was brightly breaking thereon, and showing all sorts of lines of dark and light greens.

"Now you see that we are steering dead on to that shore?" he said; and we saw that the vessel seemed to be doing that perilous business. Nearer and nearer we came upon what seemed to us, deceived by distances at sea, certain destruction. "What does it mean?" we said; "where are we going?"

"That is the first part of the astonishment you are going to have," he said. "We shall go much nearer in shore yet," and certainly we did so until all the mountain side was definable. We could perceive the difference in the foliage of the trees, and began seriously to shiver.

Our friend enjoyed our surprise, and would not enlighten us as to the way out of the difficulty that appeared so imminent—a ship steaming straight on to the shore, and now not very far off it.

"Now look out!" he said, and, doing so, we perceived that a sudden turn of the helm took the vessel round a projecting corner that had seemed a continuous part of the land before us. We had a narrow channel now to enter, and in a few moments were in it, and the way we had entered was hidden from us. High hills appeared on both sides, and also behind us. Nothing could exceed the surprise. It was a strait gate truly, and difficult to find; it had led to a narrow way also. Was it too much to think of the journey of Christian, and to hope that the land of Beulah, yet to come, would complete the parallel? It was not too much so to think, as we afterwards found.

We had gone through Tory Channel, as the gateway was called, and had now entered upon Queen Charlotte's Sound, a sheet of water that we never saw the like of, and such that, if we had all the eloquence of all the tongues that were ever attuned to talk, we could not sufficiently paint in words as we saw it on that sunshiny summer's morning.

Coleridge said that his eyes made pictures when they were shut, and we know that they did so, and that the eyes of all others such as Coleridge make pictures also. We are not all akin to Coleridge in that way. But few have picture-gallery heads and eyes that can, from poor bald print, make rich views—creative heads, that can from the raw material of the writer's art make up the finished beauties of nature. We want to tell of Picton and the approach to it, and feel how miserably short we shall fall in the feeble attempt to do so. Queen Charlotte's Sound is in length between one and two hours' steaming up to Picton from the time we entered it. Everybody wished that it would never finish. The water seemed to be about a quarter of a mile wide only. The lovely hills on both sides were plainly discernible, and all upon them, down to a stray sheep that here and there might be seen upon their sides. Now and then, in some sequestered nook, a fisherman had fixed his hut. The smooth waters over which we glided were alive with fish. No storms could get at these waters—no winds or waves devastate their shores. To live in one of those fishermen's huts, roam about these hills, and fish and sail upon these waters, away from taxes and troubles, cark and care of every kind, would woo any one to the hermit's life. We have mentioned pirates just now in enumerating those that might have dwelt here for peace and quietness, and absence of the police. Captain Kidd might have buried his treasure here, or kept it unburied with no one to disturb it or him. Had a pirate robbed a large merchantman and left her in Cook's Straits, the ship could never have found whither the robber had gone. It would have seemed that he had foundered on shore, and that all hands had gone down, as he ran his craft for Tory Channel, and got into Queen Charlotte's Sound. We see what a thorough good subject Captain Cook was, that having got into such a place, he could think of coming back again, when he had good ships and all appliances and means handy here for setting up a Robinson Crusoe kingdom on his own account. The world would have wept for his loss, as we weep for Franklin's, and he would have lived on unknown and happily as did the mutineers of the "Bounty" in their South Sea Island. Such a general and yet special effect had the scene upon us, that the same thoughts and fancies about it appeared to occur to every one. People who would not agree with us on any subject, through perversity of mind, forgot themselves now for a time, and were natural and truthful for once only. The steward had come on deck half a dozen times to give warning of breakfast, but he "took nothing by his motion." The breakfast-table waited on the beauties of nature. Queen Charlotte's Sound was the Aaron's rod that ate up all else. A company was proposed at once to settle it, for no signs of any township appeared. If there were such a thing many miles ahead, there was plenty of room and to spare for another one—near to the strait gate or midway. That idea may be carried out yet, and the settlers that shall come to this paradise will never want to leave it if they value the finest climate in the world—which New Zealand possesses just about this spot—and a life such as man was intended by his Maker to lead, for his health and happiness here, and his soul's peace hereafter.

We have seen some fans made for ladies that have a very long handle to the semicircular fanning affair at the top. The handle is the sound, up which we are going, and the radiating fan at the top represents Picton, or the site of it, for there is very little of town there yet. Green hills all around shut in this lovely valley on every side, save that on which we had come to it. Picton does but perfect the beautiful approach to it. It disappoints no anticipation, except that of being able to get anything on shore that one might happen to want. Picton is not a "seat of commerce." Very much otherwise. The people have, as they should have, but few wants, and the supplies quite correspond to the demand.

Whatever we wanted, that we could not get. How to get over an hour there was great trouble. It was too small a portion of time to go in for any great undertaking—such as a breakfast on shore, as even for that it was questionable if the mutton chops and the fish would not have to be caught before they could be dressed. The only amusements handy were a post-office and telegraph station. We each agreed to have a shilling's worth of telegraphing to strangers, and to wait for the replies which were to be requested "instanter." It really formed a lively occupation, and we can recommend it to folks hard up for an hour's amusement at little railway country stations, and out-of-the-way holes and corners. We had first to select those who were to be favoured with our ten words, and then what the ten words were to be. The half-dozen efforts produced good hearty laughter—and that before breakfast! We got several replies before we left. The messages were, of course, to people we only knew by name, and on matters that would only bewilder the recipients, and in no ways do damage beyond the payment for answer; as we spent a shilling also, that equalized matters. Our lot fell to telegraphing a clerical dignitary of the land, and we sent this query to a New Zealand head of the Church:—"Can a Protestant Englishman lawfully be married to an unbaptized Maori in Church of England, and according to its forms?" The answer cleared up all doubts about marrying any of the pretty savages we saw, according to Church of England forms. We found that such was held to be a sort of Church desecration. The time we had to stay at Picton was on account of mail receipt and delivery. We thought that the purser might have managed all that by a waistcoat-pocket arrangement in a few minutes; the time, however, had to be occupied. Those who took no part in the telegraph station performance agreed to exercise their wits in making epigrams on the place and its surroundings—a prize to be awarded to the best one, and the nearest local paper to receive it for publication, which proved to be the *Marlborough Press*. On an inspection of the efforts made, the shortest was voted to be the best, and the writer was baptized at once in the waters of Queen Charlotte's Sound—equal to Jordan—as the Poet of Picton. This should not be lost, and, as it has appeared in print once, it may as well do so again :—

> "Had Adam, other quarters seeking,
> When he lost our Eden home,
> But seen thy beauties—perfect Picton,
> He of loss had little known."

That honour may be accorded where 'tis due, it is fair to state that the second line ran originally, "When he lost his Eden home," but a little lady of fifteen mildly suggested that "our" was the better word, and everybody saw it so at once. Of course it was "our" home that Adam lost. We had all been living there, or thereabouts, now, but for the misfeasance of himself and wife, and that co-respondent, the snake. It was agreed on all sides that if any one of that summer morning's crew were ever missed unaccountably from the busy world, his friends might suspect Picton. There is warrant for so saying. We all know that the beauties of one South Sea Island haunted the minds of the crew of the "Bounty." The nature of man, and his love of nature, both broke forth in that shout with which, having disposed of all impedimenta, they set out to return thither, "Huzzah for Otaheite!"

We were in for good things all that day. If a day begins well, it often continues so; and though we were out to sea again, there was to be something yet to relieve the monotony of sea life in a coasting steamer. We were to go through a maelstrom on a small scale, to experience a little of Scylla and Charybdis, reproduced here in a nautical difficulty called "French Pass." Not a few *bon mots* were made on that name by those whom it reminded of other difficulties, at that time identified with the French and the "pass" to which their whole nation had come. This French Pass is a narrow sea-gateway on the seaway from Picton to Nelson, and, as the map will show, to go through it from Admiralty Bay saves going all the way round long D'Urville Island. The waters have only lately, two or three thousand years or so, broken away that island from the mainland, and the passage is one of shallows, rocks, and general trouble. We should not like to go through it at night—if it be ever then attempted—or to try it in a sailing vessel. It is quite sensational enough in a steamer, and brings all hands on deck and all heads forward over the bulwarks. The stream is about four steamers in width, and there is just a passage somewhere in it, of about one steamer's width, and no more, that can be got through. It is that or nothing. Failure would leave our names to be "writ in water." High are the cliffs on both sides, and much broken up here and there. The waters that rush between them have a strange appearance, showing on the surface large whirling circles, smooth in the middle and ringed at the edges. These whirling circles are not to be gone through—where they float, danger lurks. Towards one side, some one—a Frenchman, we suppose, from the name—discovered that there was depth enough for a steady vessel to pass through, and through that we had to go. He must have been an investigating navigator that went through it first. A look would satisfy most seamen, who were not in a hurry to get to their destination, or their graves. Going through the French Pass kept us as much from the dinner-table as going into Picton had kept us from breakfast, and, when we thought to go peacefully below, there was another scene for us that put dinner further back. A great school of porpoises had just gone over the maelstrom—a hundred or more, of all sizes and weights—and, that difficulty over, had laid down steadily for a regular Derby race. On all sides our steamer was surrounded by enormously-heavy fish, that bounded out of the water their whole length, three and five at a time, neck and neck, and then, side by side, splashingly dived in again. Their progress through the water was at an immense pace, leaving the steamer behind at pleasure. The sea was alive with them all around, and our vessel had apparently some attractions for them, or their vanity tempted them to display their powers to us, as a peacock or turkey-cock does his tail.

Fish that must have weighed two hundredweight or more engaged in a race that, though "flat," had jumps every now and then over imaginary fences ten feet high. The race, at a killing pace, was something better than one could see on a racecourse, and had this great advantage—it lasted nearly an hour, whereas a land steeplechase is a sensation of a few minutes only.

CHAPTER XXXVIII.

THE MAORI FAMILY—"IN TOWN."

THE great historian and essayist—the late Lord Macaulay—has told us, at the conclusion of his essay upon Van Ranke's

MAORI DRESS (MALE).

book on the Popes, in words familiar to us all, that in a day to come a New Zealander shall sit upon a broken arch of London Bridge, and sketch the ruins of St. Paul's

Cathedral. That is the great interest that we all have in the New Zealander—our successor. It has generally been assumed by writers and artists, who have lent their talent to sketching this scene on London Bridge, that the New Zealander whom Macaulay had in his mental eye was to be a descendant of the Maori race; and such is, no doubt, the impression of most readers. In a frontispiece to the first edition of the *Savage Club Papers*, published in London, we

MAORI DRESS (FEMALE).

have the whole scene before us—the broken bridge, the river Thames grown o'er with weeds and lilies, St. Paul's in the distance, with great cracks and gaps in its dome, and the artist at work, seated on the broken bridge. He is depicted as a swarthy savage, with feathers in his hair, covered only over the loins, and smoking the usual calumet pipe that is known to English eyes as a part of savage life. We question whether Macaulay did not intend that his prophetic New Zealander should be the descendant of the British, and not of the Malay, settler, but we found ourselves looking on the latter, in the popular belief that such as he was to see and do in the hereafter what Macaulay had depicted. In Auckland, we found the Maories in plenty. Queen Street, the chief street of that city, was noticeable for the number of Maori men, women, and children to be met there. We realized at once that we were in a foreigner's land. The traveller may pass through, and stop for many days in Adelaide, Melbourne, and Sydney, and see no aboriginals there, while in Tasmania he may seek them in vain. In the New Zealand towns of Dunedin, Nelson, Christchurch, and Wellington, he may fancy himself in English townships, if he stops but a short time therein; but in Auckland it is a very different matter. He meets Maories everywhere, and of all sorts. He sees, too, by their ways, that he is the stranger there, and not they. The Maori is quite out of place in a city of white people. His dress, his manners, and his habits, and her dress, her manners, and her habits, too, do not look the right sort of thing at all to European eyes. He puts a blanket round his middle, and fastens it with a skewer, showing more uncovered leg than a kilted Highlander, and that is often her attire as well. Then nothing will do but they must both sit about, dreadfully in the way, in the most prominent places. A British dog will sleep only in the centre of the road or pathway. Nothing of privacy enters into his nature—until he retires to die; and it is so with the Maori of both sexes. The white citizens are hurrying to and fro on some business, or with some object; but the Maori has neither business nor objects, and shows his utter contempt for such by getting in everybody's way, and by sitting about on the footpaths in little groups. That is generally the case about public-houses and public buildings—the post-office especially. Now, as the Maori has the happiness of never writing letters, or receiving them, it is obvious that he only gets about that and similar buildings to be in other people's way, and to force you to step over him, as one does over the dogs. We stopped amongst groups of them, again and again, to note their peculiarities. Of these, the most palpable and striking is certainly the tattoo business—it lies on the surface.

Of all the people who have set to work to improve the human face by the aid of art, the Maori stands first. In that respect he has really no second—he is so far away ahead of all others. Painting the face is again becoming fashionable

ARTISTIC TATTOOING (1).

with some white folks—a return to the fashion of our great grandmothers, who added patches of black sticking-plaster here and there on their countenances as beauty spots. The Maori is no such cobbler, but, on the contrary, is a great facial artist. We counted no less than fifteen different designs of facial decoration, well drawn, well cut, and well worked out, or rather worked in, on the Maori face. And such good, substantial work too. No need to do it over again. It looks like to the paintings on the Egyptian temples, as plain and definable as if done but yesterday, and yet we saw tattooed faces that had existed nearly a century. The Maori keeps no count of his age, and is as bad a chronicler as a woman pretends to be, but it was easy to see to what great ages some of them had attained. The tattoo that had taken but three months to do, when its wearer was but twelve or twenty,

ARTISTIC TATTOOING (2).

looked clear and plain enough when he came to be eighty or ninety. Talk about the vanity of civilized people again in our presence, and we will make answer and say that the Maori is the greater dandy. With a pair of mussel-shells, used as tweezers, he pulls all the hair that grows on the face out by the roots. Whiskers, eyebrows, moustache, and beard—out they all come, with a wrench and a squeak, and tears to the eyes. Having cleared the forest in this way, the ground is to be laid out. The plan is drawn in white paint, made of the scrapings of oyster-shells. That plan is adopted which is best suited to the countenance of the subject—most becoming to his style of beauty. Here the real artist has a fine field before him. A prominent nose, like to Wellington's or Artemus Ward's, can be well decorated on both sides—a broad one can be only so done down the bridge of it. A Walter Scott forehead can have wonders done upon its surface, and a chin like to a hand of pork, or like to the first Napoleon's, can be improved upon to any extent. Whether cheeks will look best with curved lines or straight ones, and which way the curves shall go, is all matter of art, high art. A face may be painted in designs a dozen times before that which is to stand for all time—the owner's time—is determined upon. If the subject, or patient, be of any standing or consequence, the opinion of his relatives and friends is often sought by the artist. He is sent home to them with the painted face that they may approve the design. The photographer of the present day adopts this idea when he sends us the first proof of his negative. "Take it," he says, "and ask your friends' opinion of it." When the design has been finally approved of, then trouble begins. With points and edges of sharp sea-shells the victim of vanity is painfully excoriated, and a blue colouring matter, got mostly from a shell-fish, is introduced into his wounds. A little of this work goes a long way at a time, and the skin is left to heal up. To do a whole face will take from three to six months, and really great works some of these tattooed heads look. In most European museums one of them will be found. A good trade was carried on in tattooed Maori heads many years ago, until Governor Grey stopped it, and seized a sackful of heads that had been placed on shipboard for exportation. Such exports fetched good prices, and, as the Maories have the Egyptian secret of preserving them in excellent condition, a profitable business to them seemed thus to have been suddenly crushed. Such interference with free trade was the more to be deplored because it was a business that much suited Maori tastes. Nearly all Maories, in years gone by, preserved the heads of their conquered enemies. They would eat the body and the brains, but carefully preserve the head, hanging it up in their hut to apostrophise and nag and swear at, something in this fashion : " You thought you had me then, when I slipped down, but you fell over my uplifted leg, and my meri (club) settled your business. After that you were cooked, and I ate you. I afterwards ate your two brothers. Your wife and children are now my slaves. Yah!" When the whites came to New Zealand, these heads became of value—everything can generally be turned to that by British traders—and they fetched money, and tobacco, and seeds, and potatoes, and fishing-lines, in exchange. As the demand increased, the supply had to be kept up. A man with a well-tattooed head no longer slept comfortably. His head was worth five pounds at least. War between the tribes had an additional stimulus, and the trades—we beg pardon, professions—of the tattooer and head-preserver became of increased dignity. Instead of this "native industry" meeting with protection, Sir George Grey saw fit to crush it, and yet we seem to be surprised at the Maori going to war with us— we, who have taken his land from him, and knocked his business on the head! The only European artist that can stand his ground with a Maori professor of tattoo would be that famous Mr. Worth, of Paris, the English draper's shopman that was, and the arbiter of the " Becomings " that now is. That potentate of fashion, for a ten-guinea fee, tells us in what we shall look best according to our face and figure, and how best to assist nature to look to our advantage—to his taste. In fact, he undertakes to realize the wish of Robert Burns, and make us see ourselves as others see us. A similar professor of taste is the tattoo man of the Maories. The ladies that he so ornaments are very simply decorated indeed, just a little about the chin, and one or both lips. There is about the same difference in adornment between the Maori face masculine and that feminine, as there is between the plumages of the peacock and peahen. To a European, these tattooed lips of the Maori women are very ugly indeed. To the taste of the white man, a pair of pink lips is all in all. To trace blue-black lines and figures on them is quite frightful—desecrating, we might say. A little knowledge of Maori ways and manners puts the matter in a new light. Maories do not kiss. They only rub noses instead. So simple a matter as rubbing noses together, instead of rubbing lips, opens a long train of thought to the philosopher. He will argue thence that our pleasures lie in the mind, in the fancy, the imagination, and will tell us that rubbing fingers together or noses is as pleasurable as kissing, if we only think so. Is kissing only a fashion? Will it die out some day, and shall we all rub noses or fingers, or the top of each other's heads instead? Who shall say nay?

MAORI WOMEN.

In France only the men kiss, as we all well know, and the French believe that they have always led civilization; but then they believe so many things that we don't.

There was one old man Maori, quite a patriarch, that would sit about sunning himself all day, to whom we were much attracted. In age he must have been something very great. We have but to look at the trees at Burnham Beeches to see their stupendous age. They have grown through countless years to look more like to rocks than trees. It was so with this old Maori. His great grandfather might have seen the last of the moas. He was so antiquated that he appeared to be partly fossilized. When we took his hand in ours, we were establishing a direct link with the middle of the last century. We went back to 1760 in that grasp, and lived in the early days of the third of the Georges, and saw Walpole and Pope and Johnson and Goldsmith, and the beauty of the Gunnings. There was nothing the matter with this old mortality but natural decay. He was dreadfully lumpy, and slow and lumbering, but he was cheerful in his half-torpid way. We could see that the long sleep from which he had emerged in that past age was slowly regaining him again to its embrace. "Our little life is rounded by a sleep," and so was his long one. We liked to put a cigar into his large mouth, and to light it for him, and to see him gently pull at it and smile his thanks. That he should have retained a taste for tobacco up to that age was a very curious thing to us. We thought that the sense of taste, and especially a vicious taste, would have grown dulled altogether. He had a finely-tattooed face, and a head of thick, whitish grey hair. As we sat with him, we thought probably more of his past life than he did himself. There was a large scar on his neck, and another down the side of his forehead. He had been in the wars in his time—in much war, no doubt, for the Maori delights in combat. Life is a serious matter to most of them—they just never can get enough of fighting. How many men had this old Maori eaten? we wondered, for we could not question the ancient cannibal on the subject. He was a fine old mausoleum, no doubt. Gravestone inscriptions might have been tattooed on that broad chest of his. Did he know So-and-so? we might have asked, and he might have replied, "Know him! yes, plenty well. I ate him!"—a most intimate sort of knowledge that. We looked on him much as Belzoni would upon a fine old tomb, and wondered if we could, as such, get him into the British Museum on remunerative terms.

The Maori is distinguished in several prominent characteristics besides tattoo. He cannot endure a hairy face; he never eats salt; he has no faith in a hereafter; he has no industry; he has a keen sense of insult; he has no word for, or any idea of, time, and is careless about time and life; he is largely self-reliant; he is greatly lazy; he is animally selfish; he has no respect for the dead; he has no fancy, sentiment, or imagination.

Their not eating salt is a very peculiar feature with the Maories, as it has been thought amongst us Europeans that the use of salt was a necessity of life. The strong, fine, healthy physique of the Maories shows us that our belief in salt as an essential of health is a fallacy. That is a peculiarity worth making a note and a query about by those who have time and opportunity to discuss a very interesting topic—the necessity for salt at the table.

The Maori god is an image in green-stone, fashioned much like the heads on Gothic buildings called "gurgoyles" are with us. Only the bust seems to be carved. This god is supposed to be influential only in temporal affairs—success in war, and prevention of hostilities by enemies, but to have no relation in any way to the life hereafter. The Maori chiefs assume a great and mystic religious power—that of the "Tapu"—a word which we borrow when we say that such a thing is "tabooed," meaning that it is not to be meddled with in action or speech. Every chief is holy; he is "tapued," not to be meddled with, and he can transmit the power. He can make anything as holy as he is himself—perhaps a little more so. He can draw a line across a river or road, and such is at once "tapued;" beyond that line none must tread on pain of death, which follows swiftly on any breach of this superstitious rite. The white man cannot trespass with more impunity than the Maori on anything that is "tapued." This tapu power has caused plenty of war, is a strange blending of the spiritual and temporal power in those who have authority, and is worth thinking of by those who are on the look-out for innovations in our social code. It might be good to give such powers to policemen, if one could get the rowdies to believe in it. Fancy stopping the advance of a mob by drawing an imaginary line across the road with the finger!—such is tapu power. We respect every man's religion, but that did not prevent us bringing away a Maori green-stone god.

Many Maories have strongly-marked Jewish features. The face of Taipieri, the chief of the Thames district, near Auckland, and to whom the miners pay royalty, or tribute, is very Jewish in appearance—conspicuously so. The Jewish element in them probably accounts for their dislike of all labour. What we understand by "industry" the Maori knows nothing about. 'Tis not in his nature, and never will be. He has, however, a Corsican sense of insult, and he pursues its revenge exactly as a Corsican does. A word slightingly spoken, or the lie directly given, can only be wiped out in blood; whilst the death of a man, however accidentally caused, is only to be compensated by another death, and by war of tribes, if necessary. Nothing in that way is forgotten or forgiven by the Maories. Time, in the way of revenge, or any other way, is of no consequence. What is not done to-day can be done to-morrow, and in the way of vengeance no count is kept—what has to be done will be done, some time or other. A Maori never counts his years, or his days, nor knows how old he is. He has some belief that four hundred years ago his ancestors came to New Zealand from the Malay Islands, but he cannot in any way verify his chronology. As a rule, the Maori prefers "to-morrow" and "by-and-by" in all his dealings. No one ever saw a Maori hurrying himself.

The Maori sets small value upon life, and as a sequence he is very self-reliant. He is like the famous John Toler of the many duels—afterwards Lord Norbury—ever ready to rush to battle, but he is not excitably so. In his lazy way he does even that deliberately, and plans and schemes beforehand. When it comes to personal encounter, the Maori excites himself by a war-dance, in which he works himself up to a fever by friction—getting thus into a heated state of blood and brain, and so rushing on his enemy. As a warrior, he developes great tact in choosing his ground, and raising earthworks and other defences. Long ages of battling with his fellows have made war and all its belongings part of the Maori's nature. There is the soldier in all of them. Selfishness is all in all in the Maori mind. Generosity and liberality, like all such sentiments, are unknown to Maories. We strove to find instances to the contrary, but they are so few in number, and so questionable, as to be unworthy of counting as exceptions to the rule. Nothing stands in the way of a Maori doing that which pleases him—if he can do it by fraud or force. Touchy as he is in matters of honour, in all the finer points that make the civilized gentleman he is deficient.

We could never find where the Maories buried their dead, or how they disposed of them. A native grave is nowhere to be seen. We could not find out, either from themselves or from the whites, where the dead Maories were put. They must die some time, and, perhaps, with the mysterious dead donkeys, their whereabouts after death will yet be discovered. The early white settlers had a strange notion on the subject, which would be too unpleasant to mention, but in which they afterwards found themselves to be in error, as the Maori really eats none but his slain enemies, and is now leaving off even that habit, since he has not seen that Europeans do the same.

CHAPTER XXXIX.

IN THE RICHEST OF ALL GOLD-MINES—THE CALEDONIAN.

"IF you can find our old friend Freekins anywhere out in your quarter of the world, let him know that a fortune has been left him. His friends have heard nothing of him for many years, and conclude him to have passed over to the majority." We read thus in a letter received nearly two years ago from an old London friend, with whom ourself and Freekins had, twenty-two years ago, been fellow-clerks. The missing man had never been seen or heard of by us, and as no funds were forwarded to pay for hunting him up, we dismissed the matter from our mind, our duty being only to tell him of the fortune awaiting him if he came within ken.

Freekins had nearly faded from our remembrance. Dimly we recalled him as a very easy-minded youth, who was blessed with good health and good digestion, and bothered himself with no cares or ambitions. Now, as we recalled him, it appeared all right enough that a fortune should be left to him. He would never otherwise have been likely to get one. But why did he disappear from the world that he knew and that knew him, as he appeared to have done? He was never likely to become eccentric or misanthropic, and do as Laurence Oliphant, English M.P., lately did when he left the House of Commons and his Scotch constituency and the gay world of London, and, unknown to all, buried himself for a long time in some semi-monastic society on the shores of Lake Erie, in America. Nor was Freekins likely to become criminal and to flee from justice and the faces of his fellows. We did not think it was so easy for a man to disappear out of society, to drop through a trap on the stage of life, and not be discoverable anywhere below or behind the scenes. It would seem, though, that Freekins had so done.

We had to go down to New Zealand some eighteen months or so after the receipt of the advice about our missing friend, and we can safely say that we never gave him a thought, owing to the sickness of the sea journeys there and thereabouts, or to the novelty of the new land and its different aspects. We had landed on the South Island, and travelled northwards through its townships up to the far end of the Northern Island—just as far as we could go in that direction. As we stood there, we stood as far from London as any one could be upon this globe. That was at Auckland. There were places of note to be seen thereabouts, one of which was the Thames gold diggings, situated on a barren sea-shore on the eastern coast, some sixty miles from Auckland—the most unpropitious place in appearance that it was ever our fate to look at. Fortune there, however, had hidden her largest store of gold, as Captain Kidd is supposed to have hidden his wonderful treasure, where folks would be least likely to look for it.

It fell to our fortune to be there only in January last, and it fell to our misfortune to have no "second sight;" to know nothing of the place that we were in, any more than that weary work was going on there, as elsewhere, in the hope that it might be successful. We could have bought mining shares, now gone far beyond our purse, for next to nothing. We rubbed shoulders, as it were, with the winner of the Derby, before the start, and knew nothing of his excellence, nor of what we were doing. We had gone to the furthest antipodal part of the world from our London home, and had entered the house of Fortunatus, and knew it not. We had not Aladdin's lamp to see our way, and noticed not the thousand hands that, all unseen to us, were everywhere holding out bags of gold—in front of the nose that we could not see beyond.

"Well, my word! what shall we see next?" The voice came from one who stopped our way in Pollen Street, Graham's Town, Thames Diggings. This town is situated on a strip of sea-shore, washed by the Firth of Thames on one side, and banked up by a high mountain range immediately on the other. We knew not our querist, who was dressed as a digger, and we mildly hinted that he had the advantage of us. "So has any one that's got brains," he said. "Don't you know Baldwell?" We expostulated that we could not be expected to recall the events of a lifetime at once, nor remember, at call, all the faces that had, some time or other, been familiar to us. "Well, you have not altered a bit since '48, anyhow; and how is old Slopgoose?" A touch of that familiar sort made us kith and kin at once. We knew all about it now, and twenty-three years rolled away as a mist does before the sun. "And to meet you here!" we said. "We have come a long way to see something or other, and that something, at present, appears to be you. What are you doing here?"

Our newly-discovered friend, with the good memory for faces, had, we found, been working at these Thames Gold-Mines for many months. When we had met him last, he was the well-provided-for son of a well-to-do father in London, and connected with one of the professions. Here he was, a working digger, with a horny hand, and the marks of labour everywhere upon him. The change had come about, we found, naturally enough. Nature had "thrown back" in the son to the original type of perhaps the great-grandfather. He was intended to be a labouring man of the bent back and perspiring brow, one who was to live by muscular exertion, and he had gradually declined to his destiny. It was of no use to prop him up, and think to keep erect a marble figure on the feet of clay. Here, as a digger, with a short pipe in his mouth, he was happy, and the right man in the right place. We did not say "alas," for we were quite sure, after a few minutes' talk, that all would be as happy as our friend was if they could find out their right place in the world as he had done. The labour fitted for him was to him no toil, evidently enough. "We left you a gentleman of fortune," we said, "on the high road to keep a carriage and pair, and a house in Belgrave Square; and what fortune-teller could have dared to prophesy this change?" He said, "Look here, old fellow, I am well off, and happy with a good day's work for my hands, and that I never felt myself to be while trying to work with my head. The old man tried me at everything, but it was no go; and when the money had all gone, I found, in emigration and hard work out here, just what I was fitted for. I'm all right, and am healthy, lively, and strong; what more could I wish for?"

We began to perceive that there was much to be said for our friend's view of the question, and that, perhaps, the refinements of a London life, and the exercise of the nerves and brain in place of the muscles of a man might not be the best way of getting through life happily, and coming healthily in at the finish. This man "toiled all day in the eye of Phœbus, and slept in Elysium," without doubt. We were ready to buy that sound night's sleep of him, were it purchaseable, and there were other things that we envied him the possessing.

After dinner, he would take us to his workshop "up there" —pointing to the mountain range above us. His workshop, as he called it, was the Caledonian Mine—now the Great Caledonian Mine, the rich Caledonian Mine, and to be known as the richest gold-mine that man ever opened in this world as far as history supplies a record. The Caledonian Mine was, however, nothing then. Its entrance looked but a dirty hole—a perpendicular, grave-like entrance on the bleak, seaward side of a barren mountain—a home for sea birds, and sea winds, and for nothing else. Yet that hole in that sea wall led to the house of Crœsus. Through that doorway of dirt El Dorado lay. Through that entrance came two tons weight of melted gold in two months, and that successionally. Ten thousand pounds daily, week after week, and month after month, were handed down out of that unpropitious-looking hole. To have been in the richest mine in this world is something, and to have gone into it to some purpose is something more; and we did that.

In dining with Baldwell, we heard the history of a quarter of a century, and began to perceive how long life is, and how very short also, and how a life should be measured by the number and importance of the ideas and actions that it developes, and not by the number of its years. We found that we had travelled to hear news also, and some very unexpected tit-bits in that way turned up in our talk. It seemed at last that the quarter of a century of time had been but a dream, for we got to a distinctness of memory about minutiæ that might have been the events of only last week.

We found Baldwell's superiority over us in matter of muscular work when we walked up to the mine with him. It was a terribly toilsome up-hill trudge—quite a climb. The day was hot too, and the moisture of the sea beneath us exhaled and made us suffer from that worst of warmth—a moist heat. We got faint and tired, and very perspiring, over the job. The mine was reached at last, and we entered the "drive"—a long passage of about six feet by four, into which, if we went again, we should prefer to go in a coal-sack, with two holes cut as an opening for our arms, and with a coal-heaver's fantail hat on our head. How thoughtless people are in such matters! We spoilt a good hat in that excursion, and our coat was nothing to speak of afterwards.

In the halls of this burrow we saw men working by candle-light and lamp-light all about us, and listened to all the details, and made the usual remarks that politeness demanded. We had a piece of brownish-looking stone given to us also, which we have now, in which stone, further onwards in the workings, all the masses of gold were afterwards found lurking. Anything more unlike gold than the stuff we inspected could not well be imagined. A handful of fuller's earth would be as promising a "prospect," and yet here was all the wealth that could be wanted, and more than could be imagined. When Dumas gave to Monte Christo the enormous fortune that he did, he had the great trouble of imagining how to store it away. He imbedded the hundred millions in a hill in a lonely island in the Mediterranean, and made the fame of that island for all time, and his own fame also. We were in a veritable Monte Christo place here in the Thames diggings, and in the subterranean place where we stood was buried a Monte Christo amount of wealth—existing in fact, and not in fiction. "A potentiality of wealth beyond the dreams of avarice," as Dr. Johnson phrased the brewer Thrale's fortune. That wealth could have been ours too, had we been able to see but one short month into the future. We do not shave, and that is satisfactory, or the result might be that reflecting on what we might have done in January, 1871, would be too much for our o'erwrought mind—with the razor so near to our throat.

"Here's another old Londoner," said Baldwell, smacking the shoulders of a digger standing near; and he forthwith detailed to that digger how he had met us on the shore below, and had known us twenty-five years back, in a very different place. "We little thought ever of meeting at this end of the earth," said Baldwell; "but I've lost a day to good purpose in the talk we've been having of old times." We suggested here that it would be as well to renew that talk in the evening if Baldwell would come to our lodgings and bring his friend, the other Londoner, with him. That being agreed upon, we went on to see the rest of the workings, and then to see the machinery, and then to hear of the richness of this neighbouring mine and that one, and how the lodes were all supposed to run out to sea, and how the workings there would have to be under water. "You had better take shares with us before you leave the place, for now's the time to buy before we hit the vein." So they counselled us, but we had not faith in the hitting of that vein, and had done our fair share of quartz-mining ventures away over the sea in Australia. The results there had satisfied us. For the majority they generally prove satisfactory, and that in the sense in which the worsted one in a fight answers that he has had enough. Blinded mole that we were, standing amidst moles, at moles' work too—how could we see into the middle of next month, when we could not well discern, in the half darkness, the face of those that we talked with? For instance, the face of that Londoner digger whom Baldwell had spoken to with us was but imperfectly visible, so much so that we did not know him again when Baldwell stopped him at the entrance as we were making our visit, and said, "Mind, Perkins, that you come down to Burton's to-night." We thought that we had seen the look before that Perkins wore when he nodded affirmatively to that injunction. "What did you call that man?" we said to Baldwell. He answered that he called him Perkins, and that such was his name, "and what's the matter with you?" he added. Perhaps the blood had left our cheek to assist our brains in an effort at memory called up by the look of that face seen in the daylight, and by the name of Perkins. The name was near enough to Freekins, and the face was nearer still, if we could remember faces rightly. To settle the matter we stepped up to him, and a few words told us that he was our man—the man wanted for the fortune in England! We had unkennelled him many hundreds of feet underground in this out-of-the-way corner of the earth; and though we missed our fortune in the Caledonian Mine, we gave the news of a fortune to Freekins, and had not gone down to the Thames Diggings for nothing—always supposing it to be more blessed to give than to receive.

In the evening we heard the long story told of the past life of the missing man, and a not uninteresting story it was. It greatly helped us to understand the story of the claimant of the Tichborne baronetcy. It had been mythical to us up to that time how a man could disappear from the world for a number of years, and keep himself unknown to all his friends and relatives. After hearing Freekins's story, we began to understand that such could be done, and that the Enoch

Ardens and the Tichbornes of this world are not so uncommon as we imagined. The story we heard shall be moulded some day, and told, and be told as the tale of the richest gold-mine of this world. In all but the right names we have commenced it here.

CHAPTER XL.

"THE SILVER THAMES"—WITH GOLDEN BANKS.

THE steamer that took us away from Auckland jetty came to anchor, some five or six hours afterwards, in apparently open sea, but off the shore of what is called the Firth of Thames. On one side were only water and waves, as far as sight went; on the other, between one and two miles away, lay a sandy beach and the precipitous hill-sides that run down to the water's edge here, as generally elsewhere all around the east coast of New Zealand. We were to go off in a small boat to that narrow beach, on which, as we got nearer, we could see a line of habitations built. That—yes, that—was the township of the Thames diggings. That was Shortland. The diggings, where were they? They were in the sides of the overhanging hills or cliffs; we should see the entrance here and there as we got nearer inshore. By-and-by we did so. The hill-sides are like to a large pigeon-house, and the holes appearing herein and leading to the drives of the different mines are like to the holes by which such birds make their entrances and exits. To one used to the Victorian diggings about Ballarat and Sandhurst, these Thames mines have a strange look, and the strangeness is not at all favourable. To Scott's tale of the "Talisman" we remember a frontispiece of the convent of Mâr Saba in Palestine, a rocky fortress in a valley, partly surrounded by high perpendicular rocks, from which the mountain, now cut into a monastery, and called Mâr Saba, had been rent by some convulsion of nature. In the sides of these perpendicular rocks monks had bored or tunnelled holes here and there, half-way up, to which they were let down from the top by ropes, each to his little hole, there to abide in solitude till death took him, from what we can hardly call life, in a few years' time. Except that the holes in the cliff at the Thames can be scrambled up to from the bottom by those who have strong legs and good lungs and do not mind soiled dress, the Thames mining quarter looks from the water something like to Mâr Saba's precipice. Between that and the pigeon-house appearance the choice may lie. Straggling along the beach are Shortland and Graham's Town, one a continuation of the other in a roadway called Pollen Street, and the latter now the busy part of these sea-side diggings. The glory has left Shortland altogether, and its long street of habitations is but desolation and emptiness. So fares it with all townships that depend upon gold-digging as sources of support. Business and population shift from one quarter to another until the day comes—and it always does come—when the two take leave together. It is then all "Tadmor in the wilderness" henceforth. The scrubby, useless hill or cliff-side, in which the diggings are burrowed at the Thames, is owned chiefly by a Maori named Tapieri, whose house is stuck upon some projection amongst the diggings. To that we scrambled up with some loss of wind and temper. He looks wonderfully like a Hebrew, does Tapieri, and developes something of the Semitic faculty in drawing very good revenue from the diggers who scratch upon his sterile, bleak hill-sides. Tribute or royalty is paid to him by the miners. He looks on while they toil. He has the best of it. We went from his house to the famous Long Drive Mine, in which Prince Alfred is a shareholder. That mine has this advantage: it can be entered on the level sandy beach by one doorway, again at another fifty feet up the cliff, and at another some forty feet higher than that. We chose the lowest entrance, but the closeness of the atmosphere and the dirtiness of the job soon gave us enough for our curiosity. Most of these mines extend their claims far out below low-water mark, and the miners sink shafts through the water and sandy bottom to find the continuation of the vein there that they have followed down the hill-side. This digging under the water is peculiar to the Thames. We never saw it elsewhere in New Zealand or Australia. The Botallock coal-mine at Cornwall, we know, begins at the water's edge, and runs for a great distance under the sea; but these shafts begin in the water in dams that have to be pumped out and kept thenceforth water-tight to enable the bottom to be worked. Digging is mostly arduous work. Except some alluvial diggings that we saw in Victoria in 1852, at Fryer's Creek and Eaglehawk, five feet sinking to blue clay, full of gold, we never saw any digging that looked easy. At the Thames, however, in addition to the hard work, one has first to get acclimatized; the proximity of the water to the cliff-side makes the small strip of beach there of a particularly clammy, sticky, moist, oppressive atmosphere. The new arrival, if in the summer time, like to ourself, feels very languid and inert. We did so for the two days of our stay there, and our experience was that of those who went with us. The Thames is only a digging for companies and capitalists. It was at the lowest ebb-tide of luck when we saw it in January, 1871, and a few well-remembered faces that we met there were only wishing that they could leave it as easily as we could. Fortune has since given them a smile. "Hope springs eternal in the human breast." These pigeon-holed cliffs are the evidence of that faith that here, practically, is removing mountains—or much of the insides of them. Had we had faith, we might have bought mining shares for next to nothing, and been now considered shrewd speculators. We might have bought a great many shares, too, and several entire mines—plant and all. If we didn't buy, it was not because nothing was offered—O, dear, no! We will say this for the people of the Thames, that they were willing to let strangers in—to share their fortunes—on the usual terms. They are still similarly inclined, no doubt. The place is sea breezy, moist, and perpendicular. The people are mixed, patient, hopeful—and open to offers. Surrounded by the gold that was in the mountain sides, and beneath the waters at our feet, we could find no better amusement for an hour than fishing for our dinner at the end of the long jetty that Graham, a white Tapieri who divides territory here with the Maori owner, has lately built. We found two or three others fishing likewise—folks, like to ourselves, not devoured by the greed of gold, nor excited by its presence around, nor by the offers of the people to sell us shares in their fortunes—to come. With these primitive-minded men we pursued the ancient and quiet business of fishing, with much success—taking back a full basket for the dinner-table. The folks who sat down to it seemed glad enough to eat the fish, but too busy—or too lazy—to go fishing for themselves. We had this reflection: that the fishing had been a certain good and a profit. About much of the mining going on we had just a doubt or two that kept us out of all the good things that were to be had around us—for money. Mines were pointed out—that is to say a dingy hole like to the low entrance to an Egyptian building was shown us—as being those in which Mr. So-and-so had come from Melbourne and invested so much, and in which this and that Victorian speculator held so many shares. We were glad to hear it; we smiled and looked pleased—we always do so when we find our fellow-men disbursing their capital for the encouragement of labour. How pleasant is the feeling of providing work for the unemployed, labour for the labouring man! The feeling of doing good in this way brings its reward in the present, and also in the future, when we may look back to time and money well spent, not in enriching ourselves, and leaving hoards for heirs to squander or to enrich widows for tempting baits to our matrimonial successors—but in providing for the wants of the work-a-day world—the sons of toil. Amongst the means that Providence takes for the dissemination of capital, gold-mining—especially of the quartz kind—takes front rank. Not only does it put about that which one determines upon spending for the given purpose, but it continually keeps one's good intentions in one's mind by periodical "calls." The building of churches and endowing charities was for a long time the channel for diffusing surplus wealth. If but few endowed churches and charities be found hereafter in Australia and New Zealand, let it be known that good impulses took another form—a form that did all the good in the lifetime of the doer of it, and brought him occupation of time and mind—not to say excitement—along with it. We respect Peabody. He did well with his wealth. He would not, however, have had occasion to provide houses for the labourer had he lived near to a gold-mining district. Providing labour there, for the labourers, would have exhausted the Peabody fund—had shares been taken pretty generally in the ventures going round.

One gloomy thought for the future of Shortlands and Graham's Town forced itself upon our attention. The tunnels burrowed and burrowing everywhere in the overhanging cliff would one day lead to large land-slips, and down upon the township at the water's edge would come avalanches of mountain side that would restore all things to a state of nature. The attractions of the place as a gold-field may be, fortunately in that sense, exhausted before such deluge comes; but come it must some day to a natural and an engineering certainty. No danger, of course, can be seen by those daily accustomed to the locality. We get so much used to the sight of a thing that in time we cannot see it with the eyes of others. We are blind in more things than love.

It occurred to some English speculators, about 1840, to inquire into the state of the once-productive mines in the mountain ranges of the Cordilleras in South America. An agent, accompanied by some Cornish miners, went out to the locality, and duly reported upon it. Somehow this business recurred to our mind on looking at these other mountain-side mines. We could fancy a similar commission sent out to look at the remains of the Thames diggings fifty years hence. Would similar desolation mark the scene, and a few solitary descendants of the Tapieri family be all that remained of humanity thereabout? It is very likely, but the Chinese are to come first. They ever follow the white diggers, these gleaners of the gold-fields. They are great at combination mining; fifty or more work as one man, and do wonders by such united action. They are taking to emigration largely, and to returning with their profits to their own country. They haven't come to this district yet, but will probably take it up when the white population have done with it. They will most likely wash down all these mountain sides when they come, but then they will go when done, and leave all desolate. Of the Cordillera mines it was reported that they would not pay to work with free labour, and that they never would have paid had they been so worked. Chinamen work much like to slaves, and live most meagrely whilst working. These characteristics, with their wonderfully combining faculty, explain the secret of their mining success. After the Chinamen have done with the Thames diggings, there will be this good result, that there will be no deserted mines left with long tunnels and open drives to cause future land-slips. All will be taken down and washed up, and the place be restored to the sea-birds, from whom, the proper dwellers for the place, those now usurping their territory keep it but for a little while.

Could one help lingering on deck to take a last look at this new Thames? The name had a charm for us, and for every English, and especially every Londoner's, ear. We had grown up from boyhood on the banks of "old Father Thames," and loved it as the river of our great native village. It was the "silver Thames," in the language of our forefathers, and on its bosom we had known our first English boating, and our last. Nearly twenty years ago it had floated us outwards on our start hitherwards. Leaving the new Thames of New Zealand, we did so with the natural wish that we could go quickly back to a visit to the old Thames of old England. It is but right to say that the beautiful thought we have endeavoured to express came upon us as we began to be fearfully sea-sick. Prodigal son as we were of the old Thames, it was only when trouble came upon us that we thought of returning to our father.

CHAPTER XLI.

THE WATER KING'S HEAD-QUARTERS.

A STEAMER'S journey of about sixteen hours takes one from Auckland to Tauranga (Towranghay). The steamer arrives about noon, giving full time for one to call on Mr. Fawkner at the Tauranga Hotel, and get dinner there, and chat about the place and its specialties. Tauranga is the landing-place on the east coast of the north island for those who are bound inland towards Lake Taupo, the great lake from whence the river Waikato, that the native wars have made famous, takes its rise; for those also who are wishful to see that "Gate pah" at which, a few years back, so many British soldiers and officers fell in a disastrous skirmish with the Maories who had here strongly entrenched themselves; for those also who are bound on a visit to the great twin volcanoes of Tongariro and Ruapeha—volcanoes of fire, present or past, be it understood; for those also who are bound for the lakes of hot water called Rotorua and Rotomahana; for those also who are bound for the boiling geysers, or springs, of Whakarewarewa (Walker-rueher-rueher); and for those also who are bound to Te Tarata, the grand boiling-water volcano; and for those who would see the sight of sights—in this region of Nature's wonders—the terraces of marble basins that, from the top of Te Tarata, receive its heated waters, and pass them down from basin to basin, with gradually lowering temperature to each, until they reach and run over and spread about on the great white marble floor that all around awaits their everlasting lavement. It must be admitted that, with all these attractions, it requires no excuse to go to Tauranga, and that in time to come the traveller will go thither as naturally as to Niagara ; and those in search of health will take to the waters of Rotorua, Rotomahana, and Te Tarata, as they now do to those of a far less healing nature in Germany and Switzerland. Greatly medicinal are these New Zealand heated waters. We have wandered, however, from the Tauranga Hotel, to which we return to be introduced to Mr. Peter Grant as a guide for our bush journey inland. With the horses he provides we make headway on to Maketu, distant twenty miles further southwards along the eastern coast. An accommodation house here provides supper and bed for the night. Next morning a start is made for Taheke, a sort of stopping-place half way to Rotorua, where one Bennett has kindly isolated himself from the world to keep a half-way house for the benefit of such few of his fellow-men as may come that way. Such philanthropy is exceptional and praiseworthy. Shutting his eyes to the present, Bennett can see, in mental vision, that great traffic will go his way in years to come, but that is all that he will ever see of it. His descendants —of about the tenth generation or so—may see the beginning of it. Towards evening Ohenamatu is reached, and " wonderland " is entered upon. This place is a native village that runs out far into the Lake of Hot Water, called Rotorua. It is one of the queerest of human dwelling-places. The air breathed is about half steam from the lake, and the land trodden upon is a cracked and baking crust that here and there fails to cover up the hot seething mud beneath ; where these cracks occur, steam arises all around. No mistakes must be made in one's footsteps, or one sinks into boiling mud, much as Christian did into the Slough of Despond. Mistakes that have been made in that way have not been rectified, at least not in this world. Stones are put about here and there, which are used as those similarly placed for fording shallow waters, and, stepping about upon these, Ohenamatu is reached, the village of the Hot Lake. Most of these children of the hot water—the natives—were in their element, in the evening, for it is natural that their dwelling-place should make them of an amphibious nature. Of evenings they spend two hours and more in the hot, greenish-coloured, steaming waters of Lake Rotorua. The temperature is about ninety degrees, or from that to one hundred, speaking by guess in the absence of thermometers. The habits of these out-of-the-way Maories are very simple. All bathe together, men and women, which one could see by the long hair of the gentle ones as it floated on the surface. Hilarious were they and jolly, and at play and fun with each other, these girls of the Lake Rotorua. The Turkish bath sort of life these people live agrees admirably with them, and, as a new application of the wonderful powers of steam, we took much note of it. There is something to be said in favour of Ohenamatu as a dwelling-place, though advising any emigration thither is not our thought. No fuel is wanted for cooking. No kitchen is necessary there. A kettle stuck into a hole in the ground anywhere soon gets hot. A pot or pan does the same. Potatoes are put into a flax-made bag, and sunk in the hot earth, and steamed to perfection, and so with any joint or root or grain. The drawback in the eyes of visitors seems to be the insecurity of the place. That which keeps the earth and the water hot, and the mud boiling here and there, and sending up jets of steam, cannot be very safely relied upon to go so far and never any further. The village of Ohenamatu may go up or down some day in this earthquaky, volcanic New Zealand, and is very likely to do so. Meanwhile the temperature is equable all the year round, and there can be no doubt that the natives think no other place in the world is so good as theirs. The Esquimaux, who freezes ten months out of the twelve, thinks the same; and the African, who roasts for the same period; and so why not the Rotorua man, who only simmers and steams? Our guide was of some value amongst the natives here, who knew as much of our language as we did of theirs. We got a cover for ourselves for the night, and slept the sleep of a working baker near to the oven, or something very like to it. There was the largest warm bath in the world ready to our chamber door in the morning.

The next stage took us on to the boiling geysers of Whakarewarewa—little hillocks throwing out, some feebly and some fiercely, jets of boiling water, and doing so everlastingly; for that seemed to us finite beings not the least astonishing part of it. Ten miles or so further onwards, Rotomahana, another warm lake, is reached, and has to be crossed in a boat. That being done, we bid adieu altogether to the common sort of world we have known so many years, and enter upon that which, from our childhood, we had known only from the transformation scenes in pantomimes and the landscapes in fairy burlesques and extravaganzas. Before us now rises Te Tarata, and we think that, having written that much, we had better stop until we get the shade of J. W. M. Turner, that great painter of the mystic, to assist us. As we do not, however, expect to be credited, it matters little what we say. Our writing will be memoranda for our own reference merely—to be referred to hereafter as evidence of how barren our brains were in descriptive power in the year seventy-one. Te Tarata rises before us a respectably large mount, with a reservoir of sapphire-blue water at the top. The temperature of this water is about one hundred. The reservoir containing it is of great diameter. The inside of it is coated with a pinkish or light chocolate-coloured silicious or limestone cement. From the water, beautifully blue, that bubbles in this large basin is thrown up from the centre a continuous fountain-like column for thirty feet or more above the level of the edge of the reservoir—a veritable volcano of bluish, hot water! In its fall, this column of water sends large quantities from the basin splashing over the side—the lower side of the basin, towards Rotomahana Lake. In its "play" of countless years, this grand fountain, buried in the wilderness, has worked out a wonder equal to the production in the same time, by the coral insect, of the islands in the South Seas. It has fashioned for itself a terrace of titanic basins, by which its waters grandly and gracefully descend its side. A staircase, as it were, of richly-coloured marbles, that stand there to show us what Nature can do when she condescends to architecture upon earth. The whole is something that makes Versailles and its attempts but a gingerbread affair—a mere oyster-shell and mud-pie of the gutter!

The marble basins of Te Tarata are formed of silicious matters that are contained in the blue hot waters of the volcano above. That water comes through various earths, and, heated as it is, brings up in a boiled state all sorts of stony and mineral matter. The splashing and ever-falling water works out its own basin, and the petrifying matter contained in it makes that basin's inner and outer coatings. The first one looks of the purest, whitest, transparent marble, holding thousands of gallons of the most deliciously-blue water. Over the edge of this immense basin the waters flow to the one beneath, in a perpetual cascade. A cascade of water is not sufficiently beautiful. A cascade of Honiton lace is therefore supplied by Nature as a background to the cascade of water. Inexplicable as this may look, it is of easiest explanation. The same limestone deposit that forms the basin runs with its waters, over the sides of it, and lingers and drops, like to stalactites on a cavern's roof, from the edges all around. These stalactites, or fringes, are lengthened, and crossed and re-crossed by the process of time, until they reach to the basin beneath, and here is the lace-work in marble, the lattice in stone, the tracery done by time, the knitting, netting, and crochet worked by the fair and fairy fingers of Nature!

In the many gigantic basins, so terraced down the side of the water volcano, and so receiving and passing down its blue, mysterious waters, with a peculiar falling, ringing, gurgling, babbling sound, Nature has avoided monotony to the eye. By her all-excelling, cunning hand, colour is introduced with wondrous effect. Pink marble interspaces the white basins, and the lace-work hanging around is of the colour of the basin whence it hangs. To geologists we will leave it to account for pink limestone following upon white, and white upon pink. They will possibly say that a different mineral base to the basin into which the water falls, or a different temperature of such water, has worked the wonder. It is very likely. Difficult, indeed, is it to enter into any such disquisitions when on the scene itself. The beauty of the wild scenery around ; the volcano above one, throwing up its eternal column of bluish, steaming waters; their rush, in foamy-white streams, over the crater's side ; their fall from basin to basin ; the terraced basins themselves ; their o'erhanging lace-work; the marble floor, on which all is spread beneath ; the effect of light and shade and sunshine upon the whole affair—volcano, terraced marble basins, and falling waters—is so wondrous, so exciting, and so enchantingly bewildering, that the mind cannot become practical, nor go behind the scenery, as it were, of this great stage-work, to inquire into those disappointing practicalities that we always find behind the scenes. To look and wonder, and to enjoy and worship, is all that can be done within sight and sound of gorgeous Te Tarata.

These water-basins have about three and a half feet of depth, which one can test by going into them. The temperature decreases about fifteen degrees at each fall, and the water is about lukewarm when it reaches its final marble floor. This limestone crust stretches all around for great distances, distributing the water until it reaches the main channel to the neighbouring lake. The petrifying power of the water is very strong. The body of a plucked fowl exposed to it for twenty-four hours becomes not only nicely cooked, but enclosed also in a limestone covering that effectually preserves the enclosure until wanted. A notion is contained in this announcement for a new meat-preserving company, which we here ventilate, reserving no rights—save of eating. Now and again Te Tarata has spasms, and, with one strong convulsion, sends the whole contents of her magnificent reservoir into the air, completely emptying its basin. The waters go to a towering height, and descend with a crushing rush on the basins beneath. We were told that the sight was very grand when such occurs, but we were satisfied with the grandeur that we saw, and needed no imagination of anything further. Very curative are these waters of the New Zealand lake district. They are inaccessible to the invalid at present, and for his or her stay in the place there is no accommodation. This district will be the future sanatorium of New Zealand, and possibly of New South Wales. Cutaneous disorders yield quickly to the influence of the waters, and to bathe in them daily for a period is to renovate and renew the nervous system. The three days' journey into the wilds to reach them is, however, all against their being made available to the seeker of pleasure or of health, for the present generation at least. The Lake District of New Zealand is for the tourist of time to be. Lucky tourist!—that one of the future. We found that Prince Alfred had been the last visitor to the grand scene that we have endeavoured to write about. Princes are but men, we know; but, as a common form of laudation, we may say that it was a sight fit for a prince.

CHAPTER XLII.

THE PAKEHA'S PROGRESS.

THAT which Shakspeare took from the writings of others, he has been justified in taking on the score that it was of no value where he found it, and of the greatest where he left it. The same argument applies to all that the white settler has done, and is doing, in New Zealand, except that he pays for what he takes, and gives the price demanded by those who occupied parts of the country before he came. The Arab calls his visitor Howadji, and the Maori calls them all Pakehas. The Maori is of similar old blood to the Arab; both belong to the old stock that did not believe in working. Much of what the Maori retains as law and custom is of the old Levitical character, and there is a strongly Jewish look to be seen in many of the race. We went to New Zealand with an Exeter-Hall idea of the Maori as a very superior aboriginal, who, if let alone, would develope, in a Darwinian way, into a better kind of being altogether. We soon got disabused on that score. The contact we had with Maories all through the islands disillusioned us completely. The distance and the enchantment gone, the delusion went also. The Maori had had an undisturbed possession of the three islands of New Zealand for four hundred years, and through the length and breadth of them there was nothing to show of the works of man—that he had cultivated the field and the garden, and "caused the wilderness to blossom like the rose." He had for all that time roamed these fair islands of New Zealand, from Foveaux

Straits in the south to Cape Maria Van Diemen in the north, and noted not their beauty or usefulness beyond what a wild beast might. He fought with his fellows, and as he killed them he ate them, and the strong began a war of extermination against the weak, and in that way the stronger natives of the north island nearly depopulated the southern altogether—made it a sort of hunting-ground on occasions when they wished to be festive. To this kind of beings the missionaries were sent, and we have had plenteous opportunity of hearing of the doings of these philanthropists, and now of seeing the results. The missionaries who held forth at Exeter Hall in our time in London, twenty years ago, and before that, made great capital, in every sense of the word, of their New Zealand doings. They objected at the outset to the Pakeha settlement of the place, that their good doings amongst the natives might not be interfered with. They would have had the whole country left to themselves, for the express purpose of the conversion of the Maories. It is very likely, we thought, as we saw the scanty result of all their labours, that they did not wish a Pakeha's report of how little of Christianity it is possible to get into the Maori mind. Missionaries are but men, and they like their doings to be thought much of, and to be their own reporters of it. The distance of New Zealand from Europe, and the little that was then known of the strange race that inhabited it, made these missionary reports all the more of interest. Otherwise it were better by far that the missionaries had been employed in the potteries of England, or in the mining districts, or in the "black country" there, where their efforts are more wanted, and might have had an appreciable result. We went into the little pig-like dwellings of these Maories in their dirty little villages, and to their rude cabin-like chapels, and heard them gabble over the forms of prayer and service taught them as one might teach a parrot, and understood by the Maori about as much as by the bird. It is useless to attempt to Christianize unless you at the same time humanize, and you cannot get the Maori to live like a human being. He will live in his own fashion—

that of the beasts of the field, or a very little better. As for the birds of the air, their nests are wonders of art and pleasure-palaces compared to the pigstyes in which these Maories herd together. They raise their potatoes, maize, kumeros, and taro in little patches about their huts, and these gardening operations are attended to by the women, and are on so paltry a scale that not more than a few thousand acres are under cultivation in the Northern Island, where it is computed that about fifty thousand natives own twenty million acres of land —useless land to them; and yet these are the people who quarrel and fight about land!

Before we enter upon their fighting reasons, we will dismiss their acquired religion by saying that multitudes of them have lately deserted it for a mumbo-jumbo business called the "Hau-Hau" superstition, initiated by one of themselves, who had gone mad, and inaugurated by the murder of one of their best missionaries. This new superstition is professed by all those who are antagonistic to the Pakehas. Their profession of Christianity is a wretched mumbling of a few words and the possession of a Prayer-book or Bible, printed in their own language, which latter they regard as a sort of talisman, and believe that the possession of the book, and not the reading or the practising of its precepts, is the whole matter. There are no Christian qualities in a Maori's nature.

One of the best men who was ever in New Zealand, or anywhere else, the late Bishop Selwyn, said that he could solemnly declare that, since the colony began, no act of wilful injustice had ever been committed by any one in authority against a Maori, and we believe that the same may be said of the Pakehas not in authority. Why the fighting, then? Simply this, that the Maori is of a quarrelsome nature, and must fight with some one. Fighting is, with the Maori, a disease or bias of the mind; and all diseases, it is now pretty well demonstrated, are intermittent and periodic in their nature. The partial desolation of Taranaki on the west coast took place because two or three thousand turbulent natives thereabout wanted a fight. Neighbouring tribes there were none that could be well quarrelled with, but there were neighbouring Pakehas — quiet settlers from Devon and Cornwall. These Maories owned fully three millions of acres of fertile land, of which they scarcely cultivated fifty acres, and yet they sought, by quibbles and tricks, and afterwards by fighting, to dispossess the Pakehas of a few thousand acres, which had been bought by the Government from them, and paid for over and over again. It was this triplicate payment for the land that led them doubtless to think that they could get further payments by fraud or by force. Every one knows what it is to have a "black sheep" amongst the peaceable and industrious members of a family, and how he will not work nor keep straight, but will live on the labour of the others, and pluck the weakest, and be violent when wheedling and swindling will go no further. Of such are the Maories. To satisfy their acquisitiveness, they will stick at nothing. For a two-barrelled gun a "Rangitara," or chief, will offer a hundred acres of land—that does not belong to him, or will promise this, that, or the other, or anything that will serve his purpose. He has no conscience, fears no hereafter, and has no ideas of acquiring property by any other means than swindling, robbery, or fighting. All these he considers legitimate measures. We speak authoritatively on the matter, having been for some time in company of Matene te Whiwhi, who, in 1853, began the native movement to make himself Maori king. On a three-days' journey we had this magnate and three of his kindred in our company, and treasure their signatures in our pocket-book. Matene te Whiwhi did not succeed for himself in his kingly aspirations, but became a sort of king-maker in setting up in 1858 one Wherowhero, who took the title of Potatau the First. The object of the "king" business was to consolidate the Maories against the Pakehas when any opportunity could be discovered for picking a quarrel, and, if none should be discovered, to make one.

The result of three days' intimate acquaintance on shipboard with these leading men amongst the Maories was, that we concluded the relation of the Maori to the Pakeha to resemble that of a polecat who would interfere with the progress of an ox. All our fine notions about the excellence of the Maori race are now obliterated, and we shall look on the gradual obliteration of the race as one of the dispensations of Providence, really merciful—to a better race.

That better race is the Pakeha, who has, through the New Zealand islands, done more in forty years than the Maori would do in four thousand—a safe conclusion, seeing that he did nothing in four hundred years. For that reason alone we shall be glad that he be removed from the country. That the Maori had the fair land of New Zealand to himself for four hundred years, and did no more with it than so many monkeys would, is our indictment against him. If it be thought by any missionary-lover that we are too harsh, we answer, in missionary language, that we judge but in the same spirit that he was judged who made no use of the napkin-buried talent with which he had been entrusted.

See the doings of the Pakeha through the long length of this land, and that for the little time that he has had a share of it, and how he has put the talent out at interest in his one great way of doing all things—earnest work! Running through, as we did, from Southland to Otago, and so northwards, through Canterbury, Westland, Marlborough, Nelson, Wellington, Hawke's Bay, Taranaki, and Auckland—ten provinces and their towns and hamlets—we could but echo Tennyson's rhapsody on the works of the doers of this world, and say that all we saw done, and done so well, was but the earnest of what those who had done it all would yet do. If they had done all this as a beginning, what would not the completion be like! So much done is yet so little-looking in the vastness of New Zealand.

In these ten provinces the Pakeha has raised ten chief towns, all well worthy the name, and numberless outlying townships and villages. The post-office list for New Zealand is a walking-stick in length, and might be given to students in elocution as a sort of practice over heavy ground, so far as the names are concerned. A flotilla of steamers are ever coasting south, north, east, and west, and railways have been constructed in Southland and Canterbury, and others are now initiated. The Pakeha has unearthed gold at both ends of the long length of the land, and that at the northern end, the Thames, has been unearthed in such quantities as no gold-mine ever yet yielded. The Caledonian Mine is a world's wonder in the way of gold-mines, and has enriched the city of Auckland in every conceivable way. Telegraphic wires run through the land. The plains are covered with sheep and cattle, and in wool the Pakeha exports the finest that Europe receives. In building-stone, other countries are customers to him; the new Town Hall of Melbourne is built with the produce of his Oamaru quarries. He has roamed the forests, and found trees that yield unequalled woods for purposes of commerce, and through the length and breadth of the land he has found fields of usefulness, and has put them to the best purpose. At a late national exhibition of the products of the country, held at Dunedin, specimens of gold, copper, iron, coal, limestone, and ornamental woods were sent from nearly all the ten provinces. All that a goodly land can yield is brought forth and disseminated for the good of mankind, and these doings of the Pakeha are but the work of his first forty years.

Albert Land, not hitherto named by us, deserves a few words. The northernmost part of New Zealand, from Auckland to Cape Maria Van Diemen, is two hundred miles in length, and from thirty-five to fifty-five in breadth. It stands in about the same relation to the rest of New Zealand as Devon and Cornwall do to England. Here the Kauri pine —that king of pines—attains its finest growth. The country is splendidly watered, and pretty bays and harbours indent both east and west coasts. Buried about in the earth here are found the greatest stores of a pale yellowish gum, that can be quarried almost like stone in blocks, and which, under the name of Kauri gum, is sold by the ton, and is becoming of much use in commerce. It is a most curious deposit, and various theories are ventilated about it and its origin. Little settlements are to be found here and there in this Albert Land, especially on the banks of the Kaipara river, and eastward on the shore of that wonderful Bay of Islands—a bay as magnificent as the harbour of Sydney. This part of New Zealand never gets its share of visitors, and yet it is fully deserving—a sort of Cinderella of the New Zealand family that will yet look up in the world. The Bay of Islands is the harbour to Russell—a township that once had the more famous name of Korrareka, the first Pakeha settlement in New Zealand. This place was an ocean "Alsatia" once—a no-man's land of liberty and licence of the wildest kind that sailors could delight in. It was strangely deserted soon after the British took formal possession of it because of some hostilities on the part of the natives. It was at Korrareka that the first official representative of England set up the British flag, and it was here that Heki, a New Zealander who has left his name in the story, cut the flag-staff down. This Bay of Islands is a Paradise of a scene—a lovely bay, dotted with little green islands of bewildering beauty. Here came the weary whaler and the merchantman, wanting rest and fresh water, and Kauri pine-spars for his masts. Auckland got the start when Heki and his Maories frightened the British settlers away from this place, and Korrareka has never recovered itself. Like the sleeping beauty that it is, it will be awakened some day to greatness. The Mormons talk of leaving Salt Lake City and seeking a quieter home. Let them, or some better class of emigrants, have a look at the Bay of Islands. They will never want to go any further, and they will never leave the place. It has historic interest further than we have mentioned, for to it came that French man-of-war that was to take possession of New Zealand for France, but found itself just a little too late, and from Korrareka was despatched that English man-of-war that got down to Akaroa, in the Southern Island, just in time to keep the French from taking possession there also. Here, too, Nature has been kindest in all her bestowings through the three islands. Here is the vegetation of the tropics without the tropical inconveniences of scorching heat and parching drought. Peaches, oranges, olives, and pine-apples and bananas, and all the goodly and sweet things of the south, grow here in greatest luxuriance. Some of the little settlements on the pretty harbours and bays of the east and west coasts are most romantically situated, and not least so is little Parengarenga, that sits on the nose of the North Cape—the Land's End of New Zealand. Here too, at Korrareka, was signed the "Treaty of Waitangi"—England's title-deed to New Zealand—that deed of bargain and sale between the Pakeha and the Maori which the former has always adhered to with the honesty of an Englishman, and the latter evaded, or endeavoured to evade, with the instincts of a Maori.

CHAPTER XLIII.

THE MAORI'S DECLINE.

CAPTAIN COOK estimated, nearly a century ago, that the Maories had, long before his discovery of them, seen their best days—that is, the days when their number was greatest. He thought that they had, in the hundred years preceding his visit, eaten up about one-fourth of their then number. He felt for them in a large-minded way, for the great navigator and discoverer was a liberal-hearted man, and he, in some sort, excused their manners on the score that they had no animals in the country which they could hunt and kill, and cook and eat. They had brought with them, when they migrated from the Malay Islands, only a dog and a rat. We have Shakspeare's authority for calling rats but "small deer." Better venison they had not, and hence Cook was inclined to look with a philosophic mind upon the way they had taken to for supplying the want of animal food. Had he come to the Islands of New Zealand fifty years later, the English nation might have been saved great trouble with the Maories, and the British exchequer a large outlay. It is possible that nearly all of the natives would by that time have eaten up one another, for there can be no doubt that such a taste as they were cultivating would have greatly increased by what it fed upon, and that in satisfying it a larger number would have to be killed than could have been conveniently eaten—whilst fresh. The Maori had to eat his man quite fresh, for he knew not, never knew, and does not know now, the virtues of salt as a seasoning to, or as a preservative of, his meat, or as anything else that is useful. In the mind's eye we can see the waste of such food that must have been occasioned by the Maori taste. To get one or two bodies for a meal, many must have been killed, for it is not likely that the exact quantity wanted for the week's supply could have been obtained as easily as by hunting or by purchase of animal food. It had to be fought for—to be obtained by hand-to-hand warfare. The surplus food was dealt with in this way. The head was cut off, and, the brains having been taken out, it was dried in the sun, stuffed with leaves and kauri gum, and then half baked before a slow fire. It was ever afterwards kept as a household ornament, until the white man came to the islands, when these heads were all purchased for museums and travelling shows, and the other "aids to science" for which such things go. The head being off, the body was laid upon stones that had been previously heated by fire. It was then covered up with branches of fern, and further covered with earth. The heat of the stones slowly baked it, and the covering prevented any escape of vapour. Six hours afterwards, this baked meat was uncovered, and put away until wanted on a platform supported by four sticks, where it remained until required for breakfast, dinner, or supper. Captain Cook did much to put an end to this kind of feeding, by leaving numbers of pigs on the islands, and by supplying the Maories with potatoes, turnips, carrots, maize, and corn. These latter are cultivated to this day in little patches about the Maori dwellings, and the natives live thereon literally from hand to mouth. Before they got this vegetable diet, they subsisted upon the roots of fern, upon stray rats, and upon stranded whales and sharks, and such fish as they could catch without fish-hooks. These and the "animal food" to which we have alluded constituted their sustenance. Birds there were none worth shooting for food, and, had there been any, the Maories had no powder. A moa would have made a meal for a large family for a month, had that gigantic bird existed in the Maories' time, which is very doubtful, and had the Maori possessed any means of catching a bird that could see about ten miles around him at a glance, and could run faster than an express train—a matter which is still more doubtful. The pigs we regard as having done more to suppress the cannibal taste, or to satisfy it, than anything else that can be looked for as an argument in that way. They increased and multiplied, and replenished all New Zealand, and up to forty years ago had the great honour, which pigs never before had, of constituting the whole Fauna of a large country. The wretched rat disappeared before them, and there was never a people who could, like the Maories, have so sensibly said "Please the pigs," looking to the great importance that these animals must have had in their eyes. The trouble of catching them was greatly in the pigs' favour, for a very little trouble suits a Maori who is not bent upon robbery or vengeance. A mother pig and her large young family were the easy victims, and they were not always secured without a battle, of which the Maori often could show the scars. The pigs are now the only animals in the three islands of New Zealand for the sportsman's pleasure. Prince Alfred was treated to a pig-hunt there, on his late visit, in the same way that he was treated to an elephant-hunt at the Cape. After all, the elephant looks but a larger pig, and the long-legged New Zealand boar must have given the better sport. There is a great Darwinian point about these pigs that must not be overlooked. When Captain Cook left them on the islands, the pigs were of our ordinary farmyard kind—the type of which every Englishman knows—but the constant working of the pig, in rooting at the fern-trees for food, gradually lengthened his snout to a very appreciable extent. Having to poke that nose always into the earth has lengthened it and strengthened it, until it is quite a distinct sort of snout from the snout of its ancestor and progenitor, Captain Cook's pig of a hundred years ago. Let Darwinians reflect upon this, as it bears out their theory that the grasping property of the monkey's tail was brought about by the gradual action of fear in the case of those monkeys whose hold was insecure, upon the structure of the vertebræ. To put the formula in other words, "that which is required by the necessities of animal life is furnished by nature;" and we might add, "that which is not required is taken away," as we find the fishes in the Mammoth Caves of Kentucky to have no eyes. Sight not being required there, the eyes that were not used gradually faded, and in the progress of the species were not reproduced.

We will return to our Maori, who is gradually fading too, not being reproduced at all in sufficient numbers to keep the species upon the earth. There are many more men than women now, and but few children—a sort of thing quite out of the order of an increasing people, in which there are always more women and children than men. Looking at them lying about in their dirty villages, the matter becomes understandable to us. Fighting men they are all, and bulldogs at that. That is their great characteristic. It is good in its way, no doubt, but must be allied to other qualities to make it of good to its owner. Down Whitechapel way, we could pick up any Sunday morning twenty bull-necked, bull-doggy fighting men, who, for a stake of five pounds a side, will punch each other to death for hours together. These men will fight, and will do nothing else in the way of hard work. Cadge they will without shame, and loaf about with pipe in mouth and sponge upon others, leaving their wives to wash and mangle and slave for their benefit. Work for their living, in the sense of steady labour, these men never will. All that is characteristic of the Maori. This Whitechapel breed will band together and have faction-fights with other similar breeds. That is like the Maori also. These Whitechapellers, hating labour of all kinds, will hate those who pursue it, interfering with and annoying and worrying in every way those who will work, whilst they idle. Of such is the Maori all over. Those "Roughs" of London, and their like the "Reds" of Paris, will cajole and shuffle, lie and swindle, and so also will the Maories. We were in company with three of them for four days on board a steamer in one of our coasting excursions, and had, then and there, plenteous evidence of their qualities. They were men of mark, too, amongst the Maories—one of them had tried once to make himself king over them. These men were always trying " to come the old soldier" over us in a regular Jeremy Diddler way. Borrowing was their great point, extending from money to tobacco; and borrowing was only another name for sponging or begging. Draughts and cards they would play, and always stipulate for a stake which they had no means of paying, nor inclination to pay either, when they lost. They would beg only a pipe of tobacco, and then take a handful, borrow a penknife—and pocket it, and try to sell anything that they had saleable—for six times its value. Of all sorts of meanness they were guilty, and such, we found, was not our experience alone, for we extracted from a Wellington paper the following remarks on the Parliamentary Maories whom the wisdom of the New Zealand Constitution permits to sit in the House of Representatives there. The remarks were made in the House by another honourable member, not a Maori, and it will be seen that they are quite parliamentary in style. The speaker said, "One of those Maori representatives was a great chieftain named Mete Kingi, of whom they had doubtless heard. That hon. gentleman had very peculiar notions of the functions of a legislator, and had a number of weaknesses altogether beyond political weaknesses. For instance, he had a habit of walking away with the soap and hair-brushes belonging to the lavatory. (Laughter.) He met that hon. gentleman one day on the beach at Wellington with a hair-brush sticking out of his pocket. (Continued laughter.) That hon. member also had a weakness which was unfortunately not confined to the Maori race—that of borrowing half-crowns, and never repaying them. Mete Kingi very soon found out that the best time to borrow half-crowns was just before a division; and he was sorry to say that, having acted as 'whip' for one of the parties in the House, he was very frequently the victim; and the common honesty of that party had never prompted them to repay him. (Loud laughter.) On one occasion he met with Mete Kingi and a coloured colleague coming out of a certain fishmonger's shop in Wellington, holding by the tail a shark about 3ft. long. It was a remarkable fact that for about a week after that occurrence it was utterly impossible to sit in the part of the House where the Maories were ; and every one certainly pitied the unfortunate interpreter who had to sit amongst them. (Great laughter.) Mete Kingi made a speech once, and a very fair sample it was. He said, 'England is a great nation. (A pause.) The Maories are a great people. (A pause.) The English have called us to this great house. (A pause.) We sit here.' Then came the anti-climax :—' They have pounded my cow at Wanganui.' Then he ended like an ancient chief of an Indian tribe :—' I have spoken.' That was the best speech he ever made."

We had once before, over twenty years ago, been in similar company to that of our three Maories, and that was a company which a steamer was carrying, amongst others, down the river Thames in London to a prize-fight. When we got off that steamer we had lost purse, handkerchief, gloves, and everything that could well be borrowed or filched from us. Australians have been taken to England as pugilists, and so have Americans, while negroes in plenty have entered the fistic ring ; but we don't remember that a Maori was ever taken to England for that purpose. He seems to have been overlooked by the " Fancy," and the omission should be amended. He will go readily, and will fight well, and " sell " his backers also as readily as he will fight. They may take our word for it that he will do nothing but for his own benefit. And yet, ye gods, how the Maories can fight! We were shown a spot where less than two hundred of them had withstood the British soldiery to five times the number, and that for two days and a night. The Maories had only the advantage of raised ground and some earthworks hastily thrown up. When on the second day they were appealed to by General Cameron to give in, as he was loth that such men as they had proved themselves should die, they returned the Roman answer, "Ask him which it is that he thinks is to die," and so fought on until they nearly all fell. The rest fled, still fighting. If such as they were could be got to fight for other people than themselves, we would back them, as soldiers, against all the world—including the present Prussians. We can't say more.

And yet these people decline, and decline, before the white man. His working powers paralyze the Maori, and the latter gets sulky and morose at the sight of his busy brother, and becomes careless of life and everything else. He feels that he has lost his place in the land. He is not only no longer number one there, but he is nobody at all. His proud spirit is broken. He feels that his wife cannot think much of him, and that she sees the white man work and support his wife and family, whilst she, poor devil, is called upon to work and support her lazy, do-nothing Maori lord. Do we never see the same thing amongst ourselves? We have seen it. It is not unusual to see a superior workman put his fellow's nose out of joint, and to turn the satisfied into the dissatisfied man, who will then lose energy and spirit, and become careless and reckless. It is not all of us who can stand the sight of the prosperity of others, and bear quietly to be beaten in the race of life. The Maori is not the only one who loses heart in the race when he is not only collared but passed in it. Those acquainted with animal life will tell us how many horses "shut up" entirely when that event happens to them. It is a pity, all things considered, and humanity especially, that the Maori cannot be got to leave New Zealand and go back to his own Malays, or some other island, where he might begin life anew, with the addition of an assortment of animals to rear and feed upon—to prevent a further decrease of his species. The Maori, with the form and the strength of an athletic man, has the mind of a child. He will not trouble himself to learn the English language. The Englishman has to learn the Maori's, and communicate with him therein The British Government have set up a native court at Auckland, in which justice is done in the Maori tongue. The court was sitting in January, when we were in Auckland, and we visited an English court of law doing its work in another tongue. The Maori is never satisfied with a decision unless it be in his favour; a decision against him he looks on as an injury, and broods over it in Corsican fashion. "In the case of Fox *v.* Walker, to recover from a Maori upon a promissory note, the cause of action (says an Auckland paper) has been dismissed. It appears that, in negotiating such instruments with Maories, it is essential to make them understand what they are doing. If they say they don't understand, the Maori is rid of his liability." The paragraph quoted we cut from a New Zealand paper, and it shows the difficulty of dealing with men who can say that they understand or not, just as it may suit them. A nice way of getting rid of liabilities, and kind treatment, indeed, on the part of the British! The Maori's disinclination to learn the language, and conform to the habits of the white settler, keeps him back altogether in New Zealand, and prevents him competing at anything—except fighting. He will not become servant to the settler in any way, and his only friendship for him is for what he can get out of him.

Both Pakeha and Maori are now left, by the removal of the British troops altogether from New Zealand, to shift for themselves on equal terms. The terms are not equal, however, for the white settler is thinking of working and progressing, and of leaving those who are to come after him better off than he is himself, and the Maori is thinking of nothing of the kind; he is, on the contrary, idling about and dreaming of the next cause of quarrel that he can pick, and the next fight, and of that great honour to be achieved amongst the Maories—that of being the first man in the battle to kill one of the enemy. If the white New Zealand settlers intend to hold their own, and to come out of the next scrimmage with honour, they must adopt the Prussian fashion of living, and devote much of their time to military matters and to learning a soldier's duties. To do that, the cash-book and the bank-book must be neglected for a time, and the acquisition of wealth be postponed to the more sensible question of the means of keeping it when acquired. One battle well fought and won will quiet the Maories for a long time, but the loss of one will unhinge everything, with such men as the Maories for victors. Every year fights for the white settler, however. Time is rapidly sweeping away the Maori, and he is disappearing like to the clouds that sweep his mountains' summit. His new diet is said not to nourish him as his former one did. The fern-root that he fed upon before Captain Cook introduced the

A MAORI AND HIS PIPE.

potato is said to have contained more than twice as much of nourishment. We all know the bitterness with which Cobbett spoke and wrote of the potato as an article of food for the British labourer, and his views seem to be supported by its effects upon the Maori's constitution. Consumption frequently visits his unclean and unventilated dwelling, and he has taken to bad methods of preparing his food for eating. His maize and potatoes and corn are macerated in water and left so for days, and then dried in the sun, and not eaten until they become in a half-rotten and decidedly bad-smelling state. "High" venison may be a good thing, but the "high" living of the Maori is decidedly bad. We tried to eat with them, but found nothing that our eyes or nose would let us partake of. Again, to help him out of the world, he has taken body and spirit to tobacco, which blessing of civilization makes him lazier than ever, and to which he devotes the energies of a lifetime. The female Maori does the same; the filthy pipe and the poisonous weed are never out of her hands. Tobacco, that has ruined the constitutions of half the Americans, is doing the same for the Maories. Many of them add the aid of spirits to the tobacco. We all know whither tend idle habits; bad dwellings, bad food, want of clothing, depressed energies, and the use of tobacco and spirits; and we see how many powerful agents are thus working together for the improvement of the Maori off the face of the earth.

THE END.

A Catalogue of American and Foreign Books Published or Imported by Messrs. Sampson Low & Co. *can be had on application.*

Crown Buildings, 188, Fleet Street, London,
April, 1879.

A List of Books

PUBLISHED BY

SAMPSON LOW, MARSTON, SEARLE, & RIVINGTON.

———◆———

ALPHABETICAL LIST.

A CLASSIFIED *Educational Catalogue of Works* published in Great Britain. Demy 8vo, cloth extra. Second Edition, revised and corrected to Christmas, 1877, 5s.

Abney (Captain W. de W., R.E., F.R.S.) *Thebes, and its Five Greater Temples.* Forty large Permanent Photographs, with descriptive letter-press. Super-royal 4to, cloth extra, 63s.

About Some Fellows. By an Eton Boy, Author of "A Day of my Life." Cloth limp, square 16mo, 2s. 6d.

Adventures of Captain Mago. A Phœnician's Explorations 1000 years B.C. By Leon Cahun. Numerous Illustrations. Crown 8vo, cloth extra, gilt, 7s. 6d.

Adventures of a Young Naturalist. By Lucien Biart, with 117 beautiful Illustrations on Wood. Edited and adapted by Parker Gillmore. Post 8vo, cloth extra, gilt edges, New Edition, 7s. 6d.

Adventures in New Guinea. The Narrative of the Captivity of a French Sailor for Nine Years among the Savages in the Interior. Small post 8vo, with Illustrations and Map, cloth, gilt, 6s.

Afghanistan and the Afghans. Being a Brief Review of the History of the Country, and Account of its People. By H. W. Bellew, C.S.I. Crown 8vo, cloth extra, 6s.

Alcott (*Louisa M.*) *Aunt Jo's Scrap-Bag.* Square 16mo, 2s. 6d. (Rose Library, 1s.)

——— *Cupid and Chow-Chow.* Small post 8vo, 3s. 6d.

——— *Little Men: Life at Plumfield with Jo's Boys.* Small post 8vo, cloth, gilt edges, 3s. 6d. (Rose Library, Double vol. 2s.)

——— *Little Women.* 1 vol., cloth, gilt edges, 3s. 6d. (Rose Library, 2 vols., 1s. each.)

——— *Old-Fashioned Girl.* Best Edition, small post 8vo, cloth extra, gilt edges, 3s. 6d. (Rose Library, 2s.)

A

Alcott (*Louisa M.*) *Work and Beginning Again.* A Story of Experience. 1 vol., small post 8vo, cloth extra, 6s. Several Illustrations. (Rose Library, 2 vols., 1s. each.)
—— *Shawl Straps.* Small post 8vo, cloth extra, gilt, 3s. 6d.
—— *Eight Cousins; or, the Aunt Hill.* Small post 8vo, with Illustrations, 3s. 6d.
—— *The Rose in Bloom.* Small post 8vo, cloth extra, 3s. 6d.
—— *Silver Pitchers.* Small post 8vo, cloth extra, 3s. 6d.
—— *Under the Lilacs.* Small post 8vo, cloth extra, 5s.

"Miss Alcott's stories are thoroughly healthy, full of racy fun and humour ... exceedingly entertaining .... We can recommend the 'Eight Cousins.'"—*Athenæum.*

Alpine Ascents and Adventures; or, Rock and Snow Sketches. By H. SCHÜTZ WILSON, of the Alpine Club. With Illustrations by WHYMPER and MARCUS STONE. Crown 8vo, 10s. 6d. 2nd Edition.

Andersen (*Hans Christian*) *Fairy Tales.* With Illustrations in Colours by E. V. B. Royal 4to, cloth, 25s.

Andrews (*Dr.*) *Latin-English Lexicon.* New Edition. Royal 8vo, 1670 pp., cloth extra, price 18s.

Animals Painted by Themselves. Adapted from the French of Balzac, Georges Sands, &c., with 200 Illustrations by GRANDVILLE. 8vo, cloth extra, gilt, 10s. 6d.

Art of Reading Aloud (*The*) *in Pulpit, Lecture Room, or Private Reunions,* with a perfect system of Economy of Lung Power on just principles for acquiring ease in Delivery, and a thorough command of the Voice. By G. VANDENHOFF, M.A. Crown 8vo, cloth extra, 6s.

Asiatic Turkey: being a Narrative of a Journey from Bombay to the Bosphorus, embracing a ride of over One Thousand Miles, from the head of the Persian Gulf to Antioch on the Mediterranean. By GRATTAN GEARY, Editor of the *Times of India.* 2 vols., crown 8vo, cloth extra, with many Illustrations, and a Route Map.

Atlantic Islands as Resorts of Health and Pleasure. By S. G. W. BENJAMIN, Author of "Contemporary Art in Europe," &c. Royal 8vo, cloth extra, with upwards of 150 Illustrations, 16s.

Autobiography of Sir G. Gilbert Scott, R.A., F.S.A., &c. Edited by his Son, G. GILBERT SCOTT. With an Introduction by the DEAN OF CHICHESTER, and a Funeral Sermon, preached in Westminster Abbey, by the DEAN OF WESTMINSTER. Also, Portrait on steel from the portrait of the Author by G. RICHMOND, R.A. 1 vol., demy 8vo, cloth extra, 18s.

BAKER (*Lieut.-Gen. Valentine, Pasha*). See "War in Bulgaria."

Barton Experiment (*The*). By the Author of "Helen's Babies." 1s.

THE BAYARD SERIES,

Edited by the late J. HAIN FRISWELL.

Comprising Pleasure Books of Literature produced in the Choicest Style as Companionable Volumes at Home and Abroad.

"We can hardly imagine better books for boys to read or for men to ponder over."—*Times.*

Price 2s. 6d. each Volume, complete in itself, flexible cloth extra, gilt edges, with silk Headbands and Registers.

The Story of the Chevalier Bayard. By M. DE BERVILLE.

De Joinville's St. Louis, King of France.

The Essays of Abraham Cowley, including all his Prose Works.

Abdallah ; or the Four Leaves. By EDOUARD LABOULLAYE.

Table-Talk and Opinions of Napoleon Buonaparte.

Vathek : An Oriental Romance. By WILLIAM BECKFORD.

The King and the Commons. A Selection of Cavalier and Puritan Songs. Edited by Prof. MORLEY.

Words of Wellington : Maxims and Opinions of the Great Duke.

Dr. Johnson's Rasselas, Prince of Abyssinia. With Notes.

Hazlitt's Round Table. With Biographical Introduction.

The Religio Medici, Hydriotaphia, and the Letter to a Friend. By Sir THOMAS BROWNE, Knt.

Ballad Poetry of the Affections. By ROBERT BUCHANAN.

Coleridge's Christabel, and other Imaginative Poems. With Preface by ALGERNON C. SWINBURNE.

Lord Chesterfield's Letters, Sentences, and Maxims. With Introduction by the Editor, and Essay on Chesterfield by M. DE STE.-BEUVE, of the French Academy.

Essays in Mosaic. By THOS. BALLANTYNE.

My Uncle Toby; his Story and his Friends. Edited by P. FITZGERALD.

Reflections ; or, Moral Sentences and Maxims of the Duke de la Rochefoucauld.

Socrates : Memoirs for English Readers from Xenophon's Memorabilia. By EDW. LEVIEN.

Prince Albert's Golden Precepts.

A Case containing 12 Volumes, price 31s. 6d. ; or the Case separately, price 3s. 6d.

Beauty and the Beast. An Old Tale retold, with Pictures by E. V. B. Demy 4to, cloth extra, novel binding. 10 Illustrations in Colours (in same style as those in the First Edition of "Story without an End"). 12s. 6d.

Benthall (Rev. J.) Songs of the Hebrew Poets in English Verse. Crown 8vo, red edges, 10s. 6d.

Beumers' German Copybooks. In six gradations at 4*d.* each.
Biart (Lucien). See "Adventures of a Young Naturalist," "My Rambles in the New World," "The Two Friends."
Bickersteth's Hymnal Companion to Book of Common Prayer.
The Original Editions, containing 403 Hymns, always kept in Print.
Revised and Enlarged Edition, containing 550 Hymns—

*** The Revised Editions are entirely distinct from, and cannot be used with, the original editions.

			s.	d
7A	Medium 32mo, cloth limp		0	8
7B	ditto roan		1	2
7C	ditto morocco or calf		2	6
8A	Super-royal 32mo, cloth limp		1	0
8B	ditto red edges		1	2
8C	ditto roan		2	2
8D	ditto morocco or calf		3	6
9A	Crown 8vo, cloth, red edges		3	0
9B	ditto roan		4	0
9C	ditto morocco or calf		6	0
10A	Crown 8vo, with Introduction and Notes, red edges		4	0
10B	ditto roan		5	0
10C	ditto morocco		7	6
11A	Penny Edition in Wrapper		0	1
11B	ditto cloth		0	2
11G	ditto fancy cloth		0	4
11C	With Prayer Book, cloth		0	9
11D	ditto roan		1	0
11E	ditto morocco		2	6
11F	ditto persian		1	6
12A	Crown 8vo, with Tunes, cloth, plain edges		4	0
12B	ditto ditto persian, red edges		6	6
12C	ditto ditto limp morocco, gilt edges		7	6
13A	Small 4to, for Organ		8	6
13B	ditto ditto limp russia		21	0
14A	Tonic Sol-fa Edition		3	6
14B	ditto treble and alto only		1	0
5B	Chants only		1	6
5D	ditto 4to, for Organ		3	6
	The Church Mission Hymn-Book	per 100	8	4
	Ditto ditto cloth	each	0	4

The "*Hymnal Companion*" may now be had in special bindings for presentation with and without the Common Prayer Book. A red line edition is ready. Lists on application.

Bickersteth (Rev. E. H., M.A.) The Reef and other Parables. 1 vol., square 8vo, with numerous very beautiful Engravings, 7*s.* 6*d.*

—————— *The Clergyman in his Home.* Small post 8vo, 1*s.*

—————— *The Master's Home-Call;* or, *Brief Memorials of* Alice Frances Bickersteth. 20th Thousand. 32mo, cloth gilt, 1*s.*

"They recall in a touching manner a character of which the religious beauty has a warmth and grace almost too tender to be definite."—*The Guardian.*

Bickersteth (Rev. E. H., M.A.) The Master's Will. A Funeral Sermon preached on the Death of Mrs. S. Gurney Buxton. Sewn, 6*d.*; cloth gilt, 1*s.*

——— *The Shadow of the Rock.* A Selection of Religious Poetry. 18mo, cloth extra, 2*s.* 6*d.*

——— *The Shadowed Home and the Light Beyond.* 7th Edition, crown 8vo, cloth extra, 5*s.*

Bida. The Authorized Version of the Four Gospels, with the whole of the magnificent Etchings on Steel, after drawings by M. BIDA, in 4 vols., appropriately bound in cloth extra, price 3*l.* 3*s.* each.

Also the four volumes in two, bound in the best morocco, by Suttaby, extra gilt edges, 18*l.* 18*s.*, half-morocco, 12*l.* 12*s.*

"Bida's Illustrations of the Gospels of St. Matthew and St. John have already received here and elsewhere a full recognition of their great merits."—*Times.*

Biographies of the Great Artists, Illustrated. This Series will be issued in Monthly Volumes in the form of Handbooks. Each will be a Monograph of a Great Artist, or a Brief History of a Group of Artists of one School; and will contain Portraits of the Masters, and as many examples of their art as can be readily procured. They will be Illustrated with from 16 to 20 Full-page Engravings, printed in the best manner, which have been contributed from several of the most important Art-Publications of France and Germany, and will be found valuable records of the Painters' Works. The ornamental binding is taken from an Italian design in a book printed at Venice at the end of the Fifteenth Century, and the inside lining from a pattern of old Italian lace. The price of the Volumes is 3*s.* 6*d.*:—

Titian.	Rubens.	Velasquez.
Rembrandt.	Lionardo.	Tintoret and Veronese.
Raphael.	Turner.	Hogarth.
Van Dyck and Hals.	The Little Masters.	Michelangelo.
Holbein.		

Black (Wm.) Three Feathers. Small post 8vo, cloth extra, 6*s.*

——— *Lady Silverdale's Sweetheart, and other Stories.* 1 vol., small post 8vo, 6*s.*

——— *Kilmeny: a Novel.* Small post 8vo, cloth, 6*s.*

——— *In Silk Attire.* 3rd Edition, small post 8vo, 6*s.*

——— *A Daughter of Heth.* 11th Edition, small post 8vo, 6*s.*

Blackmore (R. D.) Lorna Doone. 10th Edition, cr. 8vo, 6*s.*

"The reader at times holds his breath, so graphically yet so simply does John Ridd tell his tale."—*Saturday Review.*

——— *Alice Lorraine.* 1 vol., small post 8vo, 6th Edition, 6*s.*

——— *Clara Vaughan.* Revised Edition, 6*s.*

——— *Cradock Nowell.* New Edition, 6*s.*

——— *Cripps the Carrier.* 3rd Edition, small post 8vo, 6*s.*

——— *Mary Anerley.* 3 vols., 31*s.* 6*d.* [*In the press.*

Blossoms from the King's Garden: Sermons for Children. By the Rev. C. BOSANQUET. 2nd Edition, small post 8vo, cloth extra, 6s.

Blue Banner (The); or, The Adventures of a Mussulman, a Christian, and a Pagan, in the time of the Crusades and Mongol Conquest. Translated from the French of LEON CAHUN. With Seventy-six Wood Engravings. Square imperial 16mo, cloth extra, 7s. 6d.

Book of English Elegies. By W. F. MARCH PHILLIPPS. Small post 8vo, cloth extra, 5s.

    The Aim of the Editor of this Selection has been to collect in a popular form the best and most representative Elegiac Poems which have been written in the English tongue.

Book of the Play. By DUTTON COOK. 2 vols., crown 8vo, 24s.

Border Tales Round the Camp Fire in the Rocky Mountains. By the Rev. E. B. TUTTLE, Army Chaplain, U.S.A. With Two Illustrations by PHIZ. Crown 8vo, 5s.

Brave Men in Action. By S. J. MACKENNA. Crown 8vo, 480 pp., cloth, 10s. 6d.

Brazil and the Brazilians. By J. C. FLETCHER and D. P. KIDDER. 9th Edition, Illustrated, 8vo, 21s.

Bryant (W. C., assisted by S. H. Gay) A Popular History of the United States. About 4 vols., to be profusely Illustrated with Engravings on Steel and Wood, after Designs by the best Artists. Vol. I., super-royal 8vo, cloth extra, gilt, 42s., is ready.

Burnaby (Capt.) See "On Horseback."

Butler (W. F.) The Great Lone Land; an Account of the Red River Expedition, 1869-70. With Illustrations and Map. Fifth and Cheaper Edition, crown 8vo, cloth extra, 7s. 6d.

——— *The Wild North Land; the Story of a Winter Journey* with Dogs across Northern North America. Demy 8vo, cloth, with numerous Woodcuts and a Map, 4th Edition, 18s. Cr. 8vo, 7s. 6d.

——— *Akim-foo: the History of a Failure.* Demy 8vo, cloth, 2nd Edition, 16s. Also, in crown 8vo, 7s. 6d.

By Land and Ocean; or, The Journal and Letters of a Tour round the World by a Young Girl *alone.* Crown 8vo, cloth, 7s. 6d.

CADOGAN (Lady A.) Illustrated Games of Patience. Twenty-four Diagrams in Colours, with Descriptive Text. Foolscap 4to, cloth extra, gilt edges, 3rd Edition, 12s. 6d.

Canada under the Administration of Lord Dufferin. By G. STEWART, Jun., Author of "Evenings in the Library," &c. Cloth gilt, 8vo, 15s.

Carbon Process (A Manual of). See LIESEGANG.

Ceramic Art. See JACQUEMART.

Changed Cross (The), and other Religious Poems. 16mo, 2s. 6d.

Chatty Letters from the East and West. By A. H. WYLIE. Small 4to, 12s. 6d.

Child of the Cavern (The); or, Strange Doings Underground. By JULES VERNE. Translated by W. H. G. KINGSTON, Author of "Snow Shoes and Canoes," "Peter the Whaler," "The Three Midshipmen," &c., &c., &c. Numerous Illustrations. Square crown 8vo, cloth extra, gilt edges, 7s. 6d.

Child's Play, with 16 Coloured Drawings by E. V. B. Printed on thick paper, with tints, 7s. 6d.

—— *New.* By E. V. B. Similar to the above. *See* New.

Children's Lives and How to Preserve Them; or, The Nursery Handbook. By W. LOMAS, M.D. Crown 8vo, cloth, 5s.

Choice Editions of Choice Books. 2s. 6d. each, Illustrated by C. W. COPE, R.A., T. CRESWICK, R.A., E. DUNCAN, BIRKET FOSTER, J. C. HORSLEY, A.R.A., G. HICKS, R. REDGRAVE, R.A., C. STONEHOUSE, F. TAYLER, G. THOMAS, H. J. TOWNSHEND, E. H. WEHNERT, HARRISON WEIR, &c.

Bloomfield's Farmer's Boy.	Milton's L'Allegro.
Campbell's Pleasures of Hope.	Poetry of Nature. Harrison Weir.
Coleridge's Ancient Mariner.	Rogers' (Sam.) Pleasures of Memory.
Goldsmith's Deserted Village.	Shakespeare's Songs and Sonnets.
Goldsmith's Vicar of Wakefield.	Tennyson's May Queen.
Gray's Elegy in a Churchyard.	Elizabethan Poets.
Keat's Eve of St. Agnes.	Wordsworth's Pastoral Poems.

"Such works are a glorious beatification for a poet."—*Athenæum.*

Christian Activity. By ELEANOR C. PRICE. Cloth extra, 6s.

Christmas Story-teller (The). By Old Hands and New Ones. Crown 8vo, cloth extra, gilt edges, Fifty-two Illustrations, 10s. 6d.

Church Unity: Thoughts and Suggestions. By the Rev. V. C. KNIGHT, M.A., University College, Oxford. Crown 8vo, pp. 456, 5s.

Clarke (Cowden). See "Recollections of Writers," "Shakespeare Key."

Cobbett (William). A Biography. By EDWARD SMITH. 2 vols., crown 8vo, 25s.

Continental Tour of Eight Days for Forty-four Shillings. By a JOURNEY-MAN. 12mo, 1s.
"The book is simply delightful."—*Spectator.*

Cook (D.) Book of the Play. 2 vols., crown 8vo, 24s.

Copyright, National and International. From the Point of View of a Publisher. Demy 8vo, sewn, 2s.

Covert Side Sketches: Thoughts on Hunting, with Different Packs in Different Countries. By J. NEVITT FITT (H.H. of the *Sporting Gazette,* late of the *Field*). 2nd Edition. Crown 8vo, cloth, 10s. 6d.

Cripps the Carrier. 3rd Edition, 6s. *See* BLACKMORE.

Cruise of H.M.S. "Challenger" (The). By W. J. J. SPRY, R.N. With Route Map and many Illustrations. 6th Edition, demy 8vo, cloth, 18s. Cheap Edition, crown 8vo, small type, some of the Illustrations, 7s. 6d.

"The book before us supplies the information in a manner that leaves little to be desired. 'The Cruise of H.M.S. *Challenger*' is an exceedingly well-written, entertaining, and instructive book."—*United Service Gazette.*

"Agreeably written, full of information, and copiously illustrated."—*Broad Arrow.*

Curious Adventures of a Field Cricket. By Dr. ERNEST CANDÈZE. Translated by N. D'ANVERS. With numerous fine Illustrations. Crown 8vo, cloth extra, gilt edges, 7s. 6d.

DANA (R. H.) *Two Years before the Mast and Twenty-Four years After.* Revised Edition with Notes, 12mo, 6s.

Dana (Jas. D.) Corals and Coral Islands. Numerous Illustrations, Charts, &c. New and Cheaper Edition, with numerous important Additions and Corrections. Crown 8vo, cloth extra, 8s. 6d.

Daughter (A) of Heth. By W. BLACK. Crown 8vo, 6s.

Day of My Life (A); or, Every Day Experiences at Eton. By an ETON BOY, Author of "About Some Fellows." 16mo, cloth extra, 2s. 6d. 6th Thousand.

Day out of the Life of a Little Maiden (A): Six Studies from Life. By SHERER and ENGLER. Large 4to, in portfolio, 5s.

Diane. By Mrs. MACQUOID. Crown 8vo, 6s.

Dick Sands, the Boy Captain. By JULES VERNE. With nearly 100 Illustrations, cloth extra, gilt edges, 10s. 6d.

Discoveries of Prince Henry the Navigator, and their Results; being the Narrative of the Discovery by Sea, within One Century, of more than Half the World. By RICHARD HENRY MAJOR, F.S.A. Demy 8vo, with several Woodcuts, 4 Maps, and a Portrait of Prince Henry in Colours. Cloth extra, 15s.

Dodge (Mrs. M.) Hans Brinker; or, the Silver Skates. An entirely New Edition, with 59 Full-page and other Woodcuts. Square crown 8vo, cloth extra, 7s. 6d. ; Text only, paper, 1s.

—— *Theophilus and Others.* 1 vol., small post 8vo, cloth extra, gilt, 3s. 6d.

Dogs of Assize. A Legal Sketch-Book in Black and White. Containing 6 Drawings by WALTER J. ALLEN. Folio, in wrapper, 6s. 8d.

Doré's Spain. See "Spain."

Dougall's (J. D.) Shooting; its Appliances, Practice, and Purpose. With Illustrations, cloth extra, 10s. 6d. *See* "Shooting."

EARLY *History of the Colony of Victoria (The), from its Discovery.* By FRANCIS P. LABILLIERE, Fellow of the Royal onial Institute, &c. **2 vols., crown 8vo, 21s.**

Echoes of the Heart. See MOODY.
Elinor Dryden. By Mrs. MACQUOID. Crown 8vo, 6s.
English Catalogue of Books (The). Published during 1863 to 1871 inclusive, comprising also important American Publications.

This Volume, occupying over 450 Pages, shows the Titles of 32,000 New Books and New Editions issued during Nine Years, with the Size, Price, and Publisher's Name, the Lists of Learned Societies, Printing Clubs, and other Literary Associations, and the Books issued by them; as also the Publisher's Series and Collections—altogether forming an indispensable adjunct to the Bookseller's Establishment, as well as to every Learned and Literary Club and Association. 30s., half-bound.

⁎⁎⁎ Of the previous Volume, 1835 to 1862, very few remain on sale; as also of the Index Volume, 1837 to 1857.

—— *Supplements,* 1863, 1864, 1865, 3s. 6d. each; 1866, 1867, to 1879, 5s. each.

Eight Cousins. See ALCOTT.
English Writers, Chapters for Self-Improvement in English Literature. By the Author of "The Gentle Life," 6s.
Eton. See "Day of my Life," "Out of School," "About Some Fellows."
Evans (C.) Over the Hills and Far Away. By C. EVANS. One Volume, crown 8vo, cloth extra, 10s. 6d.
—— *A Strange Friendship.* Crown 8vo, cloth, 5s.

FAITH Gartney's Girlhood. By the Author of "The Gayworthy's." Fcap. with Coloured Frontispiece, 3s. 6d.
Familiar Letters on some Mysteries of Nature. See PHIPSON.
Family Prayers for Working Men. By the Author of "Steps to the Throne of Grace." With an Introduction by the Rev. E. H. BICKERSTETH, M.A., Vicar of Christ Church, Hampstead. Cloth, 1s.
Favell Children (The). Three Little Portraits. Four Illustrations, crown 8vo, cloth gilt, 4s.
Favourite English Pictures. Containing Sixteen Permanent Autotype Reproductions of important Paintings of Modern British Artists. With letterpress descriptions. Atlas 4to, cloth extra, 2l. 2s.
Fern Paradise (The): A Plea for the Culture of Ferns. By F. G. HEATH. New Edition, entirely Rewritten, Illustrated with Eighteen full-page and numerous other Woodcuts, and Four permanent Photographs, large post 8vo, handsomely bound in cloth, 12s. 6d.
Fern World (The). By F. G. HEATH. Illustrated by Twelve Coloured Plates, giving complete Figures (Sixty-four in all) of every Species of British Fern, printed from Nature; by several full-page Engravings; and a permanent Photograph. Large post 8vo, cloth gilt, 400 pp., 4th Edition, 12s. 6d. In 12 parts, sewn, 1s. each.
Few (A) Hints on Proving Wills. Enlarged Edition, 1s.

First Ten Years of a Sailor's Life at Sea. By the Author of "All About Ships." Demy 8vo, Seventeen full-page Illustrations, 480 pp., 3s. 6d.

Flammarion (C.) The Atmosphere. Translated from the French of CAMILLE FLAMMARION. Edited by JAMES GLAISHER, F.R.S. With 10 Chromo-Lithographs and 81 Woodcuts. Royal 8vo, cloth extra, 30s.

Flooding of the Sahara (The). See MACKENZIE.

Food for the People; or, Lentils and other Vegetable Cookery. By E. E. ORLEBAR. Third Thousand. Small post 8vo, boards, 1s.

Footsteps of the Master. See STOWE (Mrs. BEECHER).

Forrest (John) Explorations in Australia. Being Mr. JOHN FORREST's Personal Account of his Journeys. 1 vol., demy 8vo, cloth, with several Illustrations and 3 Maps, 16s.

Four Lectures on Electric Induction. Delivered at the Royal Institution, 1878-9. By J. E. H. GORDON, B.A. Cantab. With numerous Illustrations. Cloth limp, square 16mo, 3s.

Franc (Maude Jeane). The following form one Series, small post 8vo, in uniform cloth bindings:—
———— *Emily's Choice.* 5s.
———— *Hall's Vineyard.* 4s.
———— *John's Wife: a Story of Life in South Australia.* 4s.
———— *Marian; or, the Light of Some One's Home.* 5s.
———— *Silken Cords and Iron Fetters.* 4s.
———— *Vermont Vale.* 5s.
———— *Minnie's Mission.* 4s.
———— *Little Mercy.* 5s.

Funny Foreigners and Eccentric Englishmen. 16 coloured comic Illustrations for Children. Fcap. folio, coloured wrapper, 4s.

Games of Patience. See CADOGAN.
———— *Garvagh (Lord) The Pilgrim of Scandinavia.* By LORD GARVAGH, B.A. Oxford. 8vo, cloth extra, with Illustrations, 10s. 6d.

Geary (Grattan). See "Asiatic Turkey."

Gentle Life (Queen Edition). 2 vols. in 1, small 4to, 10s. 6d.

THE GENTLE LIFE SERIES.
Price 6s. each; or in calf extra, price 10s. 6d.

The Gentle Life. Essays in aid of the Formation of Character of Gentlemen and Gentlewomen. 21st Edition.
"Deserves to be printed in letters of gold, and circulated in every house."—*Chambers' Journal.*

About in the World. Essays by Author of "The Gentle Life."
"It is not easy to open it at any page without finding some handy idea."—*Morning Post.*

The Gentle Life Series, continued :—

Like unto Christ. A New Translation of Thomas à Kempis' "De Imitatione Christi." With a Vignette from an Original Drawing by Sir THOMAS LAWRENCE. 2nd Edition.
"Could not be presented in a more exquisite form, for a more sightly volume was never seen."—*Illustrated London News.*

Familiar Words. An Index Verborum, or Quotation Handbook. Affording an immediate Reference to Phrases and Sentences that have become embedded in the English language. 3rd and enlarged Edition.
"The most extensive dictionary of quotation we have met with."—*Notes and Queries.*

Essays by Montaigne. Edited and Annotated by the Author of "The Gentle Life." With Portrait. 2nd Edition.
"We should be glad if any words of ours could help to bespeak a large circulation for this handsome attractive book."—*Illustrated Times.*

The Countess of Pembroke's Arcadia. Written by Sir PHILIP SIDNEY. Edited with Notes by Author of "The Gentle Life." 7s. 6d.
"All the best things are retained intact in Mr. Friswell's edition."—*Examiner.*

The Gentle Life. 2nd Series, 8th Edition.
"There is not a single thought in the volume that does not contribute in some measure to the formation of a true gentleman."—*Daily News.*

Varia: Readings from Rare Books. Reprinted, by permission, from the *Saturday Review, Spectator,* &c.
"The books discussed in this volume are no less valuable than they are rare, and the compiler is entitled to the gratitude of the public."—*Observer.*

The Silent Hour: Essays, Original and Selected. By the Author of "The Gentle Life." 3rd Edition.
"All who possess 'The Gentle Life' should own this volume."—*Standard.*

Half-Length Portraits. Short Studies of Notable Persons. By J. HAIN FRISWELL. Small post 8vo, cloth extra, 6s.

Essays on English Writers, for the Self-improvement of Students in English Literature.
"To all who have neglected to read and study their native literature we would certainly suggest the volume before us as a fitting introduction."—*Examiner.*

Other People's Windows. By J. HAIN FRISWELL. 3rd Edition.
"The chapters are so lively in themselves, so mingled with shrewd views of human nature, so full of illustrative anecdotes, that the reader cannot fail to be amused."—*Morning Post.*

A Man's Thoughts. By J. HAIN FRISWELL.

German Primer. Being an Introduction to First Steps in German. By M. T. PREU. 2s. 6d.

Getting On in the World; or, Hints on Success in Life. By W. MATHEWS, LL.D. Small post 8vo, cloth, 2s. 6d.; gilt edges, 3s. 6d.

Gilliatt (Rev. E.) On the Wolds. 2 vols., crown 8vo, 21s.

Gilpin's Forest Scenery. Edited by F. G. HEATH. 1 vol., large post 8vo, with numerous Illustrations. Uniform with "The Fern World" and "Our Woodland Trees." 12s. 6d.

Gordon (J. E. H.). See "Four Lectures on Electric Induction," "Practical Treatise on Electricity," &c.

Gouffé. The Royal Cookery Book. By JULES GOUFFÉ; translated and adapted for English use by ALPHONSE GOUFFÉ, Head Pastrycook to her Majesty the Queen. Illustrated with large plates printed in colours. 161 Woodcuts, 8vo, cloth extra, gilt edges, 2l. 2s.

—— Domestic Edition, half-bound, 10s. 6d.

"By far the ablest and most complete work on cookery that has ever been submitted to the gastronomical world."—*Pall Mall Gazette.*

—— *The Book of Preserves; or, Receipts for Preparing and Preserving* Meat, Fish salt and smoked, &c., &c. 1 vol., royal 8vo, containing upwards of 500 Receipts and 34 Illustrations, 10s. 6d.

—— *Royal Book of Pastry and Confectionery.* By JULES GOUFFÉ, Chef-de-Cuisine of the Paris Jockey Club. Royal 8vo, Illustrated with 10 Chromo-lithographs and 137 Woodcuts, from Drawings by E. MONJAT. Cloth extra, gilt edges, 35s.

Gouraud (Mdlle.) Four Gold Pieces. Numerous Illustrations. Small post 8vo, cloth, 2s. 6d. *See also* Rose Library.

Government of M. Thiers. By JULES SIMON. Translated from the French. 2 vols., demy 8vo, cloth extra, 32s.

Gower (Lord Ronald) Handbook to the Art Galleries, Public and Private, of Belgium and Holland. 18mo, cloth, 5s.

—— *The Castle Howard Portraits.* 2 vols., folio, cl. extra, 6l. 6s.

Greek Grammar. See WALLER.

Guizot's History of France. Translated by ROBERT BLACK. Super-royal 8vo, very numerous Full-page and other Illustrations. In 5 vols., cloth extra, gilt, each 24s.

"It supplies a want which has long been felt, and ought to be in the hands of all students of history."—*Times.*

"Three-fourths of M. Guizot's great work are now completed, and the 'History of France,' which was so nobly planned, has been hitherto no less admirably executed."—*From long Review of Vol. III. in the Times.*

"M. Guizot's main merit is this, that, in a style at once clear and vigorous, he sketches the essential and most characteristic features of the times and personages described, and seizes upon every salient point which can best illustrate and bring out to view what is most significant and instructive in the spirit of the age described."—*Evening Standard*, Sept. 23, 1874.

—— *History of England.* In 3 vols. of about 500 pp. each, containing 60 to 70 Full-page and other Illustrations, cloth extra, gilt, 24s. each.

"For luxury of typography, plainness of print, and beauty of illustration, these volumes, of which but one has as yet appeared in English, will hold their own against any production of an age so luxurious as our own in everything, typography not excepted."—*Times.*

Guillemin. See "World of Comets."

Guyon (Mde.) Life. By UPHAM. 6th Edition, crown 8vo, 6s.

Guyot (A.) Physical Geography. By ARNOLD GUYOT, Author of "Earth and Man." In 1 volume, large 4to, 128 pp., numerous coloured Diagrams, Maps, and Woodcuts, price 10s. 6d.

HABITATIONS of Man in all Ages. See LE-DUC.

Hamilton (A. H. A., J.P.) See "Quarter Sessions."
Handbook to the Charities of London. See LOW'S.
—————— *Principal Schools of England.* See Practical.
Half-Hours of Blind Man's Holiday; or, Summer and Winter Sketches in Black & White. By W. W. FENN. 2 vols., cr. 8vo, 24s.
Half-Length Portraits. Short Studies of Notable Persons. By J. HAIN FRISWELL. Small post 8vo, cloth extra, 6s.
Hall (W. W.) How to Live Long; or, 1408 *Health Maxims,* Physical, Mental, and Moral. By W. W. HALL, A.M., M.D. Small post 8vo, cloth, 2s. Second Edition.
Hans Brinker; or, the Silver Skates. See DODGE.
Heart of Africa. Three Years' Travels and Adventures in the Unexplored Regions of Central Africa, from 1868 to 1871. By Dr. GEORG SCHWEINFURTH. Translated by ELLEN E. FREWER. With an Introduction by WINWOOD READE. An entirely New Edition, revised and condensed by the Author. Numerous Illustrations, and large Map. 2 vols., crown 8vo, cloth, 15s.
Heath (F. G.). See "Fern World," "Fern Paradise," "Our Woodland Trees," "Trees and Ferns."
Heber's (Bishop) Illustrated Edition of Hymns. With upwards of 100 beautiful Engravings. Small 4to, handsomely bound, 7s. 6d. Morocco, 18s. 6d. and 21s. An entirely New Edition.
Hector Servadac. See VERNE. The heroes of this story were carried away through space on the Comet "Gallia," and their adventures are recorded with all Jules Verne's characteristic spirit. With nearly 100 Illustrations, cloth extra, gilt edges, 10s. 6d.
Henderson (A.) Latin Proverbs and Quotations; with Translations and Parallel Passages, and a copious English Index. By ALFRED HENDERSON. Fcap. 4to, 530 pp., 10s. 6d.
History and Handbook of Photography. Translated from the French of GASTON TISSANDIER. Edited by J. THOMSON. Imperial 16mo, over 300 pages, 70 Woodcuts, and Specimens of Prints by the best Permanent Processes. Second Edition, with an Appendix by the late Mr. HENRY FOX TALBOT, giving an account of his researches. Cloth extra, 6s.
History of a Crime (The); Deposition of an Eye-witness. By VICTOR HUGO. 4 vols., crown 8vo, 42s. Cheap Edition, 1 vol., 6s.
—————— *England.* See GUIZOT.
—————— *France.* See GUIZOT.
—————— *Russia.* See RAMBAUD.

History of Merchant Shipping. See LINDSAY.
——— *United States.* See BRYANT.
——— *Ireland.* By STANDISH O'GRADY. Vol. I. ready, 7s. 6d.
——— *American Literature.* By M. C. TYLER. Vols. I. and II., 2 vols, 8vo, 24s.
History and Principles of Weaving by Hand and by Power. With several hundred Illustrations. By ALFRED BARLOW. Royal 8vo, cloth extra, 1l. 5s.
Hitherto. By the Author of "The Gayworthys." New Edition, cloth extra, 3s. 6d. Also, in Rose Library, 2 vols., 2s.
Hofmann (Carl). A Practical Treatise on the Manufacture of Paper in all its Branches. Illustrated by 110 Wood Engravings, and 5 large Folding Plates. In 1 vol., 4to, cloth; about 400 pp., 3l. 13s. 6d.
Home of the Eddas. By C. G. LOCK. Demy 8vo, cloth, 16s.
How to Build a House. See LE-DUC.
How to Live Long. See HALL.
Hugo (Victor) "Ninety-Three." Illustrated. Crown 8vo, 6s.
——— *Toilers of the Sea.* Crown 8vo. Illustrated, 6s.; fancy boards, 2s.; cloth, 2s. 6d.; On large paper with all the original Illustrations, 10s. 6d.
——— See "History of a Crime."
Hundred Greatest Men (The). Eight vols., 21s. each. See below.
 "Messrs. SAMPSON Low & Co. are about to issue an important 'International' work, entitled, 'THE HUNDRED GREATEST MEN;' being the Lives and Portraits of the 100 Greatest Men of History, divided into Eight Classes, each Class to form a Monthly Quarto Volume. The Introductions to the volumes are to be written by recognized authorities on the different subjects, the English contributors being DEAN STANLEY, Mr. MATTHEW ARNOLD, Mr. FROUDE, and Professor MAX MÜLLER; in Germany, Professor HELMHOLTZ; in France, MM. TAINE and RENAN; and in America, Mr. EMERSON. The Portraits are to be Reproductions from fine and rare Steel Engravings."—*Academy.*
Hunting, Shooting, and Fishing; A Sporting Miscellany. Illustrated. Crown 8vo, cloth extra, 7s. 6d.
Hymnal Companion to Book of Common Prayer. See BICKERSTETH.

ILLUSTRATIONS of China and its People. By J. THOMSON, F.R.G.S. Four Volumes, imperial 4to, each 3l. 3s.
In my Indian Garden. By PHIL. ROBINSON. With a Preface by EDWIN ARNOLD, M.A., C.S.I., &c. Crown 8vo, limp cloth, 3s. 6d.
Irish Bar. Comprising Anecdotes, Bon-Mots, and Biographical Sketches of the Bench and Bar of Ireland. By J. RODERICK O'FLANAGAN, Barrister-at-Law. Crown 8vo, 12s. Second Edition.

JACQUEMART (A.) History of the Ceramic Art: Descriptive and Analytical Study of the Potteries of all Times and of all Nations. By ALBERT JACQUEMART. 200 Woodcuts by H.

Catenacci and J. Jacquemart. 12 Steel-plate Engravings, and 1000 Marks and Monograms. Translated by Mrs. BURY PALLISER. In 1 vol., super-royal 8vo, of about 700 pp., cloth extra, gilt edges, 28s.
"This is one of those few gift-books which, while they can certainly lie on a table and look beautiful, can also be read through with real pleasure and profit."—*Times.*

KENNEDY'S *(Capt. W. R.) Sporting Adventures in the* Pacific. With Illustrations, demy 8vo, 18s.

——— *(Capt. A. W. M. Clark).* See "To the Arctic Regions."

Khedive's Egypt (The) ; or, The old House of Bondage under New Masters. By EDWIN DE LEON. Illustrated. Demy 8vo, cloth extra, Third Edition, 18s. Cheap Edition, 8s. 6d.

Kingston *(W. H. G.).* See "Snow-Shoes."

——— *Child of the Cavern.*

——— *Two Supercargoes.*

——— *With Axe and Rifle.*

Koldewey *(Capt.) The Second North German Polar Expedition* in the Year 1869-70. Edited and condensed by H. W. BATES. Numerous Woodcuts, Maps, and Chromo-lithographs. Royal 8vo, cloth extra, 1l. 15s.

LADY *Silverdale's Sweetheart.* 6s. See BLACK.

Land of Bolivar *(The) ; or, War, Peace, and Adventure in the* Republic of Venezuela. By JAMES MUDIE SPENCE, F.R.G.S., F.Z.S. 2 vols., demy 8vo, cloth extra, with numerous Woodcuts and Maps, 31s. 6d. Second Edition.

Landseer Gallery *(The).* Containing thirty-six Autotype Reproductions of Engravings from the most important early works of Sir EDWIN LANDSEER. With a Memoir of the Artist's Life, and Descriptions of the Plates. Imperial 4to, cloth, gilt edges, 2l. 2s.

Le-Duc *(V.) How to build a House.* By VIOLLET-LE-DUC, Author of "The Dictionary of Architecture," &c. Numerous Illustrations, Plans, &c. Medium 8vo, cloth, gilt, 12s.

——— *Annals of a Fortress.* Numerous Illustrations and Diagrams. Demy 8vo, cloth extra, 15s.

——— *The Habitations of Man in all Ages.* By E. VIOLLET-LE-DUC. Illustrated by 103 Woodcuts. Translated by BENJAMIN BUCKNALL, Architect. 8vo, cloth extra, 16s.

——— *Lectures on Architecture.* By VIOLLET-LE-DUC. Translated from the French by BENJAMIN BUCKNALL, Architect. In 2 vols., royal 8vo, 3l. 3s. Also in Parts, 10s. 6d. each.

——— *Mont Blanc: a Treatise on its Geodesical and Geological Constitution—its Transformations, and the Old and Modern* state of its Glaciers. By EUGENE VIOLLET-LE-DUC. With 120 Illustrations. Translated by B. BUCKNALL. 1 vol., demy 8vo, 14s.

Le-Duc (V.) On Restoration; with a Notice of his Works by CHARLES WETHERED. Crown 8vo, with a Portrait on Steel of VIOLLET-LE-DUC, cloth extra, 2s. 6d.

Lenten Meditations. In Two Series, each complete in itself. By the Rev. CLAUDE BOSANQUET, Author of "Blossoms from the King's Garden." 16mo, cloth, First Series, 1s. 6d.; Second Series, 2s.

Lentils. See "Food for the People."

Liesegang (Dr. Paul E.) A Manual of the Carbon Process of Photography. Demy 8vo, half-bound, with Illustrations, 4s.

Life and Letters of the Honourable Charles Sumner (The). 2 vols., royal 8vo, cloth. The Letters give full description of London Society—Lawyers—Judges—Visits to Lords Fitzwilliam, Leicester, Wharncliffe, Brougham—Association with Sydney Smith, Hallam, Macaulay, Dean Milman, Rogers, and Talfourd; also, a full Journal which Sumner kept in Paris. Second Edition, 36s.

Lindsay (W. S.) History of Merchant Shipping and Ancient Commerce. Over 150 Illustrations, Maps and Charts. In 4 vols., demy 8vo, cloth extra. Vols. 1 and 2, 21s.; vols. 3 and 4, 24s. each.

Lion Jack: a Story of Perilous Adventures amongst Wild Men and Beasts. Showing how Menageries are made. By P. T. BARNUM. With Illustrations. Crown 8vo, cloth extra, price 6s.

Little King; or, the Taming of a Young Russian Count. By S. BLANDY. Translated from the French. 64 Illustrations. Crown 8vo, cloth extra, gilt, 7s. 6d.

Little Mercy; or, For Better for Worse. By MAUDE JEANNE FRANC, Author of "Marian," "Vermont Vale," &c., &c. Small post 8vo, cloth extra, 4s.

Long (Col. C. Chaillé) Central Africa. Naked Truths of Naked People: an Account of Expeditions to Lake Victoria Nyanza and the Mabraka Niam-Niam. Demy 8vo, numerous Illustrations, 18s.

Lord Collingwood: a Biographical Study. By. W. DAVIS. With Steel Engraving of Lord Collingwood. Crown 8vo, 2s.

Lost Sir Massingberd. New Edition, 16mo, boards, coloured wrapper, 2s.

Low's German Series—

1. **The Illustrated German Primer.** Being the easiest introduction to the study of German for all beginners. 1s.
2. **The Children's own German Book.** A Selection of Amusing and Instructive Stories in Prose. Edited by Dr. A. L. MEISSNER, Professor of Modern Languages in the Queen's University in Ireland. Small post 8vo, cloth, 1s. 6d.
3. **The First German Reader, for Children from Ten to Fourteen.** Edited by Dr. A. L. MEISSNER. Small post 8vo, cloth, 1s. 6d.
4. **The Second German Reader.** Edited by Dr. A. L. MEISSNER, Small post 8vo, cloth, 1s. 6d.

Low's German Series, continued:—

Buchheim's Deutsche Prosa. Two Volumes, sold separately:—

5. **Schiller's Prosa.** Containing Selections from the Prose Works of Schiller, with Notes for English Students. By Dr. BUCHHEIM, Professor of the German Language and Literature, King's College, London. Small post 8vo, 2s. 6d.
6. **Goethe's Prosa.** Containing Selections from the Prose Works of Goethe, with Notes for English Students. By Dr. BUCHHEIM. Small post 8vo, 3s. 6d.

Low's Standard Library of Travel and Adventure. Crown 8vo, bound uniformly in cloth extra, price 7s. 6d.

1. The Great Lone Land. By W. F. BUTLER, C.B.
2. The Wild North Land. By W. F. BUTLER, C.B.
3. How I found Livingstone. By H. M. STANLEY.
4. The Threshold of the Unknown Region. By C. R. MARKHAM. (4th Edition, with Additional Chapters, 10s. 6d.)
5. A Whaling Cruise to Baffin's Bay and the Gulf of Boothia. By A. H. MARKHAM.
6. Campaigning on the Oxus. By J. A. MACGAHAN.
7. Akim-foo: the History of a Failure. By MAJOR W. F. BUTLER, C.B.
8. Ocean to Ocean. By the Rev. GEORGE M. GRANT. With Illustrations.
9. Cruise of the Challenger. By W. J. J. SPRY, R.N.
10. Schweinfurth's Heart of Africa. 2 vols., 15s.

Low's Standard Novels. Crown 8vo, 6s. each, cloth extra.

Three Feathers. By WILLIAM BLACK.
A Daughter of Heth. 13th Edition. By W. BLACK. With Frontispiece by F. WALKER, A.R.A.
Kilmeny. A Novel. By W. BLACK.
In Silk Attire. By W. BLACK.
Lady Silverdale's Sweetheart. By W. BLACK.
Alice Lorraine. By R. D. BLACKMORE.
Lorna Doone. By R. D. BLACKMORE. 8th Edition.
Cradock Nowell. By R. D. BLACKMORE.
Clara Vaughan. By R. D. BLACKMORE.
Cripps the Carrier. By R. D. BLACKMORE.
Innocent. By Mrs. OLIPHANT. Eight Illustrations.
Work. A Story of Experience. By LOUISA M. ALCOTT. Illustrations. *See also* Rose Library.
A French Heiress in her own Chateau. By the author of "One Only," "Constantia," &c. Six Illustrations.
Ninety-Three. By VICTOR HUGO. Numerous Illustrations.
My Wife and I. By Mrs. BEECHER STOWE.
Wreck of the Grosvenor. By W. CLARK RUSSELL.
Elinor Dryden. By Mrs. MACQUOID.
Diane. By Mrs. MACQUOID.

Low's Handbook to the Charities of London for 1879. Edited and revised to July, 1879, by C. MACKESON, F.S.S., Editor of "A Guide to the Churches of London and its Suburbs," &c. 1s.

MACGAHAN (*J. A.*) *Campaigning on the Oxus, and the Fall of Khiva.* With Map and numerous Illustrations, 4th Edition, small post 8vo, cloth extra, 7s. 6d.

—— *Under the Northern Lights; or, the Cruise of the "Pandora" to Peel's Straits, in Search of Sir John Franklin's Papers.* With Illustrations by Mr. DE WYLDE, who accompanied the Expedition. Demy 8vo, cloth extra, 18s.

Macgregor (*John*) *"Rob Roy" on the Baltic.* 3rd Edition small post 8vo, 2s. 6d.

—— *A Thousand Miles in the "Rob Roy" Canoe.* 11th Edition, small post 8vo, 2s. 6d.

—— *Description of the "Rob Roy" Canoe*, with Plans, &c., 1s.

—— *The Voyage Alone in the Yawl "Rob Roy."* New Edition, thoroughly revised, with additions, small post 8vo, 5s.

Mackenzie (*D*). *The Flooding of the Sahara.* An Account of the Project for opening direct communication with 38,000,000 people. With a Description of North-West Africa and Soudan. By DONALD MACKENZIE. 8vo, cloth extra, with Illustrations, 10s. 6d.

Macquoid (*Mrs.*) *Elinor Dryden.* Crown 8vo, cloth, 6s.

—— *Diane.* Crown 8vo, 6s.

Marked Life (A); or, The Autobiography of a Clairvoyante. By "GIPSY." Post 8vo, 5s.

Markham (*A. H.*) *The Cruise of the "Rosario."* By A. H. MARKHAM, R.N. 8vo, cloth extra, with Map and Illustrations.

—— *A Whaling Cruise to Baffin's Bay and the Gulf of Boothia.* With an Account of the Rescue by his Ship, of the Survivors of the Crew of the "Polaris;" and a Description of Modern Whale Fishing. 3rd and Cheaper Edition, crown 8vo, 2 Maps and several Illustrations, cloth extra, 7s. 6d.

Markham (*C. R.*) *The Threshold of the Unknown Region.* Crown 8vo, with Four Maps, 4th Edition, with Additional Chapters, giving the History of our present Expedition, as far as known, and an Account of the Cruise of the "Pandora." Cloth extra, 10s. 6d.

Maury (*Commander*) *Physical Geography of the Sea, and its Meteorology.* Being a Reconstruction and Enlargement of his former Work, with Charts and Diagrams. New Edition, crown 8vo, 6s.

Men of Mark: a Gallery of Contemporary Portraits of the most Eminent Men of the Day taken from Life, especially for this publication, price 1s. 6d. monthly. Vols. I., II., and III. handsomely bound, cloth, gilt edges, 25s. each.

Mercy Philbrick's Choice. Small post 8vo, 3s. 6d.
"The story is of a high character, and the play of feeling is very subtilely and cleverly wrought out."—*British Quarterly Review.*

Michael Strogoff. 10s. 6d. *See* VERNE.
Michie (Sir A., K.C.M.G.) *See* "Readings in Melbourne."
Mitford (Miss). *See* "Our Village."
Mohr (E.) *To the Victoria Falls of the Zambesi.* By EDWARD MOHR. Translated by N. D'ANVERS. Numerous Full-page and other Woodcut Illustrations, Four Chromo-lithographs, and Map. Demy 8vo, cloth extra, 24s.
Montaigne's Essays. See "Gentle Life Series."
Mont Blanc. See LE-DUC.
Moody (*Emma*) *Echoes of the Heart.* A Collection of upwards of 200 Sacred Poems. 16mo, cloth, gilt edges, 3s. 6d.
My Brother Jack; or, The Story of Whatd'yecallem. Written by Himself. From the French of ALPHONSE DAUDET. Illustrated by P. PHILIPPOTEAUX. Square imperial 16mo, cloth extra, 7s. 6d.
"He would answer to Hi! or to any loud cry,
To What-you-may-call-'em, or What was his name:
But especially Thingamy-jig."—*Hunting of the Snark.*
My Rambles in the New World. By LUCIEN BIART, Author of "The Adventures of a Young Naturalist." Crown 8vo, cloth extra. Numerous full-page Illustrations, 7s. 6d.
Mysterious Island. By JULES VERNE. 3 vols., imperial 16mo. 150 Illustrations, cloth gilt, 3s. 6d. each; elaborately bound, gilt edges, 7s. 6d. each.

NARES (Sir G. S., K.C.B.) *Narrative of a Voyage to the Polar Sea* during 1875-76, in H.M.'s Ships "Alert" and "Discovery." By Captain Sir G. S. NARES, R.N., K.C.B., F.R.S. Published by permission of the Lords Commissioners of the Admiralty. With Notes on the Natural History, edited by H. W. FEILDEN, F.G.S., C.M.Z.S., F.R.G.S., Naturalist to the Expedition. Two Volumes, demy 8vo, with numerous Woodcut Illustrations, Photographs, &c. 4th Edition, 2l. 2s.
New Child's Play (A). Sixteen Drawings by E. V. B. Beautifully printed in colours, 4to, cloth extra, 12s. 6d.
New Ireland. By A. M. SULLIVAN, M.P. for Louth. 2 vols., demy 8vo, cloth extra, 30s. One of the main objects which the Author has had in view in writing this work has been to lay before England and the world a faithful history of Ireland, in a series of descriptive sketches of the episodes in Ireland's career during the last quarter of a century. Cheaper Edition, 1 vol., crown 8vo, 8s. 6d.
New Testament. The Authorized English Version; with various readings from the most celebrated Manuscripts. Cloth flexible, gilt edges, 2s. 6d.; cheaper style, 2s.; or sewed, 1s. 6d.
Noble Words and Noble Deeds. Translated from the French of E. MULLER, by DORA LEIGH. Containing many Full-page Illustrations by PHILIPPOTEAUX. Square imperial 16mo, cloth extra, 7s. 6d.
"This is a book which will delight the young.... We cannot imagine a nicer present than this book for children."—*Standard.*
"Is certain to become a favourite with young people."—*Court Journal.*

North American Review (*The*). Monthly, price 2*s.* 6*d.*

Notes and Sketches of an Architect taken during a Journey in the
North-West of Europe. Translated from the French of FELIX NAR-
JOUX. 214 Full-page and other Illustrations. Demy 8vo, cloth extra, 16*s.*
"His book is vivacious and sometimes brilliant. It is admirably printed and illustrated."—*British Quarterly Review.*

Notes on Fish and Fishing. By the Rev. J. J. MANLEY, M.A.
With Illustrations, crown 8vo, cloth extra, leatherette binding, 10*s.* 6*d.*
"We commend the work."—*Field.*
"He has a page for every day in the year, or nearly so, and there is not a dull one amongst them."—*Notes and Queries.*
"A pleasant and attractive volume."—*Graphic.*
"Brightly and pleasantly written."—*John Bull.*

Novels. Crown 8vo, cloth, 10*s.* 6*d.* per vol. :—

Mary Anerley. By R. D. BLACKMORE, Author of "Lorna Doone,"
&c. 3 vols. [*In the press.*

An Old Story of My Farming Days. By FRITZ REUTER, Author
of "In the Year '13." 3 vols.

All the World's a Stage. By M. A. M. HOPPUS, Author of "Five
Chimnney Farm." 3 vols.

Cressida. By M. B. THOMAS. 3 vols.

Elizabeth Eden. 3 vols.

The Martyr of Glencree. A Story of the Persecutions in Scotland
in the Reign of Charles the Second. By R. SOMERS. 3 vols.

The Cat and Battledore, and other Stories, translated from
Balzac. 3 vols.

A Woman of Mind. 3 vols.

The Cossacks. By COUNT TOLSTOY. Translated from the Russian
by EUGENE SCHUYLER, Author of "Turkistan." 2 vols.

The Hour will Come: a Tale of an Alpine Cloister. By WILHEL-
MINE VON HILLERN, Author of "The Vulture Maiden." Translated from the German by CLARA BELL. 2 vols.

A Stroke of an Afghan Knife. By R. A. STERNDALE, F.R.G.S.,
Author of "Seonee." 3 vols.

The Braes of Yarrow. By C. GIBBON. 3 vols.

Auld Lang Syne. By the Author of "The Wreck of the Grosvenor."
2 vols.

Written on their Foreheads. By R. H. ELLIOT. 2 vols.

On the Wolds. By the Rev. E. GILLIAT, Author of "Asylum
Christi." 2 vols.

In a Rash Moment. By JESSIE McLAREN. 2 vols.

Old Charlton. By BADEN PRITCHARD. 3 vols.
"Mr. Baden Pritchard has produced a well-written and interesting story."—*Scotsman.*

Nursery Playmates (*Prince of*). 217 Coloured pictures for
Children by eminent Artists. Folio, in coloured boards, 6*s.*

OCEAN to Ocean: Sandford Fleming's Expedition through
Canada in 1872. By the Rev. GEORGE M. GRANT. With Illustrations. Revised and enlarged Edition, crown 8vo, cloth, 7*s.* 6*d.*

Old-Fashioned Girl. See ALCOTT.

Oleographs. (Catalogues and price lists on application.)

Oliphant (Mrs.) Innocent. A Tale of Modern Life. By Mrs. OLIPHANT, Author of "The Chronicles of Carlingford," &c., &c. With Eight Full-page Illustrations, small post 8vo, cloth extra, 6s.

On Horseback through Asia Minor. By Capt. FRED BURNABY, Royal Horse Guards, Author of "A Ride to Khiva." 2 vols., 8vo, with three Maps and Portrait of Author, 6th Edition, 38s. This work describes a ride of over 2000 miles through the heart of Asia Minor, and gives an account of five months with Turks, Circassians, Christians, and Devil-worshippers. Cheaper Edition, crown 8vo, 10s. 6d.

On Restoration. See LE-DUC.

On Trek in the Transvaal; or, Over Berg and Veldt in South Africa. By H. A. ROCHE. Crown 8vo, cloth, 10s. 6d. 4th Edition.

Orlebar (Eleanor E.) See "Sancta Christina," "Food for the People."

Our Little Ones in Heaven. Edited by the Rev. H. ROBBINS. With Frontispiece after Sir JOSHUA REYNOLDS. Fcap., cloth extra, New Edition—the 3rd, with Illustrations, 5s.

Our Village. By MARY RUSSELL MITFORD. Illustrated with Frontispiece Steel Engraving, and 12 full-page and 157 smaller Cuts of Figure Subjects and Scenes, from Drawings by W. H. J. BOOT and C. O. MURRAY. Chiefly from Sketches made by these Artists in the neighbourhood of "Our Village." Crown 4to, cloth extra, gilt edges, 21s.

Our Woodland Trees. By F. G. HEATH. Large post 8vo, cloth, gilt edges, uniform with "Fern World" and "Fern Paradise," by the same Author. 8 Coloured Plates and 20 Woodcuts, 12s. 6d.

Out of School at Eton. Being a collection of Poetry and Prose Writings. By SOME PRESENT ETONIANS. Foolscap 8vo, cloth, 3s. 6d.

PAINTERS of All Schools. By LOUIS VIARDOT, and other Writers. 500 pp., super-royal 8vo, 20 Full-page and 70 smaller Engravings, cloth extra, 25s. A New Edition is being issued in Half-crown parts, with fifty additional portraits, cloth, gilt edges, 31s. 6d.

"A handsome volume, full of information and sound criticism."—*Times.*
"Almost an encyclopædia of painting. . . . . It may be recommended as a handy and elegant guide to beginners in the study of the history of art."—*Saturday Review.*

Palliser (Mrs.) A History of Lace, from the Earliest Period. A New and Revised Edition, with additional cuts and text, upwards of 100 Illustrations and coloured Designs. 1 vol. 8vo, 1l. 1s.

"One of the most readable books of the season; permanently valuable, always interesting, often amusing, and not inferior in all the essentials of a gift book."—*Times.*

—— *Historic Devices, Badges, and War Cries.* 8vo, 1l. 1s.

Palliser (Mrs.) The China Collector's Pocket Companion. With upwards of 1000 Illustrations of Marks and Monograms. 2nd Edition, with Additions. Small post 8vo, limp cloth, 5s.

> "We scarcely need add that a more trustworthy and convenient handbook does not exist, and that others besides ourselves will feel grateful to Mrs. Palliser for the care and skill she has bestowed upon it."—*Academy.*

Petites Leçons de Conversation et de Grammaire: Oral and Conversational Method; being Little Lessons introducing the most Useful Topics of Daily Conversation, upon an entirely new principle, &c. By F. JULIEN, French Master at King Edward the Sixth's Grammar School, Birmingham. Author of "The Student's French Examiner," which see.

Phillips (L.) Dictionary of Biographical Reference. 8vo, 1l. 11s. 6d.

Phipson (Dr. T. L.) Familiar Letters on some Mysteries of Nature and Discoveries in Science. **Crown 8vo, cloth extra, 7s. 6d.**

Photography (History and Handbook of). See TISSANDIER.

Picture Gallery of British Art (The). 38 Permanent Photographs after the most celebrated English Painters. With Descriptive Letterpress. Vols. 1 to 5, cloth extra, 18s. each. Vol. 6 for 1877, commencing New Series, demy folio, 31s. 6d. Monthly Parts, 1s. 6d.

Pike (N.) Sub-Tropical Rambles in the Land of the Aphanapteryx. In 1 vol., demy 8vo, 18s. Profusely Illustrated from the Author's own Sketches. Also with Maps and Meteorological Charts.

Placita Anglo-Normannica. The Procedure and Constitution of the Anglo-Norman Courts (WILLIAM I.—RICHARD I.), as shown by Contemporaneous Records; all the Reports of the Litigation of the period, as recorded in the Chronicles and Histories of the time, being gleaned and literally transcribed. With Explanatory Notes, &c. By M. M. BIGELOW. Demy 8vo, cloth, 21s.

Plutarch's Lives. An Entirely New and Library Edition. Edited by A. H. CLOUGH, Esq. 5 vols., 8vo, 2l. 10s.; half-morocco, gilt top, 3l. Also in 1 vol., royal 8vo, 800 pp., cloth extra, 18s.; half-bound, 21s.

―――― *Morals.* Uniform with Clough's Edition of "Lives of Plutarch." Edited by Professor GOODWIN. 5 vols., 8vo, 3l. 3s.

Poe (E. A.) The Works of. 4 vols., 2l. 2s.

Poems of the Inner Life. A New Edition, Revised, with many dditional Poems, inserted by permission of the Authors. Small post 8vo, cloth, 5s.

Poganuc People: their Loves and Lives. By Mrs. BEECHER STOWE. Crown 8vo, cloth, 10s. 6d.

Polar Expeditions. See KOLDEWEY, MARKHAM, MACGAHAN and NARES.

Pottery: how it is Made, its Shape and Decoration. Practical Instructions for Painting on Porcelain and all kinds of Pottery with vitrifiable and common Oil Colours. With a full Bibliography of Standard Works upon the Ceramic Art. By G. WARD NICHOLS. 42 Illustrations, crown 8vo, red edges, 6s.

Practical (A) Handbook to the Principal Schools of England. By C. E. PASCOE. Showing the cost of living at the Great Schools, Scholarships, &c., &c. New Edition corrected to 1879, crown 8vo, cloth extra, 3s. 6d.

"This is an exceedingly useful work, and one that was much wanted."—*Examiner.*

Practical Treatise on Electricity and Magnetism. By J. E. H. GORDON, B.A. One volume, demy 8vo, very numerous Illustrations.

Prejevalsky (N. M.) From Kulja, across the Tian Shan to Lob-nor. Translated by E. DELMAR MORGAN, F.R.G.S. With Notes and Introduction by SIR DOUGLAS FORSYTH, K.C.S.I. 1 vol., demy 8vo, with a Map.

Prince Ritto; or, The Four-leaved Shamrock. By FANNY W. CURREY. With 10 Full-page Fac-simile Reproductions of Original Drawings by HELEN O'HARA. Demy 4to, cloth extra, gilt, 10s. 6d.

Prisoner of War in Russia. See COOPE.

Publishers' Circular (The), and General Record of British and Foreign Literature. Published on the 1st and 15th of every Month.

QUARTER Sessions, from Queen Elizabeth to Queen Anne: Illustrations of Local Government and History. Drawn from Original Records (chiefly of the County of Devon). By A. H. A. HAMILTON. Crown 8vo, cloth, 10s. 6d.

RALSTON (W. R. S.) Early Russian History. Four Lectures delivered at Oxford by W. R. S. RALSTON, M.A. Crown 8vo, cloth extra, 5s.

Rambaud (Alfred). History of Russia, from its Origin to the Year 1877. With Six Maps. Translated by Mrs. L. B. LANG. 2 vols. demy 8vo, cloth extra, 38s.

Mr. W. R. S. Ralston, in the *Academy*, says, "We gladly recognize in the present volume a trustworthy history of Russia."

"We will venture to prophecy that it will become *the* work on the subject for readers in our part of Europe. . . . Mrs. Lang has done her work remarkably well."—*Athenæum.*

Readings in Melbourne; with an Essay on the Resources and Prospects of Victoria for the Emigrant and Uneasy Classes. By Sir ARCHIBALD MICHIE, Q.C., K.C.M.G., Agent-General for Victoria. With Coloured Map of Australia. Crown 8vo, cloth extra, price 7s. 6d.

"Comprises more information on the prospects and resources of Victoria than any other work with which we are acquainted."—*Saturday Review.*

"A work which is in every respect one of the most interesting and instructive that has ever been written about that land which claims to be the premier colony of the Australian group."—*The Colonies and India.*

Recollections of Samuel Breck, the American Pepys. With Passages from his Note-Books (1771—1862). Crown 8vo, cloth, 10s. 6d.

Recollections of Writers. By CHARLES and MARY COWDEN CLARKE. Authors of "The Concordance to Shakespeare," &c.; with Letters of CHARLES LAMB, LEIGH HUNT, DOUGLAS JERROLD, and CHARLES DICKENS; and a Preface by MARY COWDEN CLARKE. Crown 8vo, cloth, 10s. 6d.

Reminiscences of the War in New Zealand. By THOMAS W. GUDGEON, Lieutenant and Quartermaster, Colonial Forces, N.Z. With Twelve Portraits. Crown 8vo, cloth extra, 10s. 6d.
"The interest attaching at the present moment to all Britannia's 'little wars' should render more than ever welcome such a detailed narrative of Maori campaigns as that contained in Lieut. Gudgeon's 'Experiences of New Zealand War.'"—*Graphic*.

Robinson (Phil.). See "In my Indian Garden."

Rochefoucauld's Reflections. Bayard Series, 2s. 6d.

Rogers (S.) Pleasures of Memory. See "Choice Editions of Choice Books." 2s. 6d.

Rohlfs (Dr. G.) Adventures in Morocco, and Journeys through the Oases of Draa and Tafilet. By Dr. G. ROHLFS. Demy 8vo, Map, and Portrait of the Author, 12s.

Rose in Bloom. See ALCOTT.

Rose Library (The). Popular Literature of all countries. Each volume, 1s.; cloth, 2s. 6d. Many of the Volumes are Illustrated—
1. **Sea-Gull Rock.** By JULES SANDEAU. Illustrated.
2. **Little Women.** By LOUISA M. ALCOTT.
3. **Little Women Wedded.** Forming a Sequel to "Little Women."
4. **The House on Wheels.** By MADAME DE STOLZ. Illustrated.
5. **Little Men.** By LOUISA M. ALCOTT. Dble. vol., 2s.; cloth, 3s. 6d.
6. **The Old-Fashioned Girl.** By LOUISA M. ALCOTT. Double vol., 2s.; cloth, 3s. 6d.
7. **The Mistress of the Manse.** By J. G. HOLLAND.
8. **Timothy Titcomb's Letters to Young People, Single and Married.**
9. **Undine, and the Two Captains.** By Baron DE LA MOTTE FOUQUÉ. A New Translation by F. E. BUNNETT. Illustrated.
10. **Draxy Miller's Dowry, and the Elder's Wife.** By SAXE HOLM.
11. **The Four Gold Pieces.** By Madame GOURAUD. Numerous Illustrations.
12. **Work.** A Story of Experience. First Portion. By LOUISA M. ALCOTT.
13. **Beginning Again.** Being a Continuation of "Work." By LOUISA M. ALCOTT.
14. **Picciola; or, the Prison Flower.** By X. B. SAINTINE. Numerous Graphic Illustrations.

The Rose Library, continued:—

15. Robert's Holidays. Illustrated.
16. The Two Children of St. Domingo. Numerous Illustrations.
17. Aunt Jo's Scrap Bag.
18. Stowe (Mrs. H. B.) The Pearl of Orr's Island.
19. ——— The Minister's Wooing.
20. ——— Betty's Bright Idea.
21. ——— The Ghost in the Mill.
22. ——— Captain Kidd's Money.
23. ——— We and our Neighbours. Double vol., 2s.
24. ——— My Wife and I. Double vol., 2s.; cloth, gilt, 3s. 6d.
25. Hans Brinker; or, the Silver Skates.
26. Lowell's My Study Window.
27. Holmes (O. W.) The Guardian Angel.
28. Warner (C. D.) My Summer in a Garden.
29. Hitherto. By the Author of "The Gayworthys." 2 vols., 1s. each.
30. Helen's Babies. By their Latest Victim.
31. The Barton Experiment. By the Author of "Helen's Babies."
32. Dred. By Mrs. BEECHER STOWE. Double vol., 2s. Cloth, gilt, 3s. 6d.
33. Warner (C. D.) In the Wilderness.
34. Six to One. A Seaside Story.

Russell (W. H., LL.D.) The Tour of the Prince of Wales in India, and his Visits to the Courts of Greece, Egypt, Spain, and Portugal. By W. H. RUSSELL, LL.D., who accompanied the Prince throughout his journey; fully Illustrated by SYDNEY P. HALL, M.A., the Prince's Private Artist, with his Royal Highness's special permission to use the Sketches made during the Tour. Super-royal 8vo, cloth extra, gilt edges, 52s. 6d.; Large Paper Edition, 84s.

SANCTA *Christina: a Story of the First Century.* By ELEANOR E. ORLEBAR. With a Preface by the Bishop of Winchester. Small post 8vo, cloth extra, 5s.

Schweinfurth (Dr. G.) Heart of Africa. Which see.

——— *Artes Africanæ.* Illustrations and Description of Productions of the Natural Arts of Central African Tribes. With 26 Lithographed Plates, imperial 4to, boards, 28s.

Scientific Memoirs: being Experimental Contributions to a Knowledge of Radiant Energy. By JOHN WILLIAM DRAPER, M.D., LL.D., Author of "A Treatise on Human Physiology," &c. With Steel Portrait of the Author. Demy 8vo, cloth, 473 pages, 14s.

Scott (Sir G. Gilbert.) See " Autobiography."

Sea-Gull Rock. By JULES SANDEAU, of the French Academy. Royal 16mo, with 79 Illustrations, cloth extra, gilt edges, 7s. 6d. Cheaper Edition, cloth gilt, 2s. 6d. *See also* Rose Library.

Seonee: Sporting in the Satpura Range of Central India, and in the Valley of the Nerbudda. By R. A. STERNDALE, F.R.G.S. 8vo, with numerous Illustrations, 21s.

Shakespeare (The Boudoir). Edited by HENRY CUNDELL. Carefully bracketted for reading aloud; freed from all objectionable matter, and altogether free from notes. Price 2s. 6d. each volume, cloth extra, gilt edges. Contents :—Vol I., Cymbeline—Merchant of Venice. Each play separately, paper cover, 1s. Vol. II., As You Like It—King Lear—Much Ado about Nothing. Vol. III., Romeo and Juliet—Twelfth Night—King John. The latter six plays separately, paper cover, 9d.

Shakespeare Key (The). Forming a Companion to "The Complete Concordance to Shakespeare." By CHARLES and MARY COWDEN CLARKE. Demy 8vo, 800 pp., 21s.

Shooting: its Appliances, Practice, and Purpose. By JAMES DALZIEL DOUGALL, F.S.A., F.Z.A. Author of "Scottish Field Sports," &c. Crown 8vo, cloth extra, 10s. 6d.
"The book is admirable in every way. . . . . We wish it every success."—*Globe.*
"A very complete treatise. . . . . Likely to take high rank as an authority on shooting."—*Daily News.*

Silent Hour (The). See "Gentle Life Series."

Silver Pitchers. See ALCOTT.

Simon (Jules). See "Government of M. Thiers."

Six to One. A Seaside Story. 16mo, boards, 1s.

Sketches from an Artist's Portfolio. By SYDNEY P. HALL. About 60 Fac-similes of his Sketches during Travels in various parts of Europe. Folio, cloth extra, 3l. 3s.
"A portfolio which any one might be glad to call their own."—*Times.*

Sleepy Sketches; or, How we Live, and How we Do Not Live. From Bombay. 1 vol., small post 8vo, cloth, 6s.
"Well-written and amusing sketches of Indian society."—*Morning Post.*

Smith (G.) Assyrian Explorations and Discoveries. By the late GEORGE SMITH. Illustrated by Photographs and Woodcuts. Demy 8vo, 6th Edition, 18s.

——— *The Chaldean Account of Genesis.* Containing the Description of the Creation, the Fall of Man, the Deluge, the Tower of Babel, the Times of the Patriarchs, and Nimrod; Babylonian Fables, and Legends of the Gods; from the Cuneiform Inscriptions. By the late G. SMITH, of the Department of Oriental Antiquities, British Museum. With many Illustrations. Demy 8vo, cloth extra, 5th Edition, 16s.

Snow-Shoes and Canoes; or, the Adventures of a Fur-Hunter in the Hudson's Bay Territory. By W. H. G. KINGSTON. 2nd Edition. With numerous Illustrations. Square crown 8vo, cloth extra, gilt, 7s. 6d.

South Australia: its History, Resources, and Productions. Edited by W. HARCUS, J.P., with 66 full-page Woodcut Illustrations from Photographs taken in the Colony, and 2 Maps. Demy 8vo, 21*s.*

Spain. Illustrated by GUSTAVE DORÉ. Text by the BARON CH. D'AVILLIER. Containing over 240 Wood Engravings by DORÉ, half of them being Full-page size. Imperial 4to, elaborately bound in cloth, **extra** gilt edges, 3*l.* 3*s.*

Stanley (*H. M.*) *How I Found Livingstone.* Crown 8vo, cloth extra, 7*s.* 6*d.* ; large Paper Edition, 10*s.* 6*d.*

——— *"My Kalulu," Prince, King, and Slave.* A Story from Central Africa. Crown 8vo, about 430 pp., with numerous graphic Illustrations, after Original Designs by the Author. Cloth, 7*s.* 6*d.*

——— *Coomassie and Magdala.* A Story of Two British Campaigns in Africa. Demy 8vo, with Maps and Illustrations, 16*s.*

——— *Through the Dark Continent*, which see.

St. Nicholas for 1879. 1*s.* monthly.

Story without an End. From the German of Carové, by the late Mrs. SARAH T. AUSTIN. Crown 4to, with 15 Exquisite Drawings by E. V. B., printed in Colours in Fac-simile of the original Water Colours; and numerous other Illustrations. New Edition, 7*s.* 6*d.*

——— square 4to, with Illustrations by HARVEY. 2*s.* 6*d.*

Stowe (*Mrs. Beecher*) *Dred.* Cheap Edition, boards, 2*s.* Cloth, gilt edges, 3*s.* 6*d.*

——— *Footsteps of the Master.* With Illustrations and red borders. Small post 8vo, cloth extra, 6*s.*

——— *Geography*, with 60 Illustrations. Square cloth, 4*s.* 6*d.*

——— *Little Foxes.* Cheap Edition, 1*s.*; Library Edition, 4*s.* 6*d.*

——— *Betty's Bright Idea.* 1*s.*

——— *My Wife and I; or, Harry Henderson's History.* Small post 8vo, cloth extra, 6*s.**

——— *Minister's Wooing*, 5*s.*; Copyright Series, 1*s.* 6*d.*; cl., 2*s.**

——— *Old Town Folk.* 6*s.*: Cheap Edition, 2*s.* 6*d.*

——— *Old Town Fireside Stories.* Cloth extra, 3*s.* 6*d.*

——— *Our Folks at Poganuc.* 10*s.* 6*d.*

——— *We and our Neighbours.* 1 vol., small post 8vo, 6*s.* Sequel to "My Wife and I."*

——— *Pink and White Tyranny.* Small post 8vo, 3*s.* 6*d.*; Cheap Edition, 1*s.* 6*d.* and 2*s.*

——— *Queer Little People.* 1*s.*; cloth, 2*s.*

——— *Chimney Corner.* 1*s.*; cloth, 1*s.* 6*d.*

——— *The Pearl of Orr's Island.* Crown 8vo, 5*s.**

* *See also* Rose Library.

Stowe (Mrs. Beecher) Little Pussey Willow. Fcap., 2s.

———— *Woman in Sacred History.* Illustrated with 15 Chromolithographs and about 200 pages of Letterpress. Demy 4to, cloth extra, gilt edges, 25s.

Street Life in London. By J. THOMSON, F.R.G.S., and ADOLPHE SMITH. One volume, 4to, containing 40 Permanent Photographs of Scenes of London Street Life, with Descriptive Letterpress, 25s.

Student's French Examiner. By F. JULIEN, Author of "Petites Leçons de Conversation et de Grammaire." Square crown 8vo, cloth extra, 2s.

Studies from Nature. 24 Photographs, with Descriptive Letterpress. By STEVEN THOMPSON. Imperial 4to, 35s.

Sub-Tropical Rambles. See PIKE (N).

Sullivan (A. M., M.P.). See "New Ireland."

Sulphuric Acid (A Practical Treatise on the Manufacture of). By A. G. and C. G. LOCK, Consulting Chemical Engineers. With 77 Construction Plates, drawn to scale measurements, and other Illustrations.

Summer Holiday in Scandinavia (A). By E. L. L. ARNOLD. Crown 8vo, cloth extra, 10s. 6d.

Sumner (Hon. Charles). See Life and Letters.

Surgeon's Handbook on the Treatment of Wounded in War. By Dr. FRIEDRICH ESMARCH, Professor of Surgery in the University of Kiel, and Surgeon-General to the Prussian Army. Translated by H. H. CLUTTON, B.A. Cantab, F.R.C.S. Numerous Coloured Plates and Illustrations, 8vo, strongly bound in flexible leather, 1l. 8s.

TAUCHNITZ'S English Editions of German Authors. Each volume, cloth flexible, 2s.; or sewed, 1s. 6d. (Catalogues post free on application.)

———— *(B.) German and English Dictionary.* Cloth, 1s. 6d.; roan, 2s.

———— *French and English.* Paper, 1s. 6d.; cloth, 2s; roan, 2s. 6d.

———— *Italian and English.* Paper, 1s. 6d.; cloth, 2s.; roan, 2s. 6d.

———— *Spanish and English.* Paper, 1s. 6d.; cloth, 2s.; roan, 2s. 6d.

———— *New Testament.* Cloth, 2s.; gilt, 2s. 6d.

The Telephone. An Account of the Phenomena of Electricity, Magnetism, and Sound. By Prof. A. E. DOLBEAR, Author of "The Art of Projecting," &c. Second Edition, with an Appendix Descriptive of Prof. BELL's Present Instrument. 130 pp., with 19 Illustrations, 1s.

Tennyson's May Queen. Choicely Illustrated from designs by the Hon. Mrs. BOYLE. Crown 8vo (*See* Choice Series), 2*s.* 6*d.*

Textbook (A) of Harmony. For the Use of Schools and Students. By the late CHARLES EDWARD HORSLEY. Revised for the Press by WESTLEY RICHARDS and W. H. CALCOTT. Small post 8vo, cloth extra, 3*s.* 6*d.*

Thebes, and its Five Greater Temples. See ABNEY.

Thirty Short Addresses for Family Prayers or Cottage Meetings. By "FIDELIS." Author of "Simple Preparation for the Holy Communion." Containing Addresses by the late Canon Kingsley, Rev. G. H. Wilkinson, and Dr. Vaughan. Crown 8vo, cloth extra, 5*s.*

Thomson (J.) The Straits of Malacca, Indo-China, and China; or, Ten Years' Travels, Adventures, and Residence Abroad. By J. THOMSON, F.R.G.S., Author of "Illustrations of China and its People." Upwards of 60 Woodcuts. Demy 8vo, cloth extra, 21*s.*

―――― *Through Cyprus with the Camera, in the Autumn of* 1878. Sixty large and very fine Permanent Photographs, illustrating the Coast and Inland Scenery of Cyprus, and the Costumes and Types of the Natives, specially taken on a journey undertaken for the purpose. By JOHN THOMSON, F.R.G.S., Author of "Illustrations of China and its People," &c. Two royal 4to volumes, cloth extra, 105*s.*

Thorne (E.) The Queen of the Colonies; or, Queensland as I saw it. 1 vol., with Map, 6*s.*

Through the Dark Continent: The Sources of the Nile; Around the Great Lakes, and down the Congo. By HENRY M. STANLEY. 2 vols., demy 8vo, containing 150 Full-page and other Illustrations, 2 Portraits of the Author, and 10 Maps, 42*s.* Sixth Thousand.

―――― *(Map to the above).* Size 34 by 56 inches, showing, on a large scale, Stanley's recent Great Discoveries in Central Africa. The First Map in which the Congo was ever correctly traced. Mounted, in case, 1*l.* 1*s.*

"One of the greatest geographical discoveries of the age."―*Spectator.*

"Mr. Stanley has penetrated the very heart of the mystery. . . . He has opened up a perfectly virgin region, never before, so far as known, visited by a white man."―*Times.*

To the Arctic Regions and Back in Six Weeks. By Captain A. W. M. CLARK KENNEDY (late of the Coldstream Guards). With Illustrations and Maps. 8vo, cloth, 15*s.*

Tour of the Prince of Wales in India. See RUSSELL.

Trees and Ferns. By F. G. HEATH. Crown 8vo, cloth, gilt edges, with numerous Illustrations, 3*s.* 6*d.*

Turkistan. Notes of a Journey in the Russian Provinces of Central Asia and the Khanates of Bokhara and Kokand. By EUGENE SCHUYLER, Secretary to the American Legation, St. Petersburg. Numerous Illustrations. 2 vols, 8vo, cloth extra, 5th Edition, 2*l.* 2*s.*

Two Americas; being an Account of Sport and Travel, with Notes on Men and Manners in North and South America. By Sir ROSE PRICE, Bart. 1 vol., demy 8vo, with Illustrations, cloth extra, 2nd Edition, 18s.

Two Friends. By LUCIEN BIART, Author of "Adventures of a Young Naturalist," "My Rambles in the New World," &c. Small post 8vo, numerous Illustrations, 7s. 6d.

Two Supercargoes (The); or, Adventures in Savage Africa. By W. H. G. KINGSTON. Square imperial 16mo, cloth extra, 7s. 6d. Numerous Full-page Illustrations.

*V*ANDENHOFF *(George, M.A.).* See "Art of Reading Aloud."
—— *Clerical Assistant.* Fcap., 3s. 6d.
—— *Ladies' Reader (The).* Fcap., 5s.

Verne's (Jules) Works. Translated from the French, with from 50 to 100 Illustrations. Each cloth extra, gilt edges—

Large post 8vo, price 10s. 6d. *each—*

1. Fur Country. Plainer binding, cloth, 5s.
2. Twenty Thousand Leagues under the Sea.
3. From the Earth to the Moon, and a Trip round It. Plainer binding, cloth, 5s.
4. Michael Strogoff, the Courier of the Czar.
5. Hector Servadac.
6. Dick Sands, the Boy Captain.

Imperial 16mo, *price* 7s. 6d. *each. Those marked with * in plainer cloth binding,* 3s. 6d. *each.*

1. Five Weeks in a Balloon.
2. Adventures of Three Englishmen and Three Russians in South Africa.
3. *Around the World in Eighty Days.
4. A Floating City, and the Blockade Runners.
5. *Dr. Ox's Experiment, Master Zacharius, A Drama in the Air, A Winter amid the Ice, &c.
6. The Survivors of the "Chancellor."
7. *Dropped from the Clouds. } The Mysterious Island. 3 vols.,
8. *Abandoned.   } 22s. 6d. One volume, with some of the
9. *Secret of the Island.   } Illustrations, cloth, gilt edges, 10s. 6d.
10. The Child of the Cavern.

The following Cheaper Editions are issued with a few of the Illustrations, in paper wrapper, price 1s.; *cloth gilt,* 2s. *each.*

1. Adventures of Three Englishmen and Three Russians in South Africa.
2. Five Weeks in a Balloon.

Verne's (Jules) Works, continued:—
   3. A Floating City.
   4. The Blockade Runners.
   5. From the Earth to the Moon.
   6. Around the Moon.
   7. Twenty Thousand Leagues under the Sea. Vol. I.
   8. ——— Vol. II. The two parts in one, cloth, gilt, 3s. 6d.
   9. **Around the World in Eighty Days.**
   10. Dr. Ox's Experiment, and Master Zacharius.
   11. Martin Paz, the Indian Patriot.
   12. A Winter amid the Ice.
   13. The Fur Country. Vol. I.
   14. ——— Vol. II. Both parts in one, cloth gilt, 3s. 6d.
   15. Survivors of the "Chancellor." Vol. I.
   16. ——— Vol. II. Both volumes in one, cloth, gilt edges, 3s. 6d.

Viardot (Louis). See "Painters of all Schools."

Visit to the Court of Morocco. By A. LEARED, Author of "Morocco and the Moors." Map and Illustrations, 8vo, 5s.

WALLER (*Rev. C. H.*) *The Names on the Gates of Pearl,* and other Studies. By the Rev. C. H. WALLER, M.A. Second edition. Crown 8vo, cloth extra, 6s.

——— *A Grammar and Analytical Vocabulary of the Words in the Greek Testament.* Compiled from Brüder's Concordance. For the use of Divinity Students and Greek Testament Classes. By the Rev. C. H. WALLER, M.A., late Scholar of University College, Oxford, Tutor of the London College of Divinity, St. John's Hall, Highbury. Part I., The Grammar. Small post 8vo, cloth, 2s. 6d. Part II. The Vocabulary, 2s. 6d.

——— *Adoption and the Covenant.* Some Thoughts on Confirmation. Super-royal 16mo, cloth limp, 2s. 6d.

War in Bulgaria: a Narrative of Personal Experiences. By LIEUTENANT-GENERAL VALENTINE BAKER PASHA. Maps and Plans of Battles. 2 vols., demy 8vo, cloth extra, 2l. 2s.

Warner (C. D.) My Summer in a Garden. Rose Library, 1s.

——— *Back-log Studies.* Boards, 1s. 6d.; cloth, 2s.

——— *In the Wilderness.* Rose Library, 1s.

——— *Mummies and Moslems.* 8vo, cloth, 12s.

Weaving. See "History and Principles."

Whitney (Mrs. A. D. T.) The Gayworthys. Cloth, 3s. 6d.

——— *Faith Gartney.* Small post 8vo, 3s. 6d. Cheaper Editions, 1s. 6d. and 2s.

——— *Real Folks.* 12mo, crown, 3s. 6d.

Whitney (Mrs. A. D. T.) *Hitherto.* Small post 8vo, 3s. 6d. and 2s. 6d.

———— *Sights and Insights.* 3 vols., crown 8vo, 31s. 6d.

———— *Summer in Leslie Goldthwaite's Life.* Cloth, 3s. 6d.

———— *The Other Girls.* Small post 8vo, cloth extra, 3s. 6d.

———— *We Girls.* Small post 8vo, 3s. 6d.; Cheap Edition, 1s. 6d. and 2s.

Wikoff (H.) *The Four Civilizations of the World.* An Historical Retrospect. Crown 8vo, cloth, 12s.

Wills, *A Few Hints on Proving, without Professional Assistance.* By a PROBATE COURT OFFICIAL. 5th Edition, revised with Forms of Wills, Residuary Accounts, &c. Fcap. 8vo, cloth limp, 1s.

With *Axe and Rifle on the Western Prairies.* By W. H. G. KINGSTON. With numerous Illustrations, square crown 8vo, cloth extra, gilt, 7s. 6d.

Woolsey (C. D., LL.D.) *Introduction to the Study of International Law;* designed as an Aid in Teaching and in Historical Studies. 5th Edition, demy 8vo, 18s.

Words of Wellington: *Maxims and Opinions, Sentences and Reflections of the Great Duke,* gathered from his Despatches, Letters, and Speeches (Bayard Series). 2s. 6d.

World of Comets. By A. GUILLEMIN, Author of "The Heavens." Translated and edited by JAMES GLAISHER, F.R.S. 1 vol., super-royal 8vo, with numerous Woodcut Illustrations, and 3 Chromo-lithographs, cloth extra, 31s. 6d.

"The mass of information collected in the volume is immense, and the treatment of the subject is so purely popular, that none need be deterred from a perusal of it."—*British Quarterly Review.*

Wreck of the Grosvenor. By W. CLARK RUSSELL. 6s. Third and Cheaper Edition.

XENOPHON'S *Anabasis; or, Expedition of Cyrus.* A Literal Translation, chiefly from the Text of Dindorff, by GEORGE B. WHEELER. Books I to III. Crown 8vo, boards, 2s.

———— *Books I. to VII.* Boards, 3s. 6d.

London:
SAMPSON LOW, MARSTON, SEARLE, & RIVINGTON,
CROWN BUILDINGS, 188, FLEET STREET.

LONDON:
GILBERT AND RIVINGTON, PRINTERS,
ST. JOHN'S SQUARE.

www.ingramcontent.com/pod-product-compliance
Lightning Source LLC
Chambersburg PA
CBHW051847300426
44117CB00006B/293